Community Management
Asian Experience and Perspectives

Dedicated
to the Living Memory of

Evelio Javier

October 31, 1942 – February 11, 1986

"The challenge today stands not in the battlefield but in the provinces, in the barrios. They are where leaders are needed. Yet where are those who can lead where angels fear to tread?"

—Evelio Javier, editorial written as a law student.

Elected Governor in 1971 at age 29
Antique Province, Philippines.

Evelio accepted his own challenge.

He committed himself to empowering the poor of his province.

He died in the defense of justice,
gunned down by political assassins.

May his cause endure.

Community Management
Asian Experience and Perspectives

Edited
by
David C. Korten

KUMARIAN PRESS

Printed in the United States of America
First printing 1987

Cover design by Gail S. Cleare

Typeset by Apex Typesetting Inc., New Haven, CT 06510

Library of Congress Cataloging-in-Publication Data

Community management.

    (Library of management for development)
    1. Economic development—Environmental aspects.
2. Economic development—Social aspects. 3. Community
development. I. Korten, David C. II. Title.
III. Series.
HD75.6.C65   1986   338.95   86-27691
ISBN 0-931816-43-2
ISBN 0-931816-40-8 (pbk.)

Contents

Contributors

Shaikh Maqsood Ali holds the rank of secretary in the Bangladesh Civil Service. He established and served as the first rector of the Public Administration Training Centre in Savar, Bangladesh responsible for training of all Bangladesh senior civil servants. Prior to that he was director-general of the National Institute of Public Administration in Dhaka. He is chairman of the Bangladesh Society for Training and Development. His main interest has been action training for participatory administration and planning, a field in which he has co-authored a book and published a number of articles. He has been associated with a number of committees on administrative reorganization and reform established by the Government of Bangladesh.

James N. Anderson is a professor of anthropology at the University of California, Berkeley. He has conducted intensive longitudinal field research in the Philippines and Malaysia on problems of economic, demographic, social, and ecological change. His interests in applied research and rural socioeconomic and ecological development led him to concentrate in recent years on studying the merits of indigenous agroforestry systems, especially house gardens. Anderson is the author of numerous publications dealing with Philippine society and development, human ecology, and rural development and has served as a project specialist for the Ford Foundation and as a consultant to the World Bank, several UN agencies, and USAID.

A. T. Ariyaratne is founder and leader of Sri Lanka's Sarvodaya Shramadana Movement, which has served to demonstrate the power of religion as a positive development force. For his pioneering achievements in the fields of community development and village awakening, Dr. Ariyaratne has received the prestigious Ramon Magsaysay Award for Community Leadership and the King Baudouin Prize for International Development. His contributions to interpreting the relevance of traditional Buddhist wisdom to modern day development have inspired audiences throughout the world and are well documented in his many publications as well as by numerous scholars who have made his work the subject of their own writing. See for example Joanna Macy, *Dharma and Development*, Kumarian Press, 1983.

Conner Bailey is current Assistant Professor of Rural Sociology at Auburn University. He completed his doctorate in Development Sociology at Cornell University in 1979. He has over nine years of field experience in Southeast Asia and has conducted research on marine fisheries in Indonesia, Malaysia, and the Philippines. Prior to joining the faculty at Auburn University, he was Senior Research Fellow at the International Center for Living Aquatic Resources Management (ICLARM) located in the Philippines and a Research Fellow in Marine Policy at the Woods Hole Oceanographic Institution.

J. Bandyopadhyay is one of the leading professionals in India concerned with the ecological management of natural resources. He is a faculty member of the Indian Institute of Management, Bangalore and currently is directing an ecosystems study of the Himalayas watersheds of Ganga and Yamuna for the Department of Environment, Government of India. He is the secretary of PRAKRIT, a Delhi based organization for ecology research and natural resource management.

The Bangladesh Rural Advancement Committee (BRAC) is a private voluntary organization established in 1972 to provide relief assistance to refugees who were returning to their homes after the war in which Bangladesh established its independence from Pakistan. Recognizing that relief could only serve as a stop-gap measure, BRAC soon turned its attention to mobilizing the landless poor into cooperative groups to plan and implement collective activities leading to economic and social self-reliance. BRAC has given particular attention to helping the rural poor achieve control over assets and to access the services that are supposed to be available to them from government. An active program of participatory social science research supports BRAC's programs, which have become known and respected throughout the world. BRAC has grown to a staff of 1,600 and an annual operating budget of approximately US $2.8 million, with activities in over 1,500 villages reaching more than 2 million people.

Michael M. Calavan is senior project development officer in the U.S. Agency for International Development Mission in Dhaka, Bangladesh. He was for several years head of AID's Development Studies Program, its major mid-career professional development program dealing with contemporary development issues. Before joining the U.S. foreign aid program, he taught anthropology at Illinois State University. He is a long time observer and analyst of peasant agriculture and nutrition in rural Thailand, a topic on which he has published extensively.

V. D. Deshpande is professor of economics at the Indian Institute of

Education in Pune, and president of GRAMAYAN. In addition to conducting research on social development programs, he engages in the implementation of such programs and organizes training programs for social workers. He has authored ten books and forty-five articles, including "Employment Guarantee Scheme: Impact on Poverty and Bondage among Tribals," "Struggle of the Deprived for Development 1: the Mhaisal Untouchables," and "Struggle of the Deprived for Development 2: Adivasis of Thane."

David Drucker has taught social policy development and administration to senior Third World professionals at the University College of Swansea in the U.K. He consults regularly with seven U.N. Agencies and a variety of private voluntary organizations and has been a member of consultative missions to a dozen countries in Asia. He is an enthusiastic innovator, as well as a lively chronicler, of approaches and techniques for working with communities in ways that breathe life (and fun) into top-down declarations of commitment to bottom-up planning.

Terry B. Grandstaff applies a multidisciplinary background to work on rural resource issues. He is currently doing interdisciplinary research at Khon Kaen University in northeast Thailand under Ford Foundation sponsorship, where his innovative work on rapid rural appraisal methods has gained international recognition. He did post-doctoral research on rural resource systems at the East-West Center for several years. Subsequently he worked for the Agency for International Development for four years, including a tour in Thailand.

Somluckrat W. Grandstaff taught at Thammasat University in Bangkok, where she directed the English language graduate program in economics. Thereafter she moved to Honolulu to become a research associate at the Environment and Policy Institute of the East-West Center. She is presently doing interdisciplinary research at Khon Kaen University in northeast Thailand with support from the Ford Foundation.

James Hopkins is currently assisting the Royal Thai Government's Ministry of Agriculture and Cooperatives in the development of a rainfed farming systems research and extension program in northeast Thailand. He has been implementing rural development projects in Southeast Asia for fourteen years in the fields of health, village cooperatives, and agriculture. He has acted as official interpreter for the RTG for project design teams, evaluation teams, and international conferences. His translations cover a broad range of subjects from five year national development plans to articles on Buddhism and poetry.

David C. Korten is currently Asia regional advisor on development management to the United States Agency for International Development under contract with the National Association of Schools of Public Affairs and Administration. Based in Jakarta, he works with USAID missions throughout Asia seeking to improve the performance of development projects intended to strengthen community management capacities. He also works with a number of private voluntary development agencies in Asia seeking more strategic approaches to facilitating changes in policy and institutional settings supportive of greater local control and initiative. He has lived in Asia for the past eight years, where he has also been a Ford Foundation project specialist and a visiting professor at the Asian Institute of Management. A former member of the faculties of the Harvard University Graduate Schools of Business and Public Health, he also has had extensive experience as a development management consultant, researcher, administrator, and teacher in Latin America and Africa. He is known in development circles for his numerous articles and books challenging conventional development wisdom and management practice. These have contributed to the acceptance of a number of innovative development concepts such as the learning process approach, bureaucratic reorientation, people-centered development, and community management.

Frances F. Korten is a program officer with the Ford Foundation, responsible for the Foundation's work in irrigation in Indonesia and the Philippines. She has resided in Asia for more than eight years and is widely known for her role in supporting the Philippine National Irrigation Administration in the development of its participatory approach to small scale irrigation. A psychologist by training, she has taught management at the Harvard University School of Public Health, the Central American Institute of Enterprise Administration (INCAE), the University of West Florida, and the Haile Sellassie I University College of Business Administration. She is editor of *Psychology and the Problems of Society* and co-author of *Casebook for Family Planning Management*.

Ronald L. Krannich is president of Development Concepts Incorporated, a consulting, training, and publishing firm in Manassa, Virginia. A political scientist, public administrationist, and Southeast Asian specialist, he has written extensively on local government and public policy in Thailand. He has conducted several research projects in Thailand and served as an advisor to the Thai government on decentralization. He is author of *Mayors and Managers in Thailand* and *The Politics of Family Planning Policy*. His articles appear in *Public Administration Review, Urban Affairs Quarterly, Administration and Society,* and *Asian Survey*.

Hasan Poerbo is professor of Human Settlements and Housing in the Department of Architecture at Institute of Technology Bandung (ITB) in Indonesia; and Director of the ITB Centre for Environmental Studies. He is also a member of Indonesia's National Research Council and Advisor to the Minister of Housing. He is a former dean of the Faculty of Civil Engineering, Design and Fine Arts at ITB, and former chairman of its Department of Architecture. He has been an East-West Center Fellow and served on Indonesia's National Educational Reform Committee. In addition to being a leading Indonesian academic, Professor Poerbo also is a social activist. It was through his leadership that the Cigaru experiment was established by the ITB Centre for Environmental Studies, and he campaigns tirelessly for broader applications of its lessons within Indonesia's local development programs. He has also had a leading role in organizing the scavengers of Bandung for a variety of self-help activities.

Romana P. de los Reyes is research associate of the Institute of Philippine Culture of the Ateneo de Manila University in Quezon City, Philippines. Her main interest has been in farmer organizations that manage small scale irrigation schemes. She was a member of the Communal Irrigation Committee, which assisted in the development of the participatory communal irrigation program of the National Irrigation Administration in the Philippines, and has gained international recognition for her leading role in development and application of the innovative social science methods involved in that effort. She is currently directing a nationwide study to access the impact of the participatory program on the performance of the assisted irrigation systems and the capability of their irrigators' associations.

Jeff Romm began working in community resource management as an afforestation officer in Nepal in the mid-60's. Subsequently, serving for several years as a Ford Foundation program officer in Asia, he participated in the development of community approaches for managing irrigation systems and forest and range lands in nations throughout South and Southeast Asia, and is credited by his colleagues with setting the direction of much of the Foundation's work in resource management in the region. He currently teaches natural resource policy at the University of California, Berkeley.

S. P. Salunke, Colonel, Ret. was administrator of the Pani Panchayat program for four years. At present he is a freelance writer for a number of newspapers and journals. He is author of *Pakistani PoW's in India* and has written a number of booklets on military campaigns.

H. C. Sharatchandra is assistant professor at the University of Agricultural Sciences, Bangalore. He was for several years on the research staff of the Indian Institute of Sciences, Bangalore. From 1980 to 1984 he taught ecology, environmental biology, and biogeography at North Eastern Hill University, Shillong. As a consultant to the Department of Environment, Government of India, he has developed a comprehensive management plan for a proposed biosphere reserve in the Northeast Himalayas. His research has dealt with a wide range of subjects in wildlife biology, avian biology, and natural resources conservation. His current research focuses on the conservation and management of tropical forests.

Vandana Shiva is currently a consultant to the United Nations University, Tokyo, working on problems of conflict resolution in natural resources management. Her work ranges from philosophy of quantum mechanics to farm forestry and alternative sciences. She is active in a number of ecology movements in India, and is coordinator of the Dehradun based Research Foundation for Science, Technology and Natural Resource Policy.

Robert Y. Siy, Jr. is a professor with the Rural Development Management Program of the Asian Institute of Management (AIM) in Manila and is a leading member of its Rural Development Management Group. His research interests and consulting experience have been in the areas of rural development, rural infrastructure planning, technology, and transportation. He served on the Communal Irrigation Committee of the Philippines National Irrigation Administration and regularly consults for that agency. He has done extensive research on the zanjera irrigation systems in Ilocos Norte and is author of *Community Resource Management: Lessons from the Zanjera* (Manila: University of the Philippines Press, 1982). He is currently editing a book on the development of the NIA's participatory approach to small-scale irrigation development to be published by Kumarian Press, and has been conducting research on the management problems of private voluntary development agencies in Southeast Asia.

Soedjatmoko is the Rector of the United Nations University located in Tokyo, Japan. His distinguished international career as statesman, humanist, and scholar of international development and politics has brought him countless honors, including honorary degrees from major universities in four countries. An active participant in the international debate on development and environmental issues, he has been a member of the Independent Commission on Disarmament and Security Issues (Palme Commission), the Independent Commission on International Humanitarian Issues, and the Club of Rome. He has served his own country of Indonesia as Ambassador to the United States, Advisor for Social and Cultural Affairs to its National Development Planning Agency, Personal Advisor to the Ministry of Foreign Affairs, and United Nations delegate. He has served as a Trustee of the Ford Foundation and the Aspen Institute. In wide demand as a lecturer, he has published numerous articles and books on the social, economic, cultural, and political aspects of development. His most recent book is *Development and Freedom*.

James Terrant is a Ph.D. candidate in Development Studies at the University of Sussex in England. He served as a technical advisor to the Centre for Environmental Studies of the Institute of Technology Bandung, assisting with the implementation and evaluation of the Ciamis Program. He also served as a consultant to USAID/Jakarta on the design of its Uplands Conservation Project. He has been an associate fellow of the Overseas Development Council, where he co-authored *An Alternative Road to the Post-Petroleum Era: North-South Cooperation* and *Assistance to the Third*

World on Urban Energy. Prior to that he served on the staff of a member of the U.S. House of Representatives.

Apichart Thongyu has spent many years as a village worker in rural Thailand. He is currently project administrator of the Northeast Community Development II Project of Redd Barna-Thailand; a committee member of the Inter-Religious Committee for Social Development; and Coordinator for the northeastern section of the Exchange Forum on Rural Development, a national forum of nongovernmental community development workers. Formerly he was president of the Voluntary Teacher Group in the Rural University Project of the Thailand Ministry of Education's Non-Formal Education Department. He has published numerous articles on rural development in a variety of journals. His article on "Community Analysis for Rural Development" has had an important impact on development implementation in Thailand. His latest book is *Culture and Community Analysis: A New Alternative for Rural Development.*

Norman Uphoff has been for many years chairman of the Rural Development Committee at Cornell University, with an appointment in the Department of Government and the Center for International Studies. He spent a sabbatical year 1978-79 as a research fellow with the Agrarian Research and Training Institute in Sri Lanka and has, since January 1980, spent two to three months a year working with ARTI colleagues on the Gal Oya project. He has done extensive comparative work on rural local organization and local institutional development. His most recent book is *Local Institutional Development: a Sourcebook with Cases* published by Kumarian Press in 1987.

Andrew P. Vayda is Professor of Anthropology and Ecology at Rutgers University. Formerly a Professor at Columbia University, he has taught also at the University of Indonesia and other Indonesian universities and has directed human ecology projects in Indonesia and Papua New Guinea. He has published several books and more than seventy articles. He founded the journal *Human Ecology* and served as its editor for five years.

Foreword

My participation over the past thirty years in the search for development alternatives, particularly in Asia, has kept me in close contact with the growing body of literature critiquing the relevance to the Asian context of the old model of development, and with with attempts to find alternative pathways to social change. The title of this volume identifies it as a contribution to this search.

The contemporary development debate commonly centers attention on the contest between "delivered development," which is planned from the top, with people as the objects; and "participatory development," which is planned from the bottom, with people, particularly the poor, as the subjects of the development process. *Community Management* integrates these perspectives, viewing planning as both a "top down" and a "bottom-up" process involving social mobilization and a great deal of devolution of power in a truly democratic context. In this sense the book goes beyond Asia and has lessons both for other Third World regions and for industrialized countries as well. In all countries the effects of the current world development crisis have propelled the concepts of people-centered development and of community management to the center stage of concern, among theoreticians and practitioners of development alike.

After nearly thirty-five years of "development" based on the growth model—the cornerstones of which are modernization, industrialization, and urbanization—Asian societies are drifting rudderless. They are confronted by a world historical framework in which the ideological driving forces for accumulation which pertained to economically advanced societies no longer offer a viable road to development for the less advanced. The compulsion to seek alternative driving forces for social change, even in its narrower conception let alone in wider human terms, is therefore mounting.

Not all poor societies of Asia are in the same stage of historical development. After World War II, South Asian societies along with certain other

Third World countries, were incorporated into a global system over which they had little control. Thus, they failed to make a meaningful historical transition to either capitalism or socialism. Nor have they been able to integrate their dualistic economies or eradicate the worst forms of poverty and hunger. Some Southeast Asian countries have tried to move into capitalism, though the results are far from clear.

There is indication in much of Asia of a heightening sense of alienation, as well as a waste of resources and of the available knowledge base. The list of the contradictions apparent in Asian societies is leading to political and social unrest and growing militarism, which could result in revolutionary changes or in complete destabilization and anarchy.

There is still very little understanding of the interaction between internal developments in the Asia countries and the external geopolitical constellations at work or of the forces that are sharpening micro-level contradictions. The research that has been done by Asian scholars on social change in the Asian context is still in its infancy and too often lacks interdisciplinarity. Part of the explanation is found in the lack of a coherent intellectual framework going beyond conventional neoclassical and Marxist thinking, both of which have emerged from the study of Western societies and are not by themselves sufficient to an understanding of the Asia reality. Something more than single discipline analysis, narrow quantification, and "a priori" theorizing is also needed.

In an attempt to fill this gap, which is not unique to Asia, Third World social scientists have attempted to analyze development processes from essentially two perspectives. The first line of research has been organized around the Latin American Dependency Thesis and the African Center-Periphery Thesis. The theme of Unequal Exchange, originating in the pioneering work of Raul Prebish, plays a key role in this analysis. This literature, which has been developed and deepened by Samir Amin and others, examines development at the global level in very broad terms and represents a useful tool of analysis of the dominance/dependence syndrome into which the Third World is locked. A detailed analysis, even on these lines, has yet to be made for Asia.

The second line of research, still in its infancy, takes off from the cultural and historical schools of thought in both the industrialized and Third World countries. It criticizes a predetermined universalism and stresses pluralism, including geocultural specificity. In so doing it makes an important advance over the past evolution of the social sciences based entirely on the study of Western societies—producing hypotheses and value judgements based on that historical cultural world which continues to have a strong influence on the educational, technical, and administrative systems of Third World countries.

The second line of research is exemplified by "Towards a Theory of

Rural Development"[1] and "Bhoomi Sena — a Struggle for People's Power,"[2] a collective work by four Asian colleagues and myself. It shares with the present volume the conviction that development is simultaneously a "top-down" and a "bottom-up" process. It is concerned with both national macro perspectives and the constituent micro grassroots contradictions. Development here is viewed as a process of human development, a process of social transformation in which people are the subjects and in which they participate at all levels of decision making. Self-reliance is both a means and an end in this process. It is a process that releases the creative energy of people, assures equal access to resources for all, tends to eliminate the difference between mental and manual labor, and uses technology appropriate to these social goals. This research, though giving some space to micro-macro linkages, is primarily concerned with the grassroots micro problematique. It squarely faces the issues of people's participation, conscientization, and the building of countervailing power, as part of an on-going social process—the long revolution towards social and structure change toward transformation in Asia.

It is clear that work at the global level, at the national macro level, and at the grassroots micro level not only must be integrated but also expanded and refined for different cultural settings. Some minimal conceptual work is going on, but much more needs to be done in Asia where the micro- and macro- and global issues of development are highly intertwined. At the same time many innovative practical experiments, such as referred to in *Community Management* are being undertaken throughout Asia. But too often they exist in isolation. They need to be identified, documented, analyzed, and linked as part of an on-going praxis. Even this requires a conceptual framework. If a more coherent but flexible paradigm is not evolved, what results is rhetoric for social change and development for people at one level, and a great deal of isolated and fragmented activities at the periphery on the other.

This book on *Community Management* by David Korten, with its focus on people, local resources, institutional systems and linkages, and learning systems, is an important contribution toward meeting the current need for a framework able to provide greater coherence and conceptual clarity in the search for alternative development approaches.

Ponna Wignaraja
Secretary General
Society for International Development (Rome)
and
Chairman
Participatory Institute for Development
Alternatives (Sri Lanka)

NOTES

1. Haque, W., N. Mehta, Md. A. Rahman and P. Wignaraja, "Towards a Theory of Rural Development," *Development Dialogue*, 1977:2.

2. Mehta, N., Md. A. Rahman, G. V. S. De Silva, and P. Wignaraja, "Bhoomi Sena: Struggle for People's Power" *Development Dialogue*, 1979:2.

Preface

The past two decades have seen a growing awareness of the limits of development models that look to government bureaucracies to assume the leadership in doing development for people. Too often they have resulted in programs that undermine the inherent capacity of people to meet their own needs through local initiative, leaving them dependent on centrally subsidized bureaucracies which absorb vast resources without being responsive to local needs.

One result has been a search for new and more powerful participatory approaches to development. Out of this search has emerged a growing interest in the concept of community based resource management—community management for short. Earlier approaches to the problem of participation dealt mainly with community participation in the implementation of government controlled projects and programs. Community management takes as its point of departure, not the bureaucracy and its centrally mandated development projects and programs, but rather the community itself: its needs, its capacities, and ultimately its own control over both its resources and its destiny. And it focuses on empowerment—specifically the control over and ability to manage productive resources in the interests of one's own family and community. It invokes a basic principle of control and accountability which maintains that the control over an action should rest with the people who will bear its consequences.

Community management also goes well beyond earlier conceptions of community development. It is approached as a fundamental element of a broader development strategy directed to achieving a social transformation based on people-centered development values and the potentials of advanced, information-based technologies. Its implementation necessarily includes attention to the institutional and policy context, from village social structures to the structure of national institutions and policies relating to resource control.

This volume is about community management. It follows from and elaborates on the themes of two earlier volumes published by Kumarian Press. *Bureaucracy and the Poor* took development bureaucracies as its point of departure. *People-Centered Development* addressed larger issues of theory and policy relating to the purposes, strategies, and structures of an alternative development which actualizes the potentials of people as both the means and the ends of development. Both concluded that local control and initiative must form the foundation of a people-centered development strategy.

The present volume addresses the practical implications of that conclusion, looking at the issues faced in creating an institutional and policy setting supportive of such control and initiative as well as actual community-level interventions. Its case materials reveal the ruthlessness of local corruption and factionalism as well as the depth of community feeling and capacity which make possible often heroic action in the service of the community and document a variety of interventions—both successful and otherwise—intended to strengthen local capacities for self-directed resource management. The final chapter examines community management within the context of evolving views of the nature of modernity and suggests that greater initiative and leadership in achieving the newly recognized potentials of social development must come from the private voluntary sector.

I selfishly undertook the preparation of this volume as a means of advancing my own understanding of the richness of the local processes by which people, whose interests development is supposed to serve, organize themselves and their resources to meet self-defined needs and to exploit self-defined opportunities. The result is addressed to both students and practitioners of development. Foremost among practitioners, it is addressed to those who, like myself, work in development bureaucracies and are normally out of contact with the reality of rural people. Consequently we too easily slip into assuming passivity and uniformity—assumptions consistent with the standardized, centrally initiated projects and programs that the organizations in which we work are able to create. Furthermore, trained in outmoded development models, and working in organizations structured according to outmoded organizational priciples, we must continually remind ourselves of the role of local initiative in the creation of a modern society and of the often destructive impact on valuable local capacities of well-intentioned development programs. The volume is intended not only to provide such a reminder but also to suggest viable courses of action.

At the other end of the spectrum, those development professionals who as village workers are constantly immersed in village reality may at times lose sight of the broader setting within which they work. Focused on achieving immediate improvements in well-being through local self-help action, they may overlook opportunities to contribute toward achieving the larger institutional and policy changes needed to sustain the processes of community self-reliance which they are helping to strengthen. Here the volume is intended to contribute to an awareness of sometimes neglected possibilities.

The materials for such a book might be based on experience from any number of countries and regions. As I am living and working in Asia, I currently have special access to its rich and varied experience. Also, I am among those who believe that it is in Asia where the alternative development models of the future will be forged—achieving a synthesis of Asia's rich religious and philosophical traditions with advanced Western technologies of the communications age. For both these reasons it seemed natural to limit my search to contributions based on the Asian experience. The resulting volume is, however, intended to be relevant to a much broader audience.

One conscious purpose of this volume is to strengthen respect for the values and capacities of rural people—as it is on such values and capacities that development responsive to their interests must ultimately be built. Some readers may suspect that underlying the search for such understanding and respect is a romanticized view of village life and an implicit call for a return to the simple life of the past. Certainly this would be a serious misreading of my own position and, I believe, a misreading of the contributors to this volume. There is a great deal about village life that is hardly romantic as contributions to this volume graphically reveal. But the same is true for modern society. We should not hesitate to strive for a melding of the best of each. One of the more tragic errors of development experience to date has been to presume that development demands a rejection of all things traditional in accepting uncritically the values and technology of the West.

Most contributors to this volume have substantial village-level experience and have developed a deep respect for the values and abilities of village people. They have consistently taken the community and its perspective as the point of departure for their studies and analyses—a perspective all too rare in development literature. I am deeply indebted to these colleagues for sharing their experience, insights, and research results.

While the Ford Foundation originally brought me to Asia, a contract funded by the Asia and S&T Bureaus of the Agency for International Development (AID) through a cooperative agreement with the National Association of Schools of Public Affairs and Administration (NASPAA) has allowed me to remain here and has helped fund the preparation of this volume. My thanks to Kenneth Kornher, Douglas Picket, Jean North, and Gary Hansen, who have all had a part in AID's administration of this contract; and to Al Zuck, Rudi Klauss, Beth Shields, Jean Sonner, and Louis Picard who have been involved in its administration from the NASPAA side.

While preparing this volume, I have been based with the USAID Mission in Jakarta, Indonesia, working with USAID missions throughout Asia in efforts to strengthen their programming in support of community management. I am particularly indebted to William Fuller, Mission Director of USAID/Jakarta, for his encouragement and the support provided by the Mission, and also to Eugene "Rocky" Staples, former AID Deputy Assistant Administrator for Asia, who chaired the Asia Regional Committee on Community Management which I served as Secretary, and led the effort to make community management a central policy theme of AID work in Asia. Both had key roles in insuring the continuity of my support from AID. Numerous AID colleagues who have been active in AID's community management initiative have contributed substantially to the ideas presented here and two have contributed chapters. I hasten to note that the views expressed here are those of the individual contributors and of myself as volume editor. They do not necessarily represent the views of either AID or NASPAA.

The Ford Foundation continues to contribute to my support as a dependent of Frances Korten, a Ford Foundation program officer responsible for the Foundation's work on community management of irrigation in Indonesia and the Philippines. Fran has given me constant encouragement, numerous insights into community management, and offered helpful comments on some of the manuscripts. Salehuddin Ahmed, Joanne Hale, Marty Chen, Annmarie Walsh, Mark Poffenberger, Diana Putman, Terry Rambo, Gary Bergthold and Richard Norgaard have also provided comments on individual manuscripts which have contributed in important ways to the final presentation. And Pamela Korsmeyer handled the difficult task of copy editing with uncommon care and skill.

Nanik Soeroso and Tjenni Manusama have assisted in the typing of manuscripts and handled the substantial correspondence involved in keeping in contact with the contributors.

And finally I want to express my thanks to Krishna Sondhi, Publisher of Kumarian Press, who has worked as colleague and advisor on the preparation of this volume since its inception. Her faith in the enterprise and her commitment to its publication from a very early stage have contributed immeasurably to sustaining my motivation to see it to completion.

David C. Korten
Jakarta, Indonesia

INTRODUCTION

COMMUNITY-BASED RESOURCE MANAGEMENT

David C. Korten

Public development efforts of the past few decades have seen increasing extension of state authority throughout Asia into affairs once the preserve of local custom and control. In many respects this is a natural and necessary aspect of the modernization process, drawing local communities into participation in larger national and global systems. All too often however, in its enthusiasm for modernizing and rationalizing resource management, the state has underestimated the extent and capacity of the systems by which people have learned through long and often difficult experience to manage locally available resources to meet their own self-defined needs. At the same time the state has often seriously over-estimated its own ability to manage these same resources. Without denying that the traditional systems are often inequitable and unproductive, state interventions that have chosen to ignore them have seldom fared better. Too often they have simply undermined existing local capacities, created burdens on the national treasury, and exacerbated inequities by transferring resources and power from local to national elites while doing little to increase productivity.

In the face of rapidly increasing pressures on a finite resource base generated by growing populations and rising aspirations, there is need for substantial and rapid evolution of existing resource management systems to support sustainable intensification of resource use. It is unlikely that traditional village communities can accomplish this rapid evolutionary change on their own. But neither can the state accomplish it entirely through its bureaucratic instrumentalities. There must evolve a more dynamic partnership arrangement building from the existing capacities

1

and evident self-interest of the local community and complemented by the ability of the state to support the development of enabling policies and institutional linkages.

There is growing recognition in Asia of the need for such a partnership, reflected in a wide range of initiatives supportive of a strong community role in resource management within the context of larger national systems. The more advanced of these efforts go well beyond appeals for participation in government-planned and financed projects and programs calling for strong community control of development resources within institutional frameworks supportive of productivity, equity, and sustainability. The better known of these initiatives have been in irrigation and social forestry but similar concepts are being applied in health, uplands agriculture, village credit programs, and others.

Most of the efforts are in an experimental stage. Those initiated by government invariably encounter a contradiction between the requirements of such programs and the bureaucratized structures of governmental agencies. All such efforts face the reality of local politics and corruption. Much is being learned about how to confront and overcome these and other difficulties. Many of the individuals who are at the forefront of this learning are contributors to this volume. It is reflective of this distinctive nature of the *social learning processes* involved that nearly all of these contributors are best described as *practitioner scholars,* whose writing is based on rich practical experience.

THE MEANING AND LOGIC OF COMMUNITY-BASED RESOURCE MANAGEMENT

What exactly do we mean by a community management approach to development resource management or—in its shortened form—community management? The term *community* popularly implies a group of people with common interests. But the meaning intended here comes from the field of ecology, referring simply to an interacting population of organisms (individuals) living in a common location. Competing interests are assumed to be a natural feature of human communities, and one of the concerns in the development of community management systems is with the strengthening of mechanisms for effective and equitable management of such conflict. Another distinctive feature of the community management perspective is a concern with community control and management of productive resources, which goes well beyond a more conventional concern with participation in the planning and implementation of externally controlled development projects. There is also explicit attention to confronting conflicts between the imperatives of bureaucratic administration and the requirements of broadly based local resource control.

Every community develops systems or mechanisms by which its members capture and use locally available resources to meet individual and collective needs irrespective of whether it has been the subject of external interventions—governmental or otherwise—to develop its community development capacities. Such resources include but are not limited to land, water, information, technology, money, and human energy and creativity. A given community management system may be comprised of any number of different social units, including: household, small firms, kinship groups, factions, and the whole range of local organizations from voluntary associations and cooperatives to local governments. It also includes nonorganizational mediating mechanisms such as markets and informal relationships.

The performance of a community-based resource management system is a function of its ability to mobilize available resources and to use them productively, equitably, and sustainably in meeting the needs of community members. This performance varies considerably from one community to another. The systems by which a community's resources are managed also vary considerably in the degree to which they are locally controlled and, if locally controlled, the extent to which control is broadly shared among the community's members. Though difficult to define with precision, the term community management normally is applied only when these management processes involve broadly distributed control within the community. The term is not appropriately applied where resources on which the well-being of the community depends are being managed *for* the community by persons and groups outside its boundaries, and/or by a small local elite. Thus, in assessing whether a given program is indeed building community management capacity, the test of productivity is necessary but not sufficient. The empowerment test must also be applied. A true community management intervention must strengthen and broaden the local base of effective resource control.

Unfortunately the natural dynamics of bureaucratic functioning create a substantial danger that programs promoted by government in the name of community management may instead contribute to processes of concentration and marginalization, which work against the broader community interest, as in some social forestry programs in India. (See Chapter seventeen. The reason is that the management systems of bureaucracy are control oriented and seek to insure that resource management decisions conform to centrally defined prescriptions. One result is to limit the broadly based participation in resource control that is central to the community management concept. Also, formal governmental structures almost necessarily work from the top down through existing power structures thus reinforcing those structures and providing opportunities for power-oriented elites to strengthen their control over both the local and the external resources involved in such programs. Structural, policy, and value changes that reorient these dynamics are often essential if government is to be an effective partner in a community based resource management process.

Clearly the concept of community management does not offer government an easy solution to the problem of intensifying the use of critical development resources. Indeed, as will be demonstrated throughout this volume, success is likely to depend on difficult-to-achieve policy and institutional changes. Why then make the necessary commitment? Basically the arguments are three.

1. **Local Variety:** Community life is characterized by substantial variety in natural and social ecologies and in individual preferences. Optimizing productivity and sustainability in resource use in the service of the improved human well-being depends on appropriate adaptation to this variety. Centralized bureaucracies, which function according to standardized rules, have little capacity to respond to the special needs and preferences through which such adaptation might be achieved. With their broadly distributed decision processes, community management systems have nearly unlimited potential for such adaptation.

2. **Local Resources:** When people at the local level are committed to an idea, they can often mobilize an astonishing variety of resources to realize it—from underutilized land and buildings, to skills, communication channels, and money. People will volunteer their homes and their labor, vehicles, tools, and construction materials. By contrast, the bureaucracies of central government are limited to the resources they bring from outside the community subject to their direct control. To the extent that they use local resources, they can depend only on those which they buy or can commandeer through coercive means, leaving a vast range of locally available development resources untapped. Thus, central programs are likely to be costly and wasteful relative to the potentials for meeting the same needs through community initiative.

   The difference in perspective involved in planning by central government based on national resources versus community planning based on use of local resources was graphically demonstrated some years back in a national health planning workshop. World Health Organization (WHO) consultants presented a national primary health plan they had developed for a particular country. Their plan detailed requirements for construction and staffing of numbers of primary health centers and auxiliary health posts determined by applying standard ratios of facilities required per 1,000 persons. Based on the number of new facilities called for and standard staffing tables for each type of facility, tables were developed showing the exact number of each type of health professional to be recruited and trained. Construction and staffing requirements were then translated into budget requirements. Nowhere was account taken of any existing facility or staff. The projected costs were impressive. Later, workshop participants were given case scenarios of three communities and divided into groups to develop plans for addressing priority identified health needs of each community. The resulting plans called for such actions as mobilizing volunteer labor to drain a mosquito infested swamp, mobilizing religious leaders in support of health education efforts, training indigenous practitioners by a local doctor, improving an existing mission hospital, etc. The plans were at once more relevant and comprehensive than those of the national health planners. Not one of the teams called for investment in any new facility or the hiring of a single new medical staff person.

3. **Local Accountability:** A basic principle of a democratic society is that control over an action should rest with the people who will bear the major force of its consequences. Where direct control is not possible, those individuals to whom such control is delegated should be as directly accountable as possible to those most directly affected. Generally, the link between decision and consequences is closest when decisions regarding the use of local resources reside within the local community. Such a link is no assurance of high performance but it improves the odds. If a farmer chooses the wrong technology, it is his own crop that fails. If a community allows its forest resources to be depleted, its members must invest more energy and money in finding fuel and building materials. Poor conservation practices reduce the productivity of its fields. If a business fails, it is the community that loses jobs. But the personnel assigned by central government to intervene in these decision processes are accountable only to distant superiors who are seldom aware of the consequences of their actions let alone personally affected by them. When the extension agent employed by the national ministry of agriculture gives poor advice, neither he nor his superiors in a far off capital city suffer loss of income or tenure.The health ministry doctor who fails to attend to a dying child in the remote village for which she is responsible but never visits will get no reprimand from the superior who has no knowledge of that child or her needs.

These arguments regarding the benefits of local control are not new. They are well grounded in political and organizational theory. But many political leaders and development professionals, dependent on inappropriate administrative and analytical tools, have had difficulty in coming to terms with their implications. Immersed in the bureaucracy and its imperatives, they too easily come to see development only in terms of what government and its bureaucracies do to or for people. The richness, complexity, and diversity of local life and self-help action blend into highly aggregated statistics or are reduced to the abstractions of theoretical models and, once removed from consciousness, cease to exist as a practical reality.

For these reasons efforts to improve the outcomes of development action through improving the quality of project blueprints and strengthening the control systems of central bureaucracies are themselves self-defeating, exacerbating the rigidities which are a primary cause of development failure. The need is for new organizational forms and program approaches that encourage local initiative, accountability, and self-regulation; for tools and systems that strengthen social learning processes at all systems levels in support of system adaptation; and for greater reliance on private, in contrast to exclusively public, initiative.

THE TWO DIMENSIONS OF POWER

Power represents the ability to change a future state through an act of decision. Development itself might well be defined in terms of building the power of a society, i.e., of increasing its ability to change its future as an act of choice. Thus, power may be viewed as both a resource and a product of the development process.

Many social scientists have chosen to recognize power only by its distributive dimension, which in personal terms refers to the ability of one person to force his or her will on another.[1] Looking only at its distributed dimension leads to treating power as a fixed sum resource, and defining power issues as necessarily competitive in nature. An important consequence is the denial of cooperation as a rational human behavior in areas of activity where power is at issue.

But power also has an important generative dimension, which is basic to understanding the role of empowerment in development.[2] Specifically, if one group can increase its power only at the expense of another, empowerment of the poor, by definition, can be achieved only at the expense of existing powerholders, and these powerholders must be expected to resist such efforts. But such loss is inevitable only for those who measure their own self-worth in terms of their ability to excercise arbitrary domination over others. There are other ways of looking at the potentials of the empowerment process, which are both personally and socially more liberating. The seeming conflict of interest between powerholders and the powerless is not inherent in the nature of power but only in its inappropriately narrow definition. Increasing awareness of the larger possibilities is one of the important challenges facing proponents of community management.

These possibilities are embedded in the reality that social units, whether neighborhoods, local associations, families, local governments, work groups, field offices of a bureaucracy, or corporations, vary in their capacity for action, for making effective use of the resources at their command to create a new future, i.e., in their power.[3] This capacity is a function of the strength of their organization, the commitment of their members to shared ideas and purposes, and the skills they bring to bear in the pursuit of this purpose. And these are all subject to change.

Since the ability to change a future state is not by nature fixed, it represents a capacity that is subject both to enhancement and to deterioration. Thus, all members of a society or other social unit may benefit from an increase in its power if the increments in power are broadly shared within the group. Hence, the possibility that participation in cooperative endeavors can be a highly rational individual choice in a wide range of human activities.

The theories of nonviolent action set forth by leaders such as Mohandas K. Gandhi and Martin Luther King have implicitly recognized the generative dimensions of power, their purpose being to create conditions under which each individual has maximum opportunity to be an influential member of an active and productive community.[4] The empowerment processes they advocated were based on a concept of mutuality in which the power of one person is increased by his or her simultaneous contribution to increasing the power of others.[5] By building a strengthened base of social capacity for productive action, the social energy potential of the larger sociosystem is thereby increased as well. There is no evident limit to the power that may be generated through this process.

This is not to deny that empowerment processes also involve the distributive dimensions of power. An intervention directed toward strengthening the economic power of women through increasing their capacity to manage a broad range of economic resources will reduce their dependence on their spouses. Similarly strengthening the capacity of the community to assess and act on its own health problems will reduce the community's dependence on medical personnel for dealing with common health needs. In one sense the power of the former powerholder has declined, depending in part on how that individual chooses to view and act on the new reality. However, a position of power that is dependent on the weakness of another individual is a very limited, growth-inhibiting power.

A reduction in dependence-based power reduces the original powerholder's opportunities for the exercise of arbitrary coercive power, but it can also create new opportunities for that same individual to exercise more mature forms of power. For example, the increase in family earnings provided by a more economically active female member opens new opportunities for the household to advance its situation through investment in education and productive assets. Generative additions to household power can more than offset the distributional loss to the male head of household and, if he exploits these new opportunities effectively, he may find his position within the larger community enhanced accordingly.

Or consider the case of health professionals working in a community health program. When a community is dependent on health professionals for treatment of even minor ailments, their time is consumed in routine treatments that require little of their medical training and have little lasting impact on the health of the community. By concentrating on building the capacity or power of the community to address its own basic health needs, these same medical personnel demonstrate their real power to change future events. At the same time they help to relieve themselves from routine curative tasks, allowing them to devote more time to treating the serious cases that require their most advanced skills and to diagnosing more difficult community health problems—consequently increasing their own stature.

Unfortunately in this very real world, not all powerholders are so enlightened. And dealing with the less enlightened to achieve more broadly based participation in resource control and decision making often requires more than education and appeals to their higher nature. Competition for resource control all too often involves life and death struggles in which success for the poor depends on their ability and willingness to stand firm in the defense of their rights. Such struggles are documented by several cases presented in this volume.

PAST EXPERIMENTS WITH GOVERNMENT-LED LOCAL DEVELOPMENT

Concern with local development initiative is by no means new to the development scene. Community development programs attempted for many years to take development activities directly to the village. Participatory projects have called for popular participation in project design, implementation, benefits, and evaluation. And decentralization schemes have provided discretionary funding to be used for locally defined development projects. Each of these experiments provides lessons relevant to contemporary public initiatives in support of community management.

Community Development

Though community development initiatives can be traced back to the 1920's, it was the Etawah pilot project in India that brought community development into prominence in the post-colonial era. Government-sponsored community development programs were introduced throughout much of the developing world during the 1950's, but were largely abandoned by the mid 1960's, due to a long list of well-documented failings.

It has been noted, for example, that the conflicts of interest inherent in stratified village social structures were ignored by program planners while existing power structures were accepted as given. Little or no attention was given to questions of asset control or to the structural barriers to improving the lot of the poor. Programs and targets were formulated centrally and were implemented through conventional bureaucratic structures with little regard to the willingness or capability of the people to respond. Little effort was devoted to building independent, member-controlled local organizations able to solve local problems, mobilize local resources, and make demands on the broader system. The village was treated as a self-contained development unit with little attention to either the policy context, or to the broader institutional linkages that influenced the viability of village level self-help activities.[6]

Popular Participation

In the late 1960's and early 1970's, equity and participation reasserted themselves as priorities on the international development agenda—a response to the failure of "trickle down" development to benefit the masses of the world's poor. Commitments emerged to a wide range of new projects and programs intended to get the benefits of development to the poor as quickly and directly as possible, primarily by providing publicly funded and administered social and extension services.

Though project and program plans invariably stressed the importance of popular participation, in reality meaningful participation was largely precluded by the planning procedures themselves. These procedures called for blueprinted project designs in which the key decisions regarding services, facilities, inputs, schedules, and outcomes were all centrally determined by planning experts. These experts had neither the incentive nor the means to obtain meaningful inputs from unorganized, poorly educated, and widely dispersed beneficiaries to the design of multi-million dollar projects. Once such plans were completed and accepted, the only avenue left for beneficiary participation was in providing free labor and materials to implement decisions in which they had no part.

Furthermore, these plans were implemented through centralized, hierarchical, rule-bound development agencies which allowed their local functionaries little discretionary authority to make adjustments in response to local needs or preferences. And there was little or no accountability to the people who had a direct interest in actual outcomes.

Decentralization

Where decentralization of administrative functions has been attempted in Asia, the emphasis commonly has been on the implementation of the national programs through local administrative units with little more than rhetorical commitment to development of the effective, locally accountable political structures required for responsive decision making.[7] Efforts of the latter type have consisted largely of providing central grants to local bodies to be used for small-scale, local infrastructure projects. But in both instances, central control and local dependence on central funding have been retained, often with little commitment to the more fundamental political and administrative reforms that might ultimately lead to self-managing local communities.

APPLYING THE LESSONS OF THE PAST: A CASE EXAMPLE

None of these approaches to stimulating local initiative provided a fundamental challenge to the idea that the government does development for the people, who are expected to respond with grateful acceptance of whatever guidance and assistance government chooses to offer. None challenged the nature of the government's role or the appropriateness of the structures and procedures through which government conducts its business.[8] None confronted basic issues of local social structures and resource control.

The more successful community management initiatives do seek to control these difficult issues. They define government's role in terms of enabling the self-help efforts of the people. Attention is given to reorienting the structures and procedures of public development agencies in ways consistent with this new role.[9] And community-level interventions seek broadly based empowerment in resource control and management.

One of the better known and more successful national scale, government-sponsored community management efforts is that of the National Irrigation Administration in the Philippines (NIA).[10] In the late 1970's the NIA came to realize that the major remaining opportunities for further expansion of irrigation coverage in the Philippines were found in improving the thousands of small farmer owned and operated "communal" irrigation systems which already provided approximately half of the Philippines' irrigation. Thus the NIA set about to develop its ability to provide effective assistance to these farmers in increasing the coverage and reliability of their systems. The key elements of the NIA's approach demonstrate the effective application of the lessons learned from the failures of community development, popular participation, and decentralization.

1. Major attention is devoted to building independent, member-controlled irrigator associations. Every aspect of NIA assistance in the development and improvement of system facilities is designated to provide the association with experience in problem solving, resource mobilization, and asserting itself in negotiations with NIA engineers. These associations are legally chartered by the

government as autonomous, self-managing corporate bodies with the right to assess user fees, hold and dispose of property, accept loans, and hire staff. And they are granted legally enforceable rights to the water which their system is authorized to use.

2. Prior to beginning work with any community, a socio-technical profile is prepared which illuminates existing power structures and the extent to which they represent broadly based irrigator interests. These profiles are reviewed by NIA staff in project assessment workshops at both provincial and regional levels to identify potential problems, including conflicts of interest within the community, and to plan strategies for use by NIA personnel in addressing them during implementation.

3. Organizing activities begin with the strengthening of smaller turn-out groups and the formation of numerous committees to perform tasks such as obtaining water rights, registering the association, obtaining rights of way, monitoring NIA's procurement process, and assisting NIA engineers with system layout. This broadens the base of participation, builds both leadership and followership skills, and provides members with an opportunity to see first hand which individuals are most likely to represent association interests if elected to formal leadership positions. Membership in associations is limited to actual land tillers, thus insuring the representation of tiller interests and broadening the power base within the community.

4. Community organizers fielded by NIA begin working with actual or prospective association members well before the initiation of design work on a specific system to prepare the prospective users to make effective inputs to the design. Once a design has been prepared, the engineering staff walks through the actual system with association members to insure agreement on the location and nature of every facility. Construction does not begin until the association has formally approved the plans and agreed to terms of loan repayments. The system is not considered completed until the association has accepted it as meeting specifications in a public ceremony. At this point the facilities become the formal property of the association, which assumes full responsibility for their operation and maintenance.

5. Future budgets of the provincial engineering office depend on loan repayments by the assisted associations, providing a strong incentive to the provincial engineer to insure continued satisfaction with NIA services by the association members and creating a considerable measure of local accountability.

6. In a process begun in 1977 and still continuing as of the time of this writing, NIA's top management has worked to reorient the

the agency's internal structures, planning and procedures, staffing patterns, training, and evaluation systems to reflect the requirements of the participatory approach.[11] As a consequence, the NIA has developed an essentially non-bureaucratic mode of operation based on well-disciplined, problem-solving teams at regional and provincial levels. These teams have considerable discretion in adapting assistance interventions to the specific needs and circumstances of individual communities.

Several generic features of this experience point to how community management is differentiated, as both concept and practice, from earlier community development and popular participation initiatives. Specifically: 1) assistance to each individual community group is designed and managed as a discrete project activity with its own specifications and time table responsive to the particular situation of that group, based on a careful study of existing practices, technical capacities, resource availabilities, and power structures; 2) the emphasis is on community control and management of the resource, and every aspect of the project intervention is geared to this outcome, including legal confirmation of resource ownership and legal recognition of the resource management group as an autonomous body with legal rights; 3) actual project design does not take place until the beneficiaries are fully prepared to make their needs and preferences known and, once completed, is not implemented until formally accepted by an association of the beneficiaries; 4) organizing takes account of and works within existing structures to the extent possible, while building member strength from the bottom up to insure broadly based participation by the actual producers and avoid domination by traditional leaders; 5) incentive systems within the agency are structured so as to strengthen the accountability of the project staff to assisted groups; 6) systematic, long-term attention is given to debureaucratizing agency systems and procedures, developing its capacity to work flexibly as a service agency in support of local resource management groups.

It is evident that a commitment to community management is not to be undertaken lightly by a public development agency. In the absence of such commitment, programs that adopt a community management label are likely in fact to suffer all the deficiencies of past community development, participation, and decentralization initiatives.

ORGANIZATION OF THE BOOK

Commonly development texts look at problems of resource management primarily from the view of the state on the presumption that the state represents the interests of the broader society. It is a top-down view that overlooks much of local reality, as well as the bias of the state action towards the interests of existing powerholders. A first step towards achieving a needed reorientation in development thinking and programming is to better understand the nature of the development problem as it is experienced by the people, and to appreciate more fully the nature and importance of their self-help actions, preferably from the people's own perspective. It is to this task that the present book is devoted, accepting the inherent limitation of any such effort undertaken by relatively privileged outsiders.

Part I takes a broad look at the value dimensions of development as these relate to the concept of community development. Criticizing conventional development strategies and the values that guide them, each of the three contributors to this section sees in the Asian people, their communities, and their social, religious, and philosophical traditions the basis for a more people-centered development process that nourishes the spirit as well as the body.

Contributors to Part II examine the variety of local circumstances facing both households and local governments, the essential complexity of the choices faced, and the dynamics of the local decision processes through which accommodation is made. They reveal a reality all but invisible to most bureaucratic decision makers who presume to make resource management choices for the community.

Part III illuminates the broad range of resources that local communities are able to bring to bear in addressing their needs and the complex social dynamics that both enable and constrain the effective and equitable use of their resources in the community interest. It also demonstrate the limited ability of many government agencies to get even the resources they control directly into the hands of those who are most in need.

Contributors to Part IV illustrate, through a series of case studies, the power-building processes through which external catalytic agents can contribute to the development of effective community management capacities. In so doing, they demonstrate the central role of empowerment in achieving more productive and more equitable development.

Government often assumes the lead in community management interventions with decidedly mixed results. Contributors to Part V draw on a variety of case experiences to examine the potentials and limitations of government as intervener in implementing programs intended to strengthen community resource management capacities.

While it is common for attention to focus on community-level program and project interventions, equally important are interventions directed to the creation of a favorable policy and institutional setting that motivates, protects, and mediates the conflicts of self-reliant community management efforts. Both public and private sector organizations have critical roles in the creation of such enabling settings. Part VI looks at some of the issues involved and offers specific guidance for policy makers from both sectors.

The Conclusion presents an essay examining why conventional development strategies, inspired by the economic and administrative structures and theories of 1950's industrialism, have neglected the role of communities in resource management. Observing that contemporary industrial societies are themselves undergoing a profound developmental transformation, it concludes that the strategies dominating Third World development action are based on outmoded concepts of the nature of modernization, and of the organizational forms appropriate to a modern society. The newly emerging information era opens a range of new possibilities, including resource management systems based on broadly based local control and initiative, which are at once consistent with the best of Asian values and traditions, and the most advanced of technologies and organizational forms.

NOTES

1. Typical is the argument of David Eaton that power must be viewed, "As a relationship in which one person or group is able to determine the actions of another in the direction of the former's own ends." *The Political System* (New York: Knopf, 1953), p. 143. Similar definitions of power may be found in Richard Emerson, "Power Dependence Relations," *American Sociological Review*, 27, No. 1, Feb., 1962, p. 32; and Gene Sharp, *The Politics of Nonviolent Action* (Boston: Porter Sargent Publisher, 1973). Parenti goes to the extent of suggesting that it is only the implication "of dominance, gain, and loss which make[s] power of compelling interest to students of politics." Michael Parenti, *Power and the Powerless* (New York: St. Martin's Press, 1978), p. 6.

2. The distinction between power's distributive and generative dimensions is made by Talcott Parsons, *Structure and Process in Modern Societies* (Glencoe: The Free Press, 1960), pp. 220-1. Parsons makes specific note of the tendency of social scientists to focus only on the distributive dimension.

3. This seems to be a universal reality of social units. Previous studies have attributed this to different levels of interaction-influence, which is a form or manifestation of social energy, which Soedjatmoko discusses in Chapter 1 of this volume. See Rensis Likert, *The Human Organization* (New York: McGraw-Hill, 1967). Field studies that confirm differential patterns and levels of interaction influence across organizations and cultures are reported in Arnold S. Tannenbaum *Control in Organizations* (New York: McGraw-Hill, 1969); and Arnold S. Tannenbaum, Bogdan Kavcic, Menachem Rosner, Mino Vianello, and Georg Wieser, *Hierarchy in Organizations* (San Francisco: Jossey-Bass Publishers, 1974).

4. Severyn T. Bruyn, "Social Theory of Nonviolent Action: A Framework for Research in Creative Conflict," in Severyn T. Bruyn and Paula M. Rayman (eds.), *Nonviolent Action and Social Change* (New York: Irvington Publishers, 1979), pp. 19-20.

5. McClelland makes a distinction between *personalized* and *socialized* power. Personalized power is exercised through exploitation and expropriation of the property and self-esteem of other individuals. Socialized power is achieved through increasing the sense of capacity or power of others. He reports on research demonstrating the apparent paradox that the

leader becomes truely effective only by turning his or her followers into leaders, into origins rather than pawns. David C. McClelland, "The Two Faces of Power," *Journal of International Affairs*, Vol. XXIV, No. 1, 1970, 29-47.

6. Lane C. Holdcroft, *The Rise and Fall of Community Development in Developing Countries, 1950-65: A Critical Analysis and an Annotated Bibliography*, MSU Rural Development Paper No. 2, Department of Agricultural Economics, Michigan State University, East Lansing, Michigan 48824, 1978; Norman T. Uphoff, John M. Cohen, and Arther A. Goldsmith, *Feasibility and Application of Rural Development Participation: A State-of-the-Art Paper*, Monograph Series No. 3, Rural Development Committee, Cornell University, Ithaca, New York, January 1979; and Edgar Owens and Robert Shaw, *Development Reconsidered: Bridging the Gap Between Government and People* (Lexington: Lexington Books, 1972).

7. Harry J. Friedman, "Decentralized Development in Asia: Local Political Alternatives" in G. Shabbar Cheema and Dennis A. Rondinelli (eds.), *Decentralization and Development: Policy Implementation in Developing Countries* (Beverly Hills: Sage Publications, 1983), pp. 35-57.

8. These issues are examined in detail in David C. Korten and Felipe B. Alfonso, *Bureaucracy and the Poor: Closing the Gap* (West Hartford: Kumarian Press, 1983).

9. David C. Korten and Norman T. Uphoff, *Bureaucratic Reorientation for Participatory Rural Development*, NASPAA Working Paper No. 1, Washington, D.C.: NASPAA, November 1981; and Derick W. Brinkerhoff, "Inside Public Bureaucracy: Empowering Managers to Empower Clients," *Rural Development Participation Review*, Vol. 1, No. 1, Summer 1979, pp. 7-9.

10. The most complete account of this experience currently available is Benjamin U. Bagadion and Frances F. Korten, "Developing Irrigators' Organizations: A Learning Process Approach to a Participatory Irrigation Program," in Michael Cernea (ed.), *Putting People First* (Baltimore: Johns Hopkins University Press, 1985).

11. Explicit application was made of learning concepts and methods outlined in David C. Korten, "Community Organization and Rural Development: A Learning Process Approach," *Public Administration Review*, Vol. 40, No. 5, September/October 1980, 480-511.

PART I: INTRODUCTION

DEVELOPMENT AS A HUMAN ENTERPRISE

David C. Korten

The human meaning of development is found in its contribution to actualizing the highest potentials of human life. Achieving an economic standard that insures all people the satisfaction of their basic needs is one fundamental and essential step toward this goal. But even basic needs are appropriately defined in terms of much more than consumption goods such as food, shelter, clothing, and health care. They include needs for personal security, for love, for being a respected and productive member of one's community, and for spiritual growth. All too little writing on development explores its non-material dimensions, and development programs rarely, if ever, give attention to planning for nonmaterial outcomes. Similarly, development thought and practice are prone to neglect what is perhaps the most central and yet least tangible of development resources, the social energy created by the commitments and interactions of people working toward shared goals. A concept of development measurable only in terms of the monetary value of physical production and consumption is particularly alien to the deeper cultural, philosophical, and religious traditions of Asia.

The contributors to this section are among those who are searching for a concept of development and an approach to its attainment consistent with the deepest of human values and aspirations richly articulated in Asian religion and philosophy. Universally they condemn imported development models that have been concerned with people only as producers and consumers, concentrated power in the hands of planners and bureaucrats, and marginalized rural populations. They seek a broadly shared awakening of the human spirit and the stimulation of local initiative based on a sense of shared humanity and a search for self-realization. Here community management becomes more than a means of more effi-

cient distribution of irrigation water and for preserving forest resources—
though it is this also. It becomes as well the basis of an alternative concept of the very nature of development. The perspectives of these contributors are neither anti-Western nor anti-modern. They are simply
pro-people.

Some progressive thinkers from both East and West believe the basis
for a society at once human and modern may be found in a creative
melding of the highest of Eastern spiritual and social traditions with the
most advanced of Western information age technology. One of the most
admired among such thinkers is Soedjatmoko, who in Chapter one, joins
the wisdom of a Balinese painter to the power of space age information
technology in a call for the creation of local information environments to
release the social energy of the people and accelerate the social learning
processes through which people can create their own development.

Religion is a pervasive force in the routines of daily life throughout
much of Asia. But the sterile "value-free" models of development in vogue
in recent decades have all but ignored its relevance. A. T. Ariyaratne is
one of those rare development practitioners who has devoted himself to
realizing religion's potential as a creative development force. The Sarvodaya
Shramadana Movement of Sri Lanka, of which he is founder and leader,
represents the pratical realization of his vision. In Chapter two, Ariyaratne
explicates the Buddhist origins of Sarvodaya's development philosophy
and how Sarvodaya attempts to translate it into village-led development
action through a process of individual and community awakening. In so
doing he reveals his deep respect for the values, wisdom, and basic
humanity of the rural poor.[1]

The theme of respect for village life in a predominantly Buddhist rural
society is picked up by Apichart Thongyu in a poem titled "Reflections
of a Village Development Worker" translated by James Hopkins. Apichart
is himself the development worker whose inner conflicts regarding his
role in seeking to modernize the people of a rural village in Thailand are
revealed in the poem. While some readers may find Apichart's account
to be overly romantic, surely no one should presume to intervene in a
rural community who does not share at least in part Apichart's conflict
born of deep respect for the people he presumes to serve.

These contributions set the broader context for the more focused contributions of subsequent sections.

NOTES

1. For further discussion of Sarvodaya, its programs, and the derivation of its philosophy
see Joanna Macy, *Dharma and Development: Religion as Resource in the Sarvodaya Self-Help Movement* (West Hartford: Kumarian Press, 1985).

CHAPTER ONE

Social Energy as a Development Resource[1]

Soedjatmoko

—I am moved by your work. What inspires you?
—First is religion, which nourishes the soul.
Second is art, which nourishes the heart and the feelings.
Third are the interactions of the people of my village, which create social energy.
—Balinese painter

The Hindu island of Bali is the home of a rather distinctive culture within Indonesia. It is a poor island, but the society is well-integrated, dynamic, creative, and supremely adaptive, and my painter-friend seemed to embody all of these qualities personally. I was struck by the wisdom of his answer, particularly as I realized that in his humble but profound way he had identified what may be the most potent and underutilized of development resources. I asked myself then—and these reflections today are part of my continuing questioning—how can the inherent social energy common to healthy village communities be nurtured and released in the community interest on a scale required to overcome the limitations of the failed development models of the past thirty years?

Today, more than three decades after the post-World War II development effort was launched, the world remains conspicuously and tragically beset with unacceptable suffering, want, and strife, as the gap between rich and poor continues to widen. While a great deal has been accomplished for many people, the underlying reality is that our best efforts of the past have failed to deal effectively with the problem of poverty. If anything, the scale of international poverty is even greater today than it was in the past despite the relatively higher growth rates some developing countries have achieved. Throughout the world, hundreds of millions remain in an intolerable state of degradation and despair—ill-housed and ill-cared for, gnawed by hunger which saps their physical and mental capacities. Without much prospect of productive and decently remunerated work, their real needs remain ignored by national development schemes. The great remaining problem is how to release the latent energies of these whom Gandhiji called "the last, the least, the lowest and the lost."

DEVELOPMENT AS LEARNING

For all our efforts, it remains for us to develop the social, economic, and political capacity for development, at all levels and in all component parts of our societies that will enable our nations to reduce poverty, unemployment, and inequality, and to survive and evolve in an unstable, complex, interdependent, and increasingly competitive world. Our failure is, I believe, due in part to looking on development as something we do through action or acquired skill rather than as something we learn through our own efforts and experience.

The form of learning that lies at the heart of development is the rather elusive process called *social learning*. One observer has described this as a learning form unique to the human species in that it presumes a learning environment characterized by interaction with other learning organisms.[2] It is a collective process by which neighborhoods, villages, communities, and ultimately the nation state prepare themselves not only to adjust to change, but also to direct change to suit their own purposes. In the present instance it must involve learning to break out of the mind-set that accepts passivity as the only relevant response to centuries of oppression and powerlessness; learning that the individual has rights and learning what they are; learning that people have the right and the possibility to use new opportunities; learning as a community to organize for the attainment of goals that may not have been part of traditional life; and learning as a society to enhance capacity for timely course corrections. In looking to the future, I believe that it is the capacity to learn that will determine, perhaps more than any other single factor, the viability, autonomy, and integrity of Asian societies.

Failed Development Models and Interlocking Changes

We cannot look toward the future merely in terms of advances within the framework of traditional development models and approaches. Both the successes and failures of the development experience have shown that the organized pursuit of material improvement does not automatically bring in its wake freedom, human dignity, justice, and civility. These values have in fact fallen victim to the development endeavor, even when the provision of basic services include access to education and legal protection.[3]

A further reason we cannot rely on the classic development models and approaches is that we in Asia have already experienced discontinuities with past experience such that Asian society today would be virtually unrecognizable to the early practitioner of development back in the 1950's. These changes have been driven by the impact of science and technology, uneven patterns of growth, the intrusion of alien cultures and values into traditional societies, increases in population density, heightened political awareness, growth of international communication systems, large-scale migration of peoples, and sharply altered life styles and life situations. The changes in both our reality and our thinking have been sufficiently profound that the development efforts of these past three decades have been trying to hit a moving target.

The positive or negative responses of individual Asian cultures to these changes are prefigured by the deep structure of each culture and shaped by the world view underlying it as much as they are affected by the geographical, political, or economic and social conditions prevailing in that particular country. Consequently the management of the change processes underlying Asian development must be quite setting specific.

Creating a capacity for such management involves learning needs of both a technical and a social nature. There must be a mastery of skills permitting modern science and technology to be handled constructively and adapted appropriately to social needs at all levels. At the same time, new skills are needed to keep the inevitable disparities in development manageable and within morally acceptable bounds within each community as well as within the nation as a whole. In attempting to develop these skills, we must begin to realize that development is not a linear process but rather a complex of closely interlinked changes.

Needed: The Courage to Release Control

The opportunity to organize, manage, and profit from one's own endeavors creates a motivation to learn, and, very often, a motivation to communicate one's acquired knowledge. This kind of learning takes place when circumstances encourage it between neighbors, business associates, farmers in contiguous fields, and so forth. And it is the kind of teaching and learning that has transformed some voluntary associations into the most powerful development agencies that operate in some parts of the developing world.

Recently the Self-Employed Women's Association in Ahmedabad, India sponsored a video workshop for its members in which they actually made films about their lives and experience. The joy, the sense of accomplishment, the feeling of empowerment that followed this experience was palpable, as I personally observed. Mothers' clubs, traditional savings associations, funeral societies, irrigation or forestry co-operatives, mutual assistance housing pacts, marketing co-operatives and so forth all provide examples of the successful mobilization of social energy through a social learning process.

It is important for governments to encourage and enable such initiatives, but governments have rarely been successful in creating them. Too often, political and bureaucratic institutions have been a source of obstruction rather than encouragement to local initiatives. Indeed we might as well face squarely the fact that, because they are outside the framework of bureaucratic programs, spontaneous movements that organize and share information independently are often seen as a threat to central control. And indeed in some respects they are such a threat, so it takes a degree of courage for governments to encourage them whole-heartedly. I am utterly convinced, however, that the reward for relinquishing all-embracing control is worth the risk as it creates the possibility of unleashing the social energy that is the most essential of our development resources.

Public Agencies, Private Initiatives, and Social Movements

The top-down approach to development has been thoroughly discredited by hard experience. Its failure has led to the search for alternative development theories including the bottom-up approach, the participatory approach, and the basic needs approach. None of these constitute a full-fledged development strategy: all require enabling national policy frameworks and institutional structures for them to be effective.

Traditional factors have been instrumental in determining what is perceived as a proper relationship between the governing and the governed, between state and society. They explain a great deal about the difficulties in turning a colonial bureaucracy, dedicated primarily to preserving order and collecting revenue, into a dynamic developmental agency dedicated to public service. Furthermore, modern training in development administration, with its emphasis on efficiency and technique, has unwittingly tended to strengthen deeply rooted colonial and pre-colonial paternalistic notions about the official's relationship to the public. It has further reinforced the elite's disinclination to accept the legitimacy and importance of people's participation, self-management, and self-reliance as essential vehicles for development.

We have also seen large programs of rural development mounted by international agencies that have resulted in the increase in the power of the local bureaucracy while stifling the potential for local leadership. Projects that started in the name of develpment have sometimes produced other kinds of unanticipated consequences as well.

The time has come to devote ourselves to explicit strategies for democratic structural changes that will enable people to liberate themselves from oppressive social structures which perpetuate their dependency and their powerlessness—including those of many of our public bureaucracies. Only in this way can we build societies with resilience and a capacity for autonomous creativity and continuous redefinition—the conditions essential for survival in a crowded, competitive, and rapidly changing world. Shaping such strategies will in itself require a great deal of learning.

But three decades of development experience suggest that the bureaucratic approach to the poor will have to be replaced by efforts to mobilize the social energy that normally is generated as a product of self-organized activity. Such an empowerment process must be fully reponsive to the material, social, and spiritual aspirations of the poor, as commitments to self-organized activity are only likely to be made in support of such aspirations. At the same time self-organized action can only be productive to the extent that it is directed to realizing aspirations that are consistent with the constraints as well as the opportunities—economic, social, and technological—of their situation. Ultimately only the poor can define their own aspirations and negotiate their adjustment to the possible.

To support the poor in their own learning, the more privileged members of society must learn the art of listening and be willing to recognize their past mistakes. Too often, local bureaucrats, taking their cue from the national bureaucracy, have been averse to listening to ordinary citizens. Many of the projects created and managed by governments, moreover, leave little decision making to citizens and thus generate little popular participation and support. Various studies of development "success stories" demonstrate the importance of a learning process in which local residents, both male and female, and program experts share their knowledge and display a willingness to learn from mistakes and make adjustments accordingly. Yet frequently the best-intentioned "participatory" development strategies falter because they rely on a bureaucracy unable to respond to community needs and unwilling to rely on community skills and problem-solving capacities, even though it is just such resources that time and again have proven to be basis of effective action.

With central governments simply incapable of dealing with the enormous, often inchoate social and cultural forces shaping Asian societies, we need to consider what other kinds of institutions and modes of organization might help to fashion the learning processes necessary to deal with these forces before they engulf us totally.

One problem is, of course, that we simply may not know, through any sort of ordered, rational process, which institutions may prove to be most effective. History tells us of the rise of spontaneous, unexpected currents that have altered the course of human affairs—the Gandhian movement in India is a classic example. Such forces for change and renewal, which arise outside the normal government structure, are bound to continue. Finding ways to encourage and facilitate these impulses will test the creative abilities of established structures including governments.

The Learning Agenda

As indicated by the argument above, the need to learn is not limited to the poor. It is the essence of the whole development process requiring all segments and levels of society to meet new learning needs. Communities will have to learn new lessons in the management of developmental or sectoral activities—for example, the management of community irrigation or forestry projects. Government bureaucracies and institutions will have to learn to adjust to such a system of self-management.

The kinds of adjustments that development and social change require today involve learning beyond that which takes place in the formal educatioin system as these adjustments will have to be made by all layers of society. It is a period when change compounds change, mutual learning processes in support of social, political, and organizational innovation must be stimulated in which there are no teachers and no students. It must involve the governments as well as the citizens, the poor as well as the rich, the planners and administrators as well as their targets.

The learning agenda must be broadly defined to include learning to organize for new purposes, to adjust traditional institutions to serve these ends, and to continuously scan for new technologies that might upgrade traditional capabilities. The role of non-governmental organizations and civic volunteers, who straddle the modern world and traditional cultures, will be crucial in this endeavor.

The response of formal education systems to such new needs and potentials has thus far been inadequate even in conventional education and far from what is called for in this much broader learning process. In many places a number of other institutions and organizations have gotten into the business of education, including corporations, labor unions, the military, governmental and private agencies, libraries, museums, and professional associations. In Japan, both newspapers and department stores run educational and cultural training programs. In the United States, the educational programs of the giant communications company, AT&T, enrolled nearly half a million people in 1979 before the company was broken up. This total exceeded that of the largest university system in the world, the State University of New York.[4]

Power Sharing and Political Integration

History has shown how difficult it is for any elite to learn how to share power with others, and to realize that only a constantly expanding polity will ensure the continued viability of the state to say nothing of the continuity of their own privileged position. It further demonstrates that the resort to military power is often an admission of the elite's inability to handle certain problems.

One may wonder what incentives might motivate those in power to commit themselves to learning to share power. Beyond the satisfaction of living by humanitarian ideals and responsible citizenship, there is the very pragmatic reality of the pressure that growing numbers of poor are putting on the land and water resources on which the well-being of the powerful and powerless alike ultimately depends. Increasing density in rural areas is driving people to exploit marginal lands more intensively. The communities that have traditionally lived there have worked out their own ways of working productively within ecological limits, but larger numbers of people threaten to stretch the ecological carrying capacity beyond its limits. In a sense the ecological future will depend not on what the experts in the cities think but on the decisions of the hundreds of millions of peasants in the poor countries.

The scientific basis of a more productive, sustainable way of life is already available for many kinds of ecological conditions. But the knowledge has not yet reached the people whose very survival depends on it; and their communities are not organized to use scientific knowledge even when it is available. It is not only in their interest but in the interest of all of us on this globe to make sure that we find more effective methods of delivering scientific knowledge to these end-users.

We are also in a situation in which large segments of the powerless, the marginalized and the poor in our societies no longer accept their condition as inevitable. Where they are incapable of doing something about it directly, they act indirectly. And so, millions and millions of people in Asia are on the move, either to the larger cities or across national boundaries or even across continents escaping from violence and/or seeking release from their poverty. Unemployment, of course, is often coupled with a sense of despair that leads many into escapism, criminality or purposeless rage. Urban criminality has become a major problem in the larger cities in Asia. And this is simply the tip of an iceberg, the beginning of a process of implosion of our social and political systems, whatever their ideological orientation.

History also shows that the political elites face a dilemma in dealing with these issues as attempts to share power are themselves frequently accompanied by conflict and struggle. There is therefore the need for the society to develop the adequate resilience to go through such crises as inevitable phases in the process of constant adjustment. Unless such a resilience and flexibility is developed, conflict may pass beyond the point of no return to the breakdown of the moderating center, polarization, and a continuously escalating spiral of violence.

There is a similar urgent need at the political level for learning how to integrate politically different segments of society which are at different levels of social and technical development. The assumption has been that development would automatically socialize people into the existing political system. We are now beginning to recognize—in the unceasing flare of violence and strife we see between recent achievers and those who feel left behind—that this assumption was incorrect. These tensions are, of course, all the more capable of erupting into murderous retaliation and counter-retaliation when a regressive economy makes the gaps between the two rival groups all the more apparent and harder to close. Whatever the situation, however, this is a problem that has forcefully driven home our need for mutual tolerance in different religious and social groupings.

SIGNIFICANCE OF THE COMMUNICATIONS REVOLUTION

In both city and countryside there is little question that increasingly sophisticated communications have sharply affected aspirations and life styles and led to higher levels of political consciousness. They have brought shifts in values so profound that in many cases, one can speak in terms of generational quantum jumps.

It is worth reminding ourselves that when the post-war development experience began in the early 1950's, the modern communications age was just dawning. The transistor had been invented a short time before, the first Sputnik was not yet launched, and the first communications satellite was five years beyond that feat. Microchips had not yet been devised, and the typical computer was enormously expensive, very large, and accessible only to a handful of specialists.

The new information and communications technologies proliferated at an astonishing speed in developing countries. During the late 1950's and 1960's, according to UNESCO statistics, radio ownership increased by more than a hundredfold in Latin America, by more than two hundred times in Asia, and more than four hundredfold in Africa. Television, with its even greater power to stir hopes and expectations, followed apace.

While this information revolution is having a profound impact on the rural areas of the South, this is a mere shadow of the impact the new, information-based technologies are having in the North. There, a new industrial revolution is now taking place based on advances in biotechnology. If the countries of the South do not develop the capacity to participate in this revolution, they will become even more vulnerable and dependent on the North than they are now.

We can no longer afford to think in terms of closing a knowledge gap. Rather, we will have to leap over a whole generation of outmoded technologies and theories of organization. We do not have time to repeat the mistakes of the North or even to follow passively in their footsteps picking up techniques that they have outgrown and discarded. We must cultivate the art of innovation or invent it in a form that is consonant with the real needs of our societies.

The information revolution creates possibilities in Asia for significant social innovation. Access to information is itself a kind of power, and the empowerment that independent access brings is multiplied when information can be exchanged as well as received. New information and communication technologies, ranging from those as simple as the cassette tape to those as complex as the communications satellite hold out this promise. They can be organized in a way that not only permits people to choose information from a larger and more varied menu but also permits them to participate in programming, in reporting news relevent to themselves, and in sharing what they have learned with others.

Creating Local Information Environments

The idea that bureaucratic government agencies can develop local leadership is an illusion. A more promising strategy for development and strengthening of broadly based local leadership is through the creation of local micro-information environments in which co-operation between villager and project worker can flourish. For example, such local learning environments could be stimulated by establishing decentralized radio stations and citizen-band systems through which farmers could exchange information on local crop prices, weather, and market conditions. Through the use of video tapes we might be able to revitalize oral tradtitions and bring even the illiterate into the information age.

The information environment in its totality—including every medium from wall-posters and folk-plays to television and computer data banks—must be shaped in such a way that it is accessible to all. Material that is only comprehensible to more highly educated residents works to the relative disadvantage of less educated groups and would only serve to widen the income gap. Villagers and urbanites also need specific information about their rights as citizens. Ideally, this should be allied to the knowledge of where and how to obtain legal redress for injustices, but even the basic information about individual and collective rights may encourage people to assert themselves. Above all, and this cannot be emphasised too strongly, the informatioin channels must include new or improved mechanisms for dialogue and interaction—in short, for mutual learning.

To meet the learning needs of development, there obviously must be an unprecedented flow of information into the villages and urban neighborhoods, capable of reaching the poorest as well as the traditional channels of communications such as the village headman, the extension services, and the school system. What is urgently called for is the transformation of the village from a traditional society to an "information community," capable of acting and responding creatively to the information reaching it and capable of generating its own information as well as seeking out new information as needed.

MARKETS AND SMALL ENTERPRISES AS LEARNING ENVIRONMENTS

Markets have always been important loci of information. It is interesting to note that even in several countries where private capital is not accepted as a legitimate basis for economic activity, the mechanisms of the marketplace are increasingly valued for their information-clearing functions.

Similarly in both socialist and capitalist as well as mixed economies, innovation seems to be most at home in relatively small enterprises that are allowed to exercise initiative, take risks, and gather and dispense information. The resilience of an economy depends, to a large extent, on such small enterprises. The problem, however, has been to organize the small entrepreneurial units into networks large enough to benefit from larger marketing systems, quality-control methods, technological innovations, credit systems, and other possible economies of scale.

One working model for dealing with this problem that is well worth study involves the 15,000 to 20,000 textile firms operating in the Prato area of Italy.[5] Most are very small and employ only a few workers. In these businesses, which provide work to 70,000 people directly and to another 20,000 in supporting services, traditional forms of production, social relations, and technologies survive side by side with very advanced production technologies and marketing systems. There is a blend of old and new technologies in an industry which is deeply rooted in the local historical tradition and social structures.

The Prato experience, and similar experiences elsewhere, such as in the Sakaki region in Japan, suggest possibilities for dispersed rural industrial production systems in developing countries which would be competitive with urban production centers. Such arrangements would ensure that the urban areas would no longer monopolize new economic opportunities. This in turn might lead to new and more equitable urban-rural configurations, a central issue the solution to which has so far escaped all development efforts aimed at poverty reduction. The prospects of this kind of rural industrialization hinge on a systematic effort constantly to modernize existing technologies and continuously integrate old and new technologies. It also depends on linking up traditional crafts and social infrastructure with modern, even computerized, quality control and marketing systems.

CONCLUSION

All of the evidence we have accumulated from the past three decades—during which the global community has evolved into some 160 nation-states beset by swirling configurations of power; rising ethnic, religious and cultural tensions; and millions afoot fleeing fear and hunger in quest of a better life—should teach us finally just how complex a thing the development effort is. Gone are our comfortable technocratic illusions that development success is basically achieving a kind of critical mass of skills, machinery, and capital.

Furthermore we are realizing that the ultimate purpose of development is to make the population of a country—especially its weak and poor—not only more productive but also more socially effective and self-aware. Truly humane development requires human growth in the sense of people becoming freer human beings, liberated from their own sense of powerlessness and dependency.

To achieve the innovations that are both necessary and possible there is need for new policies to remove existing structural impediments to efforts by the people to generate and apply their social energy to the social learning on which true development depends. These policies must reflect the special quality of social energy as a spontaneous creation of the inner spirit of the people. Government can control it only by destroying it and, in the process, destroying that spirit. Thus, rather than seeking its control, governments must learn how to help the people create structures which nurture and sustain that most precious of all development resources through allowing it to find productive expression.

The policies that have guided development to date—and perhaps misguided is a fairer description—have tended to do just the opposite. They have tended to suppress the very social forces on which true development ultimately depends by bureaucratizing the development process and by creating and reinforcing powerful political constituencies among the urban elites to the relative neglect of the rural masses. Of course, much needed corrective actions leading to a change in the balance between the urban and rural sectors and an integration into the national mainstream of the previously disenfranchised and marginalized will amount to a fundamental change in the distribution of economic and political power.

I do not wish to sound naive. I realize full well that such a change entails grave political risks for any government brave enough to attempt it. Given the fragility of many governments in the developing world—despite the authoritarian character of a great number of them—their capacity to make a fundamental adjustment of this kind within a short period is limited. At the same time, the risks of continuing to ignore the problem may prove even more catastrophic. There is therefore a tradeoff between present and future risks.

I believe that five general qualities will characterize the leaders and institutions of those societies that adapt successfully to these challenges.

- First they must be flexible and innovative, not frozen in old rigidities, and must be prepared constantly to take up new initiatives and directions.

- Second, they must possess a working familiarity with the latest achievements in science and technology.

- Third, they must be firmly rooted in the cultural soil of the society they seek to serve, and able to relate society's goals to currents on the international scene.

- Fourth, they must approach their very difficult learning tasks in a spirit of humility, cognizant that human endeavor is as capable of folly as of wisdom.

- Fifth, and finally, the leaders and institutions of the future must be keenly aware that development is much more than a quick technological fix. It is driven also, in very important ways, by the inner impulses of the human spirit, which often are reflected in religious or moral convictions.

In 1937 Albert Einstein, who was a great humanist as well as a great scientist, said,

> Our time is distinguished by wonderful achievements in the fields of scientific understanding and the technical applications of those insights. Who would not be cheered by this? But let us not forget that knowledge and skills alone cannot lead humanity to a happy and dignified life. Humanity has every reason to place the proclaimers of high moral standards and values above the discoverers of objective truth . . . What these blessed men have given us we must guard and try to keep alive with all our strength if humanity is not to lose its dignity, the security of its existence, and its joy in living.

NOTES

1. Based on two lectures titled "Development as Learning" delivered by the author to the Tenth Vikram Sarabhai Memorial Lectures, Ahmedabad, India, 19-20 January 1985. The author is currently Rector of United Nations University.

2. E. S. Dunn, Jr. in *People-Centered Development* (West Hartford: Kumarian Press, 1984) edited by David C. Korten and Rudi Klauss.

3. Indeed it seems to make little difference whether one started from the philosophy of growth

or that of equity. The growth models tended to founder on the resistance of elites to sharing the new wealth that came to them with this approach. The pursuit of equity led to the bureaucratization of society without accompanying economic growth. We now have a lot of experience in developing countries to show neither growth nor equity follows one another automatically.

4. C. R. Wharton, Jr., "Education 1984: Renaissance and Reform." Address to Education Commission of the States, St. Paul, Minn., 2 August 1984.

5. C. Mazzonis, U. Colombo, and G. Lanzavecchia, "Co-operative Organization and Constant Moderinization of the Textile Industry at Prato, Italy."

CHAPTER TWO

Asian Values as a Basis for Asian Development[1]

A. T. Ariyaratne

The common people of Asia have found themselves at the receiving end of grand plans from bureaucrats and policy makers, sermons from moralizers, and goods and services from a market economy. They have little or no control over the ideas, technologies, strategies, and structures that are imposed upon them from outside. To make things worse they are also made morally and legally accountable for whatever is imposed upon them through a representative democracy which in itself has become a mechanical process mostly devoid of human values.

Common people prefer personal relationships, intimate shared experiences, direct cultural and spiritual life, household and small economic arrangements, participatory democracy, and community politics. They are guided more by intuitive understanding than by organized and systematized knowledge.

Unfortunately development as practiced in much of post-independent Asian society appears to be an elitist exercise that has pushed common people to an increasing state of dependency and nonparticipation in the decision-making processes that effect their lives.

THE SOCIAL COSTS OF INAPPROPRIATE DEVELOPMENT

An increasing disparity is evident between the intuitive understanding of common people as to what development is about, and the organized knowledge and predetermined expectations of the privileged in society pertaining to development. The social cost in terms of political and communal violence, moral degeneration, economic stagnation, and increased poverty has been very heavy. These are evident in Sri Lanka as in most other Asian societies and are a consequence of the violence to our values and social institutions thrust upon our societies by an inappropriate development path. This violence is revealed in:

1. The loss of faith the individual has suffered in himself or herself.

2. A life based upon a reliance on the less worthwhile goals such as acquisition and possession of material wealth, power, position, and status and over-indulgence in the pleasures of the senses.

3. The adoption of anti-social and immoral means such as violence, deception, competition, corruption, and exploitation in order to achieve these goals.

4. The disintegration suffered by society as a consequence of the divisiveness of caste, class, creed, race, and party politics.

5. The maldistribution and improper utilization of the factors of production vis-à-vis land, labor, capital, organization, and human resources, and the resulting failure to achieve the maximum welfare of one and all in a society whose population is increasing rapidly.

6. The complete faith that is placed in the efficacy of large scale organization in the field of politics, finance, commerce and industry.

7. Excessive dependence that is placed on an export-import economy based on cash crops instead of on the sounder economy of self-reliance.

8. The subservience of the village to the city or town.

9. Relying too much on the ability of the politician and the administrator to solve both material and spiritual problems of society, while failing to evoke the inherent strength of the people to solve their own problems.

10. Failure on the part of our leadership to understand that in the performance of their public duties they themselves have to obey the very moral laws that are recognized to be applicable to the individual.

11. Lack of an integrated and coherent plan of national development giving every individual a place in its formulation and implementation.

Like the germs of a terrible disease attacking the body of a helpless victim, these evils have eaten into the very fabric of our society. A drastic change is called for to remedy them, and any delay will result in untold damage to the nations of Asia. The inherent talents and resources available and lying unused must be harvested for the good of the community through people's movements which spring from the people's will and values.

INSTITUTIONAL vs. PEOPLE'S PLANNING

Many of the disruptive consequences of development can be traced to our excessive reliance on institutional planning, the general tendency of which is to make people more and more dependent on impersonal and distant institutions. They feel more and more alienated from centers of decision making and meaningful action. Their creative nature is never manifest in worthwhile activities. People feel compelled to seek redress through petitions to administrators, *tamashas* to please political leaders, letters of introduction from influential persons and other such wasteful actions. Finally they overthrow governments by using the only power they have, the free vote—at least in those countries where this means of expression is available. But with a new government usually the vicious circle starts again, as the institutionalized economy is pressurized still more by increasing unemployment and inflation.

On the other hand, a true people's plan sets in motion a series of activities in households and local small communities that will not depend so much on the money economy, jobs, or impersonal behavior of distant institutions. It can develop itself into a mass movement aimed at the satisfaction of basic human needs principally depending on people's creativity and efforts in their own social milieu.

RECREATING A HARMONIOUS SOCIAL ORDER

During the period of industrialization in Europe and the subsequent commercial expansion towards the East, production of wealth was a material and mechanical affair from which spiritual and humanistic considerations were totally absent and was the sole economic philosophy that interested the Western capitalists. We cannot go on with this theory. In our society, the human being is just as, or even more, important as an end in himself—although we are equally anxious to increase our economic productivity to give him a higher standard of living. The dilemma we are faced with today is how to harmonize economic theory with our age-old wealth.

In Sri Lanka the old social order achieved and ensured a contented, dignified, and satisfied people for centuries on end. With the advent of commercialism from the West and the subsequent conquest of our land by foreigners, the old order broke down without being replaced by a viable new one. The new values, technologies, and socio-economic political structures never achieved a coherence comparable to that of the old society they replaced—a society in which the elements of individual, family, village, or national life fitted one into the other most beautifully, and functioned as a harmonious whole.

To achieve a comparable coherence, development should take place from the grassroots up and not vice versa and should relate itself to the cultural and spiritual values of the people. Its techniques should be adapted to the particular situation. Planners and development thinkers all over the world today are speaking such words. They are part of the responsible language of a more people-centered development. But this latest development vocabulary will remain only the self-satisfying jargon of distant technocrats unless a deeper spiritual-cultural and socio-economic meaning is given to its words.

PRINCIPLES OF BUDDHIST PHILOSOPHY

In the third century B.C., Sri Lanka became a Buddhist country, and every aspect of Sri Lankan life—be it social relationships, the political economy, art and architecture, education and literature—was nurtured in the cradle of Buddhist culture. Four-and-a-half centuries of foreign domination in Sri Lanka did not destroy this influence.

Principles for Human Emancipation

According to Lord Buddha's teachings man's suffering is mainly due to his ignorance of the true nature of things within him and around him. Buddha noted three principles of reality, which he taught must be discovered by each individual who would achieve emancipation.

1. **The Principle of Change or Impermanence:** All phenomena, whether physical or mental, social or spiritual, are caused by various factors or conditions coming together, and these conditions and phenomena are in a state of constant change.

2. **The Principle of Suffering:** One who fails to understand the fact that everything changes every moment, and who develops a strong tendency to crave for and grasp things with greed, invariably comes to grief when he has to part with them.

3. **The Principle of Egolessness:** The deceptive notion of I, me, and mine is the root cause of anger, hatred, and greed. The Lord Buddha dismissed as false the belief in a permanent unchanging personality arising from the 'Ego' or 'I' factor of the personality.

The Well-being of All

These three principles of reality have conditioned the minds of the people in Sri Lanka for centuries. They provide the basis for the core of the Buddhist philosophy, which is a respect for all life as expressed in the concept of Sarvodaya, "The well-being of all." Mahatma Gandhi perhaps realized the danger of the Western political concept of "The greatest good of the greatest number" to an Indian society already divided by race, caste, religion and language. In its place he called on his people to accept the concept of Sarvodaya as the one thought that would unify their nation ideologically and lead it towards an exploitation-free society of equal citizens. Unless one's ideological conditioning is nonfragmentary and embraces harmoniously one's own welfare with the welfare of others, one cannot go very far as an effective agent of social change.

SARVODAYA SHRAMADANA MOVEMENT: AN EXPRESSION OF BUDDHIST THOUGHT IN ACTION

The Sarvodaya Shramadana Movement in Sri Lanka represents the practical translation of the basic principles of Buddhist philosophy into a people-centered development movement. These principles are embodied in the name itself. As "Sarvodaya" signifies a thought, "Shramadana" signifies the implementation of that thought. *Sarva*, meaning "all," and *Udaya*, meaning "awakening," are Sanskrit words. The ideas of self-development, self-fulfilment, self-reliance, self-realization and nondependence, are all understood in the single word Udaya. *Shrama* literally means energy or labor, and *dana* means sharing. Shramadana means sharing of one's time, thought, and energy for the welfare of all. Thus the literal meaning of Sarvodaya Shramadana is "to awaken all through mutual sharing."

Sarvodaya philosophy, as practiced by Sri Lanka's Sarvodaya Shramadana Movement, points out a two-fold liberation objective. First, within one's own mind or thinking process there are certain defilements one has to recognize and strive to cleanse. Second, one has to recognize that there are unjust and immoral socio-economic chains that keep the vast majority of people enslaved, and that these chains have to be removed if the human being is to experience true freedom and enjoy fundamental human rights. Only those who have as their supreme goal the development of their personality to the fullest can in the long run show others the path to liberation from the spiritual and moral lapses and socio-economic ills that humanity is faced with today.

What we call a Shramadana camp is the first step taken for both individual and community development. The selected community is assisted to develop self-reliance, community participation, and a simple, practical planned program of development. The motivation comes both from the need to awaken within the individual and the group the qualities mentioned above, and from the need for an access road to the village, pure drinking water, toilets, a school building, and irrigation canal or other felt need. The maximum possible human, material, technical, and monetary resources are collected from within the community while the remaining requirements are sought from the surrounding villages. The idea is to make the village people look into themselves, examine and identify their own needs, and to find possible ways and means of satisfying them by their own efforts.

By the way it is conducted, a Shramadana camp becomes not only an exercise in organized manual work to meet one's basic needs, but it also serves to reawaken spiritual, and cultural dimensions of the participants' lives and the village community as a whole. All members of the community—men, women, and children—participate. Surrounding village communities express their solidarity through their participation. Members of these communities think together, plan together, cook together, share their meals, sing together, talk, enjoy, and learn from one another. A Shramadana camp is thus the first step in the awakening of a village community, an occasion where the villagers begin to rediscover their own collective potential on the path to self-development.

From Extension to Awakening

It took some time before we came to fully appreciate the implications of the concept of awakening. Sri Lanka is a country of 23,000 rural villages in which over 85 percent of Sri Lanka's population live. Sri Lanka's Sarvodaya Shramadana Movement started with one of these villages. Then as we tried to respond to calls from several other vilages, the idea of extension came to our minds almost involuntarily. We extended our work to a hundred villages. We were very clear at infrastructure building. We succeeded in both psychological infrastructural work, such as unifying the minds and hearts of people, and physical infrastructural work, such as linking a village to a city by a ten-mile motorable road. We did not stop with that. Still further, we extended to 1,000 villages and today more than 6,000 villages have received the Sarvodaya message and experienced at least one of our basic activities.

This of course is not a mean achievement. Many friends of Sarvodaya who were genuinely interested in us cautioned us against this expansion. We remained a popular movement, but we realized at the beginning of the second decade the conceptual contradiction we were developing by the extension approach we were voluntarily following.

Promptly we corrected ourselves. What was necessary was not extension, but awakening. Extension seeks to provide the people with leadership and with answers. Awakening builds their own leadership and their capacity to seek their own answers, using their own resources, in ways consistent with their own setting and values.

We still had much to learn in Sarvodaya and we reached a consensus that the objective of this learning should be the awakening of human personality to the fullest, in the context of the awakening of the family, the village and the urban community, the national community and the world community. We realized that these six levels of awakening are interrelated and therefore must take place in an integrated way. We also understood that awakening must take place simultaneously in all the dimensions of man and society, namely, spiritual, moral, cultural, social, political, and economic.

According to a person's ability or capacity he or she can share time, labor, knowledge, land, wealth, and any other material or nonmaterial resource to bring happiness to others. In the process of sharing, an individual cultivates four noble qualities. The thought of loving kindness towards all living beings (*Metta*), compassionate actions that help those in need (*Kuruna*), learning to secure dispassionate joy when bringing happiness to others who are in need (*Muditha*), and developing a mental capacity to accept both loss and gain, fame and blame with equanimity (*Upekkha*). This is the path to personal awakening which is the first objective of Sarvodaya.

In the process of sharing, one has to work with others. Talk to others in a language pleasant and intelligible to them. Join hands only in constructive work and not for destructive purposes. Treat others as equals without any distinction to caste, creed, race, or any other man-made difference. These four qualities of sharing, pleasant language, constructive activity, and equality form the dynamic base on which group relationships are founded by strengthening the bonds that exist between small groups. Family or group awakening can only be achieved if the members follow these principles of group conduct.

Eventually, through a similar process, family or group awakening leads to awakening of the village and urban community and ultimately to national and world awakening. A mass movement covering thousands of villages comprising diverse ethnic, language, and religious groups that participate in a united way must necessarily influence the nation as a whole and become visible to the world community as well. Its organization structure must facilitate interactive communication between the basic village/urban communities and the larger national/international communities.

The Sarvodaya Shramadana Movement of Sri Lanka has been learning and evolving for the last twenty five years. As already mentioned over 6,000 villages out of a total of 23,000 in Sri Lanka have become involved. Approximately two-and-a-half to three million people are participant beneficiaries, and each year another 2,000 vilages are being added.

DEVELOPMENT AS A PARTNERSHIP BETWEEN GOVERNMENT AND PEOPLE

We spoke above about how Sarvodaya came to realize the fallacy of assuming that its role was to provide its people with extension rather than to awaken their capacities for increased self-reliance. Government easily falls into the same fallacy.

True development must evolve from the hearts and minds of a people prepared to dedicate their lives to this cause, sometimes at considerable personal sacrifice. Neither government nor people can achieve the objective alone. Success will depend on the formation of an effective partnership between the two, which enables the people, through nongovernmental organizations and movements, to express their initiative in the development process.

NOTE

1. Abstracted from the *Collected Works* of A. T. Ariyaratne Vols. I and II, as edited by Nandasena Ratnapala and published by the Sarvodaya Research Institute. Reprinted by permission of author.

CHAPTER THREE

Reflections of a Village Development Worker[1]

Apichart Thongyu
(Translated by James Hopkins)

Old bumpy laterite road--
to the right, paddy fields and dikes;
small stream on the left, water nearly dry.
All along the road, a patchwork of grove and paddy
just past the shabby wooden bridge
resting on the stream ahead,
lies the village.....people.

Large tamarind grove, dawn awakens:
smoke drifts overhead in early morning light,
cattle, buffalo and people emerge from dwellings.
Noon passes, dusk falls:
children herd buffalo to pens, maidens draw and fetch water,
smoke arises once again.
Evening comes, only sounds of householders:
sorrow, joy, happiness, suffering.
Silence and tranquility crawl in, covering the village.

Arising early,
vanishing into the fields carrying a spade,
in my heart a question:
this? backward, undeveloped land;
this? problem people of the country;
this? symbol of ignorance;
this? symbol of malnutrition;
this? symbol of blackness, deprivation, and poverty?

Large square mesh composed of farm huts and houses.
People and their Way; one hundred and sixty years have passed,
change creeps slowly, filled with energy, yet balance.
Hot potent wind swoops in shouting unexpected turbulence;
aching and cracking.
One question drifts in on the hot wind, lingering in my thoughts:
"What am I to do here?"

After the season which has passed,
yellow wildflowers cover the paddy fields,
sunheat nearly burns crisp dried leaves.
People passing to and fro, in their hands:
workknives, baskets, fish nets.
Far in the distance, ahead lies a dry mountain.
As dusk falls, people return home carrying scrub wood,
vegetables, grass, tadpoles, crabs, fish.
Moonlight fills the sky, lustrous gold covers all;
undeveloped backwardness cannot be found.
Again the question arises: "What am I to do here?"

Sitting, reflecting on the past, reviewing sounds spoken from the
outside and their thoughts toward here: "stupid...poor...sick;"
"backward...undeveloped; not-growing...inert...lazy;"
"unhealthy...lacking education."
That is the force which pushed me here, together with the sound
floating on the wind: "You are a developer."

The village is burning with heat, everyone works in the paddy
fields; grandpa and son plow the fields, grandma and daughter
care for little children and prepare food.
Dawn till dusk, then go home.
Hot wind blows by; outside and inside, scorching heat.
Thought turns to the words of rice-eaters who have never farmed,
words which echo with a striking feeling: "Those rice farmers...
so lazy that they are poor."
Another hot blast sweeps in, leaves fall to the cracked earth;
people herd buffaloes home.

Hoey! Hoey! Hoey!
Kung king...kung king...kung king,
Small boys stuffs sticky rice in mouth,
runs and jumps upon buffalo back.
Dawn rays of silver and gold grasp the horizon,
shortly the picture will fade.

On the road from the village to the paddy fields,
no trace of "life" apart from "work,"
no trace of "education" apart from "life."

Bamboo is split open; one, two, three, four.
Enough for a house to live, only three walls is ample.
Out front a ladder leans, tied to a beam;
when leaving draw up the ladder, all villagers know...
gone to the paddy fields.
No question about morality of the village people.

No noisy sounds of confusion,
no loud sounds of people-crowds,
no heaps of noise from engines,
no sound of search for freedom,
no sound of calls for honor and rank;
only quietude,
life, and love.

One hundred sixty years of this village,
no introduction to Dharma,
no ethical theories,
no economic plan,
no articles of government,
no philosophical theory.
Only the life of people,
propagated in tranquil bliss.

Iat aat..iat aat,
bamboo leaves drift down into a pile on the ground;
Grandma sits spinning cotton.
Under the house is a buffalo pen...
a shady resting place...
a conversation spot...
where the weaving loom sits...
tomorrow...grandma's new sarong will be finished.
Sitting reflecting quietly in my heart
with the picture appearing before me,
"Is this the meaning of laziness and backwardness?"

While philosophers are investigating the answers of life,
economists are thinking and searching for economic systems,
politicians are struggling for power,
specialists are arguing over theories,

barristers are drafting laws,
social workers are speaking of freedom,
humanitarians are speaking of human rights,
monks are delivering sermons to the people,
rice farmers in the village are harvesting.

Those rice kernels
shall feed the people.

Rice is food;
vegetables, fish, birds, mice, are food.
People in the village create, make...find by themselves.
Silkworms, mulberry, cotton;
with two hands, they become clothing.
Tree roots, grass blades;
with brains, they become curatives for disease and illness.
Trees, leaves;
with labor, they are constructed into dwelling.
Ethics, virtues;
by telling and showing the way of life,
establish and thoroughly transmit values of righteousness.
What else do humans want!

Entire Khun trees blossom in yellow flowers,
today the village is exited.
Some people are saying:
"The Boss is coming today to recommend planting new crops."
The people fill the village temple pavillion;
shortly, a green vehicle glides in,
three men alight.
They start training about planting crops after the rice season,
together with exhortations not to be lazy.
People nod their heads as if they understand.
When the three men have left,
sounds of some people arise randomly:
"The plague!...only good at speaking, can they do it?...
I've planted since my father, my grandfather!
What do they know better than I?"

Grandpa, seventy-six years old,
is planting rice in the middle of the paddy field,
from morning until afternoon;
rushing the planting to catch the early rains,
and hurrying back home before dusk
because yesterday,

the district office ordered:
all villagers must prepare to enter training about:
"Conditions of Malnutrition Which Cause Ill-health and Weakness."

Jong, a small girl in the village, is carried out,
she is being taken to a hospital in the city.
White-haired grandfather prevents it;
they all take Jong to his house,
place her on the porch.
Before the Buddha altar, grandfather busily prepares things.
Shortly, the exorcist arrives;
after sitting and chanting for awhile,
a strange language bursts out.
White-haired grandfather translates,
then steps down and disappears towards the garden,
everyone sits waiting:
grandfather returns with four or five leaves,
binds them together, puts them in his mouth, chews them,
it's so confusing: I don't know, are they backward or not?
and sprays them on Jong's head.

Jong gradually moves her eyes, awakens, and regains consciousness;
Afterwards, Jong arises and walks back home;
in the evening,
I see her pushing a water cart vigorously.

Days and time change,
people change,
feelings and moods change.
I, too, am the same;
many things have changed.
I really wonder about myself:
who is actually being developed,
us, or the people in the villages?

Baskets covered and wrapped with an old sarong,
placed on wooden shelves under the house:
one...two...three...four...
five...six...
Grandmother delicately pulls them out,
unwraps the cloth carefully;
left hand swatting flies swarming around,
right hand scratching and flicking
silkworms crowded in the basket,
white and nearly full-grown.

Not too much longer,
and another new sarong will exist.

Daybreak,
another new day.
Arising slowly,
lonely and thinking of someone;
turning and seeing Grandfather sitting next to the water jar,
using an axe to cut a plow handle,
stroking it delightedly.
Loneliness disappears;
the person who turns the earth is right here.

It's nearly time to leave the village:
Mother pulls my arm and has me sit close by;
she describes the collective life of the village,
history which has never poured out in print.
Each word...each sentence
is full of life:
the story of the village in the past,
the fear of the future,
the struggle of the present.

Turning back to look once again,
to be sure.
Water in the stream is clear and clean,
Mother with a new silk skirt,
Father with a checkered sarong,
people with Virtue,
life with simplicity.
Questions are not exhausted, even at parting:
Undeveloped, really?
Backward, really?
In the time that has passed,
only one type of development was seen:
that of myself!

NOTE

1. Abstracted by David C. Korten from Apichart Thongyu "Reflections of a Village Development Worker," (Research Development Institute, Khon Kaen University, 1985). Reprinted with permisssion.

PART II: INTRODUCTION

MANAGING VARIETY

David C. Korten

The circumstances of life in rural Asia are rich in their variety. On a macro scale some areas are barely touched by rains while others experience almost perpetual moisture. Some have well developed market economies while others depend on subsistence and local barter. Some areas are rich in fertile soil while others lack even minimal top soil. In some localities population pressures make each square meter of land a precious resource. In others, nearly unpopulated, land may be freely available to any prospective user.

The diversity extends to micro-levels. The farmer working a single small field may find that both drainage and sunlight differ from one part of the field to another making productivity dependent on corresponding adjustments in cropping practices. Conditions in one locality may make it highly attractive to produce only cash crops for market. In another, subsistence production of basic grains to meet the consumption needs of the household may be the top priority. Some households will have a wide variety of employment opportunities such that the rational choice for them is to devote themselves entirely to wage employment, arranging for a sharecropper to farm their own lands. Others may have few options beyond tending their own small plot of land.

One sees among the rural communities of Asia a remarkable capacity for adaptation to varied personal circumstances and local micro-environments as individuals and households seek to optimize the use of available resources within their limits of choice.[1] This capacity is generally characteristic of community-based resource management systems, which, by their nature, are able to process the enormous quantitites of information required to make such adaptation. Where such capacity exists within a resource management system, it represents an important tool for achieving intensification of resource use without excessive input costs. On the other hand, to the extent that all control is distributed to very small local decision units, the system may have little capacity to aggregate and share risks, resources, and technical knowledge among individual units. By contrast, a bureaucratically controlled resource management system may have significant capacities to aggregate and distribute risks, resources, and technical knowledge among large areas and populations, but its limited information processing capacity normally allows for only minimal adaptation to local variety.

The ideal resource management system should combine the strength of both the community controlled and bureaucratically controlled systems, integrating responsive local decision units into larger systems able to distribute risks and developmental costs while mediating conflicts among individual local units.

The following three chapters provide an insider's view of the local variety experienced by villagers, of the processes by which local adaptation occurs, and of the barriers encountered to productive and equitable outcomes. These presentations make self-evident the reasons why bureaucratized development agencies often have a difficult time providing services perceived as relevant by their intended beneficiaries. Each chapter addresses variety at a different decision making level: the individual farmer, the household, and the local government.

Chapter four by Terry and Somluckrat Grandstaff examines the range of options facing the typical rice farmer in Northeast Thailand and the logic of his or her choices. This logic includes consideration of ecological micro-environments, taste and market preferences, and input availability. Generally, the decision is to plant several different rice varieties to accommodate different needs. Against this reality one can readily appreciate the limited relevance to the farmer of an agricultural extension agent's recommendation that all farmers adopt a single standardized rice technology package favored by government. The data for this chapter were developed as input to the design of a USAID agricultural development project demonstrating the importance of basing agricultural research on a knowledge of farmer practice. Further work along these lines is being done by the Grandstaffs and their colleagues at Khon Kaen University in Northeast Thailand. This work is demonstrating the potential power of rapid assessment methods in making agricultural research and extension more relevant to farmer needs.

Chapter five, by the research staff of the Bangladesh Rural Advancement Committee (BRAC), looks at the problem of variety from the perspective of the individual household, which must decide how to apply its economic, social, and political resources in ways that will best serve its distinctive interests. Here again, the reader's attention is directed to the extent to which these choices are at once complex, rational, and individualized. BRAC has developed a worldwide reputation for its empowerment-based local development programs, which now reach a major portion of the landless rural poor of Bangladesh. Studies such as those reported in Chapters five and eleven have given BRAC unusual insight into the local power structures and resource management systems in which it is intervening and contribute substantially to the effectiveness of its programs.

Local government/administration is also a part of the community management system.[2] In Chapter six, Ronald Krannich, who has many years experience in Thailand researching and advising on local administration, examines the problems of local government/administration through a composite case study derived from a study of small municipalities throughout Thailand. He describes a system in which locally elected officials depend on centralized national agencies for municipal staff and budgets.[3] Consequently, the locally elected officials are almost inevitably caught between the entirely legitimate demands of individual local constituents for action on a diverse range of locality and season specific needs and the demands of the central agencies for orderly compliance with administrative procedures and priorities dictated from Bangkok by officials who have no knowledge of local conditions.

NOTES

1. This does not imply that the results are optimal from either an individual or community perspective, only that the individual decision makers are generally highly rational in their adaptive behavior *within the limits of available choice,*and those choices are often quite limited.

2. By the definitions used in this book, a *local government* must be locally accountable. When the local unit is accountable only to a national administrative organization the term *local administration* is used.

3. In the case presented here, the governmental unit in question represents a combination of local government and local administration, which in part accounts for many of the conflicts reported.

CHAPTER FOUR

Choice of Rice Technology—A Farmer Perspective

Terry B. Grandstaff
Somluckrat W. Grandstaff

> We don't have the scientific knowledge to know what is possible, but the
> officials don't know the local conditions here. Nobody knows the local condi-
> tions better than we do.
>
> —Roi Et villager

In June of 1981 we undertook a week of field visits in northeast
Thailand intended to determine who does and does not use improved
rice varieties, why, and how such varieties were obtained by those who
did use them. We also wanted to know whether there were problems of
access and whether there were needs perceived by the farmers to which
the new varieties did not respond. A secondary concern was to determine
what inputs were used and how, what diseases were prevalent and how
they were treated, and the effect of flooding (submergence)[1] and drought
on yields and cultivation practices. As the interviewing proceeded, the
true complexity of the problem of technology choice became evident and
we came to realize that one could not research this subject without addressing the larger topic of what each available rice variety was used for,
on what type of field, and by whom.

The observations reported here are based on semistructured interviews
with over a hundred villagers in eleven villages of four subdistricts in
Chaiyaphum and Roi Et Provinces of northeast Thailand. While no claim
can be made for scientific precision, the experience does help to
demonstrate the value of relatively informal, rapid appraisal methods in
revealing the complexity and logic of small farmer decision making with
regard to the choice of technology in ways that more structured methods
are likely to miss.

Below we address each of our key questions in turn and summarize the insights gained from the interviews.

ACCESS

Access has two aspects: knowledge and availability. With regard to knowledge: Does the farmer know about the new varieties? Has he seen them growing? Can he distinguish among them? Does he understand the differences between photoperiod-sensitive and non-sensitive varieties?[2] With regard to availability: Is the farmer able to get the seeds he want? Can he get them free or at affordable cost from the district agricultural officer? Is there a long delay? Can he purchase them on the market? Can he get them from neighbors, etc? What is the quality of the seed available to him? These were some of the thoughts that guided our initial questioning.

In general we found that the farmers interviewed were not well informed regarding the nonnative varieties, though they had seen various types growing either in their locality or in neighboring provinces. Some did not understand there was a difference between photoperiod-sensitive and non-sensitive varieties. It was evident that more attention to communicating such knowledge to farmers using their own terminology was needed.

Demonstrations conducted by government were not always effective in building knowledge of, and confidence in, the new varieties. In one demonstration, what was supposed to have been a particular variety of rice seed proved to have the characteristics of a different variety and yielded less than the native variety against which it was being compared. One farmer commented, "They must have gotten the wrong bag." Informants reported that in another demonstration a "short" variety[3] died from submergence, just as the villagers predicted it would.

Procurement was a significant constraint in all areas visited. None of the farmers interviewed knew of any "outside" source of rice seed other than the district agricultural office. Also, no farmer interviewed reported being able to get as much as needed of the improved varieties. In the vast majority of cases, the seed had been given only to one or two families in the village who then reproduced it and made small amounts available to their neighbors.

Most villagers preferred to obtain their seed directly from government rather than from neighbors as there was greater assurance of its purity. There were several barriers here. Farmers in one district noted that they had to know the specific seed variety required , which often they did not, in order to place their order. But even if they knew exactly what variety they wanted, farmers had three common complaints about the government distribution system: (1) the type of seed they wanted was often not available; (2) the amounts were too small; and (3) the seed came too slowly or too late. The problem of availability was compounded by the fact that farmers could not find out what varieties were actually stocked at the time they placed their order. Thus, they might wait a significant period only to find that the variety was not in stock. When this occured they usually received nothing.

Village norms seem to strongly support the sharing of seed among farmers within the village. Exchange among villages appeared to be much less common. Less influential villagers might take longer to obtain a new seed variety. Also, members of the faction of the person who first receives it are likely to have their needs met before those of nonfaction members. Those toward the tail end of this distribution system are likely to find that the seed they obtain is of lesser quality, and it may also cost them more, but they will eventually get it. Normal practice involved either exchange of one seed variety for another, measure for measure, or the borrowing of seed to be paid back with or without interest after the harvest.

WHO USES IMPROVED VARIETIES

The vast majority of farmers in northeast Thailand grow rice only in the rainy season under rainfed conditions. For this reason, most farmers cannot achieve the degree of water control needed to grow the new nonphotoperiod-sensitive varieties.[4] Even in the rainfed areas however, some favored few with access to pump irrigation, usually in the dry season, are able to use these varieties, controlling water and applying fertilizer to achieve good yields.

Most farmers interviewed used photoperiod-sensitive varieties. Most were native glutinous varieties grown for own consumption as staple foods. One popular variety, *niew sanpathong*, underwent improvement by the Thailand government beginning about twenty years ago. Photoperiod-sensitive varieties of nonglutinous rice are also grown as main subsistence crops in some areas, and in many areas they are grown in smaller amounts as cash crops or for making special foods. The most popular variety of cash crop found, *dok mali*, was also an early product of government improvement.

VARIETY CHOICE

A host of factors may be involved in a farmer's preference for one rice variety over another—from agronomic conditions (weather, soil, and water) to taste preferences and knowledge. The specific characteristics of the individual variety are the key, not whether it is "improved" or "local." It became evident that, while increased knowledge regarding the newer varieties will result in the farmer being able to make better decisions, it will not necessarily lead to greater use of the nonnative varieties. Before discussing those considerations which do influence varietal choice in the villages visited, it is instructive to look first at some factors which apparently do not.

Fertilizer

All farmers recognized that fertilizer use increases yields. It was also clear to them that under some local soil conditions some application of fertilizer was essential to obtain even minimally acceptable yields. With more fertile soils farmers reported using fertilizer in the wet season only on those fields where water could be well controlled. It is interesting in this regard that the survey data for the region show that application of fertilizer vastly increases in the dry season, i.e., among those farmers with access to irrigation, and that the yield of dry season crops increases accordingly.

The reasons why most farmers in northeast Thailand use much less fertilizer than many scientists would consider optimal in the wet season are varied but fairly straightforward. The most important reason cited was lack of water control. Northeast Thailand suffers from rainfall irregularity. When there is flooding, the fertilizer is lost without effect on the crop. On the other hand when it turns out to be too dry the fertilizer is ineffective. Under either condition, use of fertilizer is an even worse investment if the crop itself is lost.

Soil texture was also a consideration. In some areas, particularly in the upper paddies, the soil is likely to have a sandy texture, which means that the fertilizer can easily wash away unless mixed with manure. This problem is less pronounced on many lower paddy areas where the soil is likely to have a greater clay content. People with sandy soils were very interested in getting a fertilizer that would not wash away but had not been able to find one. The practice of mixing the fertilizer with manure seemed to be effective but was limited by the availability of manure, much of which was trucked into the village where this practice was noted from an area where the farmers did not have this particular soil problem.

Cost was another factor in fertilizing subsistence rice (the principal need). Generally only those farmers with surplus cash could afford to put on a second dressing of fertilizer. In one area, farmers thought that even if water conditions were better, the application of fertilizer would not increase yields enough to justify the cost of the fertilizer once the risks were considered.

Considerations on the use of fertilizer did not seem to have a bearing on whether farmers chose improved over local rice varieties. They believed that all traditional rice varieties basically responded equally well to the application of fertilizer and were unconvinced that nonnative varieties would do any better, especially under local water-control conditions.[5] Thus, it appeared that decisions regarding fertilizer application were basically independent of decisions regarding choice of variety.

Diseases and Pests

Next to flooding and drought, the subject with which farmers seemed to be most preoccupied was disease and pest control. Many types of pests and diseases were discussed but in the villages visited the number one concern was the dreaded *non ko*, a type of stem borer. One farmer expressed his feelings succinctly: "If the government could solve the problem of non ko it would never have to do anything else for the farmer." Non ko was cited as the single most damaging pest or disease for rice in virtually every village visited except for some in one subdistrict in Chaiyaphum Province. In another area of the same province, it was reported that during the previous year non ko destroyed half the total rice crop of the village. Non ko was reported as being a problem for all rice varieties, in all soil types, under all water conditions, and at all times in the growing cycle from transplanting to flowering.

Here again the concerns with disease and pests did not enter decisions regarding choice of variety since non ko was considered a problem for all varieties.

One finding that should be a cause for concern is the farmers' limited knowledge of appropriate use of chemical pesticides. This was an area in which farmer ignorance was evident—a condition stressed by the farmers themselves. Most preferred not to use any *yaa* ("medicine") at all on their plants, many because they were afraid of it. In one area a farmer claimed that everyone who used Folidar got sick. In another study it was reported that elsewhere in the area three villagers had died from the use of an insecticide due to "misuse and allergy."

There were many evident problems in the local use of chemicals to treat crop disease and pests. One problem is that the classification of pests, diseases, and chemicals in general use by the villagers and by the local district stores is inadequate or inappropriate to the correct choice and application of chemicals for treatment. Partly for this reason the farmers considered most of the available treatments to be ineffective.

Prices

Prices were the first factor identified by the farmers as truly making a difference in the breeds they chose to plant. While prices at the time of harvest had varied somewhat from area to area during the previous

previous year, in general nonglutinous rice varieties obtained better prices than glutinous varieties, and government recommended varieties received better prices than local varieties.

Qualities of Harvested Rice

Qualities such as taste, cooking, texture, fragrance, and other such characteristics of the harvested rice were important determinants of price and of preferences in the rice grown for home consumption. For example, farmers in one area of Chaiyaphum no longer grow either RD1 or RD5 in the dry season, primarily because of the taste, but also because they are hard to thresh. RD7 is considered to be edible (okay), but not as nice as the wet season *dok mali*, which is known for its particularly appealing fragrance. RD7 is considered okay as a dry season crop because it tastes better than RD1 or RD5 and is easy to thresh. Dok mali is a little stickier (more glutinous) than the local *khao jao daeng*, but not enough to make a difference to most people since its smell is better and the taste is the same.

Most of those who prefer glutinous rice felt that *niew sanpathong* was strong in all aspects for farmers who had land suitable for growing this variety. The farmers in one area of Chaiyaphum who thought its grain was too hard were an exception. They were apparently unaware that this problem can usually be prevented through proper seed selection. The longer, more esthetically appealing grain of niew sanpathong was commonly cited as giving it an advantage over many local glutinous varieties.

No meaningful differences were mentioned among varieties in qualities relating to storage, cooking, or the time they could be kept for cooking. We did not focus on such factors however, and it is likely that they might become very significant in selection of any new breed that does have noticeable differences.

Land, Water, and Labor

Most research effort in rice has been directed to the nonphotoperiod-sensitive varieties, which do well under highly controlled conditions, especially in the dry season in northeast Thailand when photoperiod-sensitive varieties will not produce grain.[6] Consequently, such varieties allow individual farmers in the northeast who are near water sources and who can afford pumps to produce substantial quantities of grain in the dry season. But for most rainfed farmers, dry season cultivation of wet rice is beyond their means. Practically everyone, however, grows rice in the wet season. During this period, few farmers can control the water conditions well enough to use a nonphotoperiod-sensitive variety.

In three of the four subdistricts visited, the farmers had a classification scheme by which they distinguish between different locations within a given paddy field area with respect to elevation and water availability. They commonly spoke of *thi don* (highlands) and *thi lum* (lowlands). Some also mentioned areas as being *klang* (middle or in between). The actual differences in elevation to which these terms referred were generally no more than a few feet, but during the wet season, such seemingly insignificant differences greatly affect water conditions and thus have very real meaning for how the farmers must manage their fields.

The terms and their use by local farmers are not standardized from one area to another, which can be confusing to the outsider. But they have great influence on where the farmer will plant what type of rice. Indeed, this classification is perhaps the most important to their decision of what rice variety to plant. New rice breeds must fit within these catagories, or local "niches," or they are not adopted by local farmers. Improved varieties that happen to fit well are adopted. Where they haven't, the local breeds continue to be used.

To understand the significance of these choices, one should first understand some the major local categories into which rice varieties may be divided. One important distinction is between *khao nak* (heavy rice) and *khao bao* (light rice). Though defined in terms of polar opposites, there is actually a continuum between the two extremes. The "heavier" the breed, the later it will flower and be harvested. Farmers say the grain itself is also heavier and the height of the plant is generally greater, but these characteristics seem less important to the farmer, though farmers know that the lighter breeds produce less grain. The reason for this use has to do with the importance of timing crops to coincide with the availability of land, water, and labor. The lighter breeds are harvested earlier, allowing time for the planting of cash crops following their harvest. Also, they do better on the higher grounds as they require less water during their growing period. Farmers use native "light" varieties on higher lands because they produce best under local conditions. Farmers were particularly desirous of an improved "light" glutinous rice variety, especially one better able to withstand drought.

Soil, which is of obvious importance, is classified by villagers in many ways. But two main types were *sai* (sandy in the sense of loosely textured, large grained, and water porous) at the one extreme and a variety of terms that refer to "clayey" soil at the other. There is a general, though not universal, tendency for sandy soil to be found in higher areas and clayey soils in lower areas. Clayey soil takes longer to dry out but at the time it doesn't drain well and, when it does dry out, it becomes quite hard. Soil texture thus combines with (and influences) water availability in determining where and when a crop can be grown.

In general, then, it is a combination of water condition/elevation, soil texture, and the timing of land and labor availability that most influences what type of rice the farmer will decide to plant where. Underlying these choices is also a strong desire on the part of the farmer to first insure the production of enough rice to sustain his family. As one farmer said, "It's nice to grow rice for sale, but if one can provide adequately for year-round subsistence he ought to be satisfied."

It is typical for one household to have lands of varying elevation. According to the farmers, the first rule of thumb is that the lighter rice goes on the higher fields, middle rice on the middle fields and heavier rice on the lower fields. But this can be moderated by other factors in any given location. for example, in one village there was a scarcity of higher fields, and indeed its highest fields were not very high at all. Since its lower fields were subject to flooding, this was a cause for concern. This led farmers to plant lighter glutinous rice for home consumption mostly on the higher fields to maximize the probability of the subsistence rice surviving and to stagger harvest schedules. Niew sanpathong was planted on the lower fields as would be expected. However, the cash crop rice, dok mali, considered a "middle" rice, was also planted on the lower fields, even though it would have done better on the higher fields in this village. If it happened to be a good year, all three crops would survive and they would have some nonglutinous rice to sell. Even in a moderate year, the niew sanpathong would probably survive. In those years with the worst flooding, at least the light rice grown for consumption on the upper fields would survive.

If available, farmers in this particular village probably would have preferred a heavier nonglutinous rice to grow for sale—one better able to withstand submergence during floods. But, of the varieties available, the dok mali was the closest to meeting their needs for a variety with a high market value even though they had to harvest it when the fields were wet, stacking the sheaves on the paddy dikes. And often the crop died if too long submerged. From one perspective it could be said that the farmers were not planting the rice "correctly," but from their point of view, the available breeds were only partially meeting their needs.

Obviously the farmer's decision calculus needs to be taken into account by government researchers if they are to be responsive to actual farmer needs.

SOURCES OF TECHNOLOGICAL CHANGE

Also important to government decision makers is the broader question of the sources from which farmers obtain new technologies. A second study carried out in ten villages of northeast Thailand in February 1982 sheds additional light on this question.

Of the technical changes which had come to these villages during the previous ten years or so, the most frequently cited change source was the farmers themselves. In some instances the farmers had simply worked out their own innovations, in others they had observed them on nearby farmers' fields or during travel to more distant locations. The second most frequently cited source was the market—a local merchant in the majority of cases, or a rice mill, or the agents of a company. The government ranked third as a source. Generally the government source was an agricultural officer, but school teachers were also well represented. Radio and advertising fliers were also mentioned but were not important sources.

The variety of sources mentioned demonstrate that there is more than one way technological change gets into a village. Probably the number of such channels is continuously increasing as the countryside develops. It should not be surprising that farmers themselves play such a large role in the change process as they have the most interest and the most to gain or lose. Farmers are more readily convinced when they talk to other farmers whom they see using a technology in ways that make a difference to their living. A farmer who has made a good living for several years growing a particular crop or using a particular technique is a far more convincing example than seeing that crop or technique used on a demonstration plot. Farmers commonly use trips to the market, to festivals and fairs, to the temples, and even off-farm employment as opportunities to learn from other farmers.

The market is critical in making new materials available and in providing the information necessary to their use. The merchant has an interest in selling as much of his product as possible, but he also has an interest in seeing the farmer succeed and thus become a regular customer.

The government was the main source of technological change involving rice. One point that was clear from the interviews, however, was that the farmer looks to the agricultural extension agent in northeast Thailand not so much as a source of expert advice, but as a channel to more influential people and a source of cheap or free physical inputs. It was in part for this reason that farmers seldom took demonstration plots very seriously as source of new technology. Furthermore, the interviews suggested that farmers who participated in demonstration plots were doing so primarily because it was seen as an exchange relationship. The farmer used the offered technology on his plot primarily because it provided him access to inputs and other benefits of having a closer relationship with government officials not because he was especially interested in the particular technology being demonstrated.

Together, these two studies reveal the richness and significance of data that can be obtained through straightforward and inexpensive study methods, which at the same time have significant implications for policy and program action. The likelihood of effective programming in research and agricultural extension would seem to be slight in the absence of serious efforts to obtain and use such information. Programs that depend on extension agents of limited credibility going forth to promote varieties that do not fit the needs of the farmers as defined by their particular local reality are unlikely to have significant impact on farmers productivity or income.[7] Indeed, one might conclude in the present case that it should be the researcher who concentrates his attention on talking directly with the farmer— not to teach so much as to learn.[8] As more suitable varieties and other inputs are developed in response to such learning, the key duty of the extension agent might well be that of insuring that they are readily available.

Further study should be undertaken before attempting to restructure a research-extension system so radically but certainly the data of these studies suggest that radical innovations of this order may be appropriate.

NOTES

1. Paddy-field rice, of course, is grown in "flooded" fields. In this report, however, we follow farmer usage of the term "flood," meaning excessive water, for example, at a level above the dikes or above the tops of the rice plants themselves.

2. Most traditional rice varieties are photoperiod-sensitive. This means that the time at which the plant flowers depends on the length of the daylight hours (technically, in fact, the nighttime hours). Thus, during part of the year, a given variety will not flower or produce grain. In northeast Thailand, traditional rice varieties are "SDP's" (short day plants), i.e., each variety will flower only during a specific period of the year when nights are long enough to trigger flowering. Most photoperiod-sensitive rice in northeast Thailand is planted (in the wet season) in time to pass through its juvenile stage prior to the nights becoming long enough to trigger flowering. As long as the juvenile stage is completed prior to the nights becoming long enough to trigger flowering, all plantings of a given variety will be ready for harvest at the same time, even if plantings were staggered. In northeast Thailand, however, most farmers plant several varieties, allowing staggering of harvest times, although peak labor requirements for harvest are still quite high. Most of the more recent varieties developed by the International Rice Research Institute were nonsensitive, so that their growth cycle would be set by the time of planting and thus be under the control of the farmer rather than the sun. This would allow much more flexibility with regard to planting time and facilitate multiple cropping, assuming all other factors critical to timing, such as water availability, were also under control of the farmer. In Thailand, however, improved varieties of both types are still being developed, and the Thai Government's Rice Division has now adopted the position that photoperiod-sensitive varieties are needed for use under rainfed conditions (the reasons for this are explained in Note 4 below).

3. Many improved varieties are much shorter than traditional varieties, having been bred to put more of the growth into the grain and less into the rest of the plant.

4. The many photoperiod-sensitive varieties grown in northeast Thailand are well adapted to local conditions. While rainfall in the rainy season is generally quite erratic, the lowest variation from year to year is in the peak rainfall period in September and early October, which coincides with the period of peak growth for these varieties. For nonphotoperiod-sensitive varieties to do well under these conditions (in areas where drainage is sufficient

to prevent submergence), their planting time would have to be fixed so that their peak growth would also correspond with this period. Instead of better distributing labor, labor requirements would be even higher, probably in both planting and harvesting. Most important, risk would be much greater since the rice would have to be transplanted at a fixed time, during the much more variant rainfall period in July or August when water may be insufficient. With the already-adapted photoperiod sensitive varieties, however, labor can be better distributed and risk reduced since the rice can be transplanted from nurseries at any time during a longer period—from late June to early September, whenever water in the fields is sufficient, and still produce well even if the rains come late. Nonphotoperiod-sensitive varieties, however, would suffer drought after the peak rain period if planted this late.

5. The recent improved nonphotoperiod-sensitive varieties, of course, are specifically designed to be much more productive than traditional varieties in response to fertilizer. The few farmers with access to dry season irrigation understood this and used such varieties. For the vast majority, however, fertilizer response was not an issue since there were other limiting factors that precluded using such varieties (see Note 4 above).

6. While this has been generally true throughout Asia, research in Thailand has been more balanced. Two of the varieties in common use in northeast Thailand (*niew sanpathong* and *dok mali*) are photoperiod-sensitive varieties native to Thailand that have been improved by the Thai Government.

7. This statement is intended to make a point about the nature of research and extension in many areas of the world that lack "ideal" farming conditions. Northeast Thailand is one such area. The statement, however, is not intended to summarily evaluate all research and extension in Thailand. Even in northeast Thailand, many useful government-initiated innovations were widely adopted, such as niew sanpathong and dok mali referred to in this report. Compared to the scope and duration of the research and extension effort, however, i.e., from a program point of view, the impact has not been nearly as effective as it might be if greater and more systematic use of farmer knowledge were to be made.

8. This is by no means as easy a thing to accomplish as the present report in its finished form might make it appear. In fact, to make better use of farmer knowledge at least three instrumental changes are needed in the existing situation in many areas of the world: (1) increased awareness of the needs and values of getting such information from farmers, as is highlighted in the present report; but also, (2) well-developed methods, tools, and techniques to elicit the information effectively and efficiently, such as those recently being explored under the rubric of "rapid rural appraisal" (RRA); and (3) systematic institutional changes so that the necessary actions will be able to occur among the right people at the needed times and places. The authors believe it is necessary to promote all three of these, in the firm conviction that good intentions are insufficient to accomplish any major change unless the necessary means and support can also be developed.

ACKNOWLEDGEMENT: The authors wish to thank Viriya Limpinuntana and this book's editor, David Korten, for being very helpful with various drafts of this report, and to absolve them from blame for any remaining errors.

CHAPTER FIVE

Household Strategies in Bonkura Village[1]

Bangladesh Rural Advancement Committee

Contrary to the popular illusion, village life is far from simple. The decisions on which the fate of the rural household depends are varied and often involve complex judgements. This reality was dramatically revealed in one of BRAC's early studies of village-level resource allocation processes.

At the time of our study, the total population of Bonkura (885) was distributed between 146 households. The land owned by these households totaled 229.65 acres of which 192.14 were cultivatable and 37.51 were residential. For purposes of the study these households have been divided into five broad categories based on the size of their landholdings: surplus (above six acres); medium (2 1/2 to 6 acres); small (1 to 2 1/2 acres); marginal (below one acre); and landless (no cultivatable lands other than small residential garden plots). Table 5-1 summarized current ownership patterns.

As indicated by Table 5-1, the surplus and medium households, which constituted only 14 percent of the total population, owned 48 percent of the land. Marginal and landless households (53 percent of the total), owned only 8 percent. There have been major changes in household status with respect to these categories since 1947, when at the partition of India and Pakistan, most of the Hindu population migrated from the area—including five of the community's richest and strongest surplus households. With that migration, most of the Hindu lands were either sold to Moslem families at prices well below the normal market or were forfeited to the government. Consequently several families with the necessary political and economic resources were able to expand their holdings significantly.

Since 1974, although there have been cases where households have

Table 5-1: Current Ownership

Land Holding Category	Households			Holdings		
	Number	Percent	Total	Percent	Average	Cultivatable
Surplus	6	4%	53.41	23%	8.90	48.91
Medium	14	10%	55.94	24%	4.00	48.94
Small	48	33%	100.92	45%	2.10	86.04
Marginal	21	14%	11.40	5%	.54	8.25
Landless	57	39%	7.98	3%	.14	—
Total	146	100%	229.65	100%	—	192.14

landless. There were many restrictions on land transfer through sale, including Islamic preemption laws, supported by kinship norms, which forbid selling inherited land outside the kinship group so long as some kin could offer the market price.

Land ownership could be a complex matter. One did not become the legal owner until mutation documents had been obtained, and without these documents one could not sell or mortgage land, or take advantage of institutional credit for agricultural inputs. The legal fee for obtaining mutation documents was set at Tk. 1.40 per shareholder and Tk. 1 court fee. But actual costs, including expediting fees to officials in a position to hold up the proceedings, ran from Tk. 200 to 500, which was beyond the means of many households. Moreover, only a sizeable holding made the expenditure worthwhile, with the result that few persons obtained the documents.[2]

LAND USE DECISIONS

Land use decisions in Bonkura were complex, varied, and an important element of the household strategy for maintaining and strengthening the household's economic and political position within the village.

The first and most significant decision for most households was whether and how to obtain use rights to additional land; and, for all except the landless households, whether to work the lands to which it had use rights itself or transfer those rights to others and, if so, on what terms. A family owning land it decided not to cultivate itself had the option of leasing it out at the rate of Tk. 450 to 600 per acre per year, arranging a sharecropper who would pay one half of the gross returns for its use—which in a typical good year might net the landowner Tk. 1005 per acre—or "mortgaging" it to another family for approximately two thirds of its sales value—which gave the mortgagor use rights over the land until the mortgage was repaid.

The lease arrangement provided assurance of a small but secure income, and was the option normally preferred by absentee landlords who were willing to accept a lower return for the simplicity of the arrangement. Sharecropping provided a higher potential return but also carried greater risk. Though the landowner did not share in the cost of the inputs, he obtained no assured return if the crop failed, and had to be able to monitor yields. Mortgaging provided immediate cash but involved the risk that the land could be lost for an amount well below its market value in the event it could not be redeemed. And, of course, a household might mortgage or lease in land and then sharecrop it out.

Actual decisions varied with circumstances. One marginal farmer chose to lease out his land and invest the cash in cow rearing and money lending in the hope of obtaining enough return to buy more land. Two Hindus leased out their lands because they were fully occupied in their business. These transactions were, of course, not confined to the boundaries of the village. Some village lands were owned by outsiders but cultivated by members of the village, while some villagers obtained use rights to lands outside the village, some to government lands, others from absentee landlords. On balance the Bonkura households farmed more land than they owned.

Table 5-2 suggests the variety and complexity of the decisions involved. The landless, of course, engaged only in acquiring use rights. For all households categories rights to farm additional land were most commonly obtained through leasing in. At least one landless family leased in land, suggesting that not all landless households lacked cash reserves. Households in the small-holding category were the most likely to be engaged in sharecropping, both in and out. One surprising finding was that surplus households sharecropped out a smaller portion of their holdings than did the small-holder households. Overall, the picture was much more complex than the common stereotype of sharecropping involving rich landlords taking advantage of desperate landless families.

As these transactions were worked through, each household ended up with an amount of land over which it had use rights. In farming this land additional decisions were required regarding how much family, reciprocal, daily, or permanent labor would be used to cultivate it.

At one extreme were three cultivators who had recently achieved surplus status and had chosen to be owner-managers. They managed the work of others, including family members, but did not work directly on their own land. Although status considerations were involved, the determining factor seems to have been their heavy involvement in other businesses and occupations. All households used some family labor. Those with less than one acre used only family labor supplemented as necessary by reciprocal labor. Marginal and small farmers with more than 1 acre sup-

Tabel 5-2: System of Cultivation

Land-Holding Category	Households	Cultivable Holding	Lease		Mortgage		Share-cropping		Operational Holding
			in	out	in	out	in	out	
Surplus	6	48.91	6.66	—	.33	—	—	9	46.90
Medium	14	48.94	.66	—	—	2.66	66	—	47.60
Small	48	86.04	—	—	—	3.96	9.28	13.32	78.04
Marginal	21	8.25	5.38	1.60	—	1.60	2.19	1.07	11.55
Landless	57	—	8.84	—	1.45	—	3.65	—	13.94
Total	146	192.25	21.54	1.60	1.78	8.22	15.78	23.39	198.00

plemented family labor with daily labor as needed. The upper categories supplemented family labor with daily and some permanent labor.

The selection criteria used in employing laborers depended on whether the cultivator was an actual or aspiring political figure.[3] The non-political cultivator normally hired kin. If the available pool of kin labor exceeded his needs, he might consider skill. If the kin pool of labor did not provide enough person-days, he might hire neighbors. For the most part the assured supply of labor at critical times such as harvest was more important than skill, as in most agricultural work, degrees of skill do not differ markedly.

By contrast the political cultivator gave preference to political supporters. First preference went to kin who also provided factional support. Next he would turn to factional supporters from other kinship groups. Only when such "factional" labor was not available would he turn to less actively loyal kin or neighbors.

In Bonkura, all employers of permanent laborers had a political orientation, suggesting that the decision to use permanent, in contrast to day, labor was more a political than an economic decision representing a form of political patronage.

SELECTION OF CROPS AND TECHNOLOGY

Basic food security was the primary concern of the farmers of Bonkura in their selection of cropping patterns, and for most farmers their first priority was to produce sufficient rice to meet the subsistence needs of their families. Normally for a family of six this required roughly twenty maunds of paddy for half a year.

The extensive flooding experienced in the area was also a major factor in determining the selection of crops, as the only crop that will survive

66

the floods is a deep-water rice known locally as broadcast-*aman* or *b-aman*. The stem tissue of the b-aman has a unique ability to elongate in response to rising levels of water, sometimes reaching a height of twelve feet under conditions of extreme flooding. At the same time it requires approximately seven months to reach maturity, in contrast to the three- to five-month period required by other varieties normally chosen to produce the *aus*, aman, and *boro* crops.[4]

While there were dominant cropping patterns, there was also significant variation throughout the village. It was common for an individual family to have several small plots scattered throughout the village with lands of differing elevation and soil quality. These differences influenced cropping patterns, as did the totlal land holding of the family. Consequently a family might follow a different cropping pattern on each of its plots.

Overall, the relatively high elevation of Bonkura meant that flooding came somewhat later than in other parts of Bangladesh, thus influencing planting times and patterns. While late flooding was common, there were also some higher elevation lands that escaped flooding. Cropping patterns for these lands were adjusted accordingly.

For all farming families in Bonkura, the basis of their cropping system was a planting of the aman and aus crops simultaneously in May on lands where flooding was anticipated. The varieties of seed chosen were mixed in the hands and sown by broadcasting: an early maturing variety, which could grow in two to three feet of standing water to produce the aus crop for harvest in August before the onset of deeper flooding; and the deep-water rice commonly known as b-aman for harvest in December after the flood subsided. One-and-a-half acres devoted to this combination was expected to yield 13 1/2 maunds at the August aus harvest, which would last the family of six until late November through the floods. The aman crop to be produced by the deepwater rice variety was left to mature through the flood period and was ready for harvest in early December. The 16 1/2 maunds gained from this harvest (assuming 1 1/2 acres) might last the family into April. Those families with insufficient land to grow a surplus might be dependent on earning sufficient income to purchase sufficient rice to last them until the next harvest.

A single crop of aus planted alone on this same plot in May would have yielded eighteen maund in August. This was a smaller total yield than obtained from the combination. But it also required significantly less labor—fifty-one person-days per acre as contrasted to seventy-two days for the combination. The difference is accounted for largely by the greater difficulty of harvesting the combination. When the aus crop has been planted with the deep-water aman it is necessary to harvest each head selectively to minimize damage to the aman plants. The later harvesting of the deep-water aman is also complicated because, after the floods subside, the rice stalks (which may have reached a length of as much as twelve feet) essentially collapse into an entangled mass. The harvesters must tramp through this mass searching for the individual heads, which establish themselves in an upright position within the rice mat. Animals do not find the rice straw of the deepwater variety to be palatable. Having no other uses, it was commonly burned.

Aside from the higher total yield, an advantage of the combination of aus and b-aman was that having two crops at different times of the year reduced storage problems. Losses from rats were likely to be particularly severe during the floods when as much as a third of Bangladesh was underwater and the total rat population converged on the two thirds of the land that remained above water, which of course is where the rice must be stored. There is also a tendency for rice stored for long periods under conditions of high temperature and humidity to grow moldy. Thus, not having to store additional rice through the floods was considered a major advantage.

If there were no problems of flooding, two separate crops of the more rapidly maturing rice varieties would have been clearly the preferred choice. But for most of the land in Bonkura this was not an option.

Our calculations indicated that strictly on the basis of net economic returns it would have been advantageous for the farmers to plant jute rather than the mixed aus/aman rice crops. In fact, we found that the only farmers who planted jute were those with more than 1 1/2 acres. Price fluctations made it a relatively risky crop, and no farmer was willing to take that risk until his subsistence needs for rice were assured. Furthermore jute could be grown on higher ground where risk of flooding was minimal.

All cultivators in Bonkura grew some kind of a winter (rabi) crop on at least a portion of their holding, though this was not possible on lands on which the deepwater rice variety had been planted. Winter crops such as mustard and chiles were generally good sources of cash income. Sweet potato represented a lower cash value winter crop but required minimal land preparation.

Small, medium, and surplus households generally owned their own cows or bullocks, and ploughs. The medium and surplus households used all their cow dung and ashes as fertilizers and stored excess paddy for seed the next season. Others had to use their dung for fuel, buying small amounts of commercial fertilizers for their fields—which was less expensive than buying fuel. Commonly, marginal and landless households shared their animals and equipment at the time of tilling and bought their seed.[5]

DISPOSITION OF CROPS

There was a clear preference for selling harvests in a processed form or storing them until more favorable marketing conditions prevailed, and for selling at specialized local markets which tended to offer the better prices. For example, paddy was generally processed into rice before sale, except for small amounts of the poorest quality which were used in barter. The extent to which a household could afford to store its crop in anticipation of improved market conditions depended on its financial resources. Poorer households therefore tried to maximize their gains from the value-added by processing, as processing requires labor but little capital.

Almost all households in Bonkura engaged in some subsidiary agricultural production: poultry, dairy, or horticulture, depending on availability of land and capital. The surplus and medium households gave preference to poultry and dairy. In part this reflected the risk and capital requirements, but it was also significant that all subsidiary agricultural production was the preserve of women. Horticulture required the most labor and the sale of such items carried low status while their consumption carried high status. For status reasons surplus households preferred to conserve their female labor from doing horticulture and to consume all they produced in poultry and dairy.

Women of medium households sold a portion of their poultry, dairy, and horticulture products within the village, putting aside small savings in secret tills. The small, marginal, and landless sold more than they consumed to meet immediate needs for cash, and were more likely to sell outside the village to obtain the highest possible prices.

Households of each category had members who worked as either permanent or temporary agricultural laborers outside the village.

NONAGRICULTURAL INCOME

Only 5,672 paid person-days of labor were generated from the land in Bonkura, enough to provide 300 days of work per year to only nineteen persons. Another 9,346 unpaid person-days were generated, potentially providing full employment for another thirty-one persons. The importance of alternatives to village-based agricultural employment was clear especially for the landless and near landless.

Monu was the imam of the village mosque. He earned a token Tk. 144 per year but was paid fees for his services at weddings and special prayers. Shafi was supervisor to his brother Safdan's fuel business, for which he received Tk. 7 per day for roughly half the year. Two Hindus worked in the blacksmith foundry of another Hindu. One served as an assistant for Tk. 2400 per year; the other was a laborer for Tk. 400 per year. Limited though they were, such positions provided 1,971 person-days of paid work, which was not insignificant compared to the paid person-days of employment generated in agriculture.

Members of the community engaged in a variety of trading activities, either as a primary occupation or as a source of supplemental income.

Indeed, involvement of Bonkura residents in trading activities was greater than average because the headquarters of the Union was located in Bonkura and it was connected by an approach road at one mile distance from the main road from Dhaka. Four residents had permanent shops, one was an oil dealer, two were merchants who traded in the local markets (*hats*) which opened one or two days a week in various locations throughout the region, often specializing in certain products. Four other residents were Dhaka financed *faria* who canvassed the villages, bazaars and hats for produce to be taken to the urban centers. Four were sub-faria who supplemented their slim earnings as laborers, when there was no other work, by buying vegetables or eggs in the village and selling them at permanent bazaars or hats for a small profit of Tk. 2 to 5 a day. Sixteen were itinerant traders who bought items wholesale on credit from the market towns to sell to clientele from many villages. Another thirteen had home businesses selling groceries, husking paddy, stocking food grains for sale when prices were favorable, producing and selling snack foods, etc.

It is significant that most households with surplus cash tended to favor investing it in trade or employment rather than land. A small surplus invested in trade brought a quicker return than the same surplus invested in land. Once a surplus was earned from a small-scale or low-status business, that additional capital might be invested in a larger scale or higher status business. Only once a significant surplus had been generated was it likely to be used to buy land. Though land remained the mark of status and security, the path of upward mobility toward its aquisition was through trade.

Certain households had availed themselves of salaried, nonagricultural employment outside Bonkura in jobs ranging from construction work and selling to teaching, police, and government clerkships. Twenty-nine such jobs were held by persons who maintained a residence in Bonkura, providing a total of 9,298 person days of work per year and Tk. 93,125 in income.

Two Bonkura residents were head masters of regional schools, and four served as teachers. Only one teacher from Bonkura gained his position solely through merit. Of the other educators, one had an Awami League patron, two had relatives who wanted to invest in the education of their kin in hopes of future income security; and two others were linked to another senior school teacher referred to as a "first class broker." In at least two instances, bribes in addition to the regular subscription for teachership were paid to the Thana education officer. The uncle of one successful aspirant was known to have paid Tk. 1200 as a subscription and Tk. 1000 in bribes to obtain an assistant teachership for his nephew. In return, the nephew married his uncle's unattractive daughter whose marriage prospects were otherwise poor. As father-in-law, the patron-uncle benefited from both the salary and rations his nephew drew. The head master earned roughly Tk. 4,200 per annum; the teacher Tk. 300 less per year. All received rations of rice, wheat, sugar, kerosene, butter oil, and salt according to family size.

Two Bonkura residents, whose guardians sold land to invest in their education, had obtained clerkships in government offices through influential patrons who themselves held government jobs in the departments in which they became employed. Several sons of the Shaha community, for whom the grocery business was a hereditary occupation, had obtained salesboy and shop manager positions outside through the community's business links.

Four members from one strong kinship group in Bonkura had obtained appointments to the police force. The first of them won his appointment through the normal recruitment procedures: exam, medical tests, and standards of height and weight. Later, three of his kinsmen obtained appointments through a combination of bribes and his influence. One, for example, was known to have sold half an acre of land to pay the requisite bribe. Policemen earned Tk. 3000 per annum plus rations, in addition to whatever they accepted in bribes.

A group of nine women from Bonkura worked regularly outside the village on construction or earth-work projects.

FACTIONS AND KINSHIP GROUPS

There were seven major kinship groups in Bonkura. The leaders of the two strongest kinship groups, Azizur Rahman Master and Hashem Ali Master, were also the two faction leaders of Bonkura. Both were school teachers-hence the title "master"—and maintained union and thana-level political and administrative links. Each commanded the full support (with occasional minor challanges) of his own kin group in factional politics. Though kinship groups were fairly stable, factional loyalties were subject to change depending on the benefits the faction was able to deliver. Faction leadership, building from the power base of a kin group, was the path to broader political influence, the key being to gain factional followers from rival kin groups while maintaining the loyalty of one's own kin group. Links to the Union and the Thana were perceived to be of the utmost importance in this regard. Consequently faction leaders and certain individual residents tried to establish and maintain strong links with the elected and appointed officials of these levels who were perceived to be not only the distributors of public sector benefits but also the guarantors of private-sector rights and property. These officials could guarantee that one's land documents were legal and binding, and could determine whether one got the employment one sought or could obtain credit from institutional sources, and controlled many other rights and services that determined whether one's life and property were secure. They also controlled the various goods and services that flowed into the village through various government offices and programs, including: rations, fertilizer, insecticides, agricultural implements, tubewells, deep tubewells, power pumps, food-for-work wheat, and credit.

VALUES MEDIATING COMMUNITY STATUS

Aspirations and the means of achieving them were shaped in no small degree by the underlying value system of the village, as well as by its economic and political realities. Ultimately these value systems determined the basis of status and esteem in the eyes of the community and served as a powerful motivating force.

A man with high status in Bonkura had to possess land. Preferably he should have inherited it because this means in the eyes of the villagers that he has not done anything detrimental to the interests of others in obtaining it. It was also expected that if wealth was inherited, the person had a duty to let others benefit through labor and credit patronage. If possible, he should refrain from direct cultivation himself and hire others to work it, thus providing them with work. He was also expected to intercede on the behalf of others in many ways. The man of status should be educated, even if he did not necessarily use his education. Outside contacts also added to importance and respect.

The three essentials of status were land, income, and patronage. But in contrast to income from land, income from business was assumed to unsettle the resource system of the community as it was seen as being derived at the expense of others with no guarantee of benefiting a larger number. With his surplus, the businessman bought land and products at a cheap price for sale elsewhere, presumably to the detriment of other villagers.

TEN DISTINCTIVE STRATEGIES

All households in Bonkura were engaged in a continuing struggle to sustain, and in most instances to enhance, their social, political, and economic position within the community. The strategies they pursued were as diverse as their circumstances and the opportunities that the local political economy made available.

Ten types of household strategy can be identified among Bonkura households. These were a function of the resources controlled and the ideological and economic system of the village. They were defined for purposes of his study by examining the strategies of prototype individuals in terms of starting point, intermediate goal, means, and idiom of behavior.

For purposes of typing these individuals, attention was directed to identifying the distinguishing circumstances and the key decisions taken
among the options available at each point in their social and economic
ascent or descent. We then grouped together individuals that shared a
similar pattern and explained the logic of each strategy in relation to
economic and ideological factors.

Strategy I: Labor

For individuals who had no land or whose land was mortgaged out
with little hope of redemption, the immediate goal was survival. They
were constantly in search of any type of work from any source. Few status
differentials or political loyalty considerations operated for them, and men
of this category sought even the lower forms of employment as boatmen
and sweepers. The children worked to supplement their parents' income
and to earn favor of their parents' employment patrons by collecting and
drying cow dung, baby-siting, running errands to the market, etc.

Strategy II: Land/Labor

Generally followers of this strategy had inherited land and employment patrons. They cultivated what land they had and sought other labor
opportunities as time permitted. Their immediate goal was to regain lost
resources, particularly land, but they were also seeking to recapture lost
status and would not accept just any kind of labor. The men would not
be boatsmen or sweepers. The women would not serve as maidservants
or participate in food-for-work. The women might, however, accept work
from kin in processing paddy. Generally members of this group had
enough resources to buy fish. On the days the men worked their own
fields, they changed in the evening into fresh *genji* and *lungi* to visit the
market and school. They provided some labor employment to each other
and to those from strategy I. They had not fallen to the bottom rung, but
neither had they accumulated any savings to invest in obtaining additional
land or even in low-status business.

Where members of this group came from the medium landholding
category, they differed from other members of the category in that they
had the larger families and the smallest holdings, no other sources of income, and engaged in permanent labor outside, and daily labor inside,
the village.

Strategy III: Land/Education

Followers of this strategy commonly had improved their landholding
position relative to those in strategy II and were activating larger operational holdings. Their strategies were land based, avoiding labor if possible

and never selling their labor within the village. They were able to eat fish two or three times a week and put on clean shirts at the end of the day.

Education of their children was seen as a conscious investment. Although some poorer families might educate a third son after the first two sons had been gainfully employed on the land or elsewhere, persons following this strategy invested in the education of first and only sons. This strategy entailed an expense of roughly Tk. 100 per year per child at the primary level and Tk. 600 per year per child at the secondary level.

Strategy IV: Land/Small Business

Followers of this strategy typically invested in land and also in small, low-status (i.e. labor-dependent) business. Many also sold family labor both inside and outside the village. They aimed to improve their resource position through whatever means were open. Status considerations did not operate heavily. Their constraint was the amount of capital to invest in business so the range of opportunities open to them was paddy husking and itinerant trading in items such as rice, groceries, ice cream, and vegetables. Becoming a vegetable faria was the lowest status and required the least initial credit—roughly Tk. 50. A paddy-husking business could be financed with Tk. 150.

Strategy V: Land/Employment

People of this category were educated and earned regular salaried incomes. Their immediate goal was to buy land, having rejected the small business investment option in favor of education-based employment. They perceived their line of mobility as follows: education → employment → activation → eventual purchase of land.

Strategy VI: Land/High Status Business

All those in this category inherited land and had since improved their landholding position. They were from the top two landholding categories. Their immediate goals were to increase resources so they could pursue status and power. They maintained relatively high standards of living: quality food and dress plus social linkages. They received external patronage in their business and extended internal labor patronage. They had union-level political ambitions and were using marriage and education of their children as tools to enhance their status.

Their lifestyles were expensive relative to their income from land, and they had gone into high status business to ensure that they could be maintained. They had invested some capital in the purchase of grain stocks, which they stored for sale at optimal prices. This form of business had a certain status in that it demanded no labor from them and left them free to pursue other activities.

Strategy VII: Employment/Education

These had all inherited land and received education. They had all since divested some land to invest in the education of their children but remained upward mobile. Their main income was from employment and the surplus from this employment was invested in business or kept in savings. They all received external patronage to obtain their employment and now extended some internal patronage to their kin and neighbors. Although some were kinship group leaders, they belonged to strong neutral kin group and were not active in factional politics. Some of their surplus was invested in fancy clothing, pants and shirts, or costly *kurta-paijamas*, and motorcycles. They pursued the following line of mobility: education → employment → investment in education → savings and/or business investment.

Strategy VIII: Politics/Business

This category includes the three most active political types of Bonkura—Hashem Ali, Azizur Rahman, and Safdar Ali. The three inherited some land but had recently improved their land position. Their goals were status, power, and resources. They came from strong kinship groups and were themselves faction leaders. Their lifestyles were the highest in the village. Hashem Ali and Azizur Rahman had always earned a steady income from their teaching and had also invested some surplus in status businesses.

Safdar Ali differed from the other two in certain significant ways. He did not earn an employment income. Rather he moved upward through a series of small businesses, investing his money in whatever forms of business appeared open to him. Only recently had he invested some money in lifestyle improvements. He also seemed to pay less heed than Hashem Ali or Azizur to the patronage ideal, giving less attention to providing favors to his following.

Strategy IX: Business/Migration

All members of this category were Hindus who intended eventually to migrate to India. They all inherited the lines of business traditional to their caste. Most of them were Shahas known for grocery and other forms of mobile trading, and were educated, as the occupation demanded, in bookkeeping skills. Their line of mobility was fairly straight forward:

inherited business → reinvestment in business → savings → migration. Most were landless.

Strategy X: Land

This represented the prototype of the "traditional rich farmer" who inherited land and had not yet diversified into other sources of income. But members of this group in Bonkura associated closely with the land and did not keep a stranglehold on the village. Indeed, they remained fairly neutral, almost isolated, and left others alone. They extended some labor patronage but also engaged their own family labor on the land.

This study highlights the complex variety of the strategies followed by households of different circumstances in one small village of Bangladesh, the varied criteria that enter into their decision-making processes, and the dynamic and often highly enterprising nature of village life. It also reveals the conflicts, many of which were intense and bitter, the result of competing ambitions in a resource-scarce environment.

The government remained a somewhat peripheral and not always beneficial actor in the processes that shaped the fortunes of Bonkura's residents. Rather than serving as a judicious benefactor of the righteous and the needy, the government was accurately viewed primarily as a source of surplus economic and political resources in the form of employment, goods, and legal sanction to be exploited for personal gain and political patronage by those who had the ambition and the requisite economic and political resources.

Here then is a village turning over to a point where trade and employment, at least superficially, are increasingly significant. Yet the idiom of its struggle is faction and the logic of its values heavily land and kinship based.

So far in Bonkura, not enough resources flow through other avenues to challenge those resources that flow through kinship channels. Bonkura will probably not lose its feudal basis until the incomes from agricultural labor are of less significance and the pattern of labor use changes. Until such time, because so much of the available resources flow through kinship channels, kinship units continue to be the basic political units in Bonkura. Factions develop around the core of the major kinship group. Smaller, weaker kinship groups align with the larger kinship groups in an effort to derive some economic gain. Any resources that flow from the Union through the faction only further strengthen this kin-based factional alliance. So, although the resource base for factions is not high, the strength of factions derives from the close integration between kinship and factions, and although avenues of external incomes have become significant to Bonkura, the internal distribution of these resources and the individual villager's behavior in response to these resources has remained "traditional."

NOTES

1. This report is based on a research study titled *Who Gets What and Why: Resource Allocation in a Bangladesh Village* conducted and published by the Bangladesh Rural Advancement Committee (BRAC), 66 Mohakhali C.A., Dhaka 12, Bangladesh, first published in mimeograph form in July 1979 and issued as a published monograph in August 1983. This version is abstracted and edited for publication by David C. Korten. All names of persons and villages used in this study have been disguised. Reprinted with permission.

2. The exchange rate in 1977 was about Tk. 15 to US$1.

3. This includes faction leaders as well as individuals who actually held or sought formal public office.

4. These terms refer to crops rather than specific varieties. They may be roughly identified as follows: *aus* is harvested before the annual floods; *aman* is the crop harvested after the floods; and *boro* is the winter rice crop.

5. The overall picture with respect to cropping patterns and technology changed significantly as of 1978 with the inauguration of several deep tubewell and power pump schemes in the Bonkura area. This opened up the possibility of planting high yielding varieties of rice during the winter season, which took advantage of the cloudless days to achieve maximum photo-synthetic effect but which required reliable water supply and the application of chemical fertilizers.

CHAPTER SIX

Dilemmas of Local Administration in Thailand

Ronald L. Krannich

Municipal government was established in Thailand immediately following the Democratic Revolution of 1932, which deposed the absolute monarchy. Adapted from a Western model of local self-government,[1] the reforms sought to establish a degree of local self-government within what remains a highly centralized and unitary—in contrast to a federal—national political-administrative structure. The underlying intent of the new structure was to achieve a combination of: (1) local democracy, through election of key local officials; and (2) competent administration of urban services, through close supervision by national and provincial government. Thus, a central feature of the municipality in Thailand is its integration into a centralized administrative system preoccupied with insuring orderly adherence to prescribed administrative procedures at subordinate levels.

It is not surprising that significant tensions between the priorities and concerns of central and local levels of administration sometimes develop within this structure. While certain features of these tensions are distinctive to the particular structure of Thai municipal administration and the Thai cultural setting, others are suggestive of patterns observed in municipal administration in quite different structures and settings. Examination of these dynamic patterns can give us useful insights into the nature of local administration more generally, as well as the particular dilemmas faced in situations where efforts are made to introduce a responsive and democratic local administrative unit within a unitary national system.

URBAN ADMINISTRATION AND POLITICS

All levels of government in Thailand, from the national to the municipal, have differing interests and roles in the administration process. At the central level the emphasis is on setting performance standards, conducting routine supervisory functions, issuing orders, and processing documents. Overall, central administrators have few direct contacts with the day-to-day activities of municipal governments or their local constituencies.[2] While provincial officials have more immediate contacts with municipalities, their numerous provinicial responsibilities preclude close supervision of municipal officials; they primarily process the municipal orders and documents required by central officials.

The decision-making process at the municipal level differs markedly from the process at the other levels. Four conditions contribute to these differences.[3]

First, municipal governments deliver street-level services that are daily, visible, and locality specific, such as street paving, garbage collection, street lighting, and market cleaning. Since these are visible services that place local citizens in direct contact with city officials, residents are aware of them and thus usually are able to evaluate the quality of service delivery.

Second, Thai mayors are continuously bombarded by citizen complaints and demands for improved service delivery. Such citizen contact is much less pronounced—often absent—at the district and provincial levels of government.

Third, street level services are delivered by two categories of personnel: (1) central government appointed managerial officers—municipal clerk, assistant municipal clerk, chief accountant, and municipal engineers—whose primary accountability is to various units in Bangkok; and (2) locally recruited personnel of the municipal administrative organization.

Fourth, action on most sevice delivery demands and complaints depends upon resources and cooperation from provincial and central administrative units.

The interrelated nature of street-level services and the fragmented nature of authority over them creates a particular problem. For example, municipalities are responsible for maintaining law and order, but they do not have their own police forces. The enforcement function is performed by a special unit of the provincial police force. This situation is even further complicated because the police are relatively autonomous of the provincial governor and the Ministry of Interior. Since many municipal services depend on law enforcement (particularly traffic control and enforcement of building and sanitation codes), a mayor must have the cooperation of the provincial police. However, unless a mayor has a close personal relationship with the police chief, he seldom receives it.

Another prime example involves water and electrical services. As in the case of police services, water and electricity are not provided by municipal governments; they are the responsibility of provincial authorities—a fact few local citizens know. In additon to disrupting these services, the laying of water mains and the extension of power lines affect traffic flow, and may disrupt municipal garbage collection and street maintenance services in certain neighborhoods. As a result, many citizens complain to the mayor about the inconveniences caused. In response, the mayor may try to explain that the municipality is not responsible for these problems, meanwhile applying political pressure to officials in other administrative units to correct the problems that are causing complaints and misunderstanding. In this manner, a mayor becomes involved in administrative politics with the police chief, governor, or heads of the provincial water or elecrical authorities.

Central administratiors who are subjected to such pressures feel that the mayor is playing politics by interfering with the normal channels of communication and authority. Yet such lobbying efforts by a politically influential mayor often result in quick action.

These four conditions of Thai municipal administration tend to make municipal politics and policy making inherently unstable and unpredictable in sharp contrast to the more stable and predictable nature of policy at the provincial and central levels.

This is perhaps illustrated through the following "aggregate" case constructed from data compiled during a study of all municipalities in Thailand. The reader will not actually find a municipality by the name of Tamada on the map of Thailand, and no two municipalities share exactly the same experience. However, the situations, issues, resources, actors, problems, and decision-making styles reported in this case are more or less characteristic of those found in all municipalities throughout the country.

POLICY AND POLITICS IN TAMADA

The town of Tamada has a population of 15,000 and a municipal area of six square kilometers. Located 300 kilometers from Bangkok, Tamada is connected to the capital and several regional towns by paved roads and air, rail, bus, and telephone sevices. It functions as a provincial capital as well as a manufacturing, commercial, educational, social, and cultural center for nearby towns and villages.

Tamada's municipal budget totals $183,750: 25 percent of the budget is in the form of direct central government financial subsidies.[4] Over 55 percent of the total budget is spent on salaries and wages. With an average per capita expenditure of $12.25, Tamada is able to maintain past service levels and introduce a few new projects each year. Compared to funding of other levels and units of government, the municipality is relatively well off and is the envy of provincial officials.

Political-Administrative Structure

The formal governing structure of Tamada is illustrated in Figure 6-1. The Municipal Assembly, elected by the local residents, consists of eighteen members. The Assembly in turn selects an Executive Council consisting of a mayor and two councillors. This Executive Council is responsible for supervision of the administrative organization of the municipality. This consists of five major units, forty permanent municipal officials, thirty temporary municipal officials, and forty-five workers. A professional chief administrative officer—the municipal clerk—heads this organization. He is a university law graduate who is recruited, trained, assigned, and transferred by the Ministry of Interior in Bangkok. Immediately subordinate to him is an assistant municipal clerk who has similar training and experience.

The administrative units vary in size, importance, and functions. Measured in terms of budget, personnel, volume of activities, and community visibility, the engineering section is the largest and most important unit. Its major functions include road construction and repair,

Figure 6-1
Formal Structure of Tamada Municipality

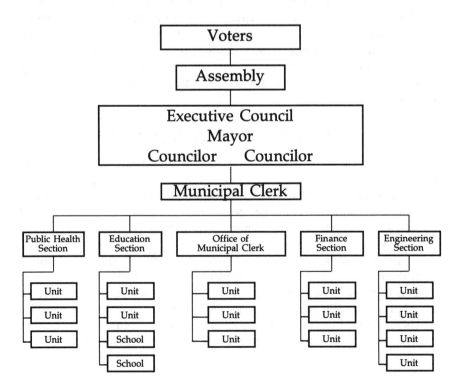

maintenance of drainage systems, refuse disposal, street and market cleaning, construction approval and inspection and vehicle maintenance.

The education section is the second largest unit. It operates elementary schools within the municipality. The finance section is third in size, but second in importance. The public health section, by far the weakest of all units, is charged with maintaining a first-class health clinic, preventing and suppressing infectious diseases, and controling the municipal slaughterhouse.

The office of municipal clerk has the status of a section. Its three units perform functions that ordinarily do not fall into the functional areas of other sections. These include routine planning; issuing letters, orders, regulations, reports, and minutes of committee meetings; maintaining records on residential movements, births, deaths, and ownership of property; and operating the fire brigade.

The Informal Structure

The formal structure communicates little of the reality of the municipal administration in Tamada. First, officials within the administrative units are divided into three informal factions based on personal relationships between their leader and former mayors and councillors. These factions cut across departmental lines. Two of them are antagonistic to one another and compete for favors from the current mayor and council members, while resisting the direction of the municipal clerk.

As the chief executive, the mayor, in theory, has the final decision-making authority. The councillors divide the responsibility for inspecting the work of the individual sections and report the findings directly to the mayor. Normally they bypass the municipal clerk and encourage individual sections heads to do the same. They view themselves not as politicians but rather as elected administrators who come from the "people" and thus know the needs of the community better than appointed administrators chosen by ministries in Bangkok. At the same time they have little real authority because of the administrative controls placed on the them by other levels of govenment.

The municipal clerk, who has the formal administrative responsibility, often complains that the members of the Executive Council, though well meaning and hard working, are ignorant of the rules and regulations, and have little knowledge of good administrative practice. It seems to him that they are too responsive to personal wishes and individual whims. At the same time he finds that few of his subordinates can be relied upon to complete a task without close supervision. Various of his presumed subordinates may be appointed by the municipal council, by the province, or by the central government and he has little real authority over them. Some may work as little as one or two hours a day while a few are local hoodlums who curse or threaten their superiors.

Services and Problems

The Tamada municipality is responsible for basic urban functions including collecting revenue, constructing and maintaining streets, markets, and drainage systems, removing garbage, preventing fires, directing basic health services, and providing elementary education on a limited scale. As noted previously, police, water, and electrical services are the responsibilities of provincial-level authorities, although many local residents still blame municipal officials for failing to perform these services adequately. Most municipal political issues and administrative problems arise from, and are dircted toward, the performance of these basic urban services.

Tamada has four continuing problems, which persistently frustrate the best efforts of Tamada administrators due to constraints of policies, authority, personnel, finance, and management.

Flooding

The most persistent and aggravating problem is flooding. Every year the southeastern section of town floods during the May-through-September rainy season. When this happens, several other problems are created: paved roads and drainage systems in this section of town are severely damaged; additional health hazards arise; traffic patterns are altered, which results in greater traffic congestion for other sections of town; and educational services are disrupted at the one municipal school located in the inundated area. Local residents have complained for years about this problem; yet, decisive action is not forthcoming from the municipality, even though all candidates in past municipal elections promised to correct it.

For municipal officials, the problem is complicated by many factors. A comprehensive flood control system with an estimated cost of US $700,000 was planned two years ago. Now the cost is estimated at US $1,000,000—over five times the total annual municipal budget. Since neither local funds not central government subsidies are available for this project, the municipality must cope through alternative means. These inlclude improving the old drainage system that contributes to the flooding; directing more landfill into the flooded area in order to confine the area inundated; instituting a flood warning system; and providing relocation and welfare services for displaced residents. Municipal officials hope these interim measures will result in substantially decreasing annual expenditures for reconditioning the damaged roads and drainage system as well as reducing the number of complaints from local residents.

Market

Tamada has one municipal market that poses serious problems. In addition to being an embarrassing eyesore, several complaints have been made of its extremely crowded and unsanitary conditions. Merchants throw garbage everywhere, both within and around the market area. Furthermore, hawkers sell their goods on the sidewalks and streets. This resulted in closing one street because it became the territory of the hawkers, increasing the volume of traffic on nearby streets and creating a serious traffic congestion problem throughout the downtown area.

Municipal ordinances prohibit such behavior, but merchants and hawkers pay no attention to them. Although the police are supposed to enforce these ordinances, they lack personnel to supervise the market area. The police also wish to avoid instigating protests from arrested violators.

Every solution has its limitations. First, funds are not availavle to build a new market. Second, it is uncertain if a new market would be profitable. Third, although additional sanitation workers can be hired, they would probably create greater congestion within the market and thus accentuate the present problem. Given these considerations, the optimal solution for municipal officials is no decision—that is, live with the problem a little longer, and in the meantime, establish a market review committee to give further thought to this matter.

Slum and Squatter Settlement

A large slum and squatter settlement has developed on government land in the northern section of town during the past three years. This land belongs to a central government unit, not the municipality—a fact few local residents know. The central government unit had plans to build an office building and housing compound there, but since the arrival of the squatters, the officials prefer not to force the people off as this would probably create a political incident having unfavorable public relations consequences for the unit.

Since the municipality lacks authority to regulate land use and enforce housing codes, it can do little except send officials from the health section and fire brigade to inspect and urge people to take preventive measures in the slum and squatter settlement. The police are unwilling to cooperate in enforcing local sanitation codes. Publicly, the police sympathize with the squatters and claim they lack the necessary manpower to enforce local ordinances. Privately, however, the police prefer avoiding this area because they fear the local toughs and because some police officers have a vested interest in keeping the houses of prostitution operating. Hence, the police acquiesce to the slum conditions and shift responsibility by blaming the municipality for allowing these conditions to develop.

The slum continues to grow as more squatters move into the area. Moreover, slum residents are particularly pleased with the extension of municipal health and sanitation services into their area. They were recently informed that the municipal schools would also accept their children. A few local politicians were especially helpful in that they promised to increase sevices to the slum area—if residents registered to vote. The slum and squatter dwellers receive free services while paying no taxes and they anticipate more services in the furture.

Cleanliness

The general cleanliness of the town is the most complicated and interrelated problem of all. Local residents carelessly litter the streets and sidewalks as well as dump garbage in open areas. This not only detracts from the natural beauty of the town, but it also clogs the open drainage systems and thus contributes to the town's flooding problem.

Municipal ordinances prohibiting littering and illegal garbage dumping are ignored by most people. The police say they cannot enforce ordinances dealing with such minor offenses because thy only have enough manpower for limited traffic control and major crime suppression. Last year the municipality spent US$4,000 on new litter barrels that were conveniently placed throughout the town. Not only were the barrels not used, but 50 percent were either stolen or vandalized. Many were thrown into the drainage ditches.

The municipality finally decided to increase its garbage collection and street cleaning services—a decision that did not depend on either local citizen compliance or police cooperation. But this decision required purchasing two new garbage trucks and hiring ten more sanitation workers. Funds are available, but both decisions must be approved by the Ministry of Interior in Bangkok. Approval is expected to take nearly ten months because of the understaffed and overworked conditions of the central units. Meanwhile, the cost of garbage trucks increases.

A previous plan for purchasing additional garbage trucks and hiring more workers had been approved. However, three months later the sanitation workers, demanding a 50 percent wage increase, went on strike. Since the municipality had to meet their demands, funds were only available for hiring five additional sanitation workers. And to further complicate the situation, two months later one garbage truck was destroyed in a serious accident. Now the municipality needs one new truck simply to restore previous service levels.

The local press criticized the mayor for his inaction and suggested that he was involved in corruption related to the purchase of new garbage trucks. Rumors and additional criticism were quickly spread among the townspeople by the merchants and hawkers in the market. With this, the mayor became angry and began to publicly blame his opposition, the governor, and officials in the Ministry of Interior for all his misfortunes in trying to sincerely solve the litter and garbage problem. Angered by the mayor's criticism, the governor initiated an investigation into the mayor's behavior and warned him to stay calm. Thereupon the mayor left town for a few days to calm his emotions and rethink his problems.

The conflicts were momentarily resolved with the return of the annual floods. The Boy Scouts and other groups were organized for a two-week community clean-up campaign. In the weeks immediately following the flood, the townspeople were more conscious of their littering habits. But in the months that followed, littering reached its former level. It would probably take another annual flood and a subsequent community clean-up campaign to again overcome the littering problem.

THE ROLE OF LOCAL ADMINISTRATION

Many of these problems require effective local coordination across technical lines and the ability to make rapid reallocations of the resources in response to situations that may constitute major crises locally but are of insufficient magnitude to capture the attention of a national agency. At the same time technical, financial, and staff resources of local government are, in many Asian countries, likely to be quite weak. They need access to the support available from larger and more specialized national agencies.

Thus, in a smoothly functioning national system, there are important roles for both central and local administration. The case of Tamada demonstrates, however, the difficulties in achieving such a harmonious outcome. Here the relationships are characterized by destructive conflicts and an inability to achieve more than limited, piecemeal responses to local needs. The reasons bear examination.

Political versus Administrative Imperatives

To some extent the differences between the viewpoints of political and administrative officials at the municipal level reflect an inevitable and universal conflict between the political imperative for quick and responsive results, and the administrative imperative for order and consistency. The elected officials stress their democratic mandate from the people, and view local policy and politics as inherently messy and unpredictable. They demand that the administrative function be more responsive and resent what they perceive to be indifference among the local bureaucarats. On the other hand, the appointed administrators stress the importance of competent adminstration, as characterized by orderly adherence to procedure, and attempt to make the political arena more stable and predictable. They resent the intrusions of the elected officials, which they view not as a necessary and appropriate response to local realities but simply as arbitrary, uninformed, personalized, and disruptive.

Toward an Integrated Local Administration

On paper the formal organizational chart for Tamada gives the appearance of an integrated local administration. In fact it is not. Tamada is in many respects a local political system imposed on top of a national administrative system, with only tenuous links between the two.

Both the mayor and the municipal clerk are "men in the middle." Neither controls the resources to discharge his duties effectively. At the same time the responsibilities of the mayor, as defined by his local political constituency, are likely to be in large measure in conflict with those defined by the Ministry of Interior for the municipal clerk, providing little basis for an effective alliance between the two. Furthermore, even if they were to combine choices, their joint ability to mobilize the required financial and human resources to achieve agreed upon outcomes would remain limited by the nature of the structures within which each works.

Any effort to improve on the situations must recognize that there will always be tensions between political and administrative imperatives and between central and local priorities. Thus, the objective is not to eliminate them but rather to find structural changes that limit the conflict while facilitating the orderly and productive mediation of those conflicts that may be forever inherent.

In the present instance this would seem to involve moving further in the direction of a true local administration in which adminstrative staff are professional, long-term employees of the local unit, and a growing portion of local financial resources are generated from local sources. Certain minimum national standards might be maintained for the hiring, training, and terms of service for such employees, but the local unit would be their employer. This would call for the national agencies involved gradually to adjust their own roles from direct admininstration of local affairs, to regulatory and support functions—changes that can be achieved only over time with significant difficulty. At the same time special training to prepare new mayors and council members for their roles might help them to understand better the requirements of public administration and how best to work with the system to achieve the desired responsiveness to local needs.

The issues involved are challenging and difficult. Addressing them will requre recognition at all governmental levels of the special role and nature of local administration within a national development process.

NOTES

1. C. Chayabutra, "A Comparative Study of Local Government in Thailand and England". Ph.D. dissertation, University of Exeter, England, 1986; and C. Karnjanaprakorn, "Municipal Government in Thailand as an Institution and Process of Self Government", Ph.D. dissertation, Indiana University, 1959.

2. R. L. Krannich and C. R. Krannich "Anonymous Communications and Bureaucratic Politics in Thailand," *Administration and Society* 11, 2, 1979, 227-248.

3. In several respects these differences correspond to Lipsky's concept of street-level bureaucracy. See Lipsky, M. "Toward a Theory of Street-level Bureaucracy", in W. Hawley and M. Lipsky, *Theoretical Perspectives in Urban Politics* (Englewood Cliffs:Prentice-Hall, 1976), pp. 126-213.

4. For convenience, budget figures are stated in U.S. dollar equivalents.

PART III: INTRODUCTION

MOBILIZING RESOURCES

David C. Korten

Underutilized resources, potentially available to meet local develpment needs, take many forms and often exist in relative abundance in even the poorest rural communities. They include technical knowledge that has not been effectively shared, under employed workers, idle or poorly utiliz- ed land belonging to government or absentee landlords, buildings unoc- cupied or unused during certain hours, and poorly deployed government extension agents. There may also be idle money hidden away as cash or ornaments, crop and animal residues, untapped or poorly used water sources, crops lost to spoilage, idle equipment and draft animals, educated youth with no outlets for their skills, unused hydro sites, etc.

Long before the days of national development budgets, projects, and programs, rural communities commonly organized themselves for sometimes extraordinary accomplishments, dependent only on their own resources. For example, the work of communities throughout Asia in developing and managing their own irrigation systems is well known. Among the thousands of case examples are some so striking as to astonish even the most experienced observer. One of these comes from an uplands area on the island of Bali in Indonesia where fifty-four farmers carved a tunnel two kilometers long through a mountain to irrigate their twenty- two hectares without formal engineering training or outside assistance. The farmers organized themselves into teams that tunneled from opposite sides of the mountain to join the tunnel in the center, allocating the work among themselves and carefully measuring individual contributions. These contribution credits translated into rights to corresponding shares of water from the completed system, which the participants strictly en- force through their association.[1]

As dramatic as this case is in demonstrating indigenous engineering and organizing skills, cases of communities mobilizing to build irrigation systems, fish ponds, roads, public buildings, and canals using only their own resources are commonplace throughout Asia. In many instances, in contrast to programs sponsored by central government, the financial resources involved may be negligible, the main resources being local technical knowledge, labor, and materials.

Yet even seemingly very poor rural communities at times demonstrate rather extraordinary ability to mobilize financial resources as well. An example of this is reported by Dian Desa, an Indonesian private voluntary development organization, from a project that involved the construction of 1,000 household rainwater catchment tanks in selected villages of Nusa Tenggara Timur Province, Indonesia. It is an area of severe poverty, partly due to the extreme shortage of water. As the project progressed, the Dian Desa team came to realize that local tradition dictated major expenditures by the beneficiaries for social and ritual observances not anticipated in the project design. By the completion of the project, Dian Desa staff estimated that the villagers had expended the equivalent of some US $28,340, all mobilized from within the community, for the whiskey and food consumed at countless meetings and ceremonies, and for the animals sacrificed to dedicate new facilities.[2] That much of this expenditure may appear unnecessary to an outsider does not negate the fact that even these extremely impoverished villages were able to mobilize substantial financial resources for needs that to them were important.

Reasons why a community can mobilize a wide range of resources inaccessible to the bureaucracy are easy to identify. Its members have an intimate knowledge of their neighbors and their skills as well as of unused lands, facilities, and materials that may exist in substantial quantities even in very poor villages. And people are more likely to come forward in volunteering the use of such resources, including their labor and personal possessions, if they feel they will have a direct hand in determining their use, will have reasonable prospect of sharing in the benefits, and will be recognized by the community for their contributions.[3] They are less likely to bring these resources to the attention of officials who are accountable only to central authorities and represent the seemingly unlimited financial resources of the state.

The following chapters document a variety of accomplishments of rural people and describe the ways in which they organize, both formally and informally. They also contrast these accomplishments, based entirely on local resources and initiative, with the consequences of government efforts to achieve similar ends using central resources. These cases do not represent statistical samples and are not intended to demonstrate that community intiative always produces results superior to those of government. Their purpose is only to challenge the implicit assumption of much development planning that development occurs only in response to government initiative, and is necessarily dependent on central government resources and direction.

In Chapter seven, Michael Calavan presents an inventory from five villages of rural Thailand of the numerous infrastructure facilities constructed, operated, and maintained by villagers using their own resources. The management of village ponds is then examined in more detail—describing the mechanisms used to set and enforce norms on fishing and maintenance. Calavan also reports on a variety of government initiative to construct and improve similar facilities, both successful and unsuccessful.

In Chapter eight, James Anderson provides useful insights into the sophistication of some indigenous agricultural technologies as demonstrated specifically by the highly developed house gardens found in selected localities throughout the region. He notes the highly productive use of scarce land resources made possible by applications of principles of plant and animal ecology largely ignored in modern Western agricultural practice. Anderson also examines the role of the house garden in testing, adapting, and disseminating new varieties through informal community channels.

In Indonesia, well financed government programs have sought to encourage the colonization of remote and under populated areas of the country with only limited success. In Chapter nine, Andrew Vayda documents a parallel process of colonization of many of these same lands, sustained entirely through self-organizing private initiative. While not all the consequences are either socially or ecologically desirable,[4] his cases demonstrate the power and vitality of unregulated, informal economic and social processes stimulated by naturally ocurring economic incentives. One wonders what might be the record of public transmigration programs if their design recognized and sought to strengthen such natural processes.

The idea of learning from and strenghthening natural processes has been applied elsewhere with good results. For example, in Chapter ten, Romana de los Reyes documents how public irrigation programs in the Philippines benefited from studying how self-formed irrigator groups organize themselves for system operation and maintenance. Results of her study, which was funded jointly by the Philippine National Irrigation Administration (NIA) and the Ford Foundation, are summarized and their uses by the NIA discussed. This is only one example of the extensive contribution made by de los Reyes and her colleagues at the Institute of Philippine Culture to development of the NIA's participatory approach to smallscale irrigation development. The highly successful NIA program is at the forefront of efforts to demonstrate the appropriate and effective use of social science knowledge and methods in the development and implementation of community management programs.[5]

Chapter eleven presents a second contribution by the research staff of the Bangladesh Rural Advancement Committee (BRAC). This study reveals the darkest aspects of local politics, showing how a small group of local elites in several adjacent Bangladesh villages gained control of external public resources and authority through illegal and anti-social means and turned these against the community they were intended to benefit. The study analyzes the complex networks of corruption that developed and how they were sustained. BRAC-assisted people's organizations documented the structure of the networks and the practices of their members, and then challenged the corrupt power holders. The case demonstrates how essential such organizing efforts can be in assuring that the benefits of government poverty programs reach those for whom they are intended and the difficult obstacles they face, setting the stage for Part V on "Interventions to Empower."

NOTES

1. N. Sutawan, M. Swara, N. Sutjipta, W. Suteja, and W. Windia, "Subak Dalam Sistem Irigasi Non-PU Dan Subak Dalam System Irigasi PU: Kasus Subak Timul Baru Dan Subak Celuk Kabupaten Ginayar," Universitas Udayana, Denpasar, Bali, Indonesia, September 1984.

2. "Report on the Water Supply Program at Kec. Kewapante, Kab. Sikka, Flores, Nusa Tenggara Timur," Yayasan Dian Desa, P. O. Box 19, Bulaksumur, Yogykarta, Indonesia, 1984.

3. Another example is provided in Chapter fifteen in the experience of the Gram Gourav Pratisthan in organizing poor farmers in arid areas to establish pump fed irrigation systems.

4. We may safely assume that the same is true for many of the government's transmigration efforts as well.

5. For other social science applications see Romana P. de los Reyes, "Process Documentation: Social Science Research in a Learning Process Approach to Program Development," *Philippine Sociological Review*, 32, 105-120; and Romana P. de los Reyes, *Sociotechnical Profile: A Tool for Rapid Rural Appraisal* (Quezon City: Institute of Philippine Culture, Ateneo de Manila University, 1984).

CHAPTER SEVEN

Community Management in Rural Northeastern Thailand[1]

Michael M. Calavan

Thai villagers accomplish a variety of significant tasks through collaborative effort. Activities regularily encountered by students of village life include: construction and maintenance of roads; construction and maintenance of wells; construction and maintenance of irrigation systems; construction and maintenance of temple complexes; organization of a regular round of cult activities and religious festivals; funeral insurance clubs; labor exchange groups such as harvesting cooperatives; and commercial cooperatives (called *hui*).

These activities provide significant services: creation of "public goods;" management of important resources; provision of "social welfare;" mobilization of labor for public and private benefit, recreation, marketing and transport of commodities; and maintenance of a degree of "social equilibrium." This paper provides examples of such activities observed during field visits to five villages in Khon Kaen and Kalesin provinces of northeast Thailand. The first part focuses on the village of Ban Kham Paum, looking at the mechanisms by which resources are mobilized and managed at village level. The latter portion concentrates on mangement of village ponds, suggesting some principles to guide government programs intended to help villagers improve fish pond structures and management.

BAN KHAM PAUM VILLAGE

The experience of Ban Kham Paum village illustrates a range of the sometimes quite ambitious projects carried out through local initiative, often with the involvement of local religious leaders.

A Village Road System

In 1973, during a period when there was a great deal of interest in "village development," a proposal for reorganizing village roads on a grid system was originated by the abbot of Ban Kham Paum's temple. The plan called for building five straight, north-south and five straight, east-west roads in place of one meandering road and several trails already in existence. The *Kamnan* (sub-district headman) called a public meeting where the plan, which would require moving 118 houses out of a total of 300 in the village, was discussed and accepted. Several substantial tasks were implied by this decision: a) house removal; b) road construction; c) buying gravel; and d) maintenance.

House removal caused inconvenience to many households. Some families discovered that they would lose all their house land to the road right-of-way and thus would be forced to buy new house land or to move to already-owned garden plots at the edge of the village. Other families lost only part of their house plots, but still found it necessary to move their houses back from the right-of-way. "Moving" a house ordinarily implied tearing it down, board-by-board and reconstructing it in the new location. It was impossible to fully repay families for expenses incurred and effort expended. However, an ingenious, and apparently satisfactory, form of "symbolic compensation" was devised. Each household that did not have to move was asked for a voluntary contribution to a compensation fund. This amount was divided equally among the 118 households that did have to move. The 130 *baht* received by each family was said to be "for nails." Inconvenienced households were further compensated by the assistance of kinsmen, neighbors, and friends in the relocation process.

Road construction was carried out over a two year period. Tools used in preparing road beds were limited to heavy hoes and bamboo carrying baskets. Necessary tasks included digging, carrying, spreading, and tamping of earth. The work was organized and supervised by the nine members of the village development committee. Straight segments through the village were completed one at a time. Work days were set during agricultural slack periods and were announced throughout the village. Most workers came from houses located close to the right-of-way on which work was planned for a given day. All households were expected to send representatives to "do their share" over the two year period. Attendance was recorded in an account book. No specific sanctions were contemplated for nonparticipating households other than gossip and ill will. The abbot organized a rotational system whereby families in each of the five village *khum* (neighborhoods) were expected to feed the workers.

After completion of the road bed, gravel was spread. The accelerated Rural Development Department provided a truck and driver, but local residents paid for gravel, gasoline, and the driver's per diem. Money was raised through contributions from village households.

The completed roads are maintained by local residents, with families expected to maintain those sections adjacent to their house compounds. Maintenance requires the same simple tools as construction. Sections of road that are heavily used and poorly maintained are sometimes adopted as special projects by the village "youth club." The kamnan ordinarily calls to the attention of the young people those sections needing special maintenance.

In 1964 the seven kilometers of dirt road leading from the village to the main highway were substantially improved in a similar manner.

A Village Electrical System

For more than six years, from 1972 to 1978, residents of Ban Kham Paum enjoyed electrical service from a system that was planned, paid for, and maintained solely on local initiative. Two nearby villages had established generator-operated systems, and the abbot proposed that local residents do the same. Under the abbot's direction, a total of 100,000 baht was raised. Some funds were contributed by local residents specifically for the electrical project; others had been contributed to the general temple fund.

The abbot and a local resident knowledgeable about generators sought a used generator in Bangkok and in several locations in northeastern Thailand. They finally located a thirty KW diesel generator in a rock crushing plant in Buriram Province for which they paid 40,000 baht.[2] The remaining 60,000 baht was sufficient to finance wiring, electrical poles, and installation. Equipment and installation were purchased in Khon Kaen.

Those households not initially connected to the system could become connected by making a request to the abbot. In such cases wiring was done by local monks, who also visited customers monthly to collect bills. One monk acted as bookkeeper for the system.

The system was closed down at the end of 1978 after more than six years in response to a government promise to connect the village to the regional grid "before the elections" of April 22, 1979. When we visited the village in late June 1979, piles of concrete electric poles could be seen along village roads. A few poles had been raised, but no wire had been attached.

The "Big Well"

The "big well" lies about one kilometer beyond Ban Kham Paum's northern boundary near a village more than 130 years old—and is nearly as old as that village. During the dry season, it supplies drinking water to residents of a number of villages in the area.

In about 1965, a widely known monk, who resides at the famous Wat Po temple in Bangkok and is a native of a nearby village, came to "sponsor" improvement work on the well. He lived at the site during the dry season and encouraged residents in the work of digging the well deeper and wider and in lining the walls with boards. The well is approximately thirty feet in diameter. Because the monk was present, all labor done, and donations of cash and construction materials could be interpreted as *tham bun* or "merit making."

Minor maintenance tasks—e.g. patching boards—are carried out by residents of the nearest village. Once a year the kamnan mobilized workers from three or four surrounding villages. On a specified day each March (when the water level is low) 170 to 180 people gathered to remove mud that had been deposited in the bottom of the well.

Tube Wells

Ban Kham Paum has a total of seven tube wells distributed rather evenly through its territory. They were dug in 1970-71. These, too, were built under the leadership of the local abbot. When people came to the temple to draw water for bathing, washing clothes, etc., from the temple ponds he would ask "why don't you get a tube well?" When they asked, "Who's going to organize the effort and pay for it?," he would reply, "I am." He would then give them each 100 baht to initiate a construction fund. Each local well was constructed at a cost of about 1500 baht by a local man. Each was provided with a hand pump, a roof, and a sign listing all contributors—with the abbot's name at the top.

Unfortunately the water provided is not of high quality. Its salinity rules out the wells as a source of drinking water. Nevertheless, the wells provide a convenient sourse of "use" water (*naam saaj*) for various cleaning tasks around the house.

The Temple Complex

Many, perhaps most, Thai villages have impressive temple complexes. A normal inventory of structures includes: one or more monks' dormitories, one or more *sala*, preaching hall (*wihaan*), and an ordination hall (*bod*). Other structures sometimes found include pagodas (*ceddi*), a library, a monks' dining hall, and funeral urns. The *wat* (temple complex) at Ban Kham Paum includes: several dormitories, a large preaching hall, a dining hall, an ordination hall, attractive gardens, five ponds, and several large tanks for capturing rain water.

The wat is impressive not only for the religious functions fulfilled but also as a repository of local wealth and source of secular sevices. Through merit making activities, villagers are able to mobilize materials and labor sufficient to build structures worth hundreds of thousands of baht. In addition, annual maintenance costs—for monks, novices, and structures—are quite high. In addition to specifically Buddhist services, residents receive a series of social benefits: the pageantry and recreation offered by religious festivals; space for public meetings in the sala; a park-like atmosphere; non-Buddhist supernatural assistance in the form of amulets, spells, potions; well water; social welfare services, e.g. food gifts in excess of the needs of the monks; party equipment for weddings, wakes, and other private ceremonies; and education.

Construction, maintenance, and provision of services are accomplished under local management through cooperation between monks and ordinary villagers with an impressive degree of efficiency.

Wat Kham Paum has had two freshwater ponds for many years. In about 1957 three additional ponds were dug by monks and novices under the supervision of the abbot. In 1964 the system was improved by construction of a small canal from the village's Large Pond to the Temple Ponds. Originally laid out by the abbot using his "naked eye," it stretched more than half a kilometer, passing under paths and roads through concrete pipes. The system worked admirably until 1978, when the government-planned, contractor-built spillway at the Large Pond was undermined and these ponds dried up.[3]

Residents were forbidden to fish in the ponds, as such behavior would be inappropriate in a Buddhist sanctuary. However, in 1978 when the ponds dried up, villagers were allowed to collect fish.

COMMUNITY MANAGEMENT OF VILLAGE FISH PONDS

It is clear that northestern Thai villages were traditionally established with an eye to the adequacy of nearby water supplies. Many are located on the banks of permanent streams or natural lakes and ponds. In other cases, villages are located near natural depressions associated with small streams (hoey), which flow for at least part of the year. Water is impounded to meet dry season needs by construction of earthen embankments. In four of the five villages visited, artificial ponds had been created in this way. The fifth village was located near a natural pond.

Water had been impounded in the man-made ponds for periods ranging from eighty to 200 years. With reasonable attention to construction and maintenance, these ponds provide useful water sources. Conventional uses include: fishing, water for livestock, human bathing, water for washing clothes and other domestic purposes, and for hand-watering of garden plots and nurseries. Northeastern Thai generally avoid drinking water from surface ponds or streams so long as rain water or pleasant-tasting well water is available.

Historically, once a new village has been established, one of the first activities of the new community is to construct a village pond—usually in an existing swampy area. Consequently development officials can expect to find man-made ponds, with well-established routines for maintenance and operation at many, perhaps most, feasible locations in the Northeast and should recognize that their village pond development projects seldom involve wholly new structures. In nearly all instances they well be engaging in upgrading of existing ponds with existing mangement systems often developed over several decades. Generally they will achieve better results if they take care to build from and strengthen what exists.

Maintenance

Once the dam/dike is constructed it must be maintained on a regular basis. In three of the four villages with artificial ponds, the work was done on an annual basis, usually during the transition between the hot and the rainy seasons (roughly May-June). At the village of Ban Ped, work was ordinarily carried out twice a year, once at the beginning of the rains and again shortly before the end of the rains, to insure maximum strength in anticipation of heavy flooding.

As in road construction, the four tasks to be performed during routine maintenance are digging, carrying, spreading, and tamping dirt. Dirt is ordinarily removed from the bottom of the pond inside the dike/dam. It is then carried a few meters to the embankment, spread and tamped into place. Work requirements are ordinarily assessed by the kamnan or *phu-jaajiban* (village headman), but specific dates and working arrangements are ordinarily decided in a public meeting called for that purpose. In general at least one worker is required from each village household. In one of the villages visited, households unable to send a representative are expected to contribute a small amount of cash (5-10 baht) or some food. Usually there is no specific sanction for avoiding maintenance tasks, but villagers and headmen agree that incurring the displeasure of fellow villagers is a heavy risk.

Labor may be mobilized on an individual, group, or team basis. Traditionally at Ban Kham Paum, the *phujaajiban* would assign a section of two or three *wa* (four-six meters) to each village household. In this case, villagers are not expected to carry out their tasks during any particular day but within a specified period of several days. If work is scheduled for three days, individuals are expected to show up on one of those days. If the group is large, it may be divided into teams, each to work on a separate sector of the dike. Workers are expected to bring hoes and carrying baskets as well as food for their noon meal.

In addition to this standard method of mobilizing labor for public works, maintenance work is carried out in two additional ways; workers may be hired with funds resulting from fines paid by those who fish illegally in the pond or those caught fishing illegally may be forced to "work off" their punishment by doing maintenance tasks. Hired workers may be paid by the day, by the number of wa completed, or by the number of cubic meters of earth moved. Those working for punishment will ordinarily be assigned a set number of wa of dike to refurbish.

Villagers are also expected to turn out in emergencies. During high water they work at raising low sectors (other than those intended as "spillways"), strengthening weak spots, and locating and plugging leaks. In areas of sandy soil these are formidable tasks and the dike is sometimes breached. In some areas this happens once every two or three years; in others it occurs once in thirty or forty years. If the dike breaks, villagers allow much of the water to escape. After floods have subsided, villagers repair the broken section with earth and stones. Invariably additional rains at the end of the season allow them to store some water.

Fisheries Management

Even without stocking by Inland Fisheries officials, village ponds support significant populations of "wild" fish. In addition, frogs and freshwater crabs, shrimp, snails, and shellfish provide significant sources of animal protein.

Systems for controlling fishing in man-made and natural ponds vary widely through time and from place to place. The natural pond at Ban Boeng Kae and the man-made pond at Ban Noon were fished without regulation. "Management" consisted of clearing aquatic vegetation at the former site and of dike maintenance at the latter. At Ban Kham Paum, Pan Naan Pond was forbidden to all fishermen for a period of at least forty years.[4] It was opened to restricted fishing only in 1973. Before this, use was limited to watering of animals, bucket irrigation of the garden plots, and drawing water for household use. Since 1973 the pond has been opened to fishing under conditions devised by the kamnan but generally accepted at a public meeting. An area of about twenty-five *rai* (total pond area is 220 rai) was set aside as a fish "sanctuary."[5] The boundary was marked by a series of wooded posts placed at intervals of about three meters.

Fishing within the sanctuary at Pan Naam Pond is forbidden through the year. Fisherman discovered within the area are ordinarily subject to fines varying from ten to 100 baht set by the kamnan. Those caught using gill nets or throw nets are assessed fifty or 100 baht fines. Those who use other, less efficient, techniques are given smaller fines. At least some villagers are willing to report their neighbors for illegal fishing.

In instances where gill nets are discovered and their owners are not, the kamnan seizes the net. If the owner does not come forth to claim it in a few days it is sold to any interested buyer. The funds received from fines and net sales are used by the kamnan to hire local people to carry out maintenance work on the dike.

At Ban Phaum Sim, the village pond was closed to fishing from September to March. The decision was normally taken (at a public meeting) to "open" the pond a few days before *Bun Dyan Sii*, a traditional holiday. The day before the holiday the pond was fished intensively, by all methods, without limitation. Soon after, bamboo poles were set out to mark the boundary of a sanctuary in the lower end of the pond. Thereafter, villagers were free to fish outside the sanctuary by any method until the pond was closed in September. After the pond was upgraded in 1977, two additions were made to these rules. A "pond committee" was established, and it was decided that all individuals who catch more than ten kg. of fish on "opening day" should surrender the excess to the pond committee. Fish thus collected were to be sold and the proceeds used for pond maintenance. The value of this regulation had not been adequately tested since the upgraded dike broke in October 1978, and fingerlings stocked in the pond a few months before were lost.

Some ponds are open to animals and others are not. Most of Naung Boeng Kii Pond at Ban Ped is protected by a barbed wire fence. Animals are able to approach the pond to drink at a few, restricted locations. Areas within the fence produced considerable grass. The right to cut grass is auctioned off at a public meeting each June or July. In 1978 this privilege was sold for 1,200 baht. The individual who makes the winning bid sells shares in the "enterprise," either by prearrangement or after the fact. At the same meeting a three member committee is elected with responsibility for dike maintenance using the funds collected from both the auction and the fines for illegal fishing. The ordinary pattern in this village election is for three individuals to be nominated and then elected by acclamation.

In the villages visited, public fisheries were "managed" to a considerable extent. Artificial ponds were built and maintained, some fingerlings have been stocked in recent years, and fishing and other uses are regulated. However, other aspects of a fisheries management system—fish nurseries, fertilization, feeding, clearing of aquatic vegetation, orderly drawdown and harvest—are generally lacking in the public ponds. An exception was identified at Ban Boeng Kae, where residents cleared their natural pond of vegetation at two or three year intervals. They did so when the pond became so clogged that use of a throw net was impossible. Lengths of rope or bamboo were dragged over the bottom of the pond, pulling aquatic plants up by their roots. There was no indication that this operation was part of a conscious management system, beyond its obvious function in clearing space for throw nets.

It is clear, though, that knowledge of fisheries management was widely dispersed in the region, as relatively sophisticated regimens are followed in private ponds in which fairly elaborate management techniques may be justified by adequate financial return. However, in larger multi-use public ponds it is difficult to calculate costs and benefits and to assign management costs on the basis of benefits received. Thus, in these ponds complex management schemes must be developed gradually or avoided altogether.

GOVERNMENT ASSISTANCE EFFORTS: MIXED RESULTS

The Department of Inland Fisheries has enjoyed some success in improving local fisheries in northeastern Thailand by upgrading and stocking existing ponds. They have enjoyed little success (indeed, have made few efforts) in introducing sophisticated management systems to public ponds. Four of the five ponds visited had been upgraded by government or with government assistance with mixed results.

Ban Ped Village

At Ban Ped the earth dike was raised in 1970, and a concrete spillway was constructed in 1971. Since then, neither dike nor spillway have broken, fingerlings have been stocked annually, and fishing has been excellent. Some residents who worked previously in Khon Kaen (about twenty km. away) have given up their jobs and become full-time fishermen. The fish were retailed in markets at Khon Kaen and elsewhere.

Ban Kham Paum Village

Inland Fisheries officials upgraded Pan Naam Pond at Ban Kham Paum in 1973. Fingerlings were stocked annually thereafter. In October 1978, the spillway broke due to gradual washing out of the adjacent embankment. Villagers say it was because the structure was seated only fifteen cm. deep in sandy soil. They believe that it should have been seated at least one meter deep but noted they had not been consulted by the contractor. In spite of this technical difficulty, the upgraded pond held water over a five-year period, and villagers were satisfied with the fishing opportunities it offered. Since the pond had been closed to fishing previously, it offered a new resource. Local residents reported that they seldom caught enough fish to sell, but that the pond made an important contribution to the local diet.

Ban Noon Village

At Ban Noon, villagers used their share of the *Kukrit* funds granted to tambon development councils throughout Thailand in 1975 to upgrade

Boeng Khii Ling. They hired a tractor to raise and enlarge the dike and a contractor to construct a spillway for 30,000 baht. Where possible, local labor was hired to carry out unskilled tasks. The Inland Fisheries Department stocked the pond for the first time two months prior to our visit. At that time fishing was unregulated, although local leaders suggest that fisherman who catch fingerlings should release them. Residents reported that there had been no significant improvement in fishing.

Ban Phon Sim Village

In 1977 the Canadian government gave a grant of 100,000 baht to the Fisheries Department to upgrade Boeng Saung Pond in Ban Phon Sim. Provincial Fisheries officials hired a contractor to raise the dike and construct a spillway. Local residents were dissatisfied on several counts:

- They felt the contractor had overcharged. Similar projects in the area had cost 20,000-30,000 baht.

- In the process of raising the dike, the contractor's workmen cleared all vegetation (including well-established bamboo clumps) which had strengthened it with a live root system.

- The spillway was constructed higher than the lowest sector of the dike. Thus it did not function as a spillway.

- Only a few local workers were hired for a few days to plant grass on the raised dike.

- They had to get permission of provincial and Fisheries officials to break up the upper portion of the concrete spillway with heavy hammers so that it could function properly.

In August 1978 the Canadian ambassador visited the village for a formal ceremony. A sign marking the occasion was posted near the middle of the dike. Two months later, the dike broke at a location only thirty or forty meters away. The people began to throw stones at the sign after that. Now it lies, twisted and rusting, on the ground. At the time of our visit the pond was nearly dry. Before the pond was "upgraded" the dike had seldom broken, and the pond had dried up previously only after two years of drought.

The original contractor, who was a member of the provincial development council, visited the village a few months prior to our visit and announced that he had been awarded a new 100,000 baht contract to repair the dike. The villagers were waiting, and beginning to think that they would have to do the work if it was to be done at all. In previous years, before the government had started providing assistance, the villagers probably would have mobilized immediately to fix such a break.

IMPLICATIONS

Where pond upgrading has been a technical success, with higher water levels, expanded surface area, unbroken dikes and spillways, and stocked fish, villagers appreciate the assistance. But in other instances it has produced dry ponds, reduced faith in government, and lessened capacity for local resource management.

Present planning and contracting procedures of the Department of Inland Fisheries tend to udercut local management capacity and initiative. Typically the village community is the lowest, weakest link in the "chain of command." Upgrading of Boeng Saung Pond at Ban Phon Sim provides an example:

Canadian Government makes a grant.
↓
Provincial Fisheries Office locates a suitable pond
and hires a contractor.
↓
Contractor carries out work assigned.
↓
Village residents receive an "upgraded" pond.

The Canadian government possesses financial leverage, the fisheries official has official leverage and the contractor receives leverage by legal arrangement. Only local residents lack significant power in this system.

Along with improved income and nutrition, future fisheries projects should stress local autonomy and capacity for community management as a development goal. The rationale is two fold:

1. Information flows will increase and improve in quality as villagers feel confident of their right to "speak up".

2. Worthwhile projects will be sustained only to the extenet that local groups and individuals take responsibility for management, maintenance, and improvement.

Fisheries officials should be encouraged to conceptualize their role as being able to offer their services to villagers in those settings where there seems to be potential for achieveing significant increases in fish production as a consequence of assistance which the department has the ability to provide. In doing so officials should:

1. Realize that their efforts will be merged with well-established local systems and historical processes, and take steps to learn something about them.

2. Suggest (not impose) management strategies that have been successful elsewhere in the region.

3. Seriously consider making some local group such as a tambon council or village development committee a third party to contracts between governmental and construction firms.

Such simple measures could go a long way toward improving the effectiveness of government assistance and improving government's image among the villagers.

NOTES

1. Data for this paper were gathered in July 1979 in preparing the social soundness analysis for a project being designed by the Agency for International Development to assist the Department of Inland Fisheries of the Royal Thai government in upgrading a number of village fish ponds. The opinions expressed here are those of the author and do not necessarily represent the views of the Agency for Inernational Development.

2. During the period the electrical system was operational the exchange rate was twenty to twenty-two bhat = U.S. $ 1.00.

3. This unfortunate event is described in more detail in a later section.

4. Fishing was banned in order to provide a "sanctuary" for fish reproduction, and prevent overfishing of the local system of ponds, streams, and canals.

5. One rai = 0.4 acres.

CHAPTER EIGHT

House Gardens—An Appropriate Village Technology

James N. Anderson

A *nipah* [palm leaf roofed] house, although small, has around it a variety of plants: jicamas, eggplants, winged beans, peanuts, string beans, hyacinths, lima beans, winter squash, bath sponge, bottlegourd, squash. It has besides, onions, tomatoes, garlic, ginger, and all around are sesame... to name a few.
—Translation of *Bahay Kubo* (Nipah House), a Tagalog folksong learned by Philippine children.

Until quite recently it was widely accepted that the "modernization" of agriculture in tropical Asia was the answer to meeting the food requirements of the region's growing populations. The transformation emphasized monocultural production of genetically selected varieties, improved irrigation, increased use of purchased production inputs, mechanization, and efficient farm management. Indeed, this Green Revolution package achieved dramatic increases in yields of cereals and various cash crops. Moreover, it brought higher productivity and profits to most of those farmers who could follow the prescriptions of the new technologies.

Yet despite the brief respite that the new agricultural technologies provided in the 1970's, in the mid-80's large numbers of Southeast Asian peoples again face serious food problems. These are attributable to such production problems as recurrent catastrophies, low prices to producers, and unbalanced and increasingly expensive production systems. Ironically, at the very height of success of Green Revolution production, during the favorable crop year of 1978, higher malnutrition rather than improved nutrition was observed in Southeast Asia.

The reason for this dilemma are complex. In part they relate to distributional issues. Food may be available but hungry or malnourished people may be denied adequate diets because the food produced is so expensive and is transported from such distances as to be unaffordable. However, the very process of intensification of agriculture is linked to other issues as well. It has increased the requirement for capital and the necessity for ever more expensive fertilizer, pesticide, and herbicide inputs—thus increasing the costs of production. It has also accelerated processes of erosion and of soil deterioration, thus stressing land and water resources and ecosystem tolerances. Yet, despite the added costs, neither small producers nor their harvests are more secure. Prices for crops produced often do not adequately compensate small producers for their new expenses.

Many small cultivators' real incomes have actually fallen. The enterprises of those who remain have been made more risky because of their dependence on the whims of commodity and credit markets. Many former small cultivators have given up farming, and a growing number of former agricultural workers have no place in most forms of "modern" agriculture. Both groups have joined the growing mass of unemployed in cities or have struggled to survive by fleeing with their families to the uplands where they attempt to squeeze some productivity out of unstable soils with declining fertility. Finally rising energy costs, the hazards of pollution from chemical inputs, and the reduction of productive land to nonproductive uses also exact their toll. Increasing the long-term sustainability of the "modern," high-energy, high-capital technologies introduced to revolutionize Southeast Asian food production is being brought into question.[1] While they have brought real advances, they are inadequate in their current form.

It is ironic that many of the tropical world's small producers, often maligned for their traditionalism and resistance to modernization, have long practiced a variety of effective, long established "alternative" production practices that apply principles now being rediscovered by ecology conscious scientists in the U.S. and Europe. Generally these involve polycropping systems featuring sometimes highly complex combinations of intercropping and relay cropping of multiple species, use of organic nutrients, and natural methods of pest control. Recent studies have shown that many of these food production systems, products of long-evolved trial and error, are both highly productive and ecologically well suited to conditions of the humid tropics.[2] They bear close examination in the search for well-adapted and sustainable approaches—combining folk and scientific knowledge—appropriate to Asia's agricultural needs.

THE INVISIBLE "GARDEN"

One of the most highly productive and nutritionally adaptive of these indigenous polycropping system—and one responsive to a wide variety of ecological and socio-economic conditions—is known variously as the kitchen, dooryard, house, compound, or traditional mixed garden.[3] It is typically a space around the house interplanted with a diverse mix of perennials and annuals that also harbors a variety of domestic animals. The house garden, while only a small part of the total farming system, plays a vital role in supplementing the diet and income of rural households. For the near landless, it may be their only secure source of food. Unfortunately households without secure tenure to a residential plot are excluded from having a house garden, much to their jeopardy.[4]

The typical architecture of the house garden of the humid tropics bears little resemblance to that of the house gardens found in the temperate zone, as illustrated by the following description by Winstedt based on observations in Malay villages.[5]

> ...the Malay holding is still an unkept tangle of vegetables, bananas, jack-fruit, gourds, onion, ginger, sugar-cane, chillies, flourishing where there is not too dense shade from coconut and aceca palms, fruit trees and rubber. Para rubber belongs to the present century and there are vegetables and fruit-trees unknown to the Malay's remote ancestors. The mango with its clean aromatic taste of dilute terpentine has an Indian name and origin. The sapodella, the soursap, the bullock's heart, the custard-apple, the guava, and the papaya were introduced by the Portuguese from tropical America.

Two things stand out in this description. First is the appearance of random chaos and second is the diversity—and in particular the number of varieties not native to the region.[6]

In spite of its chaotic appearance, the architecture of the house garden of the humid tropics has an underlying logic that may be missed by the casual observer though appreciated by the ecologist. Typically the house garden area includes a clearing with a bare surface, usually in front of the house, which provides a space for numerous social activities and an area free of snakes, dangerous insects and parasites where children can play and adults can work and rest safely. Just around this area ornamental plants, spices, and herbs predominate. Exotics may be grown here experimentally to test their suitability for more extensive cultivation. There may also be young plants and trees tended intensively in pots for later transplanting elsewhere in the family's fields.

Generally another distinctive portion of the garden will be found in an area where water from bathing or other household uses is drained away from the living area. Here will be found the water loving plants. If the water is adequate, there may even be a fishpond or a sump where small fish, frogs, snails, shrimps, and crabs may be found.

It is important to identify the vertical structure in the typical house garden of the tropics, resulting in a very high rate of energy capture as discussed below. Structure closely follows function in the house garden.

A COMPLEX ECOLOGICAL SYSTEM

The highly developed and productive system of the house garden applies many of the principles of tropical forest ecology, producing a much
higher ratio of energy output to enery input than achieved with most field
crops, with minimal, if any, requirements for commercial fertilizers,
pesticides, and herbicides. The undelying principles are particularly evident in the layered canopy structure of the mature garden. At its upper
story are found tall fruit trees. The middle story is comprised of shrubs
and shorter trees. The ground story is devoted to low-growing or climbing plants and shade tolerant tuberous and herbaceous plants. Incoming
light is thus used by successive plant layers at various heights and with
varying energy requirements. This vertical intercropping optimizes plant
and animal management in a limited available space and yields greater
(usually much greater) overall production per unit of land than typical
field crop production.

The vertical structure also contributes to the maintenance of soil fertility through the nearly closed cycling of nutrients. Leaf litter from various
canopies accumulates on the ground, or is swept together and burned
daily, the ash then distributed. Animal waste, kitchen waste, slashed
weeds and mature annuals, and litter from domestic industries carried
out into the compound are also distributed, providing mulch and eventually humus. Each item of "waste" is recycled to become a resource for
another process.[7]

The highly variable, interpenetrating root structures of diverse inter-
cropped plants capture nutrients and water that would otherwise be lost
into the subsoil. The deeper penetrating roots of large trees pull nutrients
and water up from the subsoil. The stratified canopy also reduces the force
of the wind, the heavy tropical rains, and the baking, glaring sun. The
rain thus drips and the sun is filtered through the layers rather than beating
on the unprotected ground. Rapid evaporation and drying of the soil and
rapid water loss through runoff and erosion are reduced. Both shading
of the soil and interception of frequent rain tend to cool soil and water
temperatures, optimizing beneficial insect and microbial activity, which
contributes to the building of humus.

The stratified canopies of the house garden create numerous micro-
climates and habitats for a variety of mostly beneficial insects, birds, and
reptilian and mammalian wildlife. The garden's structure also acts as a
dust screen and as a sound barrier, providing a degree of quiet and privacy
in the mist of what is often a dense village settlement. Litter, often burned at sunset, sends up smoke which moves mosquitoes and other annoy-
ing pests off to other resting places. While domestic animals such as
carabao, cattle, goats, or pigs (depending on religious proscription) are

tied or penned up, others such as dogs, cats, chickens, and ducks wander free and are mainly self-supporting.

DEVELOPMENT BENEFITS OF THE HOUSE GARDEN

An 1803 account by Zuniga suggests that the beneficial nature of the traditional house garden has long been evident to sensitive observers.[8]

> The Pangasinans [of Central Luzon in the Philippines] cluster their houses on both sides of the road, which is the best way of settling down in the Philippines for the reason that in this way the natives can have a garden beside their houses where they can raise all kinds of fruits and where they can augment their income by planting black pepper, cocoa, and other edible things. This is of great importance to the poor because, if they lack rice to feed their children, they can assuage their hunger by giving them bananas and other fruit. They never would lack anything to eat with their rice which, if not eaten with something else is unpleasantly tasteless.

Some years later, Raffles also called attention to the value of the house garden in his *History of Java*.[1]

> In the first establishment or formation of a village or new ground, the intended settlers take care to provide themselves with sufficient garden ground round their huts for stock and to supply the ordinary wants of their families. The produce of this plantation is the exclusive property of the peasant, and exempted from contributions and burden; and such is their number and extent in some regencies...that they constitute perhaps a tenth part of the area of the whole district. The spot surrounding his simple habitation, the cottager considers his peculiar patrimony, and cultivates it with peculiar care. He labors to plant and rear in it those vegetables that may be most useful to his family, and those shrubs and trees which may at once yield him their fruit and their shade: nor does he waste his efforts on thankless soil.[10]

The garden produces a continuous flow of small quantities of its varied products for harvesting throughout the year, avoiding problems of storage and seasonal market gluts. Managed in a small, accessible, intensively utilized area, problems of maintenance are eased and considerable flexibility in scheduling of its minimal labor inputs is possible. The ratio of perennials to annuals and the number and types of domestic animals are easily varied to fit specific domestic requirements, providing a living repository of critical proteins, vitamins, minerals, carbohydrates, medicinals, herbs, spices, flavoring, ornamentals, building and other materials for fabrication, and firewood. The house garden has been variously and correctly called a "living storehouse," a "living pharmacy," and a "living lumberyard."[11]

Contribution to Food and Material Needs

While the garden can contribute a small amount of carbohydrates that may be important at times of shortage, its principal contribution to the diet is in the form of critical animal and vegetable proteins, vitamins, minerals, and dietary fiber. Gardens also provide the major source of snack foods, which for rural peoples are nutritionally significant, and the primary source of the side dishes and flavorings that complement the rice which serves as the basic staple for most Southeast Asian families.

Because harvesting from the house garden takes place just before meal or snack preparation there is negligible loss of nutritional value and little spoilage. Fruits and other vegetables are picked ordinarily before birds or other predators can share in the harvest. Surpluses are shared with neighbors and kin or are taken to the market for sale. Waste is minimal.

The nutritional contribution of house garden foods is particularly important during times of normal seasonal or unusual periodic food stress when they provide an emergency resource. The better gardens are managed so as to assure that some foods will always be available during the worst time of year, the "lacking" season, and to assure that something salable is available for the purchase of energy foods such as rice needed during this low nutritional period.

The high proportion of woody perennial plants provides a basic store of fuel for cooking, building and handicraft materials, certain medicinals, ornamentals and some salable surplus of fruits or leaf vegetables. A number of the commonly planted perennials such as coconuts, bananas, and papayas bear throughout the year. Many of the potherbs, all of the many edible leaves of various trees and many vegetables and condiments are also continously available. Most other fruit trees and some vegetables bear only seasonally (although the two tropical "seasons" are long). Overall the production is spread fairly evenly throughout the year, as are labor requirements.

Low Labor Requirements

Because it takes optimal advantage of natural processes, little labor is required in establishing the house garden, and even less in its maintenance and harvesting.[12] Observations from Java, where the most intensive house gardens are found, show that about 8 percent of the total labor of household members goes into garden activities, much of that being for daily harvesting for the main meal. The garden's proximity to the house saves travel time and energy and, because monitoring is constant, also reduces risk of loss to predators, intruding stray animals, spoilage, and theft.

The benefits obtained by the rural peoples of tropical Asia from their house gardens as a consequence of applying sound agronomic and ecological principles often overlooked in "scientific" agriculture are substantial. The success of this technology attests to the value of traditional wisdom, and demonstrates the effectiveness of the management systems, often informal, which village people have long established to adapt, absorb, and disseminate valuable (but to us, little known) varieties. Both the rich traditional wisdom and existing adaptive systems of resource management should be treated as valuable resources in scientific efforts to achieve further, but sustainable, improvements in agricultural productivity in ways beneficial to all members of the society. As Robert Chambers and others have argued, the most satisfactory kinds of rural development are likely to result from an integration of traditional and modern scientific knowledge as well as the use of systems that rural people themselves understand and control.[13]

NOTES

1. See R. J. A. Goodland, C. Watson, and G. Ledec, *Environmental Management in Tropical Agriculture* (Boulder: Westview Press, 1984), pp. 1-2, 226-7; and M. Altieri, D. Letourners, and J. Davis, "Developing Sustainable Agrosystems," *Bioscience* Vol. 33, No. 1, 1983, 45-9.

2. W. S. Clarke, "The Structure of Permanence: The Relevance of Self-Subsistence Communities for World Ecosystem Management" in T. Bayliss-Smith and R. Feachem (eds.), *Subsistence and Survival* (London: Academic Press, 1977), pp. 363-84; W. M. Denevan *et. al,* "Indigenous Agroforestry in the Amazon," *Interciencia* Vol. 9, No. 6, 1984, 346-57; K. J. Pelzer, "Swidden Cultivation in Southeast Asia: Historical, Ecological and Economic Perspectives" in P. Kunstadter, E. Chapman, and S. Sabhasri (eds.) *Farmers in the Forest* (Honolulu: University of Hawaii Press, 1978), pp. 271-86; and Ignacy Sachs, "Food and Energy Production, Allies or Problems," *Development Forum,* Vol. 13, No. 6, 1985.

3. Growing recognition of the value of the home garden is reflected in a comparative study of house gardens and other polycultural agroecosystems in Southeast Asia being carried out by the Southeast Asian Universities Agrosystem Network (SUAN) with the assistance of the Environment and Policy Institute of the East-West Center and funding from the Ford Foundation. A very effective program of research, training, and extension has also been carried out at the Asian Vegetable Reasearch and Development Center.

4. Though individually small, the production of the house garden may be quite significant. Nor is their significance limited to the tropics. For example, in the Soviet Union it is estimated that though only 3 to 5 percent of total cropland is devoted to house gardens, they yield nearly one-third of total agricultural production. See W. Jackson, "The Soviet Union," in G. A. Klee (ed.) *World System of Traditional Resources Management* (New York: John Wiley and Sons, 1980), p. 131.

5. Richard, Winstedt, *The Malays: A Short Cultural History,* (London: Routledge and Kegan Paul, 1961, pp. 126-27.

6. The house garden has long served as a place where newly available species are planted on an experimental basis. Many cash crops are first adopted, tested, and grown for wider cultivation in the house garden.

7. O. Soemarwoto and I. Soemarwoto, "The Village Home Garden: A Traditional Integrated System of Man-Plants-Animals." A paper presented to the Conference of Integrated Systems Development, September 1979, Arlon, Belgium, 14 pp.

8. *Status of the Philippines in 1800,* [1803] (Manila: Filipiniana Book Guild, 1973), p. 407.

9. S. Raffles, *History of Java* (London: John Murray, 2nd Edition, Vol. 1 of 2 Vol., 1830), pp. 90-1.

10. For centuries the house garden has been a prime instrument in natural resettlement processes. As this quote suggests, the household garden is often the first thing developed by migrants to a new place. In fact, if the move does not involve a great distance, the garden maybe initiated several years before the house is moved or built on the new site. See O. Abdoellah, *Homegarden Plant Structure of the Bantarkalong Javanese Village, Pananjung, Pagandaran, West-Java* (Bandung: Institute of Ecology, Padjarjaran University, 1982), 18 pp.: and O. Abdoellah and G. Marten, *Production of Human Nutrients from Homegarden, Uplandfield (Kebun), and Ricefield Agricultural Systems in the Jatigade Area (West Java).* Working Paper of the East-West Environment and Policy Institute, Honolulu: East-West Center, 1984, 55 pp.

11. These and numerous other benefits are well documented by Terra, based on field studies in Java during the 1930s on "mixed garden horticulture" or what is locally referred to as *pekarangan.* G. J. A. Terra, "Mixed Garden Horticulture in Java," *Malayan Journal of Tropical Geography,* Vol. 3, 1984, 33-43.

12. The rare heavy tasks (tree planting, fencing, pruning, turning the soil) and the dangerous ones (climbing tall trees) are performed by men, who also tend to care for the large animals. Women usually share in planting and weeding and do most of the harvesting just prior to preparation of meals in which particular products will be used.

13. R. Chambers, *Rural Development: Putting the Last First* (London: Longman, 1983).

CHAPTER NINE

Self-Managed Land Colonization in Indonesia[1]

Andrew P. Vayda

The Buginese peoples, whose homelands are in South Sulawesi, have a well established tradition of trading and sailing throughout maritime Southeast Asia dating back to the early sixteenth century.[2] Because of the periodic conflicts in South Sulawesi, many Buginese traders, especially those from Wajo, set up new bases beyond Sulawesi for their operations. This dispersal of the traders continued after the seventeenth century, and Buginese trading colonies and emporia were established in Sumbawa, Kalimantan, Ambon, Java, Sumatra, Singapore, and Johore. Bands of Buginese adventurers and warriors sometimes followed in the wake of the traders and took part in local dynastic quarrels and wars. Some Buginese even succeeded, at least temporarily, in establishing themselves as rulers of petty states on and around the Malay Peninsula. The connections between the Sulawesi homelands and these scattered areas of Buginese trade and influence were maintained by the traders who sailed the islands in their *prahus*.

The extensive movements of Buginese traders and sailors prior to the present century gained for the Buginese in general a widespread reputation for being roving and adventurous. It should be emphasized, however, that most Buginese continued to live essentially peasant lives back in Sulawesi and to devote themselves to agriculture and fishing. The trading activity is of interest here not because it shows any generalized "love of movement" among the Buginese, but rather because it served to establish the networks along which information about opportunities in other lands could flow back to whatever potential migrants there were among the Buginese in South Sulawesi at particular times and for particular reasons.

This provides the context of extensive colonization by the Buginese of underdeveloped areas of several of the large islands of the Indonesian archipelago. The processes of this successful colonization, which was largely self-managed and financed, is of particular interest when juxtaposed with the limited success of expensive government-sponsored colonization schemes in the same and similar areas.

THE COLONIZATION OF SUMATRAN SWAMPLANDS

One of the notable accomplishments of Buginese colonization has been the development and settlement of tidal swamplands in southern Sumatra.[3] The first stage of colonization consists simply of obtaining the information that a particular area is available, feasible, and appropriate for pioneer settlement. Their history of trade and their established trading settlements gave the Buginese easy access to such information. It also provided them with information on related commercial opportunities.

The special opportunities that coastal swamps presented for agricultural colonization were related to expansion of world demand for tropical agricultural products following the development of steamships and the opening of the Suez Canal, which occurred in 1869. Much of the Buginese homeland in South Sulawesi suffered from a long dry season and erratic rainfall and was therefore poorly suited for the production of such cash crops as rubber, coconuts, and pepper. However, by virtue of the established trading networks, the Buginese knew that a voyage in a prahu could take them to lands suited to such crops—in the present instance to low-lying, sparsely inhabited coastal swamps where coconuts could be profitably grown for the production of copra which, as a source of vegetable oil, was much in demand internationally. Accordingly some farmers who hoped to benefit from the cash-crop boom moved from Sulawesi to the swampy rural environs of ports like Pontianak in West Kalimantan and Johore in southern Malaya where Buginese traders were already established.

Apparently it was in Kalimantan that Buginese farmers first learned the Banjarese techniques of digging canals for drainage and tidal irrigation to facilitate agriculture in the coastal swamps. With these techniques, they could grow rice to sustain themselves initially in what would have otherwise been an inhospitable environment. Then, as rice yields declined after a few years, they converted the farmed land to coconut groves. The proximity of ports from which Buginese prahus sailed ensured that the farmers' production could be marketed.

In addition to the desire for profit from cash crops, a motive that Buginese farmers had for emigration in the first decades of this century was the desire to escape from the Dutch administration that had just extended its sway in South Sulawesi and had imposed such new burdens on the people as a head tax, income tax, and the greatly resented obligation to work on roads and engage in other forms of corvee.[4]

Along Sumatra's eastern coast, Buginese adventurers and presumably therefore also prahu traders had been active as far back as the seventeenth century, but no established Buginese trading colonies were there to attract farmers from South Sulawesi when the cash-crop boom began. Indeed, before this development, most of the whole lowland on the eastern side of Sumatra was very sparsely settled.[5] On a few of the larger rivers, there were tiny principalities such as Jambi on the Batang Hari and Palembang on the Musi. Elsewhere, hunters and gatherers still roamed. The vast coastal swamps were almost deserted, and remained so into the present century except for the occasional village of either Malay fishermen or so-called Sea Gypsies. The first coconut-growing migrants to the swamplands were not Buginese but Banjarese, who began to settle the Indragiri coast of Riau in the first years of the century.

When the Buginese started to come, it was because colonization in previously favored areas in Kalimantan and Johore had passed beyond the stage in which new land was readily available. This was a hardship not only for new migrants who wanted their own land but also for the older ones whose adaptation had consisted of clearing new land for growing rice and other food crops as previously farmed land was converted into coconut groves. Not having land for the food crops was particularly onerous when rice could be bought only at very high prices. This was the case during the First World War (1914-18) when Buginese settlement in the Indragiri-Jambi border area is said to have begun. The oral histories collected by Lineton suggest that a common pattern was to move from one settlement area to another to seek a better livelihood.[6]

This pattern of pioneering elsewhere when opportunities diminish in areas of older settlement was to be repeated in the course of the southward-moving colonization of Sumatra's eastern coast. Apart from government-sponsored transmigration, this colonization has been, for approximately the last three decades, an essentially Buginese process. As the Buginese in Sumatra became more numerous, not only were the new settlements increasingly dominated by them but also the Buginese from particular Sulawesi districts tended to culster. The process operated much like the "chain migration" described in Price's study of southern European settlement in Australia, i.e., the first migrants recruited family and friends to join them; as numbers and security increased, a community life based on the homeland culture was gradually established; and the existence of this community life attracted more migrants, including some who might otherwise have been too old, too unenterprising, or too timorous to move. Moreover, simply getting to Sumatra had become easier and safer with the advent of regular steamship service.

The economic, social, and psychological support that migrants in the

post-pioneering stage of a colonization process receive from earlier settlers is especially noteworthy because an argument sometimes used to
justify elaborate efforts and large expenditures in programs of government-
sponsored colonization is that migrants are necessarily cut off from their
familiar social networks and that governments must therefore organize
"almost everything" for them.[7]

Lineton's dissertation, based on field work both in Jambi and in the
Wajo district of South Sulawesi, provides valuable information on the support and assistance that new migrants receive from earlier settlers in
Sumatra and from other nongovernmental agencies.[8] For making the
journey itself, sometimes there is help from Sumatra, either in the form
of money sent to cover travel expenses or in the form of a kinsman who
returns to Sulawesi to fetch the migrants and personally handle travel arrangements for them.

Many migrants receive no such help, but are still given assurances
of support upon arrival in Sumatra. It is common to employ the services
of a Buginese "migration organizer" (*pengurus rantau*), who arranges not
only the travel by ship from Ujungpandang to Jakarta and then on to the
Sumatran ports, but also accommodation in the cities and the necessary
letters of authority from the police. On arrival in Sumatra the migrant joins
relatives who assist him in finding work and accommodations. Favored
entry points, reception centers, or transit places for new arrivals are those
where their labor is needed for rice harvesting and for opening up forest
areas for agriculture.

The migration of Buginese to Sumatra and other Indonesian islands
was given a major impetus by the rebellion of Kahar Muzakar in South
Sulawesi (1951-65) which devastated their homeland and its economy. The
water buffaloes with which they plowed their fields had been taken by
the rebels and slaughtered for food. Their daughters were forced into marriage according to the rebels' dictates, and they had been forbidden, on
pain of death, to go to town to buy salt, sugar, margarine, and other "in-
fidel" foods.

What had been perhaps a constant trickle of migration to Sumatra
since the 1930s became trasformed suddenly into a flood. More than 10,000
Buginese are estimated to have passed through Tanjung Priok, the port
of Jakarta, on their way to Sumatra in 1955, the peak year for migration
during this period.[9] As a consequence Buginese settlements in the late
1950s and 1960s spread "like wildfire, leaping from one river mouth to
the next in a seemingly inexorable march towards the south."[10] In areas
like Jambi's Sungai Ayam, first opened for settlement only in 1952, land
remaining to be developed was already in short supply by 1958, and people were shifting farther south to other rivers.

The areas not yet fully opened by the Buginese for their preferred sequence of rice and coconut growing are the areas into which they were still moving (especially in southern Sumatra) at the time that the Indonesian government began developing projects there for Javanese and Balinese transmigrants. It seems likely that the Buginese would have soon completed their transformation of the swamplands into settled and agriculturally productive areas if not for the advent of the government's transmigration program. As that program moved into the implemetation phase, in some places such as Sungai Samut in the northern part of South Sumatra's Upang Delta, the government even moved away Buginese settlers who had been opening land at no cost in order to make room for Javanese transmigrants, who were being settled at a cost of several thousand dollars per hectare.[11] Questions must be raised about this policy, not only with respect to its cost but also with regard to the prospects for the success of the government-sponsored transmigrants, who were pioneering without the kinds of social-institutional supports enjoyed by Buginese migrants in Sumatra.

TRANSFORMING FORESTS TO PEPPER PLANTATIONS IN EAST KALIMANTAN

A case involving the migration of Buginese farmers from South Sulawesi to forest areas of East Kalimantan provides further insight into the working of such social-institutional support mechanisms, which have surely been a significant factor in the success of the "spontaneous" Buginese colonization process wherever it has occurred. In the case of East Kalimantan, the colonization involved a well-organized process geared to the rapid clearing and temporary settlement of forest lands for pepper farming.

Our research in East Kalimantan was concentrated in the district of Loa Janan.[12] In 1980 we found that 1,170 hectares here had been cleared of lowland dipterocarp forest and converted by Buginese migrants to plantations of pepper (*Piper nigrum*) along twenty-five kilometers of the main Samarinda-Balikpapan road. The households of the pepper growers numbered at least 770 and were distributed among four villages. Dwellings and plantations spread from either side of the main road to a distance not exceeding five kilometers.

Though there had been Buginese movement from South Sulawesi to East Kalimantan at least as far back as the sixteenth century, the number of Buginese present in the district of Loa Janan in the 1950's could, according to our infomants, be counted on one's fingers. The number began to increase in the early 1960's after construction was begun on the Samarinda-Balikpapan road, with most of the early settlers coming from the vicinity of Muara Badak, a town on the East Kalimantan coast. Many had moved to Muara Badak around 1951 when the Islamic rebellion of Kahar Muzakar drove them from their South Sulawesi homelands.

The techniques used by the Buginese for pepper farming result in rapid erosion and depletion of the soil, with the result that after approximately ten years the yields of pepper plantations in areas of poor red-yellow podzolic soils decline to the point that the plantation must be abandoned. By the early 1960's the initial cycles of pepper farming were drawing to a close at Muara Badak.

One of the first farmers to move from Muara Badak to Loa Janan said he had gone there around the end of 1961 with four friends to examine its possibilities. Though at that time access to the area was limited to a small road suitable only for motorcycles, they found it sufficiently attractive to move. After they established their plantations, their example was followed by other migrants from Muara Badak—a movement that continued for several years.

When the Kahar Muzakar rebellion in South Sulawesi ended in 1965, it became safe for Loa Janan pepper farmers to go back to their homelands to visit their relatives. From these visits a new wave of migration from South Sulawesi to East Kalimantan resulted, impelled by prospects of social and economic advancement rather than by the fear and insecurity that had driven earlier migrants to Muara Badak.

Just emerging from years of privation, the relatives and friends of the visitors found very attractive the wealth that the migrants displayed (gold, tape recorders, etc.), the gifts they brought, and the stories they told of opportunities at Loa Janan and, in some cases, even of pilgrimages to Mecca made possible by success in pepper farming. Starting a new life at Loa Janan not only held the promise of greater future rewards but also, for some, the prospects of obtaining productive farming land more cheaply and easily than restoring their own rice fields, neglected during the period of the rebellion, to full production. So, beginning in 1966, Buginese migrants to Loa Janan increasingly came straight from South Sulawesi rather than from elsewhere in East Kalimantan.

The process operating was again the familiar one of chain migration, wherby the first migrants to a place, usually young men, recruit family and friends as new migrants who, in turn, recruit others.[13] There were in addition developments through time that served to enhance the attractiveness of Loa Janan. As the Buginese increased in number, more of their own schools and mosques were built so that later comers could have the psychological comfort of finding a community life not very different from what they were leaving behind in South Sulawesi. And there were developments that made easier the task of converting forest to pepper plantations.

Specifically concessions were granted to two timber companies in Loa

Janan. One began operation in 1969 and the other in 1970. This meant that migrants could use logging roads to gain access to convertible forests and that they found the forest easier to clear because the logging companies had already selectively removed some large-diameter trees. Transportation problems were further eased by completion of the Samarinda-Balikpapan road which passed through the area. After this there were, according to the heads of the four villages of Buginese pepper farmers, at least twenty migrants arriving each month to settle.

Another factor was the presence of institutionalized services available to help migrants before their departure from Sulawesi and after their arrival at their destination—as already discussed in the first section in relation to the Sumatra migration. As mentioned there, the services provided in Sulwesi include those of the pengurus rantau. They arrange boat passage for travelers and obtain not only the tickets for them but usually all necessary official papers and letters from the provincial government and police as well. Moreover, the organizers arrange transportation to the port and then provide food and lodging there to the travelers prior to departure of their ship. For these services, the organizers in Pare-pare, the port of departure for East Kalimantan, were receiving about Rp. 12,500 (US$12.00) per migrant in 1980.[14] Rp. 9,000 of this went for boat passage. After expenses for food and lodging, the organizers usually had a profit of between Rp. 1,000 and Rp. 1,500. In cases when a ship's departure was unduly delayed, they would lose money because of the costs of providing room and board to the migrants during the waiting period. A migrant making his own arrangements normally would have to pay several thousand rupiahs more than the fee being charged by the organizers.

Many of the organizers started their business during the Kahar Muzakar rebellion and were for some years looked on with disfavor by the South Sulawesi government, which was trying to control emigration from the provinces. However, after 1970, the government granted licenses to some of the organizers to run travel bureaus. In the course of research in Pare-pare in 1980, we found there were at least seventeen licensed and unlicensed organizers. The former differed from the latter in having offices, a regular office staff, an official company name, and lists of ship arrivals and departures posted in front of their offices. Moreover, unlike the unlicenced organizers who often scoured the countryside for would-be migrants, they generally waited in their offices for customers to come to them.

Although similar fees were charged by the two types of organizers, the unlicensed ones were preferred by many migrants because they obtained ways of arranging travel even for persons lacking identification cards and travel permits. Both types of organizers used their own dwellings to lodge travelers, but conditions tended to be inferior in the houses of the unlicensed organizers. Sometimes no more than space on the ground beneath the elevated main floor of the house was provided.

While in Pare-pare, we heard of two other types of operators: (1) men who find intended travelers in the rural areas and bring them to migration organizers in Pare-pare in return for commissions; and (2) migration organizers who are in effect illicit money lenders, charging substantially higher fees but allowing payments to be deferred until the migrants have earned money in East Kalimantan. We were unable to contact these operators or otherwise verify reports of them.

Once they arrived in Loa Janan, the migrants received more help, provided to some by relatives already living in Loa Janan, and to others by so-called *penerima rantau* or "migrant receivers." There were twelve penerima rantau among the established Buginese residents of Loa Janan, and helping newcomers was for them a matter of morality and prestige rather than the kind of commercial activity in which the migration oraganizers in South Sulawesi were engaging. It was also a matter of quasi-kinship. Migrants who leave their homeland one by one and without relationship to one another become as one family in their new settlements.

The help given by the migrant receivers consisted of getting the newcomers started in pepper farming and getting them registered with the local authorities, if they had proper travel documents and identification cards. Without these or without at least references on their behalf from relatives already settled in Loa Janan, newcomers would be helped less readily by the migrant receivers. The feelings of moral obligation and quasi-kinship did not necessarily extend to everybody.

To get newcomers started in pepper farming, the migrant receivers either found jobs for them as farm workers (sometimes as employees of the migrant receivers themselves) or allocated land to them for conversion into pepper farms.

At the time of arrival of the first Buginese migrants to Loa Janan, licenses to open forest land had been granted to individuals and there had been little official control over the location and extent of the land the licensees subsequently opened. Possibly with the intention of rectifying this, in the late 1960's the government adopted new regulations whereby licenses to open land were to be granted for specific locations and were to be granted not to individuals but rather to groups, for each member of which two hectares were allotted. In applying for group licenses under the new regulations, the migrant receivers presented fictitious names so they would have land available for allocation to new migrants.

There was no direct charge by the migrant receivers for the land they allocated, except in the case of those two-hectare plots which they had already cleared with the usual techniques of slash-and-burn cultivation. The charge for such a plot in 1980 was Rp. 50,000 to 60,000 per hectare to cover expense such as for having trees with diameters of 50 cm. or more felled with chainsaws at the rate of rp. 1,000 per tree.

For new migrants without either the money to pay for all the clearing costs or the capability or desire to do the clearing themselves, it was still possible to obtain cleared plots from the migrant receivers but with the understanding that half of the pepper vines on these plots, although planted by the new migrants, would belong to the migrant receivers. It was the latter who, under this arrangement, also provided pepper cuttings for planting and the ironwood stakes, measuring 2 to 2 1/2 meters, needed for the pepper vines to climb up and around. They sometimes lent farm implements also.

Newcomers who were allocated forest land by the migrant receivers and were able to clear it and plant it themselves could establish themselves as pepper farmers, if they brought enough money with them to take care of their subsistence needs for six to eight months. After that time, the dry rice planted in the cleared plots was ready to be harvested, and some of it could be set aside for subsistence while the proceeds from selling the rest of it could be used to meet further consumption needs and to cover the costs of converting the temporary rice fields into pepper farms. Pepper cuttings might, for example, have to be bought for Rp. 150 each if not obtained gratis from the plantation of relatives or friends.

As a token of gratitude, several tins of unhulled rice from the harvest, each tin containing approximately eleven to twelve kg, would be given by the new settler to the migrant receiver who had allocated land to him. However much the migrant receivers were motivated by considerations of status, prestige, and quasi-kinship, it seems clear that they were not suffering economic losses from their activities.

The Buginese farmers cleared forest area by slashing underbrush with cutlasses and felling larger trees with axes or chainsaws. Ironwood was sequestered for later use and some other timber was kept for house-building and firewood, but most of the cleared vegetation was left to dry in the sun and was then burned. This usually occurred during the relatively dry months of August and September. The resulting ash provided nutrients critical for farming in the otherwise poor soils of Loa Janan.

For planting rice, the men made holes in the ash-covered ground with long dibbling sticks, and the rice was then sown, usually by the women. A few farmers planted corn, but most, regarding rice as their staple, made that their first crop. After harvest they used it for their own subsistence as well as selling some of it in order to have funds for buying other foods and covering other expenses.

Most of the area planted in rice was, after a single harvest, converted to pepper plantations. Some small portion might, however, be planted in rice for a second year to provide the farmers with subsistence while

while waiting for income from the pepper, which takes about three years
to develop a substantial yield.

After planting pepper on their land, some migrants also planted fruit
trees such as jackfruit, durian, rambutan, langsat, and mango. Planting
these trees might be regarded as establishing a basis for claiming permanent rights to the land, but it should be noted that, contrary to what is
often assumed about inter-island migrants, in the case of the Buginese
migrants to Loa Janan there seems to have been no dominating motivation to own land in the migration area. Holding licenses to open land in
Loa Janan or being allocated land by license-holders did not confer *de jure*
ownership. For that, certificates of ownership had to be obtained from the
government. But interviews of the local government officials and the pepper farmers themselves revealed that most of the latter had no intention
of applying for the certificates. The reasons given for not applying included
the following:

1. Slowness and expense of the certification process, which could take
   several years without resulting in a title.

2. Ignorance of the application procedures.

3. Fear that being certified as landowners would mean having to pay
   taxes.

4. Belief that certification was unnecessary for the use that the farmers
   wanted to make of the land.

Further evidence of lack of concern about ownership is the substantial
erosion and depletion of soil nutrients resulting from the practices of the
farmers in Loa Janan. The motivation of these farmers must be distinguished from that of peasant farmers who, dependent on local resources and
having no appreciable mobility, may invest considerable exertion in preser-
vation of this resource.[15]

For the Buginese migrants choosing to live in East Kalimantan, land
with primary or logged over forest that could be burned to add nutrient-
rich ash to the soil had always been available when old plantations were
to be abandoned and new ones begun. In discussing the implications of
possible difficulty in obtaining suitable lands for development of new pepper plantations, some farmers said in 1980 that they would then go to
newly opening frontiers in Central and Southeast Sulawesi to plant
cloves, cashews, or oil palm. It may be concluded that Buginese migrants
have regarded the availability of suitable, forested lands as a prerequisite
for their staying on as pepper farmers in East Kalimantan. If unsuccessful,
they would choose to move rather than find ways to re-use old land.

CONCLUSIONS

Several things are demonstrated by Buginese migration with respect to the opening up and settling of new lands.

1. Migration can happen quickly in response to new opportunities.

2. The process can effect major transformation of environments and can do so without the kind of assistance in land-clearing and settlement-building that has been received by migrants in the government's resettlement and transmigration programs.

3. Settlement by the migrants is not necessarily permanent, nor apparently is it intended by them to be so. Stays in one place were not definitely planned for any longer than the periods of profitable yield of the perennials planted there.

4. Consistent with the lack of long-term commitment to particular localities, resource use by the migrants is oriented much more toward profitability than towards sustainability.

Such spontaneous colonization efforts can be a powerful force in opening new lands, but at the same time they clearly cannot be considered an unmixed blessing. The challenge to policy makers is to recognize and make full use of the positive developmental forces involved, while at the same time finding ways to create incentives that will limit the more destructive land use practices.

NOTES

1. Based on Andrew P. Vayda, "Buginese Colonization of Sumatra's Coastal Swamplands and Its Significance for Development Planning," *Proceedings of the Jakarta Workshop on Coastal Resources Management*, edited by Eric C. F. Bird and Aprilani Soegiarto (Tokyo: United Nations University, 1980); and Andrew P. Vayda and Ahmad Sahur, "Forest Clearing and Pepper Farming by Bugis Migrants in East Kalimantan: Antecedents and Impact," *Indonesia*, 1985, in press.

2. Historical information is based on Leonard Y. Andaya *The Kingdom of Johor 1641-1728* (Kuala Lumpur: Oxford University Press, 1975); John Bastin and Robin W. Winks (eds.), *Malaysia: Selected Historical Readings* (Kuala Lumpur: Oxford University Press, 1966), Chapter 4; John Crawfurd, *A Descriptive Dictionary of the Indian Islands and Adjacent Countries* (London: Bradbury and Evans, 1856); B. Schrieke, *Indonesian Sociological Studies: Selected Writing of B. Schrieke, Part One* (The Hague: W. van Hoeve, 1966); O.J.M. Tate, *The Making of Modern South-East Asia*, Vol. 1 (Kuala Lumpur: Oxford University Press, 1971); and especially Jaqueline Lineton, "An Indonesian Society and Its Universe: A Study of the Bugis of South Sulawesi (Celebes) and Their Role within a Wider Social and Economic System." Ph.D. dissertation, School of Oriental and African Studies, University of London, 1975; and Jacqueline Lineton, "Pasompe' Ugi': Bugis Migrants and Wanderers," *Archipel* 10:173-201.

3. Available information on this colonization suggests that its stages conform in most major respects to the stages of colonization that have been reported from other places, e.g.,

J. B. Casagrande, S. I. Thompson and P. D.Young, "Colonization as a Research Frontier: The Ecuadorian Case," in *Process and Pattern in Culture*, R. A. Manners (ed.), (Chicago: Aldine Publishing Co., 1964), pp. 281-321; Gloria Davis, "Parigi: A Social History of the Balinese Movement to Central Sulawesi, 1907-1974," Ph.D. dissertation, Stanford University, 1972; and P. D. Simpkins and F. L. Wernstedt *Philippine Migration: The Settlement of the Digos-Padada Valley, Davao Province*, Yale University Southeast Asia Studies, Monograph Series No. 16, New Haven: Yale University, 1971.

4. Lineton, *Indonesian Society, op. cit.*, pp 21-23; and Lineton, *Buginese Migrants, op. cit.*, p. 21.

5. Tate, *op. cit.*, 245 ff.; and Lineton, *Indonesian Society, op. cit.*, p. 179

6. Lineton 1975, *Indonesian Society, op. cit.*, p. 180.

7. Davis, *op. cit.*, citing Joachim Hurwitz, "Agricultural Resettlement of Javanese Farmers in the Outer Islands of Indonesia before World War II," Paper prepared for Center for International Studies, Massachusetts Institute of Technology (mimeo), 1955.

8. *Op. cit.*

9. *Ibid.*, p. 24

10. *Ibid.*, p. 182.

11. Willam L. Collier, "Development Problems and Conflicts in the Coastal Zone of Sumatra: Swamps are for People," paper presented at the Programmatic Workshop on Land-Water Interactive Systems, Bogor, September 18-22, 1978, (mimeo) p. 22.

12. Much of the fieldwork was conducted by Ahmad Sahur, whose assistance is gratefully acknowledged.

13. Sixty-nine of the men in our 100-farmer sample were still unmarried when they migrated to Loa Janan.

14. In 1980: US$1.00 = approximately Rp. 625.

15. For a discussion of peasant farmers as conservators of resources, see Vandana Shiva et al., *Social Economic and Ecological Impact of Social Forestry in Kolar* (Bangalore: Indian Institute of Management, 1981), pp. 23-24. For discussion of other frontier farmers more like the Buginese see Maxine Margolis, "Historical Perspectives on Frontier Agriculture as an Adaptive Strategy," *American Ethnologist*, 4, 1977; 42-64. For a fuller discussion of clean weeding and other erosion-producing practices of the Loa Janan pepper farmers, see our article in *Indonesia*, April 1985, on which this section of the present paper is based.

CHAPTER TEN

Local Knowledge in Management of Small-Scale Irrigation[1]

Romana P. de los Reyes

The potential for increased crop production from the use of irrigation water has motivated groups of farmers in different societies to cooperatively find the means to bring water from streams to their fields. Utilizing their intimate knowledge of the local terrain, they locate the most appropriate site for diverting water from a stream and the routes for delivering the water to their fields. Because construction of the irrigation infrastructure often relies fully on manual labor, this usually extends to over a few years.

The physical construction of indigenous irrigation systems also initiates the development of the social organization for managing the system. Farmers who undertake the construction become the system owners and their leaders take on the tasks of managing system operations. Also their arrangements in the labor and material contributions for building the system become the basis for defining their responsibilities in maintaining the physical system and in allocating the irrigation water. This simultaneous development of the technical and social structures of indigenous irrigation systems creates social systems that fit the logic of the physical systems.

In the Philippines communal systems exemplify the indigenously developed irrigation systems. These farmer-owned and managed systems individually serve less than 1,000 hectares, but as a group they irrigate about half of the total irrigated lands in the country, or about the same area of land covered by systems owned and operated by the government. The prevalence of communal systems throughout the country indicates that farmers in widely dispersed communities have worked out similar solutions for managing a critical resource.

Cognizant of the important lessons that could be drawn from irrigation management methods created out of farmer experience, in late 1977
the National Irrigation Administration (NIA) commissioned the Institute
of Philippine Culture (IPC) of Ateneo de Manila University to undertake
a study of the ways in which farmers managed communal systems.[2] The
research study was intended to identify the practices that work best under
the constraints that farmers face in order to incorporate these practices
into a program for assisting less experienced and less successful communal
systems.

Taking into account factors such as geographical diversity, ethno-
linguistic distribution, and climatic variation, five (of the twelve) service
regions of NIA were designated as the regional research sites. A multistage
random sampling procedure was then followed to select the sample for
the study. This resulted in the identification of nine (of the thirty-nine)
provinces in the five regions as the sample provinces. Of the 633 communal systems in these provinces, fifty-one systems (or 8 percent) were
randomly drawn to become the sample for the study.

Data for the study were obtained through onsite inspection of sample systems, depth interviews with key informants, and interviews with
sample farmers using the system. In four of the fifty-one sample systems
a total of one month was spent in each conducting both interviews and
onsite inspection, while in each of the other forty-seven systems, fieldwork was completed in two weeks. The fieldwork activities were undertaken from November 1977 to May 1978. The key findings of the study
and the subsequent use of the research data and methodologies to
improve NIA's communal assistance program are discussed in this chapter.[3]

FARMERS' PRACTICES IN MANAGING COMMUNAL SYSTEMS

Farmers in communal systems adopt different ways of managing their
system according to system size. Farmers in systems that serve less than
fifty hectares are generally loosely organized, relying on informal arrangements for system operation and maintenance. In contrast, farmers
in most systems that irrigate more than fifty hectares are organized into
irrigators' associations. They have evolved more formal management procedures such as designating one or more water distributors, observing
a regular system maintenance schedule, requiring irrigation fees, dividing
the system's service area into smaller units, and paying leaders for services rendered.

The management of irrigation confronts farmers with a variety of questions regarding water distribution, system maintenance, paying for
operating costs, and conflict management. In many communal systems
the farmers have evolved answers to these questions over several decades.

In the process they have developed many management methods well suited to the constraints of their particular system and its environment. The specific solutions that farmers have devised to manage irrigation water are best seen through a discussion of eleven irrigation management issues.

1. Responsibility for Distributing Water

Farmers in smaller systems feel that specialized people are not needed to distribute water because, being relatively few in number, farmers can discuss and plan water distribution among themselves. But in most systems irrigating more than fifty hectares, farmers do see a need for water distributors because of the complexity of allocating water among so many people, and they frequently hire a team of such persons. The team leader is responsible for distributing the water from the dam to all parts of the system, and other members allocate water within their own areas.

2. Water Distribution Schedules

In all systems studied, farmers want to have continous supplies of irrigation water. However, they usually practice this method of water distribution only during the wet season when rainfall augments the irrigation supply. During the dry season, most farmers in systems serving less than fifty hectares are able to irrigate continuously; those in larger systems usually carry out some form of water rotation.

Within the larger systems, the level at which rotation takes place also depends on system size. A system that irrigates about 100 hectares with five branch canals, for example, has a rotational schedule based on the branch canals. When there is not enough water for continuous irrigation throughout the system, water supply is rotated within the branch canals. Those farmers with land irrigated from the first half of the branch canals draw water during the first three days of a week; downstream farmers do so during the remaining four days.

Another system serving about 4,600 hectares has rotational water distribution at two levels during the dry season. This system has two dams, each serving a specific area, and both service areas are divided into upstream and downstream zones. In one area, the two zones are irrigated alternately for two weeks; a longer period than usual but possibale for this area because it has other supplementary sources of irrigation. The zones of the other area draw water alternately one week at a time. All zones, in turn, are divided into as many as five districts which draw water at scheduled times. During its turn, each district receives all (or in some cases the majority) of the water allocated to its zone.

3. Maintaining Canals and Structures

Farmers usually consider maintenance of the dam and main canal obligatory for all farmers in the system, and maintenance of branch canals and farm ditches to be the responsibility of only those farmers who make use of the facilities. For most systems in excess of fifty hectares, groups of farmers or their representatives are often assigned on a rotating basis to maintain major canals and structures, whereas any farmer group in the smaller systems may maintain them. But in a few smaller systems, farmers arrange for a leader to maintain the dam and the initial section of the main canal. The rest of the farmers attend to the other facilities.

4. Determining Labor Obligation for System Maintenance

Farmers in systems practicing collective responsibility for maintaining the dam and main canal usually apply objective criteria in calculating the exact labor requirement of each water user. In some systems, the irrigated area of each farm determines the number of days of maintenance labor expected from each farm family. In other systems, total rice production is the criterion—the greater one's production the more one must contribute labor to maintain the system.

5. System Maintenance Schedules

Farmers in systems serving less than fifty hectares usually do not prepare a maintenance schedule in advance; they simply maintain the canals and structures as the need arises, which is often twice a year (at the beginning of each crop season). Farmers in larger systems, in contrast, tend to use maintenance schedules calling for regular and frequent work. Frequency of maintenance work ranges from once every two months to once a week, with each farmer's work day carefully specified (e.g., the first Friday of each month, or the fifteenth of each month).

6. Contacting Farmers Regarding Maintenance Schedules

Farmers in all systems, but particularly those in the larger ones, face communcation difficulties in reminding their dispersed colleagues about maintenance activities. Several ways of communicating are used to ensure that almost all farmers participate in system maintenance. Some of the ways include making house calls, posting notices at conspicuous places in residential areas, calling meetings in which maintenance tasks are planned, shouting from the highest point in the community, and beating a drum or blowing in a shell as a signal for farmers to gather for maintenance work.

7. Meeting the Cost of Operation and Maintenance

Farmers in all systems studied contribute to the cost of operating and maintaining their systems. Their contribution may be in the form of cash donations, labor for system maintenance, materials for the repair of damaged structures or the construction of new ones, food for irrigation-related occasions, and payments of penalties for violating rules.

In some systems, most of which are over fifty hectares, farmers also pay irrigation fees. Smaller systems tend to have relatively low fees which are used for little else besides compensating the system leaders. Larger systems have higher rates because they have to meet many other expenses such as payments for hired maintenance workers, costs of materials for repairing structures or building new ones, and costs of office supplies.

8. Determining Irrigation Fees

Farmers realize the importance of specifying the basis on which irrigation fees are calculated. The usual basis is either the number of irrigated hectares a farmer cutivates during each crop season or the amount of rice he uses for seed for each crop season.[4] Only one system in the study was found to have different irrigation fee rates for the wet and dry seasons. Although the rates are standardized they are often adjusted downward for farmers whose yields are low due to inadequate irrigation.

9. Collecting and Handling Irrigation Fees

Fee collectors personally contact individual farmers to facilitate collections. One person can handle this method of collection in most systems irrigating less than fifty hectares but the responsibility is often delegated to two or more persons in larger systems. Each collector is assigned his own area within those systems.

Farmers in larger systems have also found it necessary to adopt formal measures for handling the money because of the complexity of the financial transactions. Measures instituted and enforced in one system irrigating 4,600 hectares are: (1) a collector remits his collections to the association treasurer as soon as they reach US $26; (2) the treasurer deposits remittances in a bank once these reach US $53; (3) the treasurer never keeps in his possession an amount exceeding US $132; (4) only authorized farmers handle bank transactions; and (5) the financial records of the association are audited each year by designated farmers who also prepare an annual financial report, a copy of which is furnished to association members.[5]

10. Resolving Irrigation Conflicts

Many routine disputes in the systems studied are caused by unequal water distribution or by tampering with temporary water control structures along the length of a canal. Major disputes stem from such divergent issues as siting of irrigation structures, misuse of funds, sharing of a water source between two or more systems (or between old and new parts of a recently expanded system), integration of small systems into a large one, turnover of government-built irrigation structures to the farmers, and rivalry over position of leadership within a system.

Farmers are usually able to settle routine disputes by themselves. But in resolving major conflicts, assistance is often required from outside people such as the local police, elected government officials, and officials of irrigation and agricultural agencies. The intercession of irrigation officials does not necessarily resolve conflicts. Because their authority over communal irrigation is supervisory and investigative only, government irrigation officials do not have the power to settle disputes unless the disputants are willing to accept their verdict.

Given the limited authority of government officials over communal irrigation affairs, farmers ultimately fall back on their own resources to resolve irrigation conflicts. Their last recourse is the local court, but farmers usually avoid this costly and time-consuming step.

11. Assigning Operation and Maintenance Responsibilities

Underlying the various irrigation practices that farmers have devised is the concept of "mini-unit organization" found in most systems serving more than fifty hectares.[6] This concept calls for delegating responsibility for routine operation and maintenance to small groups of farmers within the system. The heads of these groups assume leadership in carrying out daily operations.

Farmers in many systems have accepted this concept and divided their service areas into small units (referred to as sectors, districts, or zones in the systems studied). These small units are defined on the basis of a system's physical layout, not in terms of residential boundaries. A unit thus may be delineated according to its location in the system (e.g.. an upstream area) or its water source (e.g., a branch canal). Farmers belonging to each unit take on operations responsibilities within each area and one farmer assumes leadership in implementing the various irrigation practices.

IMPACT OF THE RESEARCH ON NIA'S ASSISTANCE PROGRAM

The NIA sponsored this study specifically because top agency officials recognized that greater knowledge of farmer experience with irrigation management would yield important lessons for its work in assisting farmers with the improvement of their physical structures and management practices. Having the support of top agency officials, NIA staff and IPC social scientists were then able to work closely together to apply insights from the study in a variety of ways within NIA's communal assistance program. A brief review of these will help to illustrate the importance of the effective use of social analysis in programs intended to strengthen community management capacities more generally.

Development of a Planning Tool

The first application came in the development of a sociotechnical profiling methodology, which by 1980 NIA was applying nationwide for project site assessment and planning. Previously site assessment had been a fairly informal process involving only the collection of a few basic technical and economic data. Following conventional practice in irrigation, no attention was given to social characteristics of the community relevant to irrigation or to how existing irrigation activities were organized. The IPC study highlighted this critical missing dimension. Consequently NIA's leadership called on IPC social scientists to assist them in developing a more comprehensive and integrated assessment instrument, which ultimately was derived from the instruments and methodologies employed in the IPC study.[7]

In early trials of the new assessment instruments it immediately became clear that they would be useful not only in improving site selection but also in anticipating a broad range of problems relating to rights of way, factionalism, power structures, and leadership. Thus altered, the project staff could plan their strategies for addressing these in ways appropriate to the specific situation. This use of the profiles in the site assesssment workshops organized by NIA's regional staff as a routine part of the site selection and planning process have helped strengthen problem analysis in most all aspects of NIA's communal project implementation process.

Two cases serve to illustrate one type of issue, highlighted by the profiles, that can be effectively resolved only with a knowledge of local social and organizational patterns.

The profile of one candidate project indicated that the project would cover an existing system whose farmer-users were organized into two associations. When this was analyzed in a profile analysis work-shop there was much discussion about whether or not to merge the two associations. Proponents for the merger argued the need for only one association since farmers drew water from only one source and one diversion structure. Those who disagreed in turn pointed out the existing leadership roles and traditions of the two associations and the potential difficulties of merging them owing to their long established independent operations. In fact, the project profile indicated that while the leaders of the two associations had no objection to sharing the irrigation facilities that NIA would construct, they wished to continue the independent management of their respective service areas. Eventually NIA rehabilitated the existing system without changing any major aspects of its physical layout. The two associations retained their independent status but they developed arrangements for shared participation in contributing to the project construction and they agreed to their respective shares for repaying the construction costs.[8]

The profile of another project on the other hand, revealed that the project would cover two existing systems that drew water from separate sources. This information also prompted discussion on how to develop the physical system and irrigators' association. In this case, however, the farmers wanted a single organization because almost all who farmed the thirty-five-hectare area served by one system also cultivated fields in the other system, which covered eighty-three hectares. As it turned out, NIA replaced the brush dam of one system with a new concrete one and rehabilitated the damaged permanent dam of the other system, this being done under the auspices of only one association.

Input to Strategies for Developing Irrigator Associations

The IPC study, like other studies of irrigation in Southeast Asia, revealed that the stronger associations generally divided the system's service area into relatively small units based on canal layouts and assign system operations and maintenance tasks within each unit to the farmers whose fields are located there. From initiation of NIA's very first participatory pilot project, this served as a basic principle in the approach to farmer organizing developed by the NIA's staff. Organizing associations by sector and focusing early efforts on the sector groups broadened the base of participation and leadership, while building a basis for managing the completed system on a decentralized sector basis.[9]

In early 1982 NIA identified a need to provide training for farmers dealing with the operation and maintenance of the completed systems. Development of a modularized system management training manual was delegated to a working group comprised of NIA staff and individuals from a number of research and training institutions that had assisted NIA in developing other aspects of its communal irrigation program. Here again application was made of data from the study of fifty-one communal systems, illustrated by the development of the module on conflict management.[10] Data on the fifty-one systems were analyzed to identify all reported cases of conflicts encountered within these systems. This analysis revealed that such conflict can occur at a variety of levels: 1) between adjacent fields (involving farmers whose farms border on one another); 2) within the sector (between farmers whose fields are not adjacent); 3) between sectors (involving farmers whose fields are in different sectors); and 4) between the association and an external person or group (involving the association as a whole). And the analysis showed that when a given conflict is appealed to a higher level rather than being resolved at the level at which it occurs, it tends to escalate and become...increasingly difficult to resolve. As a result of this insight, the materials developed for the conflict resolution module emphasized the importance of resolving conflicts at the lowest possible system level and helped farmers think through how they might accomplish this.

CONCLUSIONS

The NIA experience demonstrates how social science research can make a useful contribution to the development of an agency program in support of community management. Indeed, the case can be made that without such research input it is very unlikely that this type of program will achieve its ends. To begin with, it is necessary simply to help sceptics recognize the extent of the potential for effective community management that exists within rural communities. But more important, it makes available to the agency the lessons that rural people have learned for themselves, often as the result of painful experience, as to how best to organize themselves to manage their resources. It helps the agency recognize the range of local conditions to which it must be able to adjust its intervention. And finally, it develops and tests methods of data collection and analysis which the agency must eventually adapt into its own planning and management systems if it is to make such adjustments.

Of course, a great deal more was involved in the case presented here than simply commissioning a research study. Agency management and staff took an active role first in defininig the study, but even more so in the analysis of the data and identification of implications for the program. They also took steps to keep the researchers engaged as resource persons during efforts to develop applications. It was an intensive, interactive process throughout, and it depended on the researchers taking an active interest in seeing their work translated into program action. Also, while for the sake of simplicity, the focus here has been on a discrete study of fifty-one communal systems, the communal program supported and drew upon a continuing flow of research inputs.

For a collaboration of this type to be effective, there must be a strong commitment on both sides to a set of shared goals, which has not often been achieved between social scientists and administrators. The future of community management interventions in Asia may well depend on the extent to which researchers and administrators are able to develop such commitment and turn it into a close collegial collaboration.

NOTES

1. Revised and excerpted from Romana P. de los Reyes, "Managing Village Irrigation Systems in the Philippines: Farmers' Practices and Implications for Government Assistance" in Thomas Wickham (ed.), *Irrigation Management: Research from Southeast Asia* (Agricultural Development Council, Inc., 1985), pp. 204-214. Reprinted by permission of Winrock International.

2. The Ford Foundation also provided support for this study through a grant to the NIA.

3. Full discussion of the research methodologies and findings are found in Romana P. de los Reyes, *Managing Communal Gravity Systems: Farmers' Approaches and Implications for Program Planning* (Quezon City: Institute of Philippine Culture, Ateneo de Manila University, 1980); Romana P. de los Reyes, *47 Communal Gravity Systems: Organization Profiles* (Quezon City: Institute of Philippine Culture, Ateneo de Manila University, 1980); Romana P. de los Reyes, Ma. Francisca P. Viado, Salve B. Borlagdan and Geosle V. Gatdula, *Communal Gravity Systems: Four Case Studies* (Quezon City: Institute of Philippine Culture, Ateneo de Manila University, 1980); and Jeanne Frances I. Illo, *The Farmers in Communal Gravity Systems: Rice Yields, Work, and Earnings* (Quezon City: Institute of Philippine Culture, Ateneo de Manila University, 1980).

4. The two criteria are closely related because all farmers use approximately the same seeding rate (quantity of seeds required to plant one hectare). The procedure is equitable because rice is essentially the only crop grown in communal systems during the wet season, and the dominant dry season crop as well.

5. All cost data have been converted to US dollars at the rate of Philippine pesos 7.60 per dollar.

6. This principle of organization, found in many indigenous systems in Southeast Asia, was earlier identified by E. Walter Coward Jr., "Management Themes in Community Systems," in E. Walter Coward Jr. (ed.), *Irrigation and Agricultural Development in Asia: Perspectives from the Social Sciences* (Ithaca: Cornell University Press, 1980).

7. For a complete description of the profiling approach, see Roman P. de los Reyes, "Sociotechnical Profile: A Tool for Rapid Rural Appraisal" (Quezon City: Institute of Philippine Culture, Ateneo de Manila University, 1984).

8. Under a policy effected by the national government in 1975, government assistance to communal systems was to be provided as a loan (i.e., no longer as a grant) and farmers were required to contribute to the costs of constructing the system during the construction period. The farmers' contributions could be in the form of cash, rights of way, materials, or labor.

9. For a full discussion of NIA's participatory communal irrigation program, see Benjamin U. Bagadion and Frances F. Korten, "Developing Irrigators' Organizations: A Learning Process Approach to a Participatory Irrigation Program" in Michael Cernea (ed.), *Putting People First* (New York: Oxford University for the World Bank 1985).

10. The other modules of the system management training for farmers include the development of plans for cropping calendar, water distribution, maintenance management, duties and responsibilities, and farm-level facilities development. For the details of the training approach and materials, see System Management Working Group, *Communal Irrigation Management Manual: Operation and Maintenance Phase* (Quezon City: National Irrigation Administration, 1982).

CHAPTER ELEVEN

Unraveling Networks of Corruption[1]

Bangladesh Rural Advancement Committee

In July 1979 BRAC became concerned about the effects of a major drought in certain parts of Bangladesh and anticipated that, by September, serious food shortages might develop. To address this need, an emergency relief program was organized in three different areas of the country. The strategy called for organizing groups of landless people in each village, encouraging them to start collective agricultural activities, using their own resources initially and then expanding to more ambitious efforts using food-for-work grains supplied through BRAC to compensate participants. In addition the landless groups were assisted in obtaining use rights to land on a collective basis through private lease and share cropping arrangements and through obtaining rights to cultivate public lands.

Through this involvement with the landless poor, BRAC staff became familiar with their situation and problems. Gradually they became aware that large scale government relief operations were going on that, if successful, would have made BRAC's work largely unnecessary. But rather than reaching the people for whom they were intended, these resources were being controlled and enjoyed by a small number of powerful men who had good connections with local government officials. It also became evident that a similar pattern prevailed in the fields other than relief operation, for example in the use of public forest lands. Although the poor were not allowed to gather small bundles of fire wood, several rich and powerful men were making large profits from the illegal cutting and sale of the timber. Combinations of economic power and threats or actual force were being used to gain control over a variety of both public and private resources. But more was involved than the economic power, followings of violent and nonviolent supporters, and official positions of a few individuals. Most significant in giving these men a disproportionate share of local power was the complex net of co-operative connections linking them into a seemingly irresistable network of corruption.

Time after time we found the landless people with whom we were working caught up helplessly in the mesh of this invisible network, only partially understanding it, and feeling powerless in dealing with it. As a result of the participatory research effort described here, they came to better understand the sources of the disparities in power between themselves and this power elite.[2] They became increasingly aware of the extent of the benefits intended for them: food-for-work, rations, education, etc., that were not getting through—being instead "caught in the net." This growth in understanding spurred their efforts to organize themselves as a means of breaking its power and restoring their own means of livelihood. This was the genesis of this participatory research effort.

Our methodology was simple and can be repeated by any field worker who can read, write, and do simple arithmetic. Our main information sources were the landless people of each village, though the power elites also supplied us with considerable information about themselves and each other. Later, we obtained help from government officials, who gave up substantial time to clarify various points for us.

We started by carefully recording all the examples of oppressive, exploitative and illegal activities we could find. The search required little effort. The landless and the poor who were the principal victims came to us. As our study continued, their interest and analytical capacity increased to the point where they brought us pens and paper, insisting that we record everything. No individual incident we recorded was news to them. But generally they were not fully aware of the systemic patterns, illuminated by the recording process, that linked individual actors and incidents across villages.

Through interviews with government officials at union and *thana* levels, we were able find out the amounts and intended uses of program resources put into the area by the government and the intended outcomes of important public policies. These were then systematically checked against what we knew was actually happening. For example, we obtained exact details of food-for-work allocations, and worked with the landless to check them against the work done and the grain actually distributed. By the act of recording and discussing the oppressive activities we demonstrated that when one person adds his knowledge to that of others and then engages in analyzing and calculating everything, it is possible to see the situation clearly for the first time—and then to see the possibilities for change. This contributed to a new consciousness and militancy among those who were working with us. As a consequence they have started taking collective action on certain issues and have achieved limited success.

After checking all details with at least four separate sources (sometimes up to fifty), we plotted all the connections involved in each incident to build up a picture of the network involved. Our charts were constantly altered and improved as our knowledge increased. Ultimately we were able to identify each of the key power brokers and their main followers. A profile was prepared on each covering their background, political and business activities, landholding and so on. By this point we limited our study to a cluster of ten villages in two unions. For each of these villages we prepared a simple village profile showing its main characteristics.

One important insight of the study is the importance of going beyond single village studies to understand how the critical linkages of the power structure extend across villages and into the different levels of government. However, in the interests of brevity and simplicity we limit ourselves here to reporting the data from just two villages, addressing the linkages between them and into union and thana levels of government.[3]

The two villages on which we report here we have chosen to call Adanpara and Kathidanga, located on either side of the border between two unions. Both are within four miles of the Indian border and three to four miles from the local thana headquarters. The area is generally hilly and 40 to 50 percent of the land belongs to the Forest Department. About 30 to 35 percent of the land in the region is still forested. Interspersed among the forest lands are many areas suitable for cultivation of paddy and certain winter crops.

It is normally a rice surplus area and also exports large amounts of timber and firewood to local towns and to Dhaka. Most of the people are involved in agriculture as farmers and laborers, or woodcutters—either individually or as part of larger operations. A significant number are engaged in trade, smuggling, and theft.

Until the 1940's the area was mainly inhabited by tribal people known as Adivasis. Changes began coming rapidly during the 1965 war as refugees from India poured into the area and many of the Adivasis emigrated to India. This process was given further impetus by the liberation war of 1971 and by the abortive rebellion of the "Kader Bahini" in 1976. Thus, unlike some other parts of Bangladesh, kinship relations among the Muslim households are not yet well developed and many of the power holders have only recently gained this status. This accounts in part for the high degree of lawlessness found in the area.

THE POWER HOLDERS OF KATHIDANGA AND ADANPARA

These two villages are adjacent to one another and their power holders are linked in several ways, as we will elaborate later.[4]

Kathidanga Village

Kathidanga, with a population of 750, is much smaller than any of its immediate neighboring villages. Of its 119 households, 6.7 percent produce a surplus on their own lands beyond subsistence needs, 16.0 percent are self-sufficient, 24.4 percent are marginal (meaning their land is insufficient to provide for their subsistence), and 52.9 percent are landless. Its main power holders are as follows.

Nazmul, age 55 who comes from an adjacent thana and fought in the British Indian Army in Burma. He arrived in 1950, the first outside settler in this Adivasi village, and worked as a day laborer until he was able to occupy five acres of Adivasi land in 1964. When the communal riot occurred in 1964, he occupied an additional 1.5 acres of government (*khas*) land and sold off the cows and G.I. sheets belonging to the Adivasis who had fled to India. With this money he bought five acres more.

Since that time he has been heavily involved in money lending as his main occupation. During 1971 he was again involved, with many other people, in looting the possessions such as copper and brass utensils, wooden door frames and other household goods of Adivasis who fled to India. Now he has ten acres. The main clients of his money-lending business are Adivasis and he maintains good relations with several Adivasi leaders by offering them hospitality and gifts even as he takes advantage of the weaker members of their community.

Farid, age 50 came in 1967 from an adjacent thana and married into the same family as Nazmul. At that time he occupied one acre of khas land and started engaging in money lending activities. Like Nazmul he does not engage in politics or other activities but concentrates on making profits through money lending. His daughter is married to the son of Kamal Member who resides in Adanpara. Now he has eighteen acres.

Matin Master, age 35[5] came from an adjacent thana, where he still had land, with his family in 1976. After arriving in Kathidanga he bought four acres from refugees. He is a high school graduate and a teacher at the Kathidanga government primary school. He is also the Secretary of the union branch of the Bangladesh National Party (BNP), which was the party in power at the time of the study, and maintained good connections with the local Member of Parliament, the Chairman of the Sundorganj Union Council, a former Minister of the Cabinet, the President of the local organization of the (BNP), the Secretary of the Thana Teachers' Association, and the President of the Central Teachers' Associations in Dhaka.

Idris Master, age 35 arrived after 1964 from an adjacent thana and married a local girl. He received one acre as a gift from his father-in-law and bought another acre from Selim Commander. He is a gambler and has since lost all but one half acres in gambling. Previously he was a teacher in Adanpara primary school, but the school has been closed since it was damaged in 1977 by a cyclone. He contested the last Union Council election and lost. Even so he remains active politically and is powerful because of a close connection with Matin Master.

Mostafa arrived with his father from an adjacent thana after the communal riots of 1964. At that time his father bought six acres. Mostafa obtained two of these and latter bought an additional acre. Formerly he belonged to a violent gang led by his uncle and another leader, now both dead. The gang also included his brother-in-law, now also dead, and a cousin. Mohiuddin, a faction leader in nearby Taluqkandi Village, was another leader of the gang until he was elected in 1977 to the Shantigarh Union Council. After his election, Mohiuddin formed his own gang and in the winter of 1978 killed Mostafa's brother-in-law in a land dispute. The next day Mostafa's cousin and another relative killed Mohiuddin's father. In late 1979 the relative joined Mohiuddin's group and, at Mohiuddin's instigation, killed Mostafa's cousin. With the death of his relatives, Mostafa became the leader of the original gang. There is a case pending against him for robbery on which his family has already spent Tk. 25,000 in bribes and other expenses.

Humayun comes from a notorious family of thieves that has lived in the region for two generations. Following the family profession, he has been in jail once and has two cases pending agianst him. He maintains close links with Mohiuddin, Salehuddin, and Kamal. He has married twice and divorced his first wife. His present wife was previously Salehuddin's third wife. He has a daughter, a son, and no land.

Factions. There are two main factions in Kathidanga Village. The first consists of persons from nearby villages, fifty households led by Mostafa, Martin Master, and Idris, but controlled from outside by Mizan, former Chairman of the Sundorganj Union Council. The second, less dominant group consists of forty-five households of refugees from India.

Adanapara Village

Adanpara is a larger village to the north of Katidanga that dominates the surrounding villages. It has a market and a population of 2,700 persons in 448 households. Of these households, 327 are setlers and 121 Adivasis. Broken down by landholdings, 2.2 percent are surplus, 5.8 percent self-sufficient, 30.8 percent marginal and 61.2 percent landless. Before 1950 there were no settlers. The major influx began after 1964. The main leaders and power holders are as follows.

Huda Master, age 60 came to the village from another part of the same District in the early 1950's and acquired five acres of khas land, of which he still has two. For about ten years he forcibly occupied khas and Adivasi land, which he in turn allocated to people coming from his former village. There were about 100 such families who came and received his "help and patronage" in return for money and services. Many of these people, however, did not actually get the land for which they paid him and became destitue. Of the 100 such families, only about twenty remain, the others having moved elsewhere. Income from these activities allowed Huda to employ several people and to buy a number of houses, including one that is quite large, plus a shop and various luxuries such as expensive furniture.

He also involved in the timber and leaf businesses,[6] and in various types of forgery and other deceptions. In 1971 the local people tried to get him involved in incidents that would get him put behind bars or killed. Even so, his good education has given him prestige and helped him in his activities. He is the retired headmaster of Motihar primary school and the father-in-law of Kamal Member.

Kamal Member, age 45 arrived in 1960 from an adjacent thana and married Huda Master's daughter as his second wife. His eldest son married the daughter of Farid from Kathidanga. When he first arrived in the village, he took employment as a laborer for Manzur Sarkar, later becoming a supervisor for Manzur and running off with about Tk. 10,000—a part of which Manzur has since recovered. Soon after he arrived he forcibly occupied two acres of land and has since increased his holdings to seven acres.

More recently he has become heavily involved in leaf and timber businesses, which are the basis of his present wealth. He was closely connected with the former Union Council Chairman and, 1977, ran against Taher Company for a position on the Union Council, but lost. After Taher was killed by the Kader Bahini, Kamal obtained the seat in a by-election, mainly through the support of Manzur Sarkar. He is now close to Mohiuddin and other Union Council Members and has good connections with the local Member of Parliament, Matin Master, the local forester, the Bangladesh Rifles (BDR, the border patrol), and the police. He is the Secretary of the Adanpara Primary School Committee and is a member of various other committees including the Madrassa Committee. His brother, Salehuddin's status as a freedom fighter had been helpful to him at various points in his career, until Salehuddin caused a clash with the local landless people (described at the end of this report), which Kamal has since been trying to settle without success.

Salehuddin, age 36, the younger brother of Kamal Member, arrived in 1960 and obtained two acres of land. He has had five wives and many mistresses. Through his elder brother he is well connected with Mohiuddin and many others, and works closely with Latif. During the day he spends most of his time drinking and gambling. At night he steals cows and other things with the help of several colleagues within the region and from across the border. There are eleven cases and three warrants against him now. He has been severely beaten by the Police and members of the Bangladesh Rifles in the market and has been sent to jail several times, but usually manages to escape through payment of liberal bribes. In 1971 he was a "freedom fighter"[7] and extracted several thousand taka from the poor, as well as from Razakars,[8] like Selim Commander of Taluqkandi Village (who was himself actively engaged in land grabbing), continuing these activities until 1973.

Hafiz, age 55 came from Assam in 1964 and obtained an allocation of 9 acres, 3 acres each for himself and his two sons. Ex-Union Council Member Lutfur from nearby Motihar Village helped him get the additional land for his sons, as well as money for three ploughs and three bundles of G.I. sheets. He assumed leadership of the refugees in the area. He has continued to be active in land grabbing schemes, as will be detailed later. He left the area for a year in 1976, but returned to continue his profession of land grabbing and resale with the help of Lutfur.

He works closely with Latif, his nephew, and has close connections with Salehuddin and Kamal Member as well as with Humayun of Kathidanga Village. He was involved with the leaf business for two years as a sub-agent. He has been married six times since divorcing two of his wives. Two current wives are engaged in collecting firewood from the forest and the other two live with their respective sons, Latif and Mofiz. Latif is the son of Hafiz's elder brother, but after his brother's death Hafiz married the brother's wife, so Latif is both his nephew and step-son.

Latif, age 35 came to the area with his uncle Hafiz and lived with him for five years until he married the first of his two wives. When Latif set up a separate household, Hafiz gave him three acres and he bought four acres of illegally occupied land from Hafiz. He has since sold off all except 3.5 acres. Latif is a heavy drinker and is closely connected with Salehuddin, Humayun, Kamal Member, Lutfur ex-Member from Motihar Village, and Mohiuddin Member of Taluqkandi Village. Also, he is a member of the Village Defense Force (VDF). He currently has six cases against him: two for robbery, others for highway robbery, attempted murder, illegal occupation of temple land, and the attempted abduction of two young women.

Mahfuz, age 36 arrived in 1960 from another part of the District and occupied five acres of khas land. In 1962 his father came and bought three acres. He has since bought seven acres more. In 1971 he was a freedom fighter and terrorized many people including Selim Commander from whom he extracted Tk. 900. He extracted Tk. 1,000 from another influential person and other amounts from less important people. Now he is the Secretry of Adanpara (west) primary school and has unsuccessfully campaigned for a seat on the Union Council. He is now trying to get the support of the local landless people to run for the Union Council in the next election. He was involved in the leaf business and has spent six months in jail. He used to drink, but currently does not.

Taher Company (now dead) was orginally from Comilla where in his youth he was involved in a murder case. He fled to Assam to escape conviction and started a business there, hence his title. In 1964 he came to Adanpara as a refugee and occupied a huge area of land temporarily abandoned by the Adivasis. By obtaining false refugee cards he got extra land allocated to him and bought a house at the thana headquarters. Later much of this land was reoccupied by the Adivasis and allocated to other refugees by the Border Magistrate.

He was deeply involved in the leaf business and bought nine acres out of the profits. As a rich and intelligent person he was often asked to give judgement at *salish*[9] and was very influential. Kamal called him his godfather-in-law, a fictitious relationship, to get his patronage. In 1977 he ran for a Union Council seat and won by spending Tk. 10,000 to bribe election officials. But when Kamal Member and Salehuddin found out on election night they got angry and said that Taher Company's days were numbered.

In the same year he was shot. He survived for a few hours, during which he told his relatives that he knew who was responsible, but for the safety of his family would not reveal their names. His relatives eventually learned the identity of the killers and were preparing to file a case when Kamal reached a settlement with them.[10] The following year Kamal was elected to the Union Council in the by-election.

Manzur Sarkar, age 72 is the biggest landowner in the area, with a total of 150 acres divided between several individual plots. During the British rule his family were *talukas*. He is influential throughout the thana and plays a "kingmaker" role during elections. He was previously involved in the timber business in a big way and was once a member of the Union Council in the adjacent union, when his uncle was Chairman. He was recently the major force enabling Kamal to become a member of the local Union Council. Now he is more or less retired from business and politics and has become "respectable."

Factions. There are three major groupings in Adanpara. The first is led by Kamal Member and consists of his own group of forty households and a group of twenty-five mainly Garo households, as well as Hafiz's small kinship group of five households, and ten households from the east *para* (neighborhood). Second is a looser grouping under several small leaders including three groups of twenty, fifteen, and thirty-seven households each, plus a group of sixty-nine Adivasi households. For certain purposes the Adivasi groups all unite under the leadership of a Garo Catholic with good connections in the Catholic Mission. Although the first faction is much smaller than the second, its tighter organization, the ruthlessness of its members, and its good connections make it the more powerful and successful.

LAND

The history of the area during past twenty years has been a continuing process of land occupation, primarily of Adivasi lands by Muslim refugees—actual or self-proclaimed. The land grabbing reached its peak in 1964-65 and 1971, when communal riots and wars forced many Adivasis to flee temporarily to India. At these times men like Selim Commander, Mohiuddin Member, Huda Master, Lutfur ex-Member and Mizan ex-Chairman were able to grab lands on a large scale and build up their present wealth and power, while Nazmul laid the basis for his money-lending business. This process is still going on and every year at transplanting and harvest times new disputes arise.

Clearly what has been involved has not been a simple matter of larger numbers of settlers arriving over the years and each occupying some land for himself. The large number of landless in the area itself refutes this theory. And the Adivasis have rarely sold productive land voluntarily in this area. In fact, the land occupation has been the work of a small number of men who, seizing a tragic opportunity, have used violence, trickery, deceit, bribery, and the forgery of official documents to expand their power and wealth and finance their vices.

As of 1976-77, with the Kader Bahini rebellion still going on, a new wave of land grabbing was underway. For the most part, the men who had assumed the lead in earlier episodes were now playing a more "respectable" role, providing protection, encouragement, and finance to a younger and more active generation—with notable exceptions such as Mohiuddin Member and Selim Commander who were still active.

Much land has already changed hands. The action, however, is shifting away from villages like Kathidanga, where 100 percent of the land has changed hands during this period, to villages like Adanpara and Motihar where land remains that has not yet been captured by the net. The methods of operation are illustrated in numerous examples including the following cases from Adanapara, for which we have detailed data supported by land documents and case numbers, as well as direct personal observation.

Recently Hafiz and his nephew Latif have been the most active in land grabbing in this village. In 1967 they forcibly occupied eight acres belonging to a *Koch*, member of the scheduled or untouchable caste who over two years filed nine cases against them and others in the Sub-Divisional Magistrate's Court. They were all arrested but released after seven days on bail while the case continued. When their conviction became imminent, they approached the Union Chairman who threatened the Koch, pressuring him to come to a compromise. As a result he kept 4.25 acres and Hafiz got 3.75. At this point the Chairman brought his influence to bear in the Court, reporting that Hafiz had never occupied any land. For his services in the case he received Tk. 1,000 from a grateful Hafiz. At the same time Hafiz was engaged in the occupation of 4.40 acres from two more Koch for which he has been able to obtain ownership documents from the Revenue Department.

In 1971 a coalition of Selim Commander and Hafiz, with the support of Kamal Member, Lutfur ex-Member and others from outside occupied 100 to 200 acres of land belonging to Adivasis who had temporarily fled to India. Much of this land was registered in the names of relatives who had since died. Since there are no proper birth and death registers in the area, the occupiers were able to maintain that the actual owners were not dead, but still in India and therefore the land was "enemy property." Any complaints from the owners to the Court were referred to the Officer-in-Charge of Police, who had been bribed by the group and simply ignored the instructions of the court to investigate. Much of this land was sold to new arrivals. Some was recovered by its owners. Hafiz kept three acres of temple land and one acre of private land obtained in this way. Latif retained three acres.

The enemy property ordinance, which figures centrally in much land grabbing, was passed after the 1965 war and was intended to be used to confiscate the property of those who had defected to India and make it available for settling refugees from India on a lease basis from the government, though often in practice it was opened for occupation. In 1967-69 a census was carried out to find out who had permanently left the country for India and to confiscate their property. We were told by senior district level officials, however, that the census officials never went to the field, but rather sat in their offices and, whenever they saw land registered in the name of a person with a non-Muslim name, they classified it as enemy property. It was a system that easily lent itself to manipulation as it was a simple matter to get land so classified. One senior official of the land settlement operation told us that in checking through classifications in part of an adjacent thana, he had found that 75 percent of "enemy property" classifications were false and that even some Muslim families had been included.

A related problem was the difficulty facing the average person in finding out how a given piece of land was classified. A senior district officer told us the story of a man who came to the Magistrate's court appealing against an enemy property classification on thirteen small plots of land. It turned out that eleven of the plots were not in fact so classified. He had been deceived by the local registrar who used his control over the local records to pretend that large amounts of land had been so classified to extract bribes on the pretense of changing the records. The remaining two classifications were false and were overthrown.

In contrast to the ease with which property can be incorrectly classified, getting a false classification corrected can be a difficult and expensive process. The owner usually has to go first to the Sub-divisional

Officer and the Additional Deputy Commissioner, and finally to the Ministry in Dhaka. Not the least of his problems is how to get inside the Ministry, which is inside a guarded secretariate building with restricted access.

One measure intended to prevent much of this type of land grabbing is a ruling by the Border Magistrate that even the land allocated to refugees in the border area is given to them only on a one year share-cropping basis and does not become legally theirs even by continued occupation. This ruling is completely ignored and ineffective.

In the face of the sophisticated system of corruption that has emerged to exploit the weaknesses in these systems, the ignorant and unorganized people on the one side of it and the senior government officers on the other side seem almost helpless.

CAPITAL

The local power elites are also able to make effective use of their near monopoly control over liquid capital, lending it out at extremely high rates of interest. Although several of the prinicipal money lenders got their start by illegally occupying land and continue to use their power over debtors to increase their holdings at low cost, the two types of operation demand different styles, connections, and methods of operation. The case of Nazmul of Kathidanga Village, illustrates the methods of the money lender.

Nazmul built up his initial capital by land grabbing and looting. In 1966 he started lending money at the rate of 100 percent per crop season. There are two main crop seasons per year: spring and summer. In that year he lent one maund of paddy worth Tk. 20 to a Garo. The Garo was unable to repay at the end of the season, and Nazmul continued to extend the loan until 1973. By that time the debt had grown to 16,384 maunds. Nazmul offered to accept Tk. 5000 in repayment and forget the rest. In 1973 he received 0.50 acres of land worth Tk. 4,980 as a final settlement.

In 1972 he lent two maunds and Tk. 200 to another Garo, who returned Tk. 200 and five maunds after one season (the price at that time being Tk. 40-50/md.). Nazmul claimed Tk. 1800 more and his debtor had to give him the use of 0.50 acres for one year. That year the yield was fourteen maunds and the following year he received another four maunds. He still claimed Tk. 1200 more. Finally his debtor paid him another Tk. 100 after selling his cow and begged to be forgiven the rest. The matter was settled, and Nazmul's profit was approximately Tk. 2,300. His business has grown over the years. This year he expects to receive 145 maunds and has already recovered forty-five.

A client of one large money lender was watching an eclipse of the moon with us one night. "Do you know what's happened to the moon?"

he said as it began to disappear. "He took a one paisa loan from the sun...."[11]

THE FOREST

Govenment forest covers an area of about 8,000 acres, or half the total BRAC project area. Two thirds of this is still forested, though large timber merchants are cutting it off at a rapid rate with the unofficial co-operation of the forestry officers. Every year for three months from February to May, large numbers of trucks come to the area and carry away large *sal* trees [a valuable timber species] to the towns for sale, and small trees and branches to the local markets for firewood. Possibly no other activity demonstrates so clearly the imbalance of power as the way in which officials treat the commercial loggers on the one hand and the poor who cut headloads of wood to sell for survival on the other.

The following is a description of one typical scheme for illegally harvesting trees from government land.

Many Adivasis have plots of private registered land inside the government forests which they do not use for agriculture because the soils are poor. Timber operators buy up these plots at Tk. 300 to 500 per acre and obtain permits from the District Forest Officer (DFO) to cut trees on this land. Though officially such permits are given free for cutting on private land, in fact they cost several thousand taka in bribes. Having obtained the permit, the operator then starts cutting down trees in the public forests adjacent to the plot. These are then carried to the plot and placed next to old stumps. The Forester is brought in to stamp the trees with a special hammer so they can be removed. A single stump may be "cut" in this manner as many as six or seven times.

The price of timber in the sub-divisional town is at least Tk. 80 per cubic foot (cft.) and the transport cost is Tk. 1,000/truck. One truck can carry about 200 cft. and the cost of cutting 200 cft. on government land is Tk. 1,400. Therefore, the sale price per truck is Tk. 16,000 and the costs Tk. 2,400 excluding bribes. Firewood is sold locally with no transport cost at Tk. 2,000 to 2,500 per truck with a cutting cost of Tk. 150. The profits are therefore Tk. 13,500 per truckload of timber and Tk. 2,000 per truckload of firewood. Bribes may take as much as one third or even half this amount. The amounts of timber and firewood cut are about equal. In three forested unions, including the BRAC project area, in the winter season of 1978-79 about forty large contractors were operating for five months, each employing an average of 100 laborers a day. Actual shipment out of the area occurs during a brief period at the end of the season. All trucks coming out of the area have to pass by the same point. A check revealed that at least twenty trucks passed that point each day for at least forty-five days, about half carrying timber and the other half firewood.

These large and profitable operations are in stark contrast with the activities of landless and destitute families who spend all day cutting a headload of firewood, then carry it on their heads to the local market where it fetches Tk. 5. According to the Forest Department, this work is only legal if the wood is broken and collected with bare hands (not cut with an axe) and if a pemit application signed by the Union Council Chairman is submitted and a fee of Tk. 1.50 paid for each headload. Because of the difficulty of conforming to these regulations, no one does, and so poor people who have no other livelihood are often harassed by the local power elites as well as by police and forest officers. An example:

On the 18th of September 1979 at 4:00 a.m. twenty-three landless laborers went from Adanpara toward the sub-divisional town carrying firewood they had cut the previous day. There was no work available and the condition of their families was serious. Some policemen returning from patrol caught them; three ran away and twenty were arrested. They had no money to pay a bribe and so were taken to the police station. Mizan, ex-Chairman of the Sundorganj Union Council and one of the area's major timber operators, spends most of his time around thana headquarters and happened to be present at this time. He became involved and negotiated a rate of Tk. 5 per head for their release. Soon their friends and relatives and other members of the landless organization arrived. With them came Amin, a faction leader of Osmanpur Village and two-time unsuccessful candidate for the Union Council. Amin was allowed entry into the police station to negotiate together wiht Mizan though the rest were refused.

On his return he told the group that by now the Forest Department had become involved and so the price had gone up to Tk. 10 per head. They refused to pay and said they were prepared to take the case to higher levels if the prisoners were not released. By this stage the prisoners were hungry and the sentry who had given permission for food to be sent in now refused. Mizan and Amin interceded with the police and got permission. After showing their sympathy in this way they gave the news that the Bangladesh Rifles had been informed by telephone and the rate had now gone up to Tk. 15 per head. The friends still refused to pay, however, and the police sent a man over to the Forestry office for co-ordination.

Then Mizan, Amin, and the police began discussions with the prisoners inside and friends outside simultaneously. They hinted that the prisoners might be beaten, kept without food, and later sent to jail. Amin reminded the prisoners that their friends would find it very difficult to go to higher levels and offered to sign a bond for their release. Eventually they agreed and each had to sign two bonds, one admitting guilt and another promising to pay Tk. 20 each. By noon they were released. Later, they paid. Out of the Tk. 400 collected, the police, BDR and Forest Department personnel each got 25 percent and the remainder was divided equally between Mizan and Amin. Although this was paid on the understanding that the case would be dropped, it has not been.

Thus the power elites are not only able to defy laws protecting the forest with impunity for their personal profit, they are also able to use the same laws to exploit and harass the poor.

FOOD

Though our area is surplus in rice and exports substantial amounts, such a high proportion of the population is comprised of landless laborers that anything that reduces their employment opportunities results in much suffering. This happened in May/June 1979 when drought seriously affected the spring rice crop and made weeding unnecessary, thus leaving most of the laborers unemployed and on the edge of starvation. This situation was repeated in September-October. In such circumstances the almost total control enjoyed by the power elite over government food supplies disbursed by the government under food-for-work and rations programs puts them in an extremely powerful position.

Food-for-Work

Normally during the winter season large amounts of wheat are made available all over Bangladesh to compensate laborers for the creation of rural infrastructure such as roads, canals, and embankments, and for the raising and leveling of land. The program is administered by the Union Councils under the supervision of the government. In 1979, because of the crisis caused by the drought, much of the wheat intended for use in the dry winter season was brought forward during the monsoon.

In the four months August to November 1979, twenty-six schemes were sanctioned, and a total of 2,100 maunds (mds) of wheat were disbursed by the Government for this program.[12] The twenty schemes we were able to check were allocated 1,825 mds. Of this, only 425 mds. 32 seers (srs.), 23.9 percent of the total sanctioned, were really distributed. The remaining 1,392 mds. 8 srs., with a market value of Tk. 139,200, "disappeared."

According to Union Council members interviewed, 30 percent of the wheat for each scheme always goes for "expenses," transport costs and the shares of the various government officers. The transport cost is actually covered separately by the government and, from BRAC's own experience, should not in any event exceed 3 percent of the total. Several levels of government are involved, from the project implementation officer, who checks all movements and certifies completion, through the thana officer in charge of development, up to the sub-division.

In December 1979, a special scheme was sanctioned for raising and leveling the Adanpara primary school field. The school is not registered or even running though its teachers continue to draw rations. This was a special scheme transferred from some other allocation, and fifty mds. were sanctioned. It was implemented by Kamal Member, Matin Master, and Idris Master. Less than five mds. were really distributed.

But the incident of the Adanpara primary school field had begun even earlier. In early October 1979 Matin Master told three marginal farmers that he had received a delivery order for 100 mds. wheat to repair the Adanpara school field, but needed money to transport it. After bargaining, the farmers bought mds. in advance for Tk. 300. He shared the money with Idris Master and Kamal Member. When the wheat finally arrived three months later, he told them that since only fifty mds. had been sanctioned and had gone on "expenses" he could not supply any.

Control over food supplies is also an effective method of patronage. Food-for-work, for example, is usually given to the relatives and faction members of the council member. This also has the advantage of keeping the amount distributed as secret as possible. It can also be denied to any rivals or dissatisfied groups. For example, once the landless people became organized and started demanding higher wages and other benefits, the Union Council denied them any further food-for-work allocations.

RESISTANCE

In recent years the landless poor and marginal farmers have been increasingly successful in organizing themselves and in challenging some of the activities of the "net."

In Adanpara there are 4.2 acres of temple land belonging to a Koch which had been claimed by Hafiz and his relatives and previously occupied by them. In 1979 the Koch made an arrangement to share this land with a landless group of seventy settlers and Adivasis. They all filed a case against the land grabbers, and because of their large number were able to transplant and harvest their crops successfully.

On a much larger scale, the big land occupation operations started in 1976 in a nearby village by Kamal and others have been successfully countered. For three years the occupiers were able to use about 100 acres belonging to all the Adivasis of the village. In 1979 when BRAC's food-for-work program was beginning, the victims began to discuss how to recover their land. By transplanting time they had organized a strong group including almost all the landless settlers and Adivasis in the village and had established good contacts with similar groups in the surrounding villages and with the local Member of Parliament. At that time the central government was giving special attention to the Adivasis. After careful

preparation, they transplanted and harvested in a large group of sixty people and have reoccupied almost all the land, though there is a case filed
against their leader.

One of many reasons why organizing has worked to increase the
power of these groups is that they have been able to agree not to hire out
to work confiscated land for members of the net nor serve as their guards.
When such agreements extend to neighboring villages, illegal land occupation becomes increasingly difficult to sustain.

As the landless began to get organized and take action, members of
the net began to strike back. During BRAC's food-for-work program, several
women's groups were organized and started joint cultivation. Salehuddin started bullying and threatening them when he was drunk. Their
leader complained to the Union Council Member, who is Salehuddin's
brother, but got no satisfaction and so contacted all the landless groups
in the surrounding villages. They decided to organize a salish among
themselves and summoned Salehuddin to attend. At the salish it became
clear that he had been threatening many people with beating and murder
if they spoke against him. Because of this, before taking the matter any
further, the landless leaders reported these threats to the police, who were
uncooperative. It was learned that they had just received a Tk. 500 bribe
from Salehuddin in another case.

One leader had been particularly active in the salish and had also
played a central role in resisting the land-grabbing activities of Salehuddin and friends. Two weeks after the salish they attacked him in the bazar
at dusk. Though he was only slightly injured, another landless leader,
Kazim, and a local rich man who had come out of the mosque to stop
the fighting were wounded in the head and hand respectively.

The landless people became angry, cutting up bamboo to make *lathis*
(sticks) and discussed whether to go to Salehuddin's house to kill him.
They decided against it. The victims went to the Sub-Division for treatment and to the thana police station to file a case. Salehuddin also filed
a counter-case against the landless leader, which was well received by the
Officer-in-Charge (O.C.) of police because of their close relationship.

The following day, 600 men marched to the police station to request
the O.C. to take action against Salehuddin, shouting the slogan: "Build
landless organization, stop robbery!" The O.C. met them on the road. He
spoke nicely and sympathetically—not his common practice with the
landless—and promised to investigate. They heeded his request that they
return home.

When the O.C. reached the police station he found 200 women, who
had come by a different route, gathered there. He gave them promises
as well and the following day came to investigate the case.

Salehuddin disappeared for some time and his assistant Latif was arrested. Salehuddin reappeared after his brother sold 0.5 acres, mortgaged 0.5 acres and paid the O.C. Tk. 3000 to avoid arrest. He then tried to negotiate a settlement with the landless organization.

Given an understanding of the local power structure, it no longer seems surprising that resources intended for "development" rarely reach the poor. The words and plans of central government mean little. The realities of power relationships at local levels determine what actually happened.

AN UPDATE

In early 1985, a little more than five years after the original study, a follow-up was carried out in the areas to assess the impact of efforts by the landless to shift the power balance in the two villages examined above. This follow-up revealed the substantial difficulties of the undertaking. The reader should bear in mind that, of the ten villages included in the original study, Kathidanga and Adanpara were chosen for attention in this article specifically because it was here that the net was particularly well entrenched and powerful. It should also be kept in mind that the border area in which the original ten study villages was located is one of the more inaccessible in Bangladesh, and had more than the typical level of lawless activity.

After reviewing developments in Kathidanda and Adanpara, we will look at a key indicator of the progress being made by the landless of the surrounding area and at some of the lessons which this experience generated for BRAC.

Kathidanga Village

In Kathidanga village the landless organization no longer exists and any impact it may have had on the village is difficult to detect. It was one of the earlier villages organized by BRAC and contributed important lessons which BRAC has since been careful to observe. When Kathidanga was being organized, BRAC had not yet instituted the practice of beginning with a comprehensive village survey which, among other things, makes it possible for BRAC workers to specificially target the landless. Nor was it considered important at that time to restrict membership to the landless class. Consequently the organization had attracted members who were not identified with the interests of the landless and who assumed a dominant role in the association. It also turned out that most of the landless in the village were refugees without established ties to the community. Unable to find employment there and having no real ties to the village, most had left the area by 1985.

Of the net members from Kathidanga, Nazmul has increased his holdings to twenty-two acres of land and 100 head of cattle through a continuation of his money lending and land grabbing activities. His three sons are active in smuggling and black market operations. Farid has had similar success with his money lending, increasing his holdings to twenty acres. His daughter has married one of Kamal Member's sons. Matin Master is still serving as a teacher in the local primary school and has engaged in some successful land transactions, but drinks heavily and has had to sell off almost all of his property to cover drinking expenses, retaining only a one-acre homestead plot. Idris Master, having lost his land in gambling, works as a share cropper in his father's village but still remains sufficiently active politically to have been nominated to serve as a union council member. A string of additional cases were brought against him for theft following the case mentioned earlier, which had already cost him Tk. 25,000 in bribes and other expenses. To meet the expenses of these cases, he eventually was forced to sell off all his land and now lives in a deplorable financial condition. Humayun is still a prominent member of Mohiuddin's gang, maintaining good relations with Salehuddin and Kamal Member.

Adanpara Village

In Adanpara Village the landless organization survives as an important force in the village, though it faces continuing and difficult obstacles including corruption among its own leadership. Kazim, secretary of the central committee of the landless organization, who had suffered head injuries in the 1979 incident with Salehuddin, received Tk. 2,200 from the members of the organization to press their case with the district court. Some days later he demanded more money to spend on the case. As he refused to give the members an accounting for the previous money, his request was denied. It was later learned that he took another Tk. 2,000 from the central committee's account, which he was only willing to say he had spent on the case. In the meantime, he convinced the organization to compromise with Salehuddin on the case. He lost the support of the landless organization, but later won an election for Union Council membership with the support of elite factions which opposed the landless organization.

Later another leader, Kalam Munsi, obtained a loan of Tk. 1,000 from the group to buy land for himself but later refused to repay the money or turn over the land. When the group was unsuccessful in reclaiming the money, it disbanded and most of its members joined another of the Adanpara people's organizations. Still another leader gave over one acre of his land to the group for collective cultivation on the condition that they clean and level it. But after the work was done, he retained the land for himself and joined with Kazim in supporting political factions that opposed the people's organization.

As for the key figures mentioned in the earlier study, Huda Master involved himself as a member of the landless organization, consistently working against its interests until the members took a strong stand against him. His economic position and standing in the village subsequently deteriorated until he finally sold off his remaining property and returned to his home village where he passed away in 1982.

After Kamal Member became a Union Council member his income increased rapidly during the first half of his term through a variety of questionable activities. In early 1983 the landless organization caught him red-handed in collecting the grain from a Food for Work Project on which no work had been accomplished. They filed a case against him at both thana and sub-division levels, but no action was taken. So they took their case to the local Member of Parliament and with his help seized the wheat sanctioned for the scheme, completed the project, and distributed the wheat to the participants. Kamal's timber and leaf business started to decline. Blocked by the landless group from further illegal profiteering from his Union Council position he has turned to cattle stealing, with two cases being brought against him in the local thana during the past year. He still maintains good relations with the Bangladesh Rifles, Forestry, and Thana (Upazilla) officials. But in the last union council election he lost badly, receiving only eighty votes.

Salehuddin, with the help of Kamal Member and the local UP Chairman who maintains frequent contact with the landless leaders, was finally successful in negotiating an agreement with Kazim, the Secretary of the central commitee of the landless organization, and the case brought against him by the landless was finally withdrawn. He later begged pardon for the incident from the landless people in a public gathering. He continues to serve as a member of Mohiuddin's gang, engages in cattle and timber theft, and does what he can to hinder the activities of the landless organization. He now has fifty acres of land.

Hafiz lost all of his land in gambling and in paying expenses of disputes over land taken from the Adivasis. He is now a poor old man of no importance suffering from various untreated diseases. His nephew, Latif, continues to practice cattle theft and robbery as a member of Mohiuddin's gang. With the help of Mohiuddin's connections with local officials and some small bribes, he has been successful in getting the six cases that were pending against him dropped, though he spent a total of two years in jail from 1979-83. He serves as a member of the Village Defense Force and owns two acres of land.

Mahfuz has increased his holdings to twelve acres. He has continued, without success, to win the support of the landless organization in bids for the union council. He remains an important social and political figure in the area.

Manzur Sarkar became a supporter of the landless organization, giving one acre of land to the Adanpara Landless Women's Organization for collective cultivation of cassava and giving support to the candidate sponsored by the landless organization for UP Chairman Candidate in the most recent election. He died in 1984, and his family continues to hold his 150 acres of land.

Union Council Elections

As the members of landless organizations have become more politically aware, they have given increasing attention to winning representation on the local Union Councils. The Union Council elections held December 1983 to January 1984 were contested by forty-two candidates from the landless groups. Ten of these were from the ten villages included in the original study, and the remaining thirty-two were from neighboring villages. Though none of the candidates from the ten villages won, twelve of the candidates from the neighboring villages did. Though this was only a minority of the landless candidates, the results were taken as an important victory by the landless who felt it marked a turning point in their endeavor to gain power.

This focus on union-level elections has been accompanied by moves toward the formation by the landless of their own union-level federation of village level associations. So far two union-level committees have been formed by the landless, comprised of one representative from each of their village organizations. These committees meet once each month to discuss issues that affect their organizations and to seek common solutions. Among the accomplishments of these committees has been a successful effort to reorganize and reactivate the landless organization in one of the ten study villages which had run into difficulties.

LESSONS

BRAC has learned numerous lessons from this experience. First is the importance of beginning involvement in a village with a comprehensive survey that clearly identifies the target population and reveals the social structure of the village. Membership in landless organizations is then limited to those who are actually members of the landless class. Mass confrontation with elites is avoided whenever possible, attempting to resolve disputes by more tactful means. Efforts are made to develop broadly based leadership to make it difficult for one person to assume a dominant role, which may be used to his personal benefit. From the very beginning, attention is given to self-managed income and employment-generating programs based on traditional skills and occupations. This contrasts with earlier BRAC programs that were oriented more to providing emergency relief to the poor and tended to create dependency.

And so the poor continue their struggle and BRAC continues to learn. There are no easy victories and each success is built on the learning from past failures. For all the set-backs the landless of the area are making progress, no longer feeling they are simply at the mercy of corrupt elites, politicians, and administrators. And as difficult as the organization-building process is, there is no evident alternative. If these people are to gain a decent livelihood and a respected place in the community, it must come through their own efforts and organization. Try as it has, it seems to be beyond the capacity of government or foreign aid agencies to achieve this for them.

NOTES

1. With the exception of countries and capital cities all names of individuals and places mentioned in this study have been fictionalized. Any similarities to names of actual persons and places are coincidential.

2. We refer to "power" elites rather than simply elites because all members of the economic elite of the village are not members of this corrupt network. Many are indeed honest and civic minded individuals who themselves are subject to exploitation by the "net."

3. The union is the lowest political level of government and is comprised of several villages. The thana (recently named Upazilla), comprised of several unions, is the lowest administrative level of government.

4. The following report is written in the present tense to retain its sense of immediacy. The study [except for the update provided at the end] was, however, completed by the end of 1979 and the statements made apply to that point in time.

5. Titles are sometimes appended to the name in Bangladesh according to one's occupation. "Master" indicates a teacher. "Company" designates a businessman. "Member" is a member of the Union Council. "Chairman" is the Chairman of the Union Council—locally a powerful position. Member and Chairman may be prefaced by "ex-" indicating they no longer hold the position.

6. This involves collection of a particular type of leaf from the forest which is used in making the local cigarettes. Marketing of these leaves is controlled by a large, government licensed monopoly through local agents such as Huda Master.

7. Some so called "freedom fighters" were little more than thugs who took advantage of the war to rob and pillage their neighbors in the name of a patriotic cause.

8. Members of the local militia who fought with the Bangladesh army in the Liberation War with Pakistan.

9. This is the village court which is formed by respected local residents to resolve a dispute. All the villagers gather to observe the proceedings.

10. They concluded that the assassination was arranged by Salehuddin, the brother of Kamal, and carried out by members of the Kader Bahini, some of whom were friends of Salehuddin.

11. A paisa is one-hundredth of a taka.

12. One maund = 40 seers. One seer = approximately one kilogram.

PART IV: INTRODUCTION

INTERVENTIONS TO EMPOWER

David C. Korten

Power, in both its generative and its distributive dimensions, is possibly the most important and the most neglected issue in rural development interventions.[1] Powerlessness and poverty are in many instances almost synonymous. The poor lack opportunities for choice, control over resources, and the opportunity to influence their future, all of which represent aspects of power. They may lack effective means of protecting even their most meager of possessions from expropriation by exploitative elites as well. And the power resources of government, which should be providing the umbrella of protection for the poor and powerless, are all too easily expropriated by ruthless elements and turned into intruments of exploitation, as demonstrated in Chapter eleven[2]

Interventions that successfully broaden the base of power in rural communities are neither new nor rare, but they are more commonly associated with private than with public development initiatives. Past efforts have contributed a body of relevant knowledge and method. While there is no intent here to provide a practioner's handbook to empowerment interventions, the contributions to Part IV are intended to provide a useful perspective on approaches and issues.

Chapter twelve by David Drucker deals with the relationship between health workers and rural communities, showing how deeply embedded professional norms of the "helping" professions place clients in a dependency situation. Drucker provides a range of suggestions, illustrated by his own rich Asian experience, for redefining the roles of health professionals and villagers in ways that simultaneously empower the community and increase the effectiveness of the professional. He also highlights the potential of children as an underutilized village development resource.

In Chapter thirteen, James Terrant and Hasan Poerbo report on a program designed to strengthen the capacity of poor upland village communities to manage their land and water resources for both productivity and sustainability. Concentrating on the generative dimensions of power, the intervention worked to strengthen village capacities to identify, test, adapt, and share a variety of improved technologies. By working with existing village structures and natural social dynamics, the intervention stimulated spontaneous replication processes which rapidly spread from one village to another. Yet the intervention had to come to terms with the distributive dimension of power as well, working quietly to change the power balance within the village structure by beginning organizing activities at the lowest levels of village society and gradually working upward to influence the formal village governance structures. This project, carried out by the Institute of Environmental Studies of the Institute of Technology at Bandung directed by Poerbo, has attracted nationwide attention in Indonesia, especially among local government officials and the private voluntary development community.

A related case, presented in Chapter fourteen by V. D. Deshpande, S. P. Salunke, and David C. Korten, comes from the work of a private voluntary deveopment agency in India that organizes the poor in a drought prone area to manage water as a scarce and valuable common property resource. The scheme concentrates on the development of community norms and enforcement mechanisms directed to the sharing of water among the largest possible number of users and thereby increasing the returns from available water to the entire community. Both the generative and the distributive dimensions of empowerment are much in evidence, particularly as the water-user groups confront government policies that are biased toward concentrating the benefits of the available water among a few farmers. Useful data on the economics of water use and distribution are included.

Continuing with the theme of irrigation in South Asia, Chapter fifteen by Norman Uphoff presents a case from Sri Lanka, in which he was a key actor, of a foreign donor project, implemented through public agencies which played a direct and effective role in empowering communities for improved resource management.[3] The project fielded institutional organizers who prepared to assume important roles in the rehabilitation and management of one of Sri Lanka's largest irrigation schemes—resulting in substantial and well-documented improvements in water management. Equally significant, officials who were originally resistant to the organizing activities, perhaps fearing that increasing the power of the farmers would reduce their own authority and status, became enthusiastic upon finding that empowered water users made them more effective in the performance of their own duties and more respected by the community. The case provides important data challenging the assumption of some theorists that individuals will not voluntarily limit their own use of a resource in the interest of the common good if the group is large and if their access is not externally restricted.[4]

NOTES

1. See the Introduction to this volume for a discussion of the generative and distributive dimensions of power and their relevance to community management interventions.

2. For further treatment of these issues see Milton Easman and Norman T. Uphoff, *Local Organizations: Intermediaries in Rural Development* (Ithaca: Cornell University Press, 1984); Coralie Bryant and Louise G. White, *Managing Rural Development with Small Farmer Participation* (West Hartford: Kumarian Press, 1984); Bruce F. Johnston and William C. Clark, *Redesigning Rural Development: A Strategic Perspective* (Baltimore: The Johns Hopkins University Press, 1982), Chapter 5; and Guy Gran, *Development by People: Citizen Construction of A Just World* (New York: Praeger, 1983).

3. Such cases involving foreign donors and public agencies unfortunately are relatively rare. In this instance it must be noted that the catalytic role [see Chapter 22]. which proved critical to the project's success, was played by Cornell University, which is an autonomous, semi-private nonprofit institution.

4. For critical reviews of the theoretical argument that a rational man will not engage in cooperative behavior, and statements of evidence confirming Uphoff's observation see Elinor Ostrom, "The Origins of Institutions for Collective Action in Common-Pool Resource Situations," prepared September 4, 1985 for presentation at the Panel on Common Property Resource Management, Board on Science and Technology for International Development, National Academy of Sciences/National Research Council; and William Erickson-Blomquist and Elinor Ostrom, "Institutional Capacity and the Resolution of a Commons Dilemma" March 5, 1984. Both papers are available from Elinor Ostrom, Workshop in Political Theory and Policy Analysis, Indiana University, 513 North Park, Bloomington, IN 47405. Also see Robert Wade, *Peasants and Public Choice: Group Action in Irrigated Open-Field Villages of South India* (Cambridge University Press), forthcoming.

CHAPTER TWELVE

Ask a Silly Question, Get a Silly Answer—Community Participation and the Demystification of Health Care[1]

David Drucker

When I was a very small boy, I lived in a slum area of London. A charitable organization provided poor children with a two-week respite in the fresh air away from the squalid streets of the city, and away I went to the seashore. The flat open green country was rimmed with sand dunes and we ran through the salt-damp defiles and sweet-smelling grasses to the long isolated beach. Barefoot in the loose sand I trod upon a half-hidden broken bottle, and the towel hastily wrapped around my damaged foot was soon soggy with blood. My small companions went to get help and returned with a distinguished-looking gentlemen, whom, I discovered later, they had found at the famous golf course nearby.

He hauled me upon his shoulders and set off along a path towards the town, the red towel flapping like a danger signal. He asked me my name and whether I knew the names of the wild flowers in the hedgerows, which I did not, and then proceeded to tell me; "ragwort" still sticks in my mind. He then asked: "What kind of car would you like to take you to the doctor?"

My experience of cars was very limited. There had been a taxi-cab driven by my cousin, and a commercial traveller uncle had also given me rides as a special treat in his 1930 Morris. However, despite my not really caring about cars, especially at that moment with my crimson swathed foot painfully throbbing, having been asked I had no hesitation in replying to my benefactor: "I would like a Rolls Royce." The odd part of this story is that my demand was precisely matched by the actual arrival of a Rolls Royce and chauffeur, and for some days after I had been stitched and bandaged, the Rolls would call for me and I was driven in splendor on a daily tour of the countryside with my leg propped up on a cushion.

Some time later newspaper men came, took my picture, and there was a long story of how the Chancellor of the Exchequer (no less), despite wrestling with tough budgetary matters in times of depression, had had time to perform an act of kindness for a ragged child in need. The journalists were particularly interested in why I had requested a Rolls Royce. I did not say so then, but one of the morals of this story is: Ask a silly question—get a silly answer!

The question of the kind of car was unexpected, strange even exotic. It was beyond expectations or need—in fact, *silly*. However, he having raised the possibility of unreality, why not the best that unreality could provide? Extravagance seemed called for in such an expansive redefining of purpose. He wanted to be generous and grand; why not help him, and put him to the test—the test of credibility.

Now almost fifty years later, I find myself wandering back to that early notoriety as I sit at international meetings and listen to what is being said about "community participation" and "primary health care," and hear sceptics reiterate the wisdom that if you ask village people what they want, they will answer: "A ten-story, fully equipped hospital." It is their version of my Rolls Royce and is supposed to illustrate how expectation of realistic participation by the community in planning projects is unrealizable.

PARTICIPATION AS PARTNERSHIP

The fact is that "participation" is fundamentally an act of partnership. Partnerships take time and effort to establish and can only succeed and continue to flourish where there is mutual trust. Trust is not too easy to come by; it has to be solicited, worked for, have exaggerated demands made upon it at first—thus testing its reality and solidarity—and it must be gradually earned and given life.

Ever since nomadic man discovered the connection between sowing and reaping and the advantages of fixed settlements, he has had to defend himself from predators. There is little experience among those engaged in agriculture of anyone coming from outside other than to further their own interests, to exploit and often to plunder. Rural people know this in their very bones. And the assurances of those of us who speak the words of development and control or represent the organizations of modern nation-states have rarely been followed by sustained action to convince rural communities that anything has yet, or will, change in this respect.

Of course "my" Chancellor of the Exchequer was not acting in any official capacity; he was a kindly, helpful adult, and was perceived as such at that moment. Although used to esteem and authority and relaxing at his club away from his cares of office, he was responding to the human urgency of the voices seeking help. He saw the task at hand clearly, as did I, the injured child. He conveyed his sense of what needed to be done; his calm, his smell which was good and clean, and the strength felt in the contact with his body were reassuring to his partner in this circumscribed drama. His question about the flowers opened up some distance between us; flowers for slum-dwellers were of little consequence (lilies for funerals, carnations in bottonholes for weddings) but one condescendingly forgave him. He was doing his best to be friendly and to distract attention from the bloody towel. His back was carrying me loftily in the right direction for both our purposes; a barrow from the local market would have ben perfectly acceptable if it had been far to go and he had grown tired.

It seems to me in a similar way that we who aim to promote development, although with the best intentions, sometimes fail to make real contact with those to be developed and create donor-dependency relationships. True partnership is what is required, and this demands new directions, new skills, new activities and new roles if the age-old fixed expectations and patterns of interlocking behavior are not to frustrate the new aspirations of development. Let me give a simple example of what is involved in practical terms.

EXPERTS AND EXPERTS

While in Burma with UNICEF to set up a new training institute, I had occasion to travel with a local medical officer on his visit to a rural community.

> Our Jeep bumps to a stop in a fairly isolated village. While I am talking to the village midwife, three or four hundred children, some carrying smaller ones, come to stare at me, the foreigner. I notice the doctor going among the children looking at their arms. I ask him what he is doing and he tells me that he is taking this opportunity to check the immunization status of the children by looking for scars on their arms. "How long will it take you?," I ask. "Perhaps 45 minutes", he says, "but it is worth taking the time since we are here."
> I persuade him to ask the children themselves each to look at the child next to him, and if there is no scar to hold up the arm. Two false starts, while the explanation is clarified and soon 450 children perhaps, with a buzz of curiosity and excitement inspect each other. I say to the doctor: "From the beginning to end the activity took 4 minutes, and now we have the 40 minutes saved to tell why we are looking, why it is important, and anything else that you think needs to be done." I add: "None of these children have had any special education or spent seven years at medical school. Yet they are the experts—experts at standing next to other children and inspecting their arms."

This is the right kind of partnership—each bringing his own expertise, in this case the lay child and the medical man, focused on a simple activity and purpose, but of real significance. What has happened is that the doctor has redefined both his own role and that of the children. He has acted differently from what is familiar and expected in the doctor/patient relationship and the children have reciprocally acted differently also. Of particular interest here is the demonstration of the expertise of children. Indeed, children constitute substantially untapped development resource. They are not usually recognized as manpower, even though a recent report states that in South Asia alone, 29 million children are gainfully employed, by ILO standards. Another fact is that children know. They know an enormous amount, and adults have failed to gather and put to use the very careful research undertaken, quite voluntarily and without guidance, by children using guidance, by children using their inherent sense of curiosity.

MORE CHILD EXPERTISE—SURVEILLANCE

With time I came to know more of child expertise during my stay in Burma. Perhaps you are familiar with the easily made tapes in three colors for measuring the mid-arm circumference of one-to-five year old children. The gradations give a quick guide to the nutritional status of children (malnutrition, not just from lack of food but more commonly from endemic parasites and poor feeding habits). A child with a large mid-arm measurement (green) is fine, one with a middle measurement (yellow) is at risk, and one with a small measurement (red) is in very poor condition. I carried a bundle of these tapes in my pocket whenever I visited a village.

> In the tea-house children come to stare at the stranger. I take out a tape and play with it for a while. As the children become curious with my "toy," I beckon to the boldest, measure his arm and show him how to do it. I suggest a small prize for any "yellow" children he can bring me, and something a little more special for a "red." Other children are eager to join in the game, and scattered through the village. One humorist wants to measure me—and needs two tapes together. We all laugh as I pat my belly and emphasize how big and fat I am, but we agree that as I am older than five, perhaps it doesn't really count.

The fact is that in rural areas, especially where the village is scattered, the experts in knowing where all the under-fives are to be found are the children. They could be important in ensuring coverage for the care of infants, and also, for example, in locating the mothers who might be most promising for family planning, etc. With a little organization, preferably as a game, children (and there are many of them) can be mobilized to undertake all kinds of development tasks, including these types of surveillance. What is more, they can do it at a fraction of the time and expense that any health personnel could manage.

CONTROL IS NOT PARTNERSHIP

Fascinatingly enough, I have found that health workers find it extremely difficult to initiate such approaches and clearly seem to be threatened by giving up their control. Over and over again I see trained personnel taking away the tapes from the children and insisting upon doing the measuring themselves—to insure that it is done "properly." The same holds true for weighing, height-taking and so on, which with a little guidance (health education?) mothers could organize and do for themselves. This would also avoid the all too common experience of health workers prying reluctant, sometimes screaming babies from their mothers arms so that the nurse can take charge of the situation. Finally the nurse enters the result on what to the mother and the village must seem like a secret and mysterious document which emphasizes the nurse's power (the health chart).

That the community should accept this dependent and passive role and be patient in the face of health expertise seems almost to be embedded in the medical ethic. Perhaps it is reassuring to the health worker to feel he or she is in control, but accepting a more active role for the community is likely to produce better results. It is of utmost importance to recognize that this controlling approach to the health worker/patient relationship is very much counter to the principles of community development and to the need for community self-determination, where active initiatives and perhaps a degree of impatience on the part of the community are more appropriate.

EXPERTS—IN WALKING

Another example from my Burma experience is that of the immunization workers who, I discovered, carry a forty-eight hour supply of vaccines in vacuum flasks, and spend a very large proportion of their time walking to and from remote villages to a central cold-chain pick-up point in the area. The community could easily be organized so that it is responsible for assigning a reliable person to do the walking to the market town where the cold chain is situated. Shopping and the collection of the vaccine flask could be combined and would only need to be done perhaps once in three months. The trained health worker would then merely need to travel straight from village to village instead of walking repeatedly to the town, and would be assured of a fresh vaccine supply relayed to each village along his or her way.

It might also happen that the community, having understood (health education?) the need for taking such responsibility, would make sure that its members were assembled for vaccination, as one of their own people had travelled a long way on their behalf. At present the health worker's

scheduled arrival time is poorly adhered to and many workers arrive when
convenient mainly to themselves; if the communities are eager for vaccination or other help, the implication is that they had better quickly pass
the word around that the worker has come and they must hustle before
he/she takes off again. There seems to be a real resistance by health workers
to solicit more effective partnerships with the community. This seems to
have roots in the health worker's reluctance to place control (and possibly
justifiable grounds for recrimination) in the hands of the community,
which the community might exercise if the worker did not fulfill his/her
part of the bargain by actually turning up as agreed.

Once one begins to look for these invidious types of behavior, which
will certainly undermine all attempts to promote participation, one will
find them everywhere. Controlling behavior by professionals is almost a
basic element in our present social structure. Although the health field
provides telling examples, the problem is widespread.

PROFESSIONALS LOCKED INTO THEIR "CULTURE"

Unfortunately most of our training programs and certainly our higher
level educational institutions are grounded in urban elitist traditions. For
example, in some attempts to provide rural training for medical students,
the fact is that neither the doctors under training nor the centers in which
the training takes place seem to have accommodated their knowledge or
their "style" (bedside or city clinic manner) in any way to the conditions
of village life. The whole atmosphere is usually strikingly doctor-centered
rather than patient-centered, let alone community-centered. In a very compelling sense, the "institutional" ambience and the relationships set up
in the centers are indistinguishable from those in the crowded clinics in
towns. The villagers can either take it or leave it. Many studies tell us that
a large proportion leave it and the main reason is the "uncordial behavior
of the staff."

In the context of primary health care, with its accent on health rather
than disease, on the unreached rural masses rather than the urban elites,
and on active community participation rather than passive patient acceptance, the time has come for restructuring our institutions and the style
and relationship they impose upon the medical professional and those
whom he serves. Much exploration is called for if this is to be achieved.

TURNING AROUND TO FACE THE COMMUNITY

One approach from the right direction was demonstrated by a medical
team I worked with in Karnatika State in India led by a quite remarkable
Indian doctor.

> The medical team unrolled a mat on the steps of a temple in view of the
> whole community; the doctors and health workers literally turned around from

facing the patient to facing the community. Such an unusual event brings about a swift assemblage of village people. Instead of hiding from the crowd in his own sheltered space to do his secretive work, the doctor gives a public performance; and the crowd becomes the prime target for the health team. The doctor acts as a group leader, encouraging the "audience" to become participatory members in a joint activity.

Patients (especially those suffering from common ailments such as scabies, wounds, diarrhea, etc.) are drawn from the audience and the professional examines the patient in full view, explaining to the audience as he does so, in very simple and appropriate language, what is being done and what the signs and symptoms are. The questions to the patient and his replies, along with the whole procedure, are conducted in the nature of a public case-conference discussion, in terminology that the villagers are helped to understand. A simple explanation of the problem is given, followed by appropriate information ragarding how such conditions come about and what action can be taken to prevent or minimize them. The treatment and management of the condition is carefully explained. The preventive aspects are emphasized. The audience is then asked if there are others among them who have similar complaints. The professional briefly examines them and where there is some doubt, separates them for more extensive examination, He puts in a group all the patients who, he confirms, have correctly identified themselves as having problems similar to those of the demonstrated case.[2]

As small groups are formed this way, the health messages and instructions are reinforced by another member of the team. Treatment is provided to the entire group, and management regimes such as cleaning of wounds, boiling of water, preparation of dressings, etc. are viewed in detail with both the patient and their accompanying family members, with demonstration as appropriate. Questions are invited and answered.

EMERGENCE AND TRAINING OF COMMUNITY HEALTH WORKERS

In another site I saw how readily the approach lends itself to the recruitment and training of village health workers. For example volunteers can be called upon from each group to act as permanent focal points in the community for specific symptoms and conditions. To begin with, only simple single tasks should be undertaken by those wishing to volunteer.

"Alright, it is agreed that you become the Scabies lady. We will train you. Here is the lotion your village will need. Let's review and write down all the things you have to do. (The writing down constitutes a "How to deal with Scabies" guide). Everyone must hear that you can help when this happens . . . We will teach you to look out for conditions which can be mistaken for scabies and for which different help should be sought . . ."etc.

The same is done for diarrhea, with an explanation of the serious threat which is posed by dehydration. "So you will be the diarrhea worker? Everyone must know that you can help when this problem occurs. We will train you. This is what you must look for . . . what you must do . . . here are your 'tools' and medicines . . . Let's review and write down" ("How to deal with Diarrhea" guide).

In this way the villagers saw exactly how their own village-based worker had become an obvious asset. They saw the nature and content of the training so that they too understood it and could support the volunteer and minimize the mystery and superiority arising from it (good health education).

Too many programs introduce primary health care as an organizational activity and neglect the element of village people being actively introduced to an understanding of the ways and wherefores of primary health care and the value of village health workers. Selection of workers is commonly precipitous and somewhat arbitrary and is influenced by who is well connected rather than by who connects well.

In one project in India with which I am familiar, a period of nine months passed with profit before the need and value of a primary health care worker was understood and a worker was satisfactorily selected. The pressure to fill training places at a time determined by remote administrative convenience rather than by a community's readiness is to be avoided. Training of such workers should be on an item-by-item basis thus meeting a need clearly recognized by the community, and enabling the worker to demonstrate his utility and skill before responsibilities are increasingly piled upon him. Often community health workers are trained extensively in a bit of everything at once. Then the training investment becomes a heavy loss if he drops out. His training and responsibilities should be cumulative.

I SPY GAMES—VILLAGE SURVEYS

I find myself, after much experience of "top-down" planning, emphatically insisting on demystification and claiming that "planning is child's play."

It once occurred to me that it might be possible to involve children in preliminary health inspection work. This might be managed in the form of "I Spy" games.[3] One such game, for example, might call on the children to look for every conceivable water source in the surrounding area. The children could work in pairs or teams, leaving some kind of marker or agreed "secret sign" at each source discovered so that the same source is not claimed more than once by any "player," and so that a proper claim is made of each "find" and can be judged to belong to the first finder. Some kind of points system and reward for the most points could be devised. All the information from this I Spy game would then be brought together and displayed on the largest possible area on which an outline map of the village or community can be marked out—the school playground, a sportsfield, a market square, the side of a house. The map could be outlined with chalk, stones, or bamboo, or scraped on the dry earth. The children could make models with mud, coconut shells, cardboard, anything. Then with sections of the map allocated to pairs of children, they would fill in the map, marking all the water sources.

A village leader, a health worker, or a youth group might organize the whole game. Better still, an enterprising schoolteacher might use a water I Spy game to teach and link many aspects of the curriculum, preferably as a practical activity illustrating what the school is supposed to be teaching anyway—map making, charts, graphs, handicrafts, hygiene, social studies, essay writing—or as a valuable learning project in its own right.

Children could be asked to write on "Twenty-four hours of water use in my family" describing where the water comes from, how it is collected and stored, how much is used for what, and something about the seasonal variations. They could be set the task of producing a wall mural (children paired, each pair taking a small section of the wall) illustrating water use in the village. All of this clearly has direct relevance to the school curriculum.

From this basic game, we might move on to an I Spy "Sanitary Inspector" game. Teams would again be formed and rewards given, this time to the team that identifies from all the sources the most water risk danger situations: cattle drinking, bathing, clothes washing, open wells, defecation (having been told all about these beforehand). They would place a sign to mark the danger and to claim the site for their team. The sign could be semi-permanent so as to mark the site until the risk was eradicated.

Now the risk would be added (big red spots) to the sources plotted on the huge map. These water games might be linked appropriately to local water festivals such as Holi, Mahathingyan, and so on. When the whole layout is satisfactorily completed, the village leaders and the whole village should be invited to attend a ceremonial inspection of the map. The whole thing would be explained (perhaps by the children themselves) and a full presentation made on "Our Village Water Conditions and What Might be Done for a Clean Village Water Supply."

Variations can be prepared or experimented with in relation to malaria, nutrition (what is in the market week by week and is cheapest), agriculture, irrigation, forestry, husbandry, transportation, marketing, and so on.

Of course, these games and the whole procedure expect much of the schoolteacher or whoever, and might require a campaign to back them up, with an orientation and practice sessions, sponsored by the education, welfare, or health authorities.

What has been illustrated is a child-contribution approach to planning. However, the principle is the same even where an adult group is to take responsibility rather than the children.

The information and the community involvement and interest engendered by these "game" activities are the fertile ground upon which specifically local, tailor-made plans can be sown.

AN AID TO PLANNING WITH THE COMMUNITY

While working in Bangladesh with UNICEF I had an opportunity to witness such an application. In this case a new water supply was the focus.

At a large village gathering everyone is invited to list all the things that they foresee will need to be done. The emphasis is on activities. Bearing in mind the low level of literacy, someone is invited to do a drawing of each activity. (No great artistic skill is necessary; matchstick men and crude representations serve nicely, although it is surprising how often a village artist is discovered!) Each drawing is pinned on the wall until all the actions have been mentioned and everything seems to have been covered.

The activities are then considered in order of precedence chronologically, clustering the pictures where activities have to be undertaken simultaneously. When the sequence has been pinned around the meeting place to everyone's satisfaction, consideration is given to praticalities such as seasons, wet/dry, sowing/harvest, festivals and so on, so that agreed dates for each activity are placed above the appropriate picture.

Using this approach, without talking the language of planning, the community will have produced their own flow charts and chronological bar chart representations! How many people, what skills, tools and resources, represented under each of the drawings and at some point who exactly will be involved in each activity is worked out and added: a manpower plan!

Inadequate attention to estimating costs and accurate book-keeping has long been the curse of local development efforts and has caused the failure of many cooperatives. Thus, I was particularly interested in another device used to clarify such matters even for those poorly endowed with numeracy, as even those who have difficulty with addition and subtraction normally have skills in counting cash.

Plastic bags are placed under each activity and play-money (as in the game of Monopoly) used to count out what each activity is expected to cost. Where there is to be some revenue, from selling water or some other produce, a similar estimating and counting out is enacted and shown against costs. (Later, as money is collected or dispersed, it is moved from one plastic bag to another.) There now exists a very visible representation of the community budgeting for the project, and the whole collection of pictures and bags remains in the community publicly displayed and can be used for monitoring and further discussion as project implementation proceeds.

LINKING "PLANNING-UP" WITH "SUPPORT-DOWN"

Once the whole picture of the step-by-step development and the activities necessary at the community level has been laid out, it should then be possible and somewhat more familiar to work back up the administrative and technical agency structures and to tie into the community timetable and flow of activity the inputs and support required from outside, detail by detail. Where there are activities determined by technical and administrative imperatives that cannot neatly gear into the community pace and way of doing things, these points of discord must be given special consideration and replanned in the community. The range, content, and timing of the activities must eventually all lead to a service that is satisfactory to the community and the authorities, and from the technological point of view.

When these plans have been jointly examined and agreed upon, they should then become the basis for some kind of formal contractual agreement. In skillful hands this planning process at the community level can result in the enhancing of social cohesiveness; health and development education; and the establishment and improvement of community/government operational relationships—a critical aspect of practical nation building.

Underlying all this is the principle that services must be "made to measure" (measure up to the local community, that is) rather than being presented as a "standard uniform off the rack."

In community matters the golden rule is that the community will know best, if pains are taken to involve them in their own problem-solving processes. We must be prepared to take time and energy, and develop our skills in assisting them with gathering and considering information they can use, and in offering realistic methods for planning and harnessing their full development potential.

Inherently there must be a realistic understanding that if trust has been built, outsiders can work with communities and the communities will know what to do if the assistance given is realistic and important enough to them. The worker must function through appropriate relationships and institutional forms that stimulate and reinforce community participation step by step, action by action.

NOTES

1. David Drucker retains the copyright to this article and does not relinquish it in giving permission to publish here.

2. Of course, not all patients need to be dealt with in this way although this should be the major "visible" style of practice. It appeals to the curiosity and even to the entertainment qualities of village life and plays down the mystification and "confidentiality" of Western middle class medical ethics. Even so, in accordance with village values, one is careful to avoid public display of matters which may affect social life chances, such as acceptability in marriage, and so on. A village-oriented health worker should soon become sensitive to what these special matters are.

3. The original game goes like this: Someone says "I Spy with my little eye something beginning with . . . " A letter is shouted, and the other players have to guess what object in sight, beginning with that letter, has been selected. When a player guesses correctly it is his turn to set the game in motion again.

CHAPTER THIRTEEN

Strengthening Community–Based Technology Management Systems

James Terrant and Hasan Poerbo

In Indonesia, as in many other countries, erosion and flood control problems in river basins with high population densities have become widespread phenomena and a national concern. In part, the problem is rooted in the poverty and farming practices of the people who live in these river basins. Attempts at corrective action by government have had only marginal effect. Highly centralized in their management and heavily subsidized, they become mired in their own rigidity and are too costly for replication on a large scale.

In 1980 the Center for Environmental Studies at the Institute of Technology in Bandung (CES-ITB) undertook a participatory action research program in the uplands of the Citanduy River Basin in Ciamis District (kabupaten) of West Java, Indonesia. Through an action learning process, this program sought to develop experience with a different approach in which the people mobilize their own resources to address the problem, with government assuming the role of enabler and service provider.

THE SETTING

Of the total 446,000 hectares that comprise the Citanduy River Basin, 27 percent are classified as uplands devoted to small farmer cultivation. The population density of 654 persons per square kilometer is quite high by world standards, especially for uplands areas. The average size of agricultural land holdings is 0.5 hectares per household. There is also a sizeable landless population.[1]

Thirteen percent of the land area in the basin is classified as "critical land," which means that it is too degraded to sustain a permanent staple agricultural crop, though in fact some of these lands are still cultivated—providing at best only a marginal return. Fortunately the condition of these lands is usually reversible through proper soil and water management practices.

The Indonesian Government has been aware of the need for improved watershed management for some time, leading in 1980 to the USAID-funded Citanduy II Project, which sought to develop the capacity of local and regional governments working collaboratively with the Ministry of Agriculture to implement a program of watershed improvement. This program provided substantial subsidies to groups of farmers to motivate them to establish ten hectare terraced demonstration plots on which an approved uplands farming system technology package was applied. Working out of the demonstration plots, extension agents encouraged farmers in an expansion area around the site to adopt the same practices, offering them somewhat smaller subsidies as an incentive.

At roughly the same time as Citanduy II was being initiated, the newly formed CES-ITB was asked by the Ministry of Population and Environment to undertake a policy review of the Government's upland development effort. The center's study concluded that existing government programs suffered from the fact that programs were being planned and implemented without an adequate knowledge of traditional attitudes and farming practices. These programs also used inappropriate approaches and incentives in their attempts to induce farmers to change their existing practices, with the result that they often reverted back to their old practices as soon as the subsidies were no longer available. Members of the center felt that the best way to substantiate their findings would be to demonstrate the validity of an alternative approach.

THE EXPERIMENTAL PROGRAM

The experimental program was initiated in two sites in late 1980: Sagalaherang Village, with a population of some 4,000 persons; and Cigaru Hamlet, with a population of about 700.[2] Both sites were characterized by a substantial independence of individual households in decision-making and income-generating activities. Participation in joint decision making and cooperative activities was limited at both hamlet and village levels.[3]

Cigaru, though socially relatively more homogeneous, was much the poorer of the two sites. A sizable portion of its male labor force spent substantial time away from the community in search of income-earning opportunities. This gave them less time for activities such as terracing and irrigation development to improve the productivity of their lands. Available data indicated that crop yields were declining in the late 1970's and early 1980, especially in Cigaru.

Sagalaherang was more socially stratified. A relatively small number of larger landowners had become heavily involved in cash crops, especially tree crop agriculture. A larger number of middle-level farmers marketed some surpluses from their production. The largest group of households consisted of small subsistence farmers. The first two groups dominated village decision making especially on economic matters. The third group had little access to this process.

Preparatory Activities

The first year of the program was devoted to the collection of baseline data and the formation of a program strategy, followed by initial field motivation and organizing efforts. A variety of techniques were used to engage the villagers in a critical assessment of their reality and of the measures they might take to improve their situation. These included brainstorming, directed discussion of specific community problems, simple simulations, and the reading and discussion of passages from the Qur'an. Considerable attention was given to "critical introspection" aimed at identifying the major attitudinal and organizational barriers confronting community-wide development. Villagers were helped to look at problems logically and to examine their systematic causes. This was intended to be a process of self-education and attitudinal change as well as a stimulus to organized action.

As the program progressed, staff came to recognize that women were active members of the agricultural labor force in both settings. Though they played only a minor role in public functions, in the household they were equal partners with their husbands in decision making. Consequently attention was given to involving them more actively in the discussions and simulations. This led to a number of women's activities centered on intensification of home gardens, animal husbandry, child and health care, housing improvement, etc.

Reactions to the program were significantly different in Sagalaherang and Cigaru. In Sagalaherang, the point of entry had been through the village head and his assistants. It was a new village, recently created through the division of another village that had grown too large in population for efficient village administration. Here the village head insisted that the CES-ITB work with and through the formal village government rather than calling mass meeting for discussion and informal education as was done in Cigaru. Yet the village head and the official governing council of the village made little effort to inform or involve other village residents in the initial motivation, planning, and organizing efforts. This seriously weakened the program from the start, a problem that was never overcome and was reflected in the limited results achieved there.

By contrast the hamlet chief in Cigaru was open-minded and himself a small farmer. He was also the village dresser, informal veterinarian, and birth attendant[4] who was genuinely respected and regularly consulted for guidance by the villagers. He facilitated the broad participation of the hamlet residents in the program and was active in the formation of the subsequent work groups. Consequently it was possible in Cigaru to develop a broad organizational base from which a strong, community-base development program emerged.

Developing an Action Program

In May 1981 residents of both communities were asked to come up with a list of priorities for an action program. In Cigaru they listed: 1) an improved road, electricity, potable water supply, and improved seeds and agricultural inputs. In Sagalaherang they listed: 1) improvement of the village council, better seeds and agricultural inputs, electricity, and improved village market facilities. The choice of activities such as roads and market assumed a significant marketable agricultural surplus that did not yet exist in Cigaru and, in the case of electricity, a level of income and management capability far beyond their actual situation. The need for improvements in land and water management as a basis for other economic development efforts was not mentioned. These issues were explored with the residents in mass meetings. Then project staff invited the residents to visit a nearby experimental project site at Panawangan that demonstrated terracing and cropping system improvements. The result was a decision to start with a simple program of bench terracing and improvements in water distribution and drainage, along with experimentation with dry season planting of various legumes and other vegetables.

In both communities, bench terracing and integrated farming techniques were demonstrated on a plot of 0.5 hectare—the size of the typical small farm plot—donated by the communities. Working voluntarily on the demonstration plot, farmers learned the terracing techniques, which were later applied to their own lands.

To carry out the arduous terracing their own fields, the Cigaru farmers formed themselves into *kelompok hamparan* (coverage groups). Generally such a group was comprised of farmers who tilled adjoining plots in single mini-watershed area. Their activities were initially coordinated through meetings of the *rembug desa*, the traditional mass meetings held to coordinate village matters. Generally the CES-ITB team joined in these events.

Similar groups were formed in Sagalaherang, but it became evident that the program was being implemented mainly by the larger elite farmers, who dominated village decision making, only on their own lands and through the use of hired laborers to do the terracing—and without explaining its purpose. Only a relatively small area was improved. The CES-ITB field team eventually decided to abandon their activities in Sagalaherang.

Further Evolution of Village Structures in Cigaru

With time and experience, the effort in Cigaru continued to evolve, and farmers experimented with different organizational structures as they became aware of the need for internal coordination of their efforts. As household agricultural plots tended to be both small and widely scattered due to inheritance patterns and new purchases of land, some farmers found that they belonged to more than one *kelompok hamparan*. This resulted in an uneven distribution of obligations for labor sharing.

This problem led them to form what they called *kelompok domisili* (domicile groups) based on neighborhood blocks of approximately twenty-five to thirty-five households each. The total area of terraced farmland increased by 41 percent over the original plan as a result of the improved division of labor. The kelompok domisili became the locus for further efforts to improve local resource management and integrate new technologies into community and household production systems. These groups also undertook a vide variety of new initiatives including housing rehabilitation, resettlement of homes on steep, erosion-prone slopes, animal husbandry, intensification of home gardens, home processing and cottage industries, cooperative child care, introduction of energy-saving stoves, etc. They became particularly important in the village communication process, serving as communication nodes for discussion of community issues and the sharing of ideas and technologies.

During the first year, CES-ITB also encouraged the development of functional groups, e.g., dry-land farmers' groups, irrigation-user groups, sheep-pen groups, etc. The domicile groups linked the various functional groups to communities and became part of the social fabric of the village.

At one point the community needed to acquire a sprayer to combat a blight through application of pesticides. The CES-ITB field team used the opportunity to call a meeting between the dry-land farmer groups to buy a sprayer that would be shared among them. This led to the establishment of the *kelompok usaha bersama ekonomi* or KUBE, a hamlet-level cooperative organization. Once formed, this group assumed a growing range of functions that strengthened the base-level organizations and helped link them into the larger governmental and market structures while protecting members from exploitation from other political and economic power holders including the official village council, larger commercial farmers, traders, and money lenders. Specific function of the KUBE included the following:

1. Providing a forum within which members coordinated their cropping systems to facilitate collective purchase and distribution of agricultural inputs such as seeds, fertilizers, and insecticides, as well as the cooperative marketing of their increased agricultural produce.

2. Providing a management body for pre- and post-agricultural processing and support activities such as compost making, animal husbandry, seed nurseries, and processing and storage facilities.

3. Operating a savings and loan association for the community, thus generating relatively small amounts of capital for individual needs such as home construction and improvement and agricultural inputs, as well as for community undertakings.

Legally cooperatives can only exist at village level and above in Indonesia in the form of the Government-sponsored KUD (Village Unit Cooperative). This arrangement has several limitations. First, as a village level organization, it is often physically distant from individual hamlets so that the frequency of its use is limited. Moreover, formal membership in the KUD is frequently limited to farmers with relatively large land holdings or those participating in a government agricultural program and more specifically the government's rice production program. KUD participation by farmers with half a hectare or less is rare. Second, its function is limited largely to distributing inputs and marketing crops, thus preventing it from becoming a more integral part of the wider village economy. Third, as a government-sponsored institution, it is governed by the village elite acting partly on the basis of directives coming from district and subdistrict levels of government. And, as is true in much of Asia, there is a widespread distrust of government-sponsored cooperatives because of the past history of mismanagement.

In all these respects, the structure and the function of the KUD generally reflect the wider problem of limited participation by the weaker members of the community, especially those in upland, rural settlements. The KUBE provided the basis for an alternative structure that may ultimately transform and strengthen the KUD. It is an intermediate cooperative organization which itself is a direct outgrowth of the smaller functional organizations and domicile groups whose activities created a demand for its creation. Thus, it has a strong base in activities specifically geared to the interests of, and controlled by, the formerly weak members of the community. The resulting structure might be represented as shown in Figure 13-1

By this time the whole hamlet had become structurally transformed, becoming a kind of a "development module" available for replication by other hamlets.

Figure 13-1
Structure of the Cigaru Model

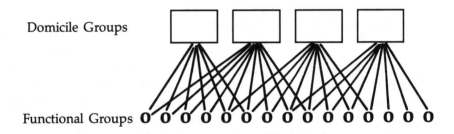

EXPANSION TO OTHER HAMLETS

The program gained considerable visibility and stature within the area as a result of a visit to Cigaru from the Minister of State for Environment in August 1981. Responding to the interest expressed by surrounding communities, the CES-ITB field team encouraged some Cigaru farmers to teach visitors from other hamlets what they had learned. They called on the Qur'anic injunction that a wise and good man shares his knowledge rather than use it only for private gain. Soon meetings were being organized in the farmers' fields attended by as many as 200 people at a time.

The villages represented at these meetings were at different levels of economic development, resource endowment, and village institutional strength. Some were lowland villages where the major economic activity was production of irrigated rice. Each brought back ideas suited for adaptation to their specific needs. Some formed irrigators' associations. Others started with land consolidation and reapportionment.

Usually there was attention to development of organizations that approximated the Cigaru structure. Indeed, in some of the villages near Cigaru, the farmers organized themselves more quickly and with a higher level of participation, both in numbers and degree of involvement, than occurred during the corresponding period in Cigaru the year before. In part, this was a result of their being able to take note of what worked and what didn't in Cigaru. At the same time, it must be recognized that Cigaru had been one of the least developed village in the region and was burdened

Figure 13-2
Map of Ciamis District

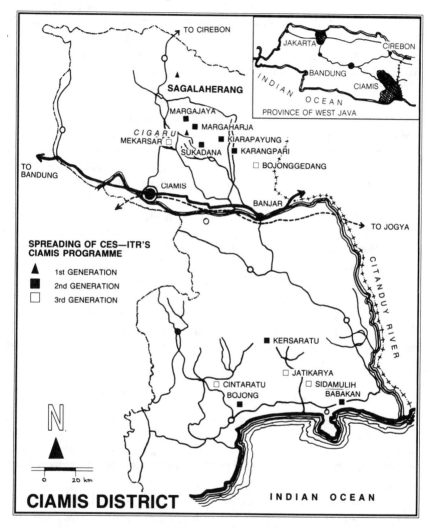

by a steady flight of its working age population, as well as a weak and remote relationship with the district level government.

By mid-1983 participation in what was now being called the "Cigaru Model" had spread to at least twenty-four hamlets of fourteen villages in Ciamis district. And some 3000 hectares had been terraced without direct subsidies.[5] (See Figure 13-2.) The cases of Sukadana and Karangpari villages illustrate the two different models of dissemination of the Cigaru Model.

Sukadana is representative of "second generation villages" in which the CES-ITB took the initiative in inviting village leaders to visit Cigaru and later assisted them in implementing the program in their own villages, with some of the best group leaders from Cigaru acting as "instructors." Generally the CES-ITB team was called in only when there was a question that the farmer "instructors" from Cigaru were not able to explain, and Sukadana's leaders came to the team asking for advice. Thus, the CES-ITB presence was much less than it had been in Cigaru itself.

Karangpari represented a "third generation village" in which the transfer was entirely spontaneous. The leader of a sub-hamlet in Karangpari heard about Cigaru's experience and went to have a look. He came back from Cigaru convinced that this sub-hamlet could replicate, and perhaps even improve on, what Cigaru had accomplished. He invited all of the households in the sub-hamlet to organize a "picnic" to Cigaru and have a discussion with the Cigaru community. Within three months his sub-hamlet had implemented all they had learned and more becoming in turn a model for the other sub-hamlets in Karangpari. Within a year the entire village had adopted the Cigaru model, with minimal assistance from CES-ITB.

In addition to the twenty-four hamlets specifically identified earlier by CES-ITB as having adopted the Cigaru Model, there were others which built on the experience of the second and third generation villages which the CES-ITB did not monitor. As of early 1986 CES-ITB estimated that the model had been adopted by some forty to fifty hamlets in twenty-six villages.

CREATING AN AREA-ORIENTED DEVELOPMENT FOUNDATION

By mid-1982 the Ciamis Program had become so complex and had been extended to so many villages that CES-ITB could no longer adequately respond to the growth in technical and training needs at the level of attention required. It was evident that the participating villages would need to draw on government sources for more of their needs. In some instances this was already occuring, but in others there was need for a brokering role to help both parties learn to work together productively. There was need for an intermediary organization that would perform such a brokering role between the hamlet-level organizations and the public and private sector organizations with which they needed to establish and manage relationships.

To perform this function it was proposed to form a nonprofit, area-oriented development foundation. Among its tasks would be:

1. To act as broker/consultant to KUBEs in their negotiation with government rural banks to obtain larger agricultural and economic

development loans using a trust fund developed from the KUBE's savings and loan association as collateral.

2. To serve as a clearing house for technical assistance in addressing environmental and agro-economic problems peculiar to the upland areas of the Citanduy River Basin.

3. To provide training for community cadres (village farmers, women, and youths) to support practical application of techniques of integrated rural environmental development within their own communities and to serve as trainer/disseminators for other communities.

4. To train and up-grade extension officers from agriculture and other ministries in the motivational and organizational techniques involved in the Cigaru Model.

5. To monitor and evaluate progress toward integrated rural environmental development in Ciamis district and identify key constraints.

In 1985 with the encouragement of the Ciamis District Head who had been a constant supporter of the Ciamis Program, the *Yayasan Bina Lingkungan Hidup* (YBLH, Foundation for the Advancement of the Environment) was established in the Ciamis township. The CES-ITB field team formed the core staff of the new foundation. Financed by a small grant from the Canadian University Service Organization (CUSO), the *Lembaga Studi Pembangunan* (LSP, Institute for Development Studies), a national nongovernmental organization, assumed many of the technical support functions previously provided to the team by the CES-ITB.

The Chairman of the YBLH also served as Chairman of a local Cooperative High School Foundation (SMAK), which it was intended would train young people from the villages for managerial responsibilities in the KUBE's after their graduation.

LESSONS AND FUTURE DIRECTIONS

The foundation of the success of the Ciamis Program was established by inducing one hamlet, Cigaru, to come to grips with the need to improve the management of its land and water resource base, creating grassroots organizational structures compatible with the traditions and skills of its people, and incrementally building up their capacity to confront more and more complex problems. It was perhaps fortunate that this occurred in one of the most backward communities in the immediate area. This made Cigaru's success all the more impressive for the surrounding communities and left them confident that if Cigaru could do it, so could they—perhaps even better.

From there the dissemination was lateral, from hamlet to hamlet and farmer to farmer. Program personnel mainly facilitated this process, allowing farmers to share the hard-won lessons of their own experimentation, in addition to what they had learned from the "experts." Villagers learned about the potentials of what could be accomplished through application of their own social energy and improved management of locally available resources. They also learned the values of cooperative action. They were strengthening their own technology management sytems, by which they captured new ideas from a variety of sources, tested and adapted them to varied local conditions, and then shared them with one another.

Once sufficient KUBE's have been formed, the intention is to form them into an association that can operate as a KUBE-owned, nonbank institution linking them into the larger resources of the national banking system. Eventually this association may be integrated into the KUD system, thereby gaining a legitimacy that will facilitate access to other government programs, while the control over resources is retained by the KUBE's.

The Ciamis Program experience demonstrates that a transformation of the traditional village social fabric is possible through a bottom-up social learning process that mobilizes the social energy of the people as a critical development resource. And it makes a small contribution toward a better understanding of how this may be accomplished on a broader scale through a combination of public and private initiative. But the challenge of achieving effective vertical integration into the larger social, economic, and political structures remains. And there is a long road yet to be traveled in obtaining a general acceptance of such an approach by national policy makers and adapting it for implementation on a larger scale.

NOTES

1. USAID Indonesia, Citanduy II Project Paper, Washington, D.C., August 1980.

2. The *kampung* or hamlet is the lowest formal settlement unit in Java.

3. Judistira Carna and Ade Emka (eds.), "Studi Pengetahuan, Sikap dan Praktek Masyarakat Kampung Cigaru Dalam Program Lingkungan Pedesaan Terpadu," Bandung: PSLH-ITB, 1983.

4. This was a very unusual position for a male in Sunda culture.

5. Apart from small initial amounts of capital, seeds, fertilizers, pesticides, and equipment, which farmers repaid directly to the program or by revolving contributions to other communities, the only subsidy of the Ciamis Program was in the time of the program staff.

CHAPTER FOURTEEN

Water for People

V. D. Deshpande, S. P. Salunke, and David C. Korten

While easily taken for granted in areas where it is abundant, in areas of scarcity, as in much of India, water is rightly recognized as among the most valuable of resources, the basis of all life and productive activity. Control over water readily becomes the foundation of both economic and political power. The *Pani Panchayat* (water council) movement founded by the *Gram Gourav Pratisthan* (GGP) in Pune District of Maharashtra State in India represents an experimental people-centered effort to improve the conservation and equitable distribution of water resources in drought-prone areas.

Conditions in Maharashtra State are characteristic of those throughout much of India. Seven thousand of its villages, accounting for one third of its population and cultivatable land, have been classified as drought prone. These areas receive on the average only 250 to 500 mm of rain a year and even this is erratic; uncertain in any given year, and tends to occur as brief heavy rains during the October-November monsoons, rapidly running off in seasonal streams and rivers.[1]

ORIGINS

The origins of the GGP movement can be traced to an experience of its founder and current managing trustee, Shri V. B. Salunke, during one of the region's more severe droughts in 1972.[2] Total failure of the monsoons for two consecutive years had created a threat of famine throughout the rural areas of the state. As an emergency measure, the government drew on available food stocks to initiate a food for work program, which emphasized road construction.

Aware of the tragic consequences of the drought, Salunke and his wife, Kalpana, made a visit to several of the affected areas of Purandhar

Taluka to study the conditions for themselves. What they found grieved them deeply. Thousands of people—men, women, and children—were working in the blistering sun breaking stones by hand to produce gravel. There was no shade and supplies of potable water were meager. The grains supplied to the workers were of poor quality and provided little protein. Payment for the work hardly covered bare food subsistence. When a death occurred, the family could not afford to take even a few hours for mourning as if would mean they would not eat that day. Pregnant women worked until the hour of delivery and could afford no more than one day of rest before returning to their labor. Some with whom the Salunkes talked felt they would be better off to commit a crime and seek imprisonment. This would at least assure them two meals a day and the work would be less strenuous.

The Salunkes concluded that the relief programs were attacking the symptoms of the drought rather than the causes of rural poverty and thus were largely futile. The emphasis should be on increasing rural productivity, in particular through the improved management of water resources. So they talked to the people about what might be done. The people said they must have ways to store water. Salunke found that the potentials for impounding water for irrigation were not being adequately exploited, and where irrigation facilities had been developed, little attention was being given to equitable distribution of the water. At the same time he observed the successful efforts of farmers who were bunding their fields to reduce soil erosion, improve moisture retention, and speed the recharging of wells. In some instances these activities enabled them to produce a second crop. But such practices were known in only a few locations.

Acting on the insight of these observations, Salunke proposed to government officials that their food for work programs should concentrate on improving facilities for local soil and water management. Some officials appreciated his argument but noted that they lacked the technical personnel to do the necessary surveys and plans. So Salunke enlisted several senior students from the Engineering College of Poona to work under his direction. They produced plans worth 500,000 rupees within fifteen days.

Encouraged by this success, a bolder scheme was tested. Ten young men with limited formal education were selected from among the laborers working on a stone-breaking project and trained in project preparation. Working under Salunke's direction, within three months they produced proposals worth three million rupees. These were presented to authorities for implementation. The success of these initiatives convinced Salunke that simple private initiative could accomplish things that seemed beyond the means of government officials whose postings were too short to allow for effective action and who were intimidated by the rules and regulations within which they worked.

THE EXPERIMENT AT NAIGAON

Other experimental activities followed. Salunke had been taken with the idea of finding a tract of land in a drought prone area that could be used to test the ultimate potential of improved soil and water management practices. Such a farm would serve as an experimental and training site for the development and dissemination of tested management practices appropriate to the region.

In 1974 he acquired a lease for forty acres of barren unirrigated village common lands in Naigaon village, one of the most drought-afflicted villages in the area. The land was so poor that it was considered unsuited for cultivation. The village had been renting it out for 400 rupees per annum as grazing land to provide for maintenance of the village temple. The villagers were delighted to accept Salunke's offer of 1,200 rupees a year for a fifty year lease. The Gram Gourav Pratisthan was established in Naigaon village as a charitable trust to manage the land. Committed to learning for themselves what might be done with the resources that were locally available, Salunke moved to the village with Kalpana and their children, where they devoted themselves fully for three years to the task of developing the site into a model experimental farm.

The forty acre plot was located on a micro-watershed of about 200 total acres. A percolation tank capable of storing a million cubic feet of water was constructed on the land. The fields were contour bunded, leveled, ploughed; stones were removed and an open well was dug at the base on the downstream side of the tank. A 7.5 h.p. pump was installed and pipes were laid underground to distribution chambers. A key to the design was the theory that water collected in the tank or used in higher fields would percolate into the ground and raise the water table in lands at lower elevations. For five years alternative cropping patterns were tested, including use of improved seeds, fertilizers, and insecticides, to determine which would provide optimal production of food and income.[3]

Of the total of forty acres, twenty-four were brought under protective irrigation, six were forested, and the remaining ten were devoted to the percolation tank, well, field bunds, and other infrastructure. The local villagers paid little attention initially—convinced that these city people were engaged in a futile exercise. But gradually the results became apparent. The twenty-four acres of previously discarded land which had been brought under cultivation were producing 200 quintals of food grains, while forty acres of village lands outside the experimental area were producing barely ten quintals. Besides record food grain production, the farm generated full-time employment for fifteen people, supported fifteen animals, 4000 trees on the rocky rimland, and 2000 fruit trees along its field bunds. A three-quarter-acre plot was in grape production.[4]

When the villagers saw these results with their own eyes they flocked to Mr. Salunke requesting that he help them with similar schemes. A meeting was held with forty families of various socio-economic levels from the nearby area. They decided to form a Pani Panchayat (water council), agreeing that they must share the water equally, a central idea around which all subsequent experiments have revolved. Building on the experience of the experimental farm, the first of many Pani Panchayats to follow was established to test the theory that village water resources could be used to the benefit of all members of the community, not only those few who by force of circumstance were able to capture them for exclusive benefits.

INDIVIDUAL VERSUS COMMUNITY INTERESTS

The experience of government irrigation schemes in Maharashtra had demonstrated the conflict between the community interest and the interest of those few individuals in a position to capture the bulk of the irrigation water. Two phenomena were evident in the government schemes. First, only a fraction of the land in the intended command areas of these schemes actually received reliable water supplies. Second, those farmers who did obtain water had a strong preference for growing sugar cane. A study done by the Gram Gourav Pratisthan explained this preference while demonstrating the extent to which it ran contrary to the broader community interest. The thrust of its argument was as follows.

In most government irrigation schemes there is little effective control on the allocation of water, with the result that those toward the head of the system are reasonably free to take as much as they want at no cost to themselves. With additional units of water being essentially free, the rational economic choice for the individual is to maximize returns per hectare of irrigated land without regard to the amount of water used. For those in this enviable position, the preferred crop is sugarcane. It is among the highest value crops grown in the region but requires relatively little labor input.[5] Furthermore, government subsidized credit is available to finance the inputs for sugarcane production. Thus, all things considered, the rational economic choice for most individual farmers who have access to limited supplies of essentially free water is to plant sugarcane.

To understand the significance of this choice from the community perspective, one must recognize that in the drought-prone areas of Maharashtra even large tracts of land have little economic value if they have no access to irrigation water. The food they produce hardly compensates for the physical energy required to work them. Consequently the incentive to increase holdings of unirrigated land is limited, and most people who desire such land can normally obtain it. But once irrigated this land becomes highly productive and gains substantially in value. Thus, in this locale the critical division is not between landed and landless but rather between those who few farmers with irrigation and the many farmers without it. Consequently it is the distribution of water rather than of land per se that is the key to both productivity and equity within the region.

The critical constraint on irrigation is the amount of water available. And of all the crops grown in the region, sugarcane is by a substantial margin the most demanding of water. It requires half again as much water per hectare as the next most water-demanding crops: fruit trees and grapes. The same water required for one hectare of sugarcane will irrigate 4.2 hectares of onion, 8.5 of maize or wheat, 10.7 of ground nut, or thirty of millet. But more to the point, from the standpoint of community need, is the fact that the production of one hectare of sugar generates a demand for only 360 man-days of labor. That is an important advantage to the lucky farmer with free water.

But from the standpoint of a community with a serious labor surplus, generating only 360 man-days of work with that precious unit of water is a disaster. The 4.2 hectares of onion would have generated 1,680 man-days of labor. And the thirty hectares of millet would have absorbed 2,700.[6]

Table 14-1
Water Requirements and Production Per Hectare by Crop

Crop	Qty. of water required per Irrigation in Hectare cm	Total number of Irrigations required	Total water required in Hectare cm	Produced in Quintal	Value per Quintal Rs.	Total Value Rs.
Sugarcane	10	30	300	1000	25	25,000
Grape	7	28	196	200	300	60,000
Fruits	7	28	196	100	300	30,000
Vegetables	7	15	105	100	100	10,000
Cotton	7	10	70	20	500	10,000
Onion	7	10	70	200	60	12,000
Rice	7	10	70	35	200	7,000
Potatos	7	6	42	200	75	15,000
Wheat	7	5	35	20	200	4,000
Maize	7	5	35	300	25	25,000
Groundnut	7	4	28	15	350	5,250
Sorghum	7	3	21	20	180	3,600
Gram	5	3	15	10	250	2,500
Millet	5	2	10	17	250	4,250

Source: Gram Gourav Pratishthan

Table 14-2

Value and Employment Generated By 300 Hectare Centimeters of Water

Crop	Area irrigable with 300 hectare CM of water (In Hectares)	Value per hectare in Rupees	Value of production from area irrigated	Man-days of work generated from area irrigated
Sugarcane	1.0	25,000	25,000	360
Grape	1.5	60,000	90,000	2,160
Fruits	1.5	30,000	45,000	1,080
Vegetables	2.8	10,000	28,000	1,008
Cotton	4.2	10,000	42,000	630
Onions	4.2	12,000	50,400	1,680
Rice	4.2	7,000	29,400	420
Potatos	7.1	15,000	106,500	1,278
Wheat	8.5	4,000	34,000	1,020
Maize	8.5	7,500	63,750	765
Groundnut	10.7	5,250	56,175	963
Sorghum	14.2	3,600	51,120	1,704
Gram	20.0	2,500	50,000	1,800
Millet	30.0	2,500	75,000	2,700

Note: 1 Hectare CM = the amount of water required to cover 1 hectare to a depth
       of 1 centimeter
Source: Gram Gourav Pratishthan

The GGP analysis suggests that overall, from the standpoint of total benefits to the community, sugarcane is probably the least rational choice among all of the crops grown in the region. By planting any other crop common to the area, water could be allocated over a larger area of land (See Figure 14-1 & Table 14-2) And thus benefit a larger number of farmers, to produce other crops of higher total value per unit of water while productively absorbing substantially more of the area's surplus labor (See Table 14-2).

ORGANIZING PRINCIPLES

The central idea behind formation of the Pani Panchayats is that in a drought-prone area, no individual should be deprived of a rightful share of the limited water resources on which life and livelihood depend. The Pani Panchayat was created as an instrument through which all members of a community could have a voice in water-use decisions within guidelines intended to insure reasonably equitable water allocation. The guidelines were framed as follows with the intent of insuring each family, at

Figure 14-1
Hectare of a Given Crop that Can Be Irrigated with
300 Hectare CM of Water

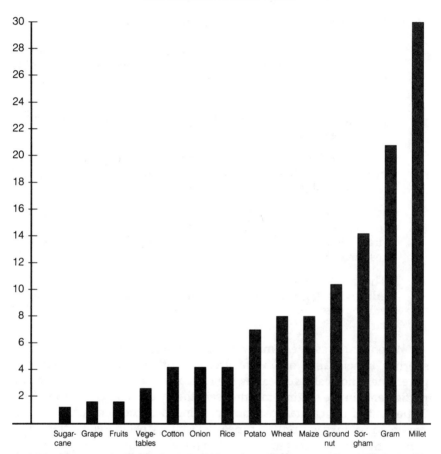

minimum, enough water for its own staple food requirements plus a small income from cash crops.

1. Assistance would be provided only for group schemes, to foster a sense of shared community responsibility.

2. Water would be shared on the basis of the number of family members, irrespective of age, not in proportion to land holdings. The experimental farm had established that, with proper methods of water management, half an acre of irrigated land would reasonably sustain one person. So this became the basic standard in system design and water allocation. Thus, a family of five would receive an allocation for a maximum of two-and-a-half acres. This

would encourage intensive cultivation of the irrigated land, producing much higher returns per unit of water. Each family would
have one vote in the affairs of the Pani Panchayat.

3. Rights to the water would belong not to the land but to the scheme
   managed by the community. Each individual living within the
   scheme area would have a right to water to increase his or her individual agricultural income. But if the land were sold, the rights
   to the water would revert to the Pani Panchayat concerned.

4. Beneficiaries would share 20 percent of the cost of the lift irrigation project, thus insuring active participation and a stake in the
   project's success.[7]

5. The project beneficiaries would administer and operate all aspects
   of the project themselves, thus recognizing and enhancing the
   leadership skills of the rural people.

6. While participants would be given wide latitude in deciding how
   to use their water allocation, sugarcane cultivation would be flatly
   prohibited as inconsistent with the principles of responsible
   resource use.

7. The landless would receive the same share of water as the landed, giving them a strong bargaining chip in negotiating sharecropping arrangements with farmers who have extra unirrigated
   land.

When first presented, many of these concepts were new to the prospective beneficiaries and were greeted with skepticism. Aware that
government normally subsidizes the full costs of irrigation development,
participants in the original meeting said they were too poor to contribute
20 percent of the capital cost. But, convinced of the benefits, they later
presented Salunke with 20,000 rupees which they had raised on their own,
demonstrating the extent to which even the very poor can mobilize capital
resources if convinced of the benefit. Once farmers from surrounding
villages observed the results of their efforts, eight more schemes soon
became operative in Naigaon and the number of requests grew rapidly.

GGP SUPPORT FOR WATER USER ASSOCIATIONS

A procedure was quickly established for dealing with such requests
which, as of this writing, GGP continues to use. First, it is determined
in a preliminary discussion whether: a) there is adequate water available;
b) the group is sufficiently unified in its resolve to develop the scheme
on a cooperative basis; and c) there is a possibility of getting power connection and permission to lift water from Government tanks. The number
of prospective beneficiaries is also determined as is the general layout of

the command area, including the number of hectares to be served and the extent to which they are reasonably contiguous.

The project proponents are then given a date on which a survey will be conducted to determine whether their proposed scheme is feasible in its existing or modified form. Before the survey is initiated they are required to present a 500-rupee deposit as an indication of their commitment. This amount is refundable on completion of the system. But if after a favorable survey result they abandon the project, the deposit is forfeited.

After completion of the survey, detailed plans and cost estimates are prepared by GGP. Before actual work is undertaken, the group has to raise and deposit with GGP an amount equal to 20 percent of the estimated capital cost. Normally each beneficiary has to raise and deposit with the scheme leader his or her share based on the amount of land held that will benefit from the scheme. In some instances this involves considerable sacrifice. Some sell their cattle, sheep, and/or goats. Others have had to sell their household utensils. And in a couple of cases they have even sold the small amount of gold from the necklace every married woman wears while her husband is alive—for many families their only valuable possession. This is painful, and some might claim unfair, but it results in a commitment and a sense of true ownership seldom found in programs where no such demands are made and is considered by GGP to be a crucial step toward growing self-reliance.

From the beginning each group assumes responsibility for administration of its own project. To provide an ongoing management structure, a manager or group leader is elected by the beneficiaries of each scheme. There are no other officers and no executive body, as it is intended that problems will be resolved by the body as a whole to insure broadly based participation.[8] Each Sunday the group leaders of all the schemes in a given area meet together. They also hold meetings of their own groups at least twice a month to discuss system management, cropping problems, and social and economic conditions affecting the productivity of their farms.

A suitable *Patkari*, or water distributor, is appointed by the Pani Panchayat for each scheme to assure fair day-to-day allocations of water to all its beneficiaries. He is usually from a neighboring village, not directly involved in the scheme itself, and is paid a modest stipend of 200 rupees a month.

Further support is provided by the GGP through its training center. Here extension workers are prepared to work with the assisted communities. The program calls for an intensive period of initial training, plus continuing refresher courses. During the initial training the prospective extensionists are paid a stipend by the Pani Panchayat that sponsors them, in return for serving as Patkari. Once they graduate, their responsibilities to the local association are expanded to include advising on farming

practices. Continuing support and training are provided by GGP staff.
A farmer group can fire its extension worker at any time if his or her services are unsatisfactory. On the other hand, to the extent that farmer incomes improve as a result of their assistance, the extensionists salary is
increased accordingly.

RESULTS

An evaluation survey conducted in January/February 1982, only two
years after the program was initiated, found forty-four lift irrigation
schemes in place in twenty-five villages with total membership of 1,338
and facilities serving 839 hectares, which had cost a total of 4,038,200
rupees. Only nine of these schemes were actually in operation, however,
due to difficulties in obtaining electrical connections.[9]

The problem of obtaining electrical connections continues to plague
the effort. While the Indian Government maintains that 100 percent of
rural villages are electrified, the service does not extend beyond the central population areas. The Electrification Board of Maharashtra operates
on the principle that installation of a new power connection must provide a return of 20 percent on capital investment. It has proven highly
reluctant to extend lines to remote irrigation schemes for small pumps to
benefit a few small and marginal farmers. A sit-in by several hundred
farmers organized by the GGP at the offices of the Electrification Board
in Pune brought promises but no action.[10]

Another critical barrier has been a government regulation that no more
than 5 percent of the area irrigated by a government constructed water
tank can be by lift irrigation. The remainder must be served by gravity
feed only, thus systematically excluding a major portion of the population, those living in the tank's catchment area, from participation. Many
of the more attractive opportunities for Pani Panchayat development depend on use of pumps to tap the resources of existing government constructed percolation tanks. Thus, this rule has presented a serious constraint to expansion of the program, even though most of the tanks have
excess water remaining at the time of the annual rains, and members of
the Pani Panchayats consistently make far more efficient use of water than
the downstream sugarcane farmers who are served by the gravity fed
systems.

Difficulties in obtaining electical connections, and restrictions on use
of water from existing tanks have severely resticted further expansion efforts, though as of August 1985, thirty-six schemes involving 939 families
and 679.47 hectares in twenty villages were in actual operation. Nineteen
additional schemes involving 507 families and 334.88 hectares in seven
villages were awaiting power connections.

An analysis of the original six Naigaon systems concluded that per hectare costs of the schemes were generally comparable to those of small-scale government irrigation schemes, even though the former took a more comprehensive approach to: a) land development and land shaping; b) field channel development and maintenance; c) group actions; and d) extension services.[11] And unlike conventional government schemes, the costs of development were borne in part by the beneficiaries.[12]

Among the less tangible social outcomes reported were an increased sense of community spirit and an increase in the time beneficiaries devoted to cultivating their own lands. Nomadic shepherds had settled on their lands, and some persons whose lands were far from their village had constructed thatched huts on them so they could live there and spend more time on agricultural work. A couple of groups had used their lift irrigation system to solve their drinking water problem, saving women's time and labor which could be devoted to tending the fields. At the same time the increased opportunities for productive work had reduced the time available for participation in community meetings and collective activities, and children of families that had settled on fields far from the village sometimes had a long walk to school.

The 1982 evaluation studied the experience of two schemes in considerable depth, providing useful insights into the early benefits and challenges involved in initiating a new irrigation system and helping farmers adapt to irrigated agriculture for the first time.

The Tukai Scheme: First Year

Work on the Tukai Lift Co-operative at Kothale, about eight kilometers from Naigaon, began in February 1979 and was completed after only a year. With its water supply fairly well assured by the Nazare dam located only a few kilometers away, it was irrigating sixty-one hectares in the *Rabi* season, 48.6 in the *Kharif* season, and 28.3 throughout the year. Beginning with eighty-nine members, it had already grown to 128. None of its members had access to any other source of irrigation. Generally the rule that water would be provided on the basis of .5 acre per family member was being observed.[13] The association was keeping accurate records of the value of the crops produced by its members, with most reporting gross returns of between 1,000 and 3,500 rupees per acre.

A special survey was conducted of a sample of thirty-two members to examine changes in cropping patterns and income as a result of irrigation. Most of those surveyed previously had grown only the traditional staple cereal crops such as sorghum and millet, and prior to receiving irrigation they had been able to produce barely half a quintal (fifty kilograms) per acre in a reasonably good year. By the time of the study they were reporting production of from three to four quintals per acre for these crops, with no addition of purchased fertilizer or improved seed.[14] Respondents reported that the increased production allowed them a commensurate reduction in the amounts of these grains they would otherwise have had to buy to sustain themselves and their families. Among the new food crops introduced with irrigation, wheat was the most popular. Most families kept this wheat for home consumption, considering it an improvement in their quality of life over dependence on the coarser sorghum and millet as their staple grain.

Three other new crops, onion, groundnut, and cotton, had been tried on small tracts of land, specifically to produce cash income. Data were collected in the survey on cash costs including wages paid, purchased inputs, water fees, and marketing costs in order to determine actual cash returns. The most popular cash crop was onions (twenty-two of thirty-two farmers). While one farmer incurred a small loss on onion, four farmers had net returns of 4,000 to 4,500 rupees per acre—demonstrating the potential of this crop. The more limited results of other farmers could generally be explained on the basis of lack of experience with onion cultivation, late planting, and inadequate water supply. Results for cotton and groundnuts as well as for a wide variety of other crops, were generally less satisfactory though the ranges were substantial. Those interviewed felt they would do better with these crops as they became more familiar with them. For most of the respondents this was their first experience in producing for market.[15]

The Mhasoba Lift Irrigation Scheme: Second Year

Mhasoba Lift Cooperative, located in Naigaon, was the first of the lift schemes developed by the GGP. Its results generally substantiated those of the Tukai system regarding the value of irrigation water, but in Mhasoba water supplies had proven quite unreliable from year to year, causing difficulties not encountered in Tukai. Though the command area had been estimated at 100 acres, the results of two years of experience suggested that the actual potential was much less. While it was reported that water availability had been a good deal better for 1979-80, the maximum area under irrigation at any one time for the 1980-81 growing seasons was just over twenty-four acres.[16] Subsequently the problem was corrected by drilling a four-inch bore hole to a depth of fifty feet inside the open well. This considerably increased water yield even during the summer months and enabled operation of the pumps for an additional six hours a day.

A survey of thirteen members produced a very disappointing picture with respect to cash crops. While all thirteen undertook onion cultivation, seven of these suffered heavy losses when they found there was no water to support the crop after transplanting. The remaining six who did receive water earned 500 to 2000 rupees per acre. Two members made a net profit on cotton, but two who tried vegetables earned nothing due to inadequate water. No one reported attempting groundnuts or wheat.[17] Though the results for Mhasoba were comparatively disappointing, they underline the importance to the farmer of assured availability of irrigation water. And as the first such scheme undertaken by GGP, the fact that anticipated accomplishments proved overly optimistic is not surprising, especially after the results of the much more controlled situation of the model farm. As reported below, the results for Mhasoba did improve substantially with further experience. As shown in Tables 14-3 and 14-4, by year five of system operation, the average family had increased its gross income from farming ten-fold over preirrigation experience.

Table 14-3
PANI PANCHAYAT VALUE OF MEMBER PRODUCTION
Five Systems 1979 through 1984 — First Year Reported is Pre-Project

| | Members | Year | Value of Crops/Member | | | | | |
			1979	1980	1981	1982	1983	1984
Mhasoba	26	1980						
Average			279	389	688	883	1757	2927
Low			180	200	300	700	1000	1900
High			500	600	900	1200	3000	4000
Babawadi	38	1980						
Average			212	574	818	1542	2326	3482
Low			150	300	600	900	1700	2500
High			400	900	1100	2000	3000	5000
Shivshankar	26	1982						
Average					4404	5065	6162	7958
Low					1500	1500	2000	3500
High					8500	8500	11000	12500
Bhairavnath	17	1982						
Average					224	245	332	450
Low					200	200	250	300
High					300	325	450	600
Savitribai Phule	16	1982						
Average					412	703	962	1881
Low					200	400	800	1000
High					600	950	1200	2500

Source: Based on data provided by Gram Partishthan

Data from Five Systems: Third to Fifth Years

In 1985, GGP compiled data from five systems, two with a five-year history, and three with three years. In each instance the total gross value of farm production, whether consumed, or sold, was reported for each participating household for the year prior to system completion and for each year thereafter.[18]

Table 14-4
PANI PANCHAYAT INDEX OF AVERAGE CROP VALUES
Five Systems — 1979 through 1984
Year 0 (Pre-Project) Crop value = 100

	Year 0	Year 1	Year 2	Year 3	Year 4	Year 5
Mhasoba	100	139	247	316	630	1049
Babawadi	100	271	386	727	1097	1642
Shivshankar	100	115	140	181		
Bhairawvnath	100	109	148	201		
Savitribai Phule	100	171	233	457		

Source: Based on data provided by Gram Gourav Pratishthan

The results reported in Tables 14-3 and 14-4 demonstrate the very sustainable difference that a small amount of irrigation water can make to the income of a household. In four of the villages, involving ninety-seven households, the highest value of farm production for any household prior to the introduction of irrigation was Rs. 600, with the average for the largest and poorest group being only Rs. 212. In Mhasoba, the village discussed above, even families with as much as six to ten hectares of unirrigated land were reporting farm production valued at Rs. 200 or less. In three villages, average value of household farm production had increased by more than three-fold by the third year of the scheme. The most impressive percentage increases were obtained in Babawadi—a sixteen-fold increase in the value of farm production over five years though thirty-four of the thirty-eight families involved each had only .4 hectares under irrigation.[19]

These results also reveal the length of the learning curve for an individual village in gaining full benefit of the irrigation resource. For each system on which we have data, the increases in the value of crops produced during the first and second year of operation were relatively modest compared to the increases achieved in subsequent years. The largest absolute annual increases are shown by the two systems that had been in operation for five years, and these came in the fourth and fifth years.

The reasons for the impressive outyear performance of Mhasoba and Babawadi point up the many variables bearing on system performance.

First, greater than average rainfall during the fourth and fifth years made more water available for irrigation. Second, market prices for their cash crops improved. Third, increased incomes allowed farmers to use more appropriate quantities of manure and chemical fertilizers and to use insecticides. Fourth, farmers were able to purchase improved seeds rather than using the seeds produced in their own fields as they did during the first three years. The data in hand demonstrate the potential for making premature judgements regarding the economic returns to efforts that depend on farmers simultaneously learning new technology, new crops, and new markets. They also demonstrate the influence of uncontrollable circumstances such as rainfall and market prices, the erratic nature of which, as in the villages assisted by GGP, introduces a substantial factor of risk and uncertainty.[20]

CONCLUSIONS

There are a variety of ways to manage distribution of a scarce common resource. Three are widely discussed in the literature: 1) use market forces by charging fees; 2) give responsibility for allocation to a strong central authority; or 3) establish community based mechanisms for self-enforcement by users according to mutually agreed norms. A fourth model, based on a queuing principle, seems to be applied in the case of the government irrigation schemes discussed in this report—the first in line takes as much as he or she likes, passing any unwanted remainder to the second in line, etc. That the queuing approach probably results in the least equitable and socially optimal allocation of the available resource requires little elaboration.

Most any other approach seems preferable. The case provides no example of the use of market forces to solve the allocation problem, though one could imagine a procedure for selling water rights to the highest bidder. If enforced, this probably would have led to improvement in overall economic returns to the scarce water resource by inducing the production of crops that produce a higher return per unit of water, thereby putting more land into production and absorbing more labor. But it would have kept resource control forever out of the hands of the poor and, with time, would probably lead to increasing concentration of both land and water resources in the hands of those wealthy enough to be successful in the initial bidding.

In theory a balance between equity and productivity might have been achieved through exercise of strong central administrative authority to enforce equitable distribution of water on a per capita basis, but administrative practice commonly diverges dramatically from theory in the direction of favoring more economically and politically powerful interests over those of the poor. At best, the costs of such a mechanism can be considerable, including: 1) maintenance of a costly bureaucracy; 2) a reduced sense of individual and community responsibility; and 3) the subordination of individual freedom of expression to bureaucratic prerogative. Furthermore, bureaucratic approaches with their demands for standardization can never hope to reach the level of intensification achieved through subtle adaptations to local soil and hydrological conditions. Such adaptations are required in order to achieve the type of productivity demonstrated by the original experimental farms at Naigaon.

It can be argued that, in most all respects, for the type of allocation problem addressed in this case, reliance on a community management mechanism provides important advantages over other alternatives. While allocation on the basis of equal shares may not produce the most economic result in terms of the highest value added per unit of resources, it provides a considerable stimulus to increased productivity while recognizing the right of every individual to access to those resources basic to life and livelihood. Furthermore, community management approaches do have a considerable potential for adaptation to diverse and changing local conditions, a capacity that may be crucial to achieving improvements in living standards in resource poor drought prone areas.

The GGP has demonstrated the feasibility of a community management approach to water management in drought-prone areas. Yet its capacity for implementation of the approach on a significant scale is limited, particularly in the face of constraints such as the availability of electricity and access to water supplies from government created reservoirs. Government controls many of the critical resources and sets the policies on which the success of programs such as those of the GGP depend. Therefore, it might be argued that the lead in implementing community management approaches is more logically left to government—if governments were able to demonstrate a capacity to work effectively with the poorer elements of the community in ways that contribute to their empowerment. Cases demonstrating such capacity among government agencies are few.

Both private and public agencies are handicapped when it comes to implementing community management approaches on their own. This suggests a need to look for ways of achieving greater collaboration between the two as partners, with each contributing its distinctive strengths in meeting shared objectives. In this instance government might, through its study of GGP experience, give serious attention to reassessing and reorienting critical policies such as those bearing on water allocation and electrification from the standpoint of both productivity and equity outcomes. At the same time government might recognize and encourage the distinctive role of private agencies such as GGP in training and organizing the poor for an effective role in resource control and management.

NOTES

1. Col. S. P. Salunke, *Pani Panchayat: Dividing Line between Poverty & Prosperity* (Pune, Maharashtra: Gram Gourav Pratisthan, November 1983), pp. 2-4.

2. V. B. Salunke is a successful engineer and businessman who continues to manage his own firm, Accurate Engineering Company, in addition to attending to the affairs of GGP.

3. Col. S. P. Salunke, *op. cit.*, p. 4.

4. *Ibid.*, pp. 4-5.

5. Fruit will produce 20 percnet more in value per hectare but it requires twice the labor input of sugar. Grapes will yield 240 percent more in value per hectare than sugar, but require four times the amount of labor.

6. This is certainly not to suggest that community interests would best be served if irrigation water were committed only to the production of millet. Not all land can be economically reached by irrigation. The amount of labor absorbed might well exceed availability, especially on a locality specific basis. The returns to labor are quite low as well, providing little opportunity for more than a bare subsistence living—though preferable to starvation.

7. In the original Naigaon scheme the remaining 80 percent was divided between a government subsidy and an interest free loan provided by the Gram Gourav Pratisthan. The local arrangements vary, however, from scheme to scheme depending on the availability of government funding.

8. Registration of the societies under the Cooperatives Act has been specifically avoided because of the very poor experience with cooperative societies in India, which have tended to serve only the interests of wealthier members of the community.

9. V. D. Deshpande, "Pani Panchayat: A Movement for Conservation and Equitable Distribution of Water," Indian Institute of Education, Pune (mimeo.), p. iv-1. By August 1985, eight of these schemes were still awaiting power connections.

10. Farmers from systems often complain that the electricity is only available at night because the Board gives preference during the day to its industrial customers. This can work considerable hardship on them due to the difficulty of supervising water distribution at night. First, it is difficult for the Patkari to know whether the farmer to whom he is releasing water is in his field. If not present, the water may be wasted or even collect in a particular portion of the field and actually damage the crop. Even if the farmer is present, it is difficult for him to accurately channel the water to where it is needed in the dark. Furthermore, farmers observe that the fee charged the association by the Board for electricity is based on the horsepower rating of their pump, irrespective of whether power is actually provided.

11. Deshpande, *op. cit.*, pp. ii-4 to 6.

12. There was of course still a considerable subsidy involved in making these projects economically viable for the small farmer beneficiaries, and there are serious doubts as to whether such schemes can be made viable on a wholly self-financing basis. See Deshpande *op. cit.*, Chapter iv, pp. 21-25. Of course, existing irrigation schemes benefiting larger and relatively more well-to-do farmers are heavily, if not completely, subsidized. Thus, the operant question is not wheter to subsidize irrigation but rather whether the available subsidies should go to allowing the poor a decent livelihood, or to increasing the profits of the already relatively well-to-do.

13. *Ibid.*, pp. iv-2 to 3.

14. There farmers were characteristically reluctant to use purchased inputs for crops grown for consumption, which thus generated no cash to repay their costs.

15. Deshpande, *op. cit.*

16. *Ibid.*

17. *Ibid.*

18. Costs of production are not reported, so net incomes could not be determined. Nor were data available giving distribution between subsistance and market production.

19. Farmers in Shivshankar had better water availability from the start and so were already planting more cash crops.

20. One knowledgeable expert, Gilbert Levine, was particularly impressed by the degree of risk that the farmers assisted by GGP seemed willing to accept in the face of highly erratic and uncertain water availability. Personal Correspondence with the authors.

CHAPTER FIFTEEN

Activating Community Capacity for Water Management in Sri Lanka

Norman Uphoff [1]

Asian farmers are well known for their traditional capacity to construct and manage irrigation systems, sometimes extending to thousands of hectares, without government assistance.[2] Yet until recently there has been some question whether similar capacity can function in large-scale, government operated systems and whether it can be activated by government initiative. The experience from the Gal Oya irrigation rehabilitation project in Sri Lanka, reported in this case, suggests a tentative yes to both questions.[3]

AN INAUSPICIOUS SETTING

Situated in southeastern Sri Lanka, the Gal Oya irrigation system serves 125,000 acres and was prior to Mahawell, the largest irrigation scheme in Sri Lanka. The system was completed in the early 1950's in an underpopulated area of the island into which some 15,000 farm families from all parts of Sri Lanka had been settled by the mid-1960s. In 1979 a major rehabilitation project was launched by the Sri Lankan government and USAID in Gal Oya's Left Bank area—chosen because its physical structures were the most severely deteriorated and its farmers were the poorest in the area. The capacity of its long and complex canal structure had been greatly reduced by erosion and siltation, and most of the control structures had been damaged or destroyed by farmers seeking to increase their water supply. Main system management was haphazard as water was regularly controlled and measured at only seven points for the entire Left Bank.[4]

Rice yields and farmer incomes were low because of a combination of water shortages, soils ill suited to irrigation, and unwillingness of its poverty-stricken farmers to invest in modern inputs given uncertain water deliveries. Most obtained only one properly irrigated crop per year, though the system had been designed for two.

Unauthorized settlement in the upper reaches of the Left Bank, mainly by children of the early settlers, had expanded the irrigated area by about 50 percent with the consequence that farmers in the lower third of the command area were seldom, if ever, able to get water. The situation was further complicated by the fact that most of the cultivators in the tail areas were Tamil speakers settled from nearby coastal areas while most of the upstream cultivators were resettled Sinhalese.[5]

The Gal Oya Water Management Project funded by USAID was mainly directed to physical rehabiltation. Almost as an afterthought the project paper stated that the 19,000 farmers in the Left Bank area (the actual number was closer to 30,000) would be organized by the end of the project's fourth year. Their "participation" was conceived mostly as contributing free labor to rehabilitate all field channels, for which no budgets had been provided under the project. As the government's Irrigation Department (ID) was mainly interested in the reconstruction of the main system facilities, this aspect of the project plus related socio-economic studies were delegated to the Agrarian Research and Training Institute (ARTI) of the Ministry of Agriculture. Technical support to ARTI was provided by Cornell University.[6]

Considered an undesirable place to live, many of the original Gal Oya settlers had come only reluctantly. Some had been sent by village headmen who wanted to get rid of troublemakers. Even after thirty years few patterns of village cooperation or solidarity had developed, and the settlement areas still had not been given names, being referred to only by the numbers assigned in the original plan. Social relations were strained. Residents had a low self-image and were regarded as rough, quarrelsome, even criminal persons by the government officials who considered Gal Oya a hardship posting. Relations between farmers and Irrigation Department officials were marked by mistrust and recrimination.

These were among the features of the project setting noted by a joint ARTI-Cornell team which visited Gal Oya in January 1980 to begin work on the participatory aspects of the rehabilitation effort.[7] After a second ARTI-Cornell team visit the following June, the ID's Deputy Director for Water Management observed that "if progress can be made in improving water management in Gal Oya, progress can be made anywhere in Sri Lanka."

Pardoxically these conditions may have worked to the advantage of the subsequent interventions. Expectations of what could be done were low, while many participants felt challenged to put forward their best efforts. Most important of all, after thirty years of hardship and neglect, the farmers were ready for a more self-reliant approach, having learned the hard way that if they didn't help themselves nobody else would.

THE APPROACH

In contrast to the approach of the project paper, which looked to farmer participation mainly to complete otherwise unbudgeted functions under the direction of the ID, the ARTI-Cornell team decided to build from the experience of indigenous farmer managed irrigation system throughout Asia and to prepare farmers for a substantial role in system operation and management.[8] The first step would be to establish small informal groups at the field channel level, which would later be joined into formal, legally recognized organizations at D-channel (distribution channel) and higher levels.[9] The organizing work would be accomplished by a cadre of institutional organizers (IOs) recruited, trained, and supervised by ARTI who would live in the villages and work with farmers as "catalysts" for local institutional development. Sri Lanka has had a history of government-instigated rural organizations being started by officials who called large farmer meetings during brief village visits. Most organizations so formed perform poorly.[10] The more intensive "catalyst" approach was based on encouraging precedents in the related experience of the Philippine National Irrigation Adminstration (NIA)[11] and the Nepal Small Farmer Development Program.[12]

The first group of IOs, recruited from among the ranks of unemployed university graduates with farm backgrounds, was fielded in March 1981 after two weeks of "formal" training in Colombo and four weeks of field orientation in the project area. Recognizing that this was a new undertaking for ARTI for which there was little directly transferable experience, a phased "learning process" approach was used.[13] Rather than try to organize the entire Left Bank straight away, work began in a large pilot area, building up a competent and committed cadre of organizers and refining the methodology through practice and continuous self-evaluation.

The initial organizing area to which IOs were assigned covered 5,500 acres around Uhana at the head of the system and 1,200 acres around Gonagolla in the middle. (See Figure 15-1) The choice of Uhana at the head was largely dictated by the fact that this was the first area scheduled for rehabilitation, and if the farmers were to have any meaningful input, the organizing work had to proceed in step with the redesign and reconstruction work of the ID since farmers were expected to desilt and reshape field channels in support of ID efforts.[14]

The Gonagolla area was chosen for work because it was closer to the middle of the system, where we expected it would be easier to organize farmers. At the head, water supplies are normally abundant irrespective of whether or not facilities are well maintained or farmers cooperate with one another. On the other hand, toward the tail-end of the system water was often so scarce that the supply was inadequate for farmers to manage so there seemed to be no basis for mobilizing sustained cooperation. We expected that farmers in the middle of the system could get the most benefit from their own self-help efforts. We were also interested in seeing how much improvement farmers could make in water availability and distribution without major investments in new physical facilities. To some extent, we did see farmer organization taking off faster in Gonagolla than in Uhana.[15] This observation was reinforced when organizing work began in a second phase covering 8,500 acres in the Weeragoda area in September1982 as this was also in the middle reaches of the system. IOs who worked in both Uhana and then Weeragoda found farmers in the latter area more responsive. Still, there were enough irrigation and related problems in the Uhana area to make farmers' initiative and responsibility there impressive as well.

Additional areas were added in March and October 1983 and in early 1984, bringing the area to about 20,000 acres with more than 8,000 farmers. Some of this area had to be dropped as IOs left the cadre to take more permanent positions elsewhere, but by the middle of 1985, the area covered was up to 25,000 acres with over 300 field channel organizations and over 400 farmer-representatives in the Sinhalese-speaking areas of the Left Bank. Organizing efforts started in 1984 in an additional 10,000 acres with a specially recruited and trained cadre of Tamil-speaking IOs had to be suspended due to troubles caused by secessionist militants operating mostly elsewhere in the country. The concentration of organizing efforts in Sinhalese areas was strategically justified since, unless farmers in the head and middle areas were organized and started using water more efficiently, there would not be enough water for the Tamil-speaking farmers downstream, some of whom had not received irrigation water for many years.

In each area, IOs began work by first meeting individually with farmers in the fields during the day or in their homes in the evening, explaining the objectives of the program and building personal rapport. Once acquainted with the people and their community, the IOs began getting farmers together in small groups to discuss their experience and needs. Eventually a meeting would be called of all farmers on a particular field channel to identify important problems relating to irrigation and to discuss what the farmers might do about them, first by their own group action and then by seeking outside assistance. This focus on problem solving has been a central theme of the program.

Once a consensus was reached on "next steps," the farmers would choose an acting spokesman or ad hoc committee to organize the activity, which might involve desilting field channels, rebuilding a broken canal bund, introducing a water rotation system so tail enders would get a fair share, meeting with the irrigation engineer about the timing and amount of water deliveries, etc. Only after the group had made progress in coping with its identified problems would the IO encourage farmers to form a more structured, though usually still informal, organization at this level. The intent was to demonstrate the value of group action so as to create a demand for organization (rather than simply provide a "supply") and to have an organization of the farmers' own creation. But also the plan was to introduce formal-legal organizational structures only at the distribution channel level and above. The field channel groups were intended to remain informal.

SOME RESULTS

Any effort of this complexity and difficulty, no matter how successful it may ultimately be, inevitably produces its share of setbacks and outright failures. Gal Oya is no exception though space does not allow enumeration and analysis of these here.[16] The focus here is on the possibilities demonstrated by Gal Oya of a development approach directed to activating latent management capacities of the farmers themselves even under such adverse circumstances.

Water Saving Measures. When the IO program was initiated at the beginning of the dry season in 1981, the supply of water in the reservoir was only about half its usual level, which was itself inadequate to serve the whole area. Within six weeks after the organizing began, farmers on 90 percent of the field channels in the pilot area had begun implementing one or more of the following measures:

- Cleaning channels through work groups doing traditional voluntary (*shramadana*) labor.
- Rotation of water among fields so tail-enders could get a fair share.
- Saving water for downstream farmers by closing gates to field and distribution channels as soon possible, using rocks or tree stumps where the gates were broken.

The latter two measures reflected unusual farmer trust and solidarity since the Irrigation Department did not always adhere to its schedule of water delivery and seldom informed farmers in advance of changes. This meant that individuals who cooperated in water saving ran some risk of not getting water unless other farmers were willing to make further adjustments.[17]

Most remarkable, given the tensions that exist between the two groups generally in Sri Lanka, were cases where Sinhalese farmers took steps to save water for Tamil farmers in tail-end areas. For example, a farmer on a short D-channel at the head of the Gonagolla branch proposed that they close their gate after four days of water issue to send the rest downstream. One farmer was unwilling to agree. So the first farmer took his dissenting neighbor on his bicycle several miles down the bumpy canal road to see for himself the situation of the tail-enders who lacked water even for drinking and washing, let alone growing a crop of rice. The dissenter came back so moved that he proposed they close the gate for two days rather than only one in an effort to send more water downstream. Such incidents were key in changing the attitudes of ID engineers, most of them Tamil, regarding farmer capacity for fair-minded cooperative behavior—an essential step in gaining the engineers' support for a more participatory approach to system development.

Farmer Initiatives. Two months after forming informal groups at the field channel level in the pilot area, farmer representatives suggested having regular meetings with the ID and other officials in their respective areas though we had envisioned this occurring only in later stages of the program. These meetings, planned and chaired by farmer representatives, eventually became established on a monthly basis in the three main areas of Uhana, Gonagolla, and Weeragoda and contributed significantly to improved working relations between farmers and officials. This improvement was demostrated during an outbreak of ethnic violence in Gonagolla in August 1981 when some huts of Tamils were burned by Sinhalese hooligans. Sinhalese farmer representatives in the area went to the homes of the ID's technical assistant (TA) and maintenance overseer (both Tamils) to give them protection. This had an important impact on attitudes of the engineers, especially since only a few months before, farmers in the area had strongly criticized the TA in a public meeting for what they considered inadequate performance of duties.[18]

Though the maintenance of distribution channels was officially the ID's responsibility, farmers on their own intiative desilted many of these channels, restoring some to operable condition for the first time in five, ten, or even fifteen years. They also used shramadana labor to improve roads and other facilities. And there were numerous instances of farmers undertaking "preventive maintenance" to keep channel bunds or other structures from deteriorating further and causing more costly damage.

Bargaining with Officials. As a consequence of the continuing acute shortage of water, the ID announced in February 1982 that farmers would be allowed to plant only 5,000 acres in the coming season, less than one-third the usual dry season allocation and mainly in the head-end areas. Some ninety farmer representatives met with the government agent, the top administrator for the district, to request that the authorization be increased. He was so impressed with the farmers' seriousness and sense of responsibility that he authorized 12,000 acres and invited them to select three among themselves to attend meetings of the District Agriculture Committee (DAC), made up of district heads of government departments.

The area actually planted that season turned out to be nearly 18,000 acres. Yet the farmers were careful enough in distributing the water that they obtained nearly average yields with a water allocation much less than normal for that acreage.[19] Farmer representatives took their participation in the DAC meetings very seriously, meeting together before DAC meetings to decide what items they wanted to put on the agenda and developing agreed positions to articulate.

Contributions to Rehabilitation. IOs began organizing "design meetings" between farmers and engineers within weeks of arriving in the Uhana area, pointing out to the engineers that by consulting with farmers on plans for improving facilities and water distribution, farmers would likely be more willing to contribute their labor to field channel rehabilitation and to subsequent operation and maintenance. The experience of engineers spending hours talking to groups of twenty to twenty-five farmers and walking along channels with them to inspect problems, began to reduce farmer hostility toward the ID. For their part, the engineers came to see that farmers had legitimate grievances and constructive suggestions. At one such meeting farmers suggested that a drainage problem might be solved at less cost by putting in only one new channel and using an existing canal rather than tearing it up and constructing parallel drainage and irrigation channels. The engineers later wondered privately why they had not thought of this. Farmer suggestions proved particularly useful in getting water to fields where elevations given in surveys were wrong.

Improvements in the Middle Reaches. One distributary channel (M5) in the middle of the system had to serve 2,500 acres, ten times the average area for a D-channel. Water supply was so unreliable that much of the area was no longer cultivated in the dry season. That it straddled the Sinhala and Tamil areas only made a bad situation worse. Farmers said murders had occurred over water in this area. Channel maintenance had been minimal for many years, especially where both Sinhalese and Tamil farmers cultivated along the same channel. Within four months after organizing was initiated, farmer representatives for the shramadana groups to clean them and worked out a system for rotating water deliveries among the channels.

The significance of what the farmers accomplished was striking. During my visit in January 1983, I observed fifteen Tamil and twelve Sinhalese farmers finishing the cleaning of M5.4.4. The thickness of the tree root that had grown through the channel and which the farmers were chopping out by hand when we arrived was mute evidence that water had not reached the tail in some twenty years. The farmers worked together for three days to get the channel cleaned, just in time for arrival of the season's first water delivery.

As M-5 received water on five-day rotations (five days with water and five with none), the farmer-representatives planned a schedule so that the first four channels off M5 were closed for the first two days of a water issue, using rocks or other makeshift arrangements, so that it could reach the three tail-end channels and their subsidiaries. The four upstream channels then received water for the last three days.

As a consequence of such activities, over 1,000 acres usually left fallow during the dry season were brought under cultivation through the cooperative efforts of farmer representatives and ID field staff. Over 300 families benefited, with most being able to get a rice crop in both wet and dry seasons,[20] Physical rehabilitation work done during 1984 improved water control, allowing a reduction in the amount of water issued to M5 without jeopardizing yields. But most of the command area had already been brought under cultivation in both seasons. Farmers reported with pride in January 1985 that there were no more conflicts among them over water.

Responsibility for Structures. In March 1983 water came a few days late and was inadequate for reaching the end of some long D-channels. Under cover of darkness some farmers broke six newly constructed measuring weirs they thought were obstructing the flow of water. Though done by individuals, the farmer organizations offered to pay for repairs, but the deputy director of the ID declined the offer on the ground that the department was also at fault because of the delays and some mistakes in design and construction. Such acceptance of responsibility on both sides was unprecedented.

Reduction in Water Use. The ID decided to start the 1984-85 cultivation season with generous deliveries to show that water could now reach all points in the system. As this was more water than needed, the engineers later told farmer representatives they wanted to reduce the water issue. In January 1985 I attended a meeting called by the ID with farmer representatives from the Weeragoda area to request farmer cooperation. The representatives readily agreed to a 30 percent water reduction, noting that if less water was used from the reservoir for supplemental irrigation in the rainy season, more would be available for use in the following dry season. They also offered suggestions for cutting back on the water supplied to them during the land preparation period.

Total water issue from the reservoir for that season was only two-thirds the national norm (and less than half the usual issue in Gal Oya) though rainfall was less than average. The following dry season, the whole Left Bank area was cultivated for the first time in many years though the

Figure 15-1

Left Bank Area of Gal Oya Irrigation Scheme

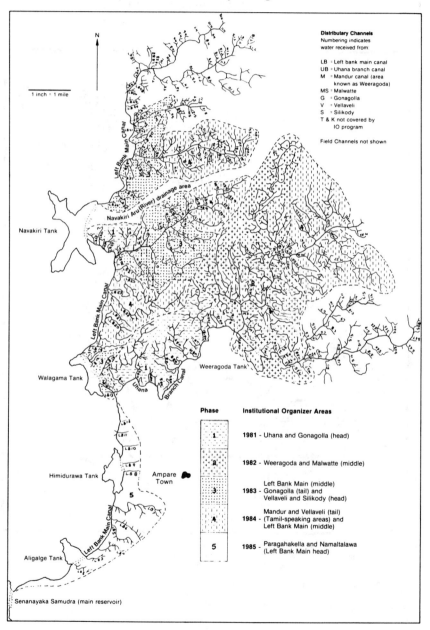

N

1 inch = 1 mile

Distributary Channels
Numbering indicates
water received from:

LB = Left bank main canal
UB = Uhana branch canal
M = Mandur canal (area
        known as Weeragoda)
MS = Malwatte
G = Gonagolla
V = Vellaveli
S = Silikody
T & K not covered by
        IO program

Field Channels not shown

Navakiri Aru(River) drainage area

Navakiri Tank

Left Bank Main Canal

Walagama Tank

Weeragoda Tank

Uhana Branch Canal

Himidurawa Tank

Ampare Town

Left Bank Main Canal

Aligalge Tank

Senanayaka Samudra (main reservoir)

Phase	Institutional Organizer Areas
1	1981 - Uhana and Gonagolla (head)
2	1982 - Weeragoda and Malwatte (middle)
3	1983 - Left Bank Main (middle) Gonagolla (tail) and Vellaveli and Silikody (head)
4	1984 - Mandur and Vellaveli (tail) (Tamil-speaking areas) and Left Bank Main (middle)
5	1985 - Paragahakella and Namaltalawa (Left Bank Main head)

Figure 15-2

**Distribution of Uncultivated Land during Dry Seasons
along M-5 Distributory Prior to 1983**

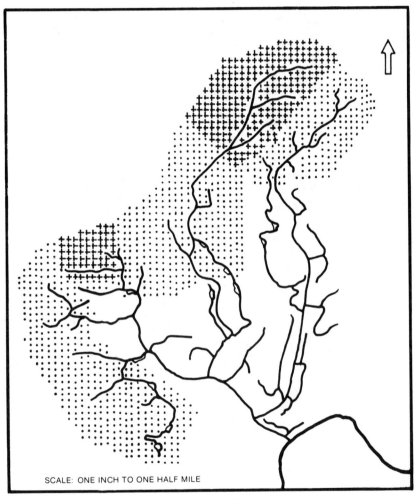

SCALE: ONE INCH TO ONE HALF MILE

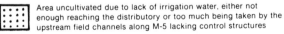 Area uncultivated due to lack of irrigation water, either not
enough reaching the distributory or too much being taken by the
upstream field channels along M-5 lacking control structures

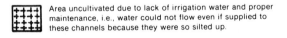 Area uncultivated due to lack of irrigation water and proper
maintenance, i.e., water could not flow even if supplied to
these channels because they were so silted up.

reservoir supply was not greater than average. With physical rehabilitation and better main system management, the ID could distribute water
more precisely, but farmer cooperation in not tampering with gates and
in using water efficiently within and between field channels was crucial
to reducing water use by about one-third.

Farmer Convention. In October 1984 a committee of representatives
from Uhana, Gonagolla and Weeragoda organized a convention to observe
"the third anniversary of their program." They raised 13,000 rupees from
members and invited the ministers of agriculture and lands, as well as
the district minister, as their guests. Some 2,500 farmers attended in an
auditorium designed for 900. Steering committee members reported their
organizations' accomplishments and presented to the ministers a number
of resolutions from their organizations, including a request for legal
recognition. While not all of the requests were accepted, the minister of
lands promised to get recognition for the water user associations and their
representatives. The minister also announced that the system of farmer
organization would be extended to other irrigation schemes in Sri Lanka.
The farmers have offered to help extend the program both within Gal Oya
and to other schemes.

The government of Sri Lanka has been sufficiently impressed to agree
to creation of a permanent IO cadre to extend farmer organization to other
major irrigation schemes and to perform organizational maintenance functions in Gal Oya. Whether the IO cadre can be absorbed into the regular
government service without significant loss of morale and effectiveness
remains an unresolved question.

ARTI's costs for the organizing effort were about 5 percent of total project costs. An analysis by C. M. Wijayaratna comparing measurable benefits
and costs for the first two years alone found a ratio of two to one.[21] Though
the funds available did not allow for the level of training and monitoring
we felt advisable, deficiencies were made up by unusual levels of effort
by farmers, IOs, and program supervisors.

METHODOLOGY FOR MOBILIZING COMMUNITY
MANAGEMENT CAPACITY

While the "social technology" developed in this case cannot be
transferred wholesale to another setting with the expectation of producing the same results, some of the principles and techniques involved may
prove useful to others seeking to promote community management
elsewhere as a basis for evolving approaches appropriate to their
circumstances.

Structure. The organizing process created the structure of farmer
associations from the bottom up, beginning with the creation of base units

or "building blocks" comprised of ten to fifteen farmers whose fields were served by a common field channel.[22] These units provide the benefit of solidarity in a group, which allows for close individual interaction and broadens the power base within the larger organization that links them. Our plan was subsequently to join these field channel groups into a larger organization representing all such groups on a D-channel. Still later these would be formed into an area assembly of all representatives from the area served by a branch channel. At the apex would be a project-level committee where representatives of all farmers in the system could meet with engineers and other officials to plan and coordinate irrigaiton and other agricultural activities.

In fact the process took on a dynamic of its own as farmer representatives "leap-frogged" the process by initiating informal cooperation at D-channel levels, starting monthly meetings with officials in the summer of 1981 when field channel groups were still getting established. Then in early 1982 they accepted representation on the District Agriculture Committee so the third and fourth tiers were formed before the second tier was formally organized. The strength of the field channel groups and the quality of their leadership made this acceleration possible with positive results. IOs began filling in the second tier on a more formal basis in 1984 with twenty-seven of thirty-seven planned D-channel organizations operating by mid-1985. Not being tied to a blueprint, the program accepted this "deviation" as positive and adapted to it.

Leadership. The more typical organizing process in which government officials call a meeting of farmers to hold "elections" for leaders normally limits selection to established leaders whose status is ascriptive rather than achieved. By working first on an informal basis, there was opportunity for a cadre of leaders to emerge who were more truly representative of the needs and interests of farmers and whose status could then be confirmed by their formal selection as farmer representatives. As there was no compensation or formal authority, the farmer representative (FR) role was not particularly attractive to persons mainly oriented to power.

When time came for formal selection of FRs at field channel level, two techniques were developed. First, FRs were selected by consensus rather than formal election. Consequently all farmers on the channel would have publicly given their assent to the FR's authority to act on their behalf. If several persons enjoyed significant support, the position could be rotated among them. No problems were experienced in working through this consensus.

Second, before selecting a representative, it was suggested the group take some time to discuss selection criteria. What did they expect him to do? What qualities would he require? This resulted in tactfully screening out unqualified candidates. If farmers agreed publicly that the FR should not have a quick temper, or should have enough time to devote to the work, or should not be identified with any political party, the range of candidates was tacitly narrowed to those who met agreed criteria without directly criticizing anyone. Attention turned to those who were not implicitly disqualified. The discussion also subtly informed the chosen person what the group expected of him.[23]

The majority of representatives thus chosen were conscientious and effective, including some who proved to be outstanding leaders. About 10 percent of the FRs so selected were poor choices, and another 20 percent were not as active as desirable. In most cases the farmers themselves have replaced those who do not meet their needs, realizing that it is their loss if their leaders are ineffective or divisive.

Party politics are quite important at local levels in Sri Lanka, but the farmers have been emphatic that such politics be kept out of their organizations and generally consider individuals with partisan attachments unsuited for leadership of their organizations. Membership on the DAC was rotated so that nobody would develop a vested interest or become a "professional leader." In general, keeping self-aggrandizing persons out of leadership positions encourages less self-seeking leaders to come forward.

Doctrine. The doctrine of "self-reliance" stressed in IO training has gradually been operationalized around the priniciple that problem-solving action should begin at the lowest possible level. Specifically:

1. Farmers should first identify and act on those problems which they can handle or alleviate by their own individual or collective efforts.

2. Those problems that cannot be solved by group action are to be taken up with government staff at local levels.

3. Remaining problems requiring more competence and resources than farmers and local officials together can muster are referred to sub-district levels for needed assistance.

Our initial expectation had been that local officials, who had been generally uncooperative with farmers and who were widely disliked by them, were a major part of the problem. We came to realize that the poor performance of officials had been in part a consequence of the fact that they simply did not have the resources to meet all the demands being placed on them and thus avoided contact with farmers or put them off. Most officials were not pleased to be as unhelpful as their situation made them. With farmers meeting more of their own needs, these officials were able to make more effective and equitable use of their limited resources, and this in turn stimulated further farmer initiative.[24] Thus, we observed an interactive process between farmers and engineers where a positive change in one group stimulated reciprocating change in the other.[25]

Phasing. Not knowing how quickly farmers would respond to the IOs' efforts, no precise timetable was set at the beginning. The speed at which work could proceed and the area an organizer could handle had to be determined by experience. Also, during the first year or two we had to work more slowly and deliberately to acquire experience, to develop techniques, and to build up a cadre with skills and motivation. The slower and more intensive work at the outset had to be regarded partly as an investment, so the initial rate of progress could not be taken as a norm. Indeed, subsequent acceleration was possible. We found in our practice that Korten's stages of program development were quite relevant: (a) first achieving *effectiveness*, (b) then attempting to increase *efficiency*, and (c) finally undertaking *expansion*.[26]

The first IOs were fielded on a more intensive basis, one IO per 100 to 150 acres or approximately two to three field channels, though assignments were made on a team basis as discussed below. By the time the third batch was fielded, assignments were made on the ratio of one IO per 300 to 400 acres and we found it possibe to form field channel organiztions within one year rather than two years, which the first organizations sometimes required. New IOs could now be trained in an apprenticeship mode by experienced IOs, while farmer representatives also gave new IOs guidance on the best methods of working with farmers. Once the program was well established and the IO cadre more experienced, IOs could handle 500 acres or more and get groups started within one season.

We also found it useful to think of the process as following three stages: 1) intensive organizing focused on formation of field channel groups and selection of farmer representatives (approximately one year); 2) consolidation through formation of D-channel and higher level organizations supported by continued training as farmers gain in experience (a one year period during which fewer IOs are required for that area, some being transferred elsewhere); and 3) sustained maintenance with a few IOs covering a much larger area to train new representatives, trouble-shoot, serve as ombudsman, monitor progess, etc.

Program Management. Fielding organizers in teams facilitated decentralized self-management and a problem-solving approach, as the groups met regularly to asess progress, identify problems, and provide one another mutual support thus limiting the need to wait for guidance from ARTI on every matter.[27] Each team had a coordinator appointed by ARTI. We later realized that this was inconsistent with our philosophy and that coordinators should have been selected by the group with the responsibility rotating at regular intervals.

A government official assigned on a half-time basis as the IO field supervisor supported the IOs in development of their own weekly and monthly plans of work. This participatory, problem-solving style of managing IO operations set an appropriate example for IOs in their interactions with the farmer organizations and in turn for the farmer organizations themselves. It was important that ARTI and Cornell maintain a similar style of interaction in their own activities since organizations tend to replicate in their environment the values and working relationships they follow internally.

Encouraging IOs to identify and discuss their own errors was an important theme throught. They were told in training that it was expected they would make some mistakes and that they would not be reprimanded for mistakes made in good faith. We would be unhappy only if avoidable errors occurred because IOs had not discussed openly and critically among themselves their experience and learning, negative as well as positive. IO job satisfaction has been high due to the trust placed in them, the visible progress achieved, and the vocal appreciation of farmers for their assistance.

Outside Support. The IOs have been catalysts for the farmers' efforts. ARTI has been a catalyst for the IOs' efforts, and the Cornell Rural Development Committee has been in turn a catalyst for ARTI. The potential for achieving such results had existed in each for some time but remained to be energized. The important catalyst role can be performed by any of a number of types of organization.[28] Such catalysts can provide many of the inputs required for mobilizing community capacity that may otherwise be lacking in governmental agencies. These include:

1. Ideas about new approaches, many based on experience elsewhere.

2. Continuity of involvement so that a learning process can occur.

3. Status and legitimacy to get the innovation accepted, at least as a trial.

4. Relative objectivity in evaluating progress and results.

5. Flexibility in providing discretionary funding, rewriting formal job descriptions, recruiting personnel on an improvised basis, etc.

These were the main elements of the methodology applied in the Gal Oya situation. They have been described very cursorily but have been and will be analyzed and evaluated in more detail elsewhere.

CONCLUSIONS

The case illustrates many of the reasons for applying a learning process approach in efforts to mobilize community management capacity.

Most of the methodology evolved in the field in the course of solving problems, many of which could not have been anticipated. More and better
planning might have been done, but the need for much improvisation
would still have remained. It is important to stress that adopting a learning
process approach does not imply doing away with advanced planning.
Such planning is essential in thinking through the problem and preparing for contingencies, but it is indicative and tentative rather than determinant and fixed and assumes a continuous re-examination of both ends
and means throughout implementation.[29]

We were struck by the extent to which, in our experience, the principles derived by Peters and Waterman from their study of the most successful American corporations applied equally to rural development.[30]
These include:

- A bias for action, expecting to learn from experience rather than
  trying to anticipate and provide for all possible contingencies in
  advance.

- Staying close to one's clientele, in our case the farmers.

- Encouraging autonomy and entrepreneurship within the enterprise, such as in our team approach supported by a decentralized
  management style.

- Seeking productivity through people, stressing human potential
  more than technology and expecting the enterprise to move forward on the basis of people's best efforts and ideas.

- Hands-on, value-driven leadership intimately involved in all operations and not hesitant about articulating normative purposes.

- Central staff kept small with few layers of administration that can
  impede the flow of information.

- A climate of dedication to the central values of the enterprise combined with tolerance and scope for all persons who support these
  values.

But while much of the focus here has been on the organizing process
from the perspective of the outside catalysts, it is important to remember
that catalyst agents are just that—catalysts of community management
capacity, which comes basically from members of the community. The
human capacities being called forth are not created by the catalysts, but
rather are only activated, much as in a chemical reaction. Part of this activation comes from the affirmation of values such as equity and participation, two core values promoted in the Gal Oya program. These have been
promoted not just for their own sake, but for the contribution they can

make to the greater productivity of water, soil and human resources. The value dimensions of social processes are difficult to assess and to replicate. But they are nonetheless real and essential to successful practice. The value aspect of social processes is difficult to isolate and assess, but both analysis and practice will be less fertile to the extent that value dimensions are excluded from consideration and promotion.

NOTES

1. I would like to thank Benjamin Bagadion, Jr., Gerard Finin, Nancy St. Julien, C. M. Wijayaratna and David C. Korten for helpful comments on earlier drafts of this chapter.

2. These include the *subaks* in Indonesia [Clifford Geertz, "Organization of the Balinese *Subak*," in E. Walter Coward, Jr. (ed.), *Irrigation and Agricultural Development in Asia: Perspectives from the Social Sciences* (Ithaca: Cornell University Press, 1980); and Aubrey Birkelback Jr., "The Subak Association," *Indonesia* (Ithaca: Modern Indonesia Program, Southeast Asia Program, Cornell University, 1973)]; the *zanjeras* of the Philippines, which may serve as many as 7,000 hectares under one coordinated system, [Henry Lewis, *Illocano Rice Farmers: A Comparative Study of Two Philippine Barrios* (Honolulu: University of Hawaii Press, 1971); and Robert Y. Siy, Jr., *Community Resource Management: Lessons from the Zanjera* (Quezon City: University of the Philippine Press, 1982)]; the Chattis Mauja scheme in Nepal covering 3,000 hectares with a three-tiered organization based on fifty-four village committees [Prachanda Pradhan, "The Chattis Mauja Irrigation Scheme," in *Water Management in Nepal: Proceedings of a Seminar on Water Management Issues* (Kathmandu: Agricultural Projects Service Centre)]; and the indigenous systems in Sri Lanka [E. R. Leach, *Pul Eliya: A Village in Ceylon* (Cambridge: Cambridge University Press, 1961); and Michael Roberts, "Traditional Customs and Irrigation Development in Sri Lanka," in Coward, *loc. cit.*, pp. 186-202.]

3. Another example from Sri Lanka comes from the 15,000-acre scheme at Minipe. See N. G. R. de Silva, "Farmer Participation in Water Management: The Minipe Project in Sri Lanka," *Rural Development Participation Review*, Vol. 3, No. 1, 1981, 16-9.

4. Main system management is inadequate in most government-managed schemes in Asia, as discussed by Robert Wade and Robert Chambers, "Managing the Main System: Canal Irrigation's Blind Spot," *Economic and Political Weekly*, Vol. 15, No. 39, A107-12. On main system management in Gal Oya specifically, see D. Hammond Murray-Rust, *Irrigation and Water Management in Sri Lanka: An Evaluation of Technical and Policy Factors Affecting the Operation of the Main Channel System*, unpublished Ph.D. thesis, Dept. of Agricultural Engineering, Cornell University.

5. In fact, a majority of the engineers operating the system were Tamil, so the water shortages of the tail were not a matter of ethnic discrimination. Given the excess of demand in the upper reaches and the lack of water control, the supply that could be gotten to the lower reaches was inadequate.

6. Cornell's involvement was funded seperately under a Cooperative Agreement with AID.

7. In addition to the ARTI Water Management Study Group headed by C. M. Wijayaratna, the team included three Cornell consultants: E. Walter Coward, David Korten, and the author.

8. See E. Walter Coward, Jr. "Irrigation Management Alternatives: Themes from Indigenous Irrigation System," *Agriculture Administration*, No. 4, 1977, 223-7.

9. Norman Upoff, "Contrasting Approaches to Water Management Development in Sri Lanka," in *Third World Legal Studies: Law in Alternative Strategies of Rural Development* (New York: International Center for Law in Development, 1982). In the Gal Oya system the hierarchy was main canal, branch canal, distributary or D-channel, and field channel.

10. Norman Upoff and R. D. Wanigeratne, "Rural Development and Local Organization in Sri Lanka," in Norman Uphoff (ed.), *Rural Development and Local Organization in Asia*, Vol. I: South Asia (New Delhi: Macmillan, 1982), pp. 479-549.

11. Benjamin U. Bagadion and Frances F. Korten, "Developing Irrigators' Organizations: A Learning Process Approach to a Participatory Irrigation Program," in Michael Cernea (ed.), *Putting People First: Sociological Variables in Rural Development* (New York: Oxford University Press, 1985), pp. 52-90.

12. Md. Anisur Rahman (ed.), *Grass-Roots Participation and Self-Reliance: Experience in South and South East Asia* (New Delhi: Oxford University Press and IBH Publishing House, 1984), pp. 121-57. Cross-national evidence of the economic and social productivity of catalyst roles is presented in Milton J. Esman and Norman Upoff, *Local Organizations: Intermediaries in Rural Development* (Ithaca: Cornell University Press, 1984), pp. 163-5 & 253-8.

13. The approach used was based on principles described by David C. Korten, "Community Organization and Rural Development: A Learning Process Approach," *Public Administration Review*, Vol. 40, No. 5, 1980, 480-511.

14. While ARTI and Cornell objected to the requirement that farmers provide free labor without having been consulted, this requirement turned out to give the farmers some unanticipated leverage over the engineers. If the latter did not consult with farmers about problems needing correction through rehabilitation, the farmers might not cooperate in finishing the rehab work on field channels, thereby diminishing the effectiveness of the whole project.

15. The fact that Gonagolla farmers knew their area was scheduled for rehabilitation had some effect on farmer decision making. Therefore, we could not fully "test" our hypothesis that major improvements in performance could be achieved solely through farmer organizational efforts at a fraction of the cost of physical rehabilitation.

16. A formal end-of-project evaluation was done by the International Science and Technology Institute, Washington, D.C., *Final Evaluation of the Sri Lanka Water Mangement Project (No. 383-0057)*, December 1985, with a more extensive evaluation done by ARTI during the latter part of 1985. This report, *The Gal Oya Water Management Project: End-of-Project Impact Assessment* is sceduled for publication in 1986.

17. As the risks were high, we insisted that the IOs avoid promoting any particular water saving regime, leaving the farmers who would have to live with the consequences to work out the details of any program for themselves. Some of the rotations had to be abandoned, particularly where farmers who were not members of the field channel groups because they were using drainage water from the system for unauthorized cultivation broke open the closed gates—which confirmed that the water saving efforts of members were indeed reducing offtakes from the main system.

18. The meeting is reported in D. Hammond Murray-Rust and Mick Moore, *Formal and Informal Water Management Systems: Cultivation Meetings and Water Deliveries in Two Sri Lankan Irrigation Schemes*, Cornell Studies in Irrigation No. 2 (Ithaca: Cornell Irrigation Studies Group, Cornell University). There was no further ethnic violence in the project area through mid-1985, despite escalation of communal strife in other parts of the country. Once I asked the farmer-representatives whether because of language problems the Sinhalese and Tamils should have separate federations of water user associations. "Only one," was the response. "There are no Sinhalese farmers and no Tamil farmers, only farmers."

19. Fortunately for all concerned, there were some unexpected rains toward the end of the season.

20. I. Ranasinghe Perera, "Gal Oya Farmers Organizing Programme: Progress and Prospects," (Colombo: Agrarian Research and Training Institute, 1984) p. 80, draft.

21. This was an informal and very conservative estimate. A more complete analysis is being prepared by Wijayaratna for his Ph.D. thesis in agricultural economics.

22. The benefits of starting with small groups at the base had already been identified by Norman Uphoff and Milton J. Esman, *Local Organization for Rural Development: Analysis of Asian Experience* (Ithaca: Rural Development Committee, Cornell University, 1974). See updated version Uphoff, *Rural Development and Local Organization in Asia*, Vol. 3 (New Delhi: Macmillan, 1983), 263-338.

23. This provided an exmple of what Schon terms "organizational learning in practice." Donald Schon, *The Reflective Practitioner: How Professionals Think in Action* (New York: Basic Books, 1983).

24. Similar experiences are reported by de Silva, *op. cit.*; and K. K. Singh, "Farmers' Association in Large Irrigation Projects: The Pochampad Experience." Paper for workshop of Social Sience Research Council and Indian Institute of Management, Bangalore, January 4-7, 1984.

25. This proved an important stimulus to the process of bureaucratic reorientation discussed by David C. Korten and Norman Upoff, *Bureaucratic Reorientation for Participatory Rural Development*, Working Paper No. 1, National Association of Schools of Public Affairs and Administration, Washington, D. C., 1981.

26. See Korten, *op. cit.*

27. Actually the initial reason for deploying IOs in teams was that we wanted to experiment with using women organizers but feared it would be unacceptable for unmarried women to live and work by themselves in the villages. Thus, we arrived at a team concept. The women proved at least as effeactive as the men and added a lot to the program.

28. A growing body of experience suggests that they may be private donor organizations such as the Ford Foundation, knowledge building institutions such as the Asian Institute of Management, ARTI, and Cornell University, or even government agencies such as the Agricultural Development Bank in Nepal. The subject of catalysts is treated in Esman and Upoff, *op. cit.*, pp. 163-6 & 262-4.

29. These same notions are advanced by Dennis Rondinelli, *Development Projects as Policy Experiments: An Adaptive Approach to Development Administration* (London: Methuen, 1983); and Albert O. Hirschman, *Development Projects Observed* (Washington: Brookings Institution, 1967). Esman and Upoff, *op. cit.* have characterized this as "inductive planning," a variant of the learning process approach.

30. Thomas J. Peters and Robert H. Waterman, Jr., *In Search of Excellence: Lessons fron America's Best-Run Companies* (New York: Warner Books, 1982).

PART V: INTRODUCTION

GOVERNMENT AS INTERVENER

David C. Korten

Third World development efforts of the past three decades have reflected a prevailing assumption that the lead role in development properly rests with central government. Accordingly government planners have determined national priorities and allocated public resources to projects and programs implemented through public ministries and agencies, acting on the belief that the most efficient allocation of resources could be achieved only through strong centralized decision making and control. The centralization of power was also seen as essential to creating a modern state with a strong national identity that could eliminate local political fiefdoms and contain the forces of local separatism. And, not incidentally, it served the needs of ambitious national leaders intent on consolidating their personal power. These forces all contributed to the bureaucratization of development.[1]

The centralized resource allocation mechanisms, standardized programs, and blueprinted projects that resulted were reasonably suited to addressing a range of priority development needs, including the development of physical and social services delivery infrastructure. They were less effective in targeting development to the specific needs of the poor, or in stimulating the people to exercise initiative and to mobilize their own resources—areas in which more differentiated, locality specific action is required.

For example, central resource allocation and bureaucratic administration have been more effective in directing investment resources into large capital intensive enterprises than in providing supporting services to geographically dispersed, small and micro-enterprises. They have been more effective in the development of large, centrally managed irrigation systems than in the strengthening of locally financed and managed small scale systems. They have been more effective in serving the extension and credit needs of large, export-oriented agricultural estates and of irrigated lowland farmers who work under relatively uniform and controlled soil and water conditions than those of rainfed uplands farmers who deal with highly varied micro-environments. They have been more effective in the development of professionally staffed hospitals and clinics than in the development of village-based community health programs. And they have proven better suited to commercial exploitation of established forests than to managing forest lands as a resource that contributes to the livelihoods of local populations.

Overall, bureaucratized development approaches were reasonably well suited to the early priorities of new nations. But increasingly the governments of Asia are finding a need to deal with new classes of problems that do not lend themselves to centralized resource allocation and standardized service delivery programs. In general, community management approaches are more appropriate to addressing more recently identified priorities, but the existing structures, procedures, and norms of public agencies introduced to serve earlier purposes now prove to be a significant barrier to achieving desired outcomes.

Experience establishes that the reorientation, essentially the de-bureaucratization, of public agencies is possible. But it is a difficult undertaking and the cases demonstrating success are few.[2] Contributors to Part V examine the problems encountered by central government when it seeks to intervene at local levels to stengthen community management capacities.

The section opens with Chapter sixteen by Jeff Romm who, during his years as a Ford Foundation Program Officer in South and Southeast Asia, was instrumental in laying the groundwork for subsequent efforts to address the community management dimensions of irrigation and forestry in several countries of the region. Beginning with an examination of the arguments that have stimulated government interest in community based approaches to resource management, Romm moves on to inventory the actions available to government to strengthen community roles and capacities in resource management. But, as Romm notes, such actions place new demands on the responsible agency. Outcomes become less predictable and needs are created to generate and process a much richer flow of information as a basis for agency decision making. This leads to a number of important organizational choices, which Romm examines.

The transition to a community management approach seems especially necessary and difficult in the forestry sector. In most countries there is a deeply entrenched tradition of public ownership of forest lands, giving forestry ministries legal control not only over the forests themselves, but also over vast tracts of land. In Indonesia, for example, the Ministry of Forestry has primary jurisdiction over 74 percent of the nation's total land area. The emergence of a commitment within Ministries of Forestry to social forestry, where the concern is with putting forest lands in the hands of the people to manage in ways which jointly benefit themselves and the national interest, represents a substantial departure from established modes of forest management. It calls for a substantial reorientation of the roles and norms of the professional forester who has been trained to plant trees, protect them from people, and supervise their commercial harvesting. Consequently translating new policy commitments to social forestry into effective program action represents a difficult challenge of uncertain outcome.

In Chapter seventeen, Vandana Shiva, H. C. Sharatchandra, & J. Bandyopadhyay examine the experience of an early social forestry initiative in India. The program that these authors studied encouraged private land owners to plant tree crops with the stated expectation that this would make fuel wood more readily available to the poor. Unfortunately key issues of asset control and market incentives were neglected leading to what, in hindsight, would appear to have been predictable outcomes quite contrary to those by which the project was justified. The case demonstrates the complexity of the program design issues faced in community management interventions, as noted by Romm in Chapter sixteen.

The inhibiting impact of bureaucratic culture on efforts to engage government officials in promoting village self-help initiative is examined in Chapter eighteen by Shaikh Maqsood Ali. He presents two Bangladesh cases, in which he was a prinicipal actor, of efforts to engage government officials in village development work, and explains why both efforts ultimately floundered. In so doing, he demonstrates how the bureaucracy nurtures and reinforces a set of norms wholly contrary to those appropriate to empowerment interventions, and concludes that government might be better advised to stay with what it is best equipped to do and encourage private voluntary development agencies to take lead in village-level organizing efforts.

One of the few exceptions to the generally dismal history of performance by public agencies in support of community management is the case, noted earlier, of the Philippine National Irrigation Administration (NIA) program of assistance to small irrigator associations. The NIA is also responsible for the development and management of much larger irrigation systems, involving facilities of a scale requiring professional management. These large systems raise particularly complex issues of water user-agency relationships, especially when a new project calls for construction of a large, government managed system in an area already served by a number of smaller, farmer managed irrigation systems. Such a situation provides the setting for the case presented by Robert Siy in Chapter nineteen. Siy's case provides a dramatic demonstration of the issues at stake and how the NIA's leadership averted a potential tragedy by an action that is probably unprecedented in the history of modern irrigation development. Unfortunately the problem is commonplace among large, centrally planned development projects throughout the world, but decisive and appropriate corrective action of the type taken by the NIA is not.[3]

NOTES

1. For an insightful analysis of this experience and the issues involved see Ambassador Soedjatmoko, *The Primacy of Freedom in Development* (Lanham, Maryland: University Press of America, 1985).

2. The case of the Philippine National Irrigation Adminstration discussed in the Introduction to this volume is one of the best known. The Gal Oya Project in Sri Lanka described by Upoff in Chapter fifteen demonstrates a successful intervention at the project level.

3. Documented examples may be found in Cheryl Payer, *The World Bank: A Critical Analysis* (New York: Monthly Review Press, 1982); Walden Bello, David Kinley and Elaine Elinson, *Development Debacle: The World Bank in the Philippines* (San Francisco: Institute for Food Development Policy, 1982); and Guy Gran, *Development by People: Citizen Construction of a Just World* (New York: Praeger Publishers, 1983). While these reports focus on the World Bank, the Bank has no monopoly on ill-conceived development projects. In the case reported by Siy one may ask why this project was undertaken in this area with such a questionable need. An important fact is that the initial impetus for the project was to bring irrigation to the village of then president Ferdinand Marcos. But this village was far from the water source necessitating construction of a long and very expensive main canal. One theory is that the costs of constructing this canal could be justified economically by the donor using cost benefit methods only by extending coverage to a much larger area and essentially ignoring the fact that this area was already adequately served by indigenous irrigation associations. The theory seems plausible, as the practice of expanding the scope of a project to produce assumptions supporting a positive cost benefit ratio is not unusual in large donor assisted projects.

CHAPTER SIXTEEN

Frameworks for Governmental Choice

Jeff Romm

Community resource management has become a significant theme of rural development strategy throughout Asia. In attempting to promote it, however, governments confront some fundamental tensions of purpose. They seek to improve cooperation between villages and the state in the control and management of natural resources, but they do so with an inescapable commitment to the state's interests. They use natural resource management to initiate broader social and economic change, but they must do so through technical agencies that are prepared to accomplish specific tasks rather than stimulate broader social effects. And in reforming agencies for the purpose of community resource management, they encounter the basic dilemma between establishing structures that secure predictable and consistent performance or maintaining flexible organizations that can adapt readily to new experience and knowledge. How governments respond to these tensions—of role, of purpose, and of organization—influences what they do and how they do it. They typically respond with choices that have been useful in conventional circumstances but that may have little relevance to the problems of community resource management.

Of particular significance is the government tendency to rely upon conventional frameworks for obtaining and using the information upon which agencies plan, organize and evaluate their activities. This paper examines the relevance of these frameworks and suggests alternatives that may improve the effect of government activities on community resource management without necessarily sacrificing the coherence and control that government agencies require. The first section introduces the context in which community resource management has developed. The second outlines the common instruments that community resource management activities contain. The third section looks at alternative frameworks for choice among governmental actions. The final section considers some implications of these frameworks for government organization.

CONTEXT

One universal aspect of the national development process is the extension of state authority into the affairs of local communities. While central governments in the past have been interested in local communities primarily as sources of revenue, the needs of the modern state lead it to seek control over a broad range of resources that the community has traditionally viewed as its own. The intrusion increases potentials for both conflict and cooperation between state and local interests. It has disrupted existing local systems that were often effective when isolated from external pressures. It has also created new systems that may be more beneficial than their predecessors but at a troubling cost in local autonomy. Important to government and the communities involved is the government's ability to choose forms of intervention that are likely to relieve conflict and promote cooperation with the diverse communities in which they occur.

Community resource management is a classic example of these dynamics of the development process. During the past decade, governments throughout Asia have focused increasingly on the improved use and control of the natural resources upon which rural production depends. Irrigation, forest, watershed, fisheries, and range management programs have grown to comprise a dominant theme of rural development strategy, reflecting a shift from past emphasis on crops to the environments in which crops are or might be produced. The reasons for the shift display interesting interactions between economic and political concerns in national development.

The economic reasons are widely appreciated. The impact of "green revolution" crop technologies upon agricultural production had reached a plateau. Although the need for agricultural gains had not diminished, production was constrained increasingly by: (1) the inadequate control of water regimes; (2) the limited amount of land that could respond productively to improved crop technologies; and (3) the needs of most rural households to secure subsistence crops as well as to produce for sale. In such conditions, the majority of rural people continued to apply relatively extensive patterns of resource use that could only satisfy a growing population by the additional opening or degradation of land. More often than not, their actions damaged their own future prospects as well as the public interests in maintaining adequate food supplies, productive forests, healthy watersheds and smaller burdens of flood and silt on downstream settlements. In economic terms, there was critical need to get water to sites where and when its impacts on productivity would be greatest and/or to develop land management systems that would make the most productive use of available moisture.

But these economic reasons do not explain why technical changes should be sought through community resource management rather than by the more conventional means—direct bureaucratic implementation and market and R&D policies—that maintain clear state dominance. The political reasons for the shift toward community resource management are significant in this regard. Improved resource management requires control of resource access and use. While states claimed ownership to most land, forest, and water, they lacked the capacity to enforce thier formal authorities over those who used these resources. Villagers did not "own" the resources but they used them heavily and with the authority of local custom. In this nebulous separation of ownership and use, neither the villages nor public authorities could control these resources sufficiently to increase their productivity or reduce the larger consequences of their degradation. Additionally, outside of central agricultural areas, the flows of influence between villages and the state were too weak to support the development of cooperation around mutual interests; hostility and aliena-tion often characterized the relationship.

In these terms, governments had reason to want to use village capacities to extend their organization of resource control; villagers had reason to want a better relationship if they gained secure rights to land and water and expanded their influence in the process, and both needed improved resource control if sustainable gains in productivity, from their diverse points of view, were to be attained. The economic possibilities of improved resource management could develop only through cooperation between villages and the state.

PROGRAMS

Community resource management programs treat the weak control of land and water as a primary constraint on the intensity and quality of rural production. Although programs have developed throughout Asia and for a diverse array of physical resources, this core concern has led to remarkably similar program features, wherever or for whatever resource programs are implemented.

An Improved Technology: A technology is introduced to increase the productivity of the resources and the returns to village management ef-fort. The technology may be an agroforestry combination of crops, a water storage or distribution system, or range fences and forage improvements. It may be designed specifically to distibute benefits in a manner that favors village collective action, village equity, or the satisfaction of national in-terests. Its productivity and distrubutive characteristics determine the probable degree of village cooperation. Government may subsidize application with financial and technical assistance.

Village Organization for Resource Control: Villagers organize to protect, operate, and maintain a technical improvement. The ease of organizations depends upon the expected productivity of the technology and the expected distribution of its benefits within the village. The strength of the organization may determine the form that the technology assumes relative to state preferences or the production and distribution characteristics it must possess to be viable. Government may influence village organization through the technologies it favors, the support it provides, and the terms of agreement it and a village negotiate.

An Agreement between Village and Government: Villagers and the responsible state agency establish an agreement, formal or informal, regarding the rights and obligations of each party. The agreement serves as a proxy settlement of deeper issues regarding property ownership. It may include the choice of technical design, a land or water management plan, a schedule of respective contributions or possible repayments, and an understanding about the flat fees or shares of product that government will receive. The village's share affects its motives for cooperation and the productivity gains that are necessary to sustain them. The agreement may include government protection of weaker segments of the community, such as land-poor village classes or the "tail-enders" of irrigation systems, from discrimination in how benefits and responsibilities are distributed.

Government Services: In addition to its direct village involvements, government may help develop markets for the products that community resource management yields, increasing the economic returns to village efforts and the village motives for cooperation. For example, it may support cottage industries that use agroforestry products or it may improve livestock markets and veterinary services. It may buy products itself at a presumably advantageous price and sponsor the development of technologies through research and development programs.

Administrative Reform: The responsible agency reforms its own structure to provide the community-oriented services to which it is committed. It thereby presumably increases the effectiveness of its contributions and the strength of village motives to cooperate. Reforms commonly include the development of a community extension wing in agencies that were previously devoted to the management of state controlled lands and waters, changes in the content of in-service training and in the skills that are recruited for employment, and the formation of planning and monitoring mechanisms specifically for community projects.

Policy Reform: Agencies, villages and political units of government change policies that adversely affect the context for community resource management. Taxation, land, and commodity market policies may be modified to increase the benefits and security that participating villages expect to obtain. Interagency relationships may be restructured to exploit the potential complementarities among public programs and to reduce their contradictory influences. Program decisions may be centralized, regionalized, or decentralized to smaller territorial units, depending upon their relative needs for local information, interagency coordination, and specialized central control.

These features create a fertile system of interdependent choices of governmental activity. They also present unusual problems of development for an implementing agencey. Their possible combinations challenge the capacity of any government agency to decide what it does, and clash with government's practical needs for simplicity. Their complexity and novelty hit organizations that are too formative to either assess the choice criteria they use or to do without the guidance that such criteria provide. The system of related choices that they describe includes critical village/ state relations that conventional agencies can leave to political processes, yet the available guides to decision making have been developed by conventional agencies for their simpler needs.

Community resource management agencies face a difficult question: Should they proceed with conventional frameworks for the guidance they need or should they explore others that may better serve their puposes? As agencies' criteria for choice determine the information that they selectively seek, absorb, and use—thus the kinds of organizational knowledge and abilities they develop—the answer to this question has some significance for the future of community resource management.

FRAMEWORKS FOR CHOICE

Community resource management agencies have strong reason to adopt conventional frameworks for choice. These frameworks are designed to assure predictable and accountable actions by the civil servants who work within them. Simple and uniform procedures enhance the accountability of staff actions and the effectiveness of organizational controls.

But the procedures also filter and channel the information that a government agency must absorb to make its choices. Their simplicity is gained at the cost of information. Their selective screening of information determines the agency's interpretation of the circumstances upon which it is to act, its assessment of the consequences of its possible actions, and its evaluation of the outcomes its actions create. Their selectivity determines as well the growth of the agency's capabilities to accomplsh its mission.

The competitive needs for organizational control and stability on the one hand, and fulsome flows of information on the other, produce a particular dilemma for community resource management agencies. If the first need is given excessive importance, the flow of information can be so confined as to prevent an organization from understanding the village conditions it is supposed to affect: it will fail in its mission even before the mission has been clearly identified, but if the flow of information is totally unrestrained, the agency's adaptability will exact a possibly fatal loss in internal control. Also, new orgnizations have little basis of their own for judging which intermediate course is likely to best serve their purposes and interests.

Community resource mangement offers cogent examples of the stress between the information frameworks that agencies use and the social purposes they are created to satisfy. The agencies have tended to adopt conventional frameworks that were developed for other problems and organizations or for purposes of bureaucratic control. These frameworks typically treat the objective of community resource management as a commodity, a service, a technique, or a project rather than as a productive set of relationships between village and state that secure the beneficial control of a resource. For lack of alternatives, agencies make their choices based upon information about how their actions are projected to achieve goals that may suit other problems but are inappropriate for their own.

The conventional frameworks screen out information that would help answer the critical questions in community resource management. How and why do villagers manage resources as they do? How do changes in their circumstances affect what they do? By what means can government best achieve changes that favor beneficial village/state cooperation in natural resource management? What governmental structures do these means and their supporting information flows require?

Answers to these questions begin in the village. The conventional frameworks answer the last question—about governmental structure—by imposing screens of information that distort how community resource management is perceived and how agencies develop to serve its needs. Alternatives may offer a more productive balance between information and control.

The "Project" vs. the "Village System" of Resource Use

The "project" is a common framework for government planning and evaluation of localized activities. In project planning, actions are chosen because they are expected to produce specific outcomes that serve agency objectives. Furthermore, the relationship between actions and outcomes is assumed to develop primarily in a specified area and in a relatively predictable environment. "Spillovers," the effects that are transmitted to other places or affect interests other than agency's, are treated as incidental to the relationship between the actions and outcomes that matter. So, too, are "confounding factors," or unplanned forces in the environment of the project that affect its outcomes.

The "project" framework determines the information that an agency seeks and does not seek in order to plan or evaluate its activities. Because of its handiness, simplicity, and conventional acceptance, it has become widely used in community resource management programs. A project plan specifies that actions of both agency and village, in establishing a village plantation or communal irrigation system for example, and the outcomes that these actions are expected to achieve. The outcomes are typically defined in terms of the agency's own production objectives—increasing fuelwood and rice yields for example. In subsequent evaluation, the agency assesses the extent to which its expectations were satisfied and considers how different actions might have satisfied them more effectively.

The "project" has obvious advantages as an instrument for organizational control, holding agency personnel accountable for the achievement of specified targets, but it has shortcomings as a screen of information about community resource management, which involves both governmental and village decisions.

First, spillover effects, such as the impact of project actions on other village resource and public forest use, are commonly the dominant outcomes of the project and affect agency objectives more strongly than those a project plan anticipates. The reason is that villagers decide what they do in the project in terms of its effects on all aspects of their livelihood; these effects are never confined within project boundaries. The "project" bounds the assumed system of cause-effect relationships by what a government agency does, and where and with whom it does it, rather than by where the causes of project outcomes and the affects of agency and village actions are likely to occur. It does not incorporate the range of community behavior that determines what vilagers do, why they do it, how the project will change what they do, and with what effects. It assumes that government is in control.

Second, confounding factors in the project environment tend to have greater effect on project outcomes than do the actions that are identified in the project plan. For example, market forces and climatic variations govern how villagers allocate their time among their mix of crop, grazing, forest, nonfarm and project activities; a planned village contribution of effort, however agreeble initially, cannot be insensitive to these basic influences upon what people do. Although the agency does not control these conditions, they are certainly more than unplanned aberrations in an otherwise sound project.

In these circumstances, the project statement of physical or economic targets misses the point: the real issue is how well a village and an agency can interpret their changeable situation and achieve mutually satisfying responses to it. The objective is the vitality of the relationship between them, and the test of a framework is the quality of information it provides to this end.

Demonstations of an alternative framework—the village system of resource use—place the "project" in perspective. Consider a village that uses an array of land qualities for different purposes. It crops some sites; it grazes and forages upon others. It treats different sites and activities with different intensity. Villagers presumably distribute their efforts in a manner that best fulfills their needs. If relative agricultural prices shift or rainfall declines, the villagers adjust their activities among crops accordingly. If nonfarm wages rise, they spend less time in agriculture, reducing the amount of land they use or the intensity with which they use it. Similarly, governmental influences that alter the relative values of village activities change the amount of land used, the distribution of activities within that area, and the intensity of effort that different activities absorb.

When government initiates a community irrigation, forestry, or range project within this village system, the outcomes of the project depend upon village incentives for supporting it relative to other activities the villagers can undertake. These incentives are shaped by other government policies and programs that affect the same system. As a project, the government initiative may appear to be viable. As a modification of opportunities and constraints in the whole village system, it may be more or less viable than it appears. To predict the outcomes of this government intervention, i.e. to plan the project, the implications of systemwide responses to it must be considered. To assess the intervention, i.e. to evaluate the project, the overall responses of the village system to it must be analyzed.

A hypothetical community forestry project illustrates the concept. A forest department and a community establish a village plantation to reduce the trouble villagers have in obtaining fuelwood, thus reducing their dependence upon the destruction of a nearby "government" forest, and to also provide them with wood products to sell. The project is planned in a manner such that: (1) full cooperation is achieved among villagers, and between community and government; (2) the plantation is located on a good site that is agreeable to all; (3) the composition and management of the plantation fully reflect village preferences; (4) the best available techniques are used; and (5) the products of the plantation are equally distributed among village members, who protect and manage it on a cooperative basis. The plan projection of outcomes is very positive. But what will the actual outcomes be, and why? The following is not atypical.

Establishing the plantation removes 100 hectares of land that had previously been available for village grazing. As nothing in the project plan reduces the number of livestock, grazing pressures do not decline.

Instead, they shift into surrounding "public" forests and increase their degradation, defeating at least one government purpose of the project. If people are willing to go only a short distance to graze their livestock, grazing pressures turn in upon the plantation itself, making its protection more difficult and perhaps eventually destroying it. This outcome may be hastened by another government program promoting livestock production, or by a rise in the value of livestock products.

By treating the plantation as isolated from the broader dynamics of village land use, a project plan misses key variables—livestock in this case—and almost invariably produces a fallacious prediction of the effects of the planned intervention on community resource management. Nor will this framework help in explaining what eventually occurs or in identifying corrective actions. Indeed, government typically blames villagers for the failure of a plan thereby justifying a stronger role for itself and undermining the cooperation the project is intended to foster.

Communal irrigation systems offer another example. Improved water control can increase crop production, but it requires a continuing investment in operations and maintenance. This takes effort which then is not available for other purposes, and this effort will be forthcoming only to the extent that the villagers see that it produces more benefits when applied to irrigation than to other activities. Government interventions can influence the level of irrigation benefits and costs that the villagers must absorb, but their effects can be assessed only within the context of the larger system of opportunities and constraints in which villagers make their choices.

Consider two villages with the same social and ecological conditions. The first has a profitable market for its unirrigable upland crops; the second does not. The government plans identical irrigation projects for both communities. From a project frame of reference, identical outcomes would be predicted for the two communities, but the "project" misses a key variable: upland crops. The first community has less incentive to maintain its system than does the second—a reality that the "village system" perspective would anticipate—and identical outcomes would be achieved only by appropriately unequal government support to the two communities.

An effective government role in community resource management requires information about how one or another intervention affects the distribution of effort throughout the village system and what the consequences for resource mangement are likely to be. The "project" framework is convenient, but it screens out critical information about what villagers want and do. Using it, agencies will tend to implement poorly chosen activities with relative efficiency.

The "village system" framework obtains the quality of information that can produce strong choices. It has other implications as well. First, it will lack the simplicity taht an agency values until its key variables in different village circumstances are more clearly identified. Perhaps the identification process is an appropriate focus for structural design of the agency as a whole. Second, an agency alone cannot satisfy the information requirements of the framework. Relative to the "project," the "village system" framework increases the information that villagers themselves must provide and thus the interdependence between the agency and the village. Third, the framework comprehends behavior that has mutual importance for both village and state interests. It provides a common base of information that fulfills the needs of both and can support the continuing negotiation of adjustments between them. Thus, it serves the fundamental objective of community resource management: to sustain village/state cooperation in regimes of resource control despite changes of circumstance to which villagers must respond.

The "Program" vs. the "Policy System"

Changes in village conditions are due partly to governmental influences over which an agency for community resource management, if using a conventional "program" framework, assumes it has little direct control. The "program" framework is the structure of allocations an agency makes to achieve its target number of projects. The framework screens out information that does not serve this relatively self-contained purpose. When applied to "village systems" rather than conventional projects, it incorporates information about the effects of other governmental policies and programs on village actions, but it still excludes information about the motives behind and sources of leverage upon these policies and programs.

Instead of a "program" view of its choices, the agency has reason to allocate resources for information about other governmental activities affecting the village context and to exert influence upon them. It needs to become an effective actor in the more general "policy system." This framework encourages the agency to seek and use information for practical choices that determine its influence upon the context, not just the specific content, of community resource management.

The tension between "program" and "policy system" frameworks is apparent in a common choice that forestry agencies face in organizing activities in community forestry. Should the agency implement its activities wholly through its own staff and structure or through district government? The answer depends upon the information framework the agency uses to consider its choice.

The "program" framework suggests that the agency should maintain full control of its activities, thereby insuring that its projects will be implemented. The "policy system" framework suggests that the agency implement its activities through district governments, which have greater ability to know about village conditions and to coordinate the activities of other agencies—in community development, agricultural extension and livestock production, for example. The "program" framework places the entire information burden on the agency. The "policy system" framework uses the information available in district governments and limits the agency's needs to information it must have—e.g. about characteristics of different classes of "village system"—to influence district choices. The agency gains simplicity and diversifies its political support at the cost of direct control and increasing interdependence.

Communal irrigation offers a second example. Should an irrigation agency specialize in the provision of physical water control structures, leaving organizational and agricultural features of water control entirely to the villages, or should it work with villages on all aspects of irrigation management?

The "program" framework suggests the latter course: the agency should develop the comprehensive talents that effective irrigation management requires. The "policy system" framework suggests that villagers should be left the challenge and opportunity to mobilize the organization and nonengineering supports they need; other agencies will be attracted to provide such supports by virtue of the opportunities for successful intervention that water control structures afford. The framework uses villages and other agencies to mobilize the requisite information. It limits the agency to the information it needs to be sure of the suitability of its structures for diverse villages conditions and to catalyze village and other agencies' responses that will make its specialized actions productive. In exchange for its loss of direct control and greater dependence on others, the agency maintains its internal cohesion by simplifying the information it requires and gains the capacity to serve many more villages than would otherwise be possible.

The examples illustrate the range of strategies that a resource management agency can adopt to influence the context in which its village activities develop. The "policy system" framework does not preclude "program" choices if these are the best in prevailing circumstances. It does mean that these choices are made upon a different information base than occurs when the "program" is adopted as convention.

AGENCY STRUCTURE AND INFORMATION FLOW

The conventional resource management agency is organized to control land and water that are assumed to be under its umambiguous authority.

Its staff hierarchies are structured to sustain this control through the downward flow of supervisory authority. Staffing requirements are determined by a desired ratio of staff to land area—the presumed unit of management—and by preferred professional backgrounds that are presumed to insure relatively predictable performance. Flows of information are designed primarily to monitor staff compliance with agency goals and to protect the agency's jurisdiction against possible encroachment.

Community resource management seriously challenges the utility of the conventional framework. In acknowledging the reality, if not the legitimacy, of village authority in resource use decisions, for example, it introduces the need for agency structures that support staff within the ambiguous setting in which control of their actions flows from the village as well as from agency superiors. In defining the primary relations of the agency in terms of people, it creates the need for the staffing that is based on a ratio of staff to people rather than to land; it necessitates the recruitment of staff who are able to deal with people as well as things. Community resource management requires an organization that cooperates rather than controls.

Other aspects of community resource management have equally profound implications for agency structure. An agency must operate in highly diverse village conditions and with experimental techniques, both of which are poorly understood. It operates in a policy context that is littered with competitive incentives, actions and jurisdictions. And it operates in a milieu that is dynamically responsive to changing economic and environmental conditions and cannot be held still for the benefit of professional plans. The central feature of agency organization in these circumstances is not its structure of authority but the structure through which it seeks and uses information.

What kinds of information should an organization seek and use? The village and policy system frameworks are bases for selecting more useful information than conventional frameworks allow. More importantly, they highlight relationships with the village and with other governmental bodies through which such information can be made available. And most important, these relationships mark channels that must be structured to insure continuous negotiation and mutual adaptation among the parties involved if the benefits of community resource management activities, however different from initial plans, are to be durable. The village and policy system frameworks can be viewed as guides to the structuring and screening of information flows within the agency.

How does an information-based agency remain adaptable without loss of necessary internal stability? The village and policy systems frameworks create patterns of interdependence that can help stabilize the agency's external environment, reducing its threats, and increasing its support.

They also can simplify internal structure by focusing it specifically upon the information that these relationships require.

The agency can shift its information structures from staff to line functions. Planning, monitoring, education, public relations, and research are conventionally organized as staff services that are used to maintain the accountability of line personnel. In an agency that is organized for information rather than authority, their functions are not primarily to control but to guide and serve the continuing adjustments that the organization must make to be stable and effective in a dynamic environment. Instead of their currently peripheral functions, they become the core "line" around which all else is organized, and they become the core resource with which the agency serves and influences its village and policy environment.

Government support for community resource management is still in a formative stage, and there remains a lack of needed knowledge about the problems these activities address, the reasons these problems occur, and the means for overcoming them. In this respect, contemporary programs must be considered as experimental tests of new approaches.

One thing is clear. Effective agencies for community resource management will be much more interdependent with villages and other governmental units than are conventional agencies. They will inevitably prove to be transitional, their primary role being to generate the information and the associated relationships upon which new institutional structures can be established that are consistent with control needs of more intensified resource use. These efforts will be the more productive to the extent that they are guided by frameworks that take the realities of the village and policy environment, rather than bureaucratic conventions, as points of departure in assessing appropriate actions.

CHAPTER SEVENTEEN

Social Forestry for Whom?[1]

Vandana Shiva, H.C. Sharatchandra and J. Bandyopadhyay

Throughout Asia declining forest reserves and related environmental deterioration have brought a substantial interest in the concept of social forestry, which looks to the community to assume a major role in forest management. The Indian government has been at the forefront of this interest, adopting an ambitious social forestry program based on broad participation in forest management to rebuild the country's forest wealth while directly meeting the needs of rural populations for the forest products. While the program has contributed to an expansion of forest cover through the stimulation of private forestry, the primary beneficiaries have been landowners and industry and, contrary to its stated objectives, it has in fact contributed to a decrease in the availability of both forest and food products to the rural poor. This study documents the nature and causes of the gap between an enlightened policy based on the concept of community management and the results of the program through which that policy has been implemented.

THE SETTING

Between 1947 and 1977, India's forest cover decreased from 40 to 20 percent, with only about 11 percent of the total land area actually under adequate tree cover.[2] Besides having a deleterious effect on agriculture, deforestation has caused severe ecological damage in many areas of rural India and hardship for the 90 percent of the Indian population that continues to depend on forests for its domestic needs, fodder for animals, poles and posts for housing, and for organic fertilizer for agriculture.

For centuries prior to British rule, the rural people of India had made use of forestry products according to locally agreed upon practices that ensured their continued supply and distribution to those who needed them. The roots of the current problem trace back to British rule and the policy of reserving large forest areas for the monopolistic use of the British government. This resulted in a sudden and drastic reduction both of the public forest lands open to public use, and the forests belonging to the local *panchayats* (village councils). An irreversible trend in forest management and land-use was thus initiated involving the alienation of the whole rural population from the forest, which in its eyes, now came under the exclusive control of such "external" authorities as forest officers and contractors. The sudden restriction of the population's access to large parts of the reserved forest led, in the absence of any alternatives, to the remaining panchayati forests being rapidly stripped of their trees to meet the needs of the local people. The reserve forests, in the meantime, dwindled through inefficient management oriented to commercial exploitation.[3]

The structure and orientation of forestry management which had led to this sorry state was adopted from the British by the Indian government after the close of British rule. The problem was subsequently exacerbated by the food production priorities of the Indian government during the 1960's, which brought thousands of hectares of forest land under the plough.

SOCIAL FORESTRY: THE CONCEPT

Under the joint crisis of unsatisfied basic needs and ecological instability, the rebuilding of India's forest wealth has, in recent years, become one of the major issues in land-use policy, and social forestry has been proclaimed as the leading instrument for forest regeneration. The announced aim of the government's social forestry program is primarily the development of firewood resources, since the shortage of domestic energy, predominantly firewood for food preparation, is expected to be more critical in future years than shortages of food itself. Furthermore, the fuel crisis diverts agricultural waste and dung from its use as organic manure to fuel for cooking, thus sabotaging sustainable agricultural activity. It also undermines agricultural activity by diverting some 20 percent of available farm labor and 18 percent of domestic household labor to firewood gathering.

Of course, forests also provide a wide variety of other products essential to rural life, including fodder for draught animals and timber for housing. This is in addition to the role of forests in stabilizing both hydrological and soil systems. By planting trees in areas now devoid of tree cover, social forestry aims to prevent soil erosion and the silting up of tanks and reservoirs; to arrest the surface run-off of rain water from hillsides; to recharge springs, streams, and underground water aquifers; and finally, in areas which have been severely deforested, to halt the process of desertification.

The basic concept of social forestry is quite simple. Young saplings planted on common lands are likely to be quickly ruined by uncontrolled grazing if the local community is not committed to their protection. They must feel they have a stake in insuring the productive development of the forest resource to meet their own needs for forest products, both for consumption and for income generation, and they must be organized to enforce the rules upon which they agree regarding the management of that resource.

SOCIAL FORESTRY: THE KARNATAKA PROGRAM

In 1980 the government of Karnataka submitted a proposal to the World Bank requesting Rs. 600 million for a five-year social forestry program. The stated aim was to combat ecological degradation and meet the basic firewood, fodder, and timber needs of the rural population. The scheme called for development of 110,000 hectares of private land as forests—some 60 percent of the total area of the scheme. A significant feature of the proposal was that the main species to be encouraged was eucalyptus. No mention was made of such traditional farm trees as *honge*, *neem* and mango.

A quotation from the proposal expresses the lofty expectations of its drafters regarding expected benefits for the rural population.

> [The purpose of social forestry] is the creation of forests for the benefit of the community through active involvement and the participation of the community. In the process, the rural environment will improve, rural migration will reduce, rural unemployment substantially cease. ...The overall concept of social forestry aims at making the villages self-sufficient and self-reliant in regard to their forest material needs.[4]

The present study examines the early results of the on-going social forestry scheme in the Kolar district of Karnataka, in which essentially the same program model proposed to the World Bank has been in operation for a number of years. The evidence from this experience suggests that this particular approach to social forestry, far from achieving its goals, has in many ways exacerbated the problems it sought to solve.

In part this is because the emphasis has in fact been on private farm forestry to the neglect of communally owned forests from which the entire community may benefit. It also relates to the choice of species, since eucalyptus, which the program emphasizes, fulfills fewer ecological functions than traditional tree species. It cannot be browsed by animals and provides no fodder, it produces no fruit or nuts, and it is not favored as a fuel.[5] There is also evidence that the development of eucalyptus plantations results in the displacement of labor.

To understand the actual and prospective impact of the program currently being implemented, it is necessary to put it in the context of the traditional agricultural pattern in the area.

Traditional Agriculture in Kolar: Private versus Communal Ownership

Traditionally agriculture in Kolar featured a rich variety of predominantly rain-fed food and cash crops, though a few areas are sustained by well and tank-fed irrigation systems. These crops have been supplemented by a mixture of carefully chosen, multipurpose farm trees like honge (Pongamia sp.), *ala (Ficus* sp.), tamarind (*Tamarindus* sp.), pale (*Acacia* sp.), and neem (*Melia Azadiraenta*). These preferred tree species provided a broad range of benefits to the local population. For example, the most popular among them in the Kolar region was the honge. Its leaves provide fodder and green manure. Its oil is used for lighting. And its wood makes an extremely good fuel. Neem is used as a pesticide, and as medicine, food, oil and firewood. Tamarind, mango, and jackfruit provide fruits that are an essential part of the diet. This mix of species made the local population self-sufficient with respect to a number of needs without making conflicting demands on the land for food, fodder, fuel, and manure.

Some were planted on privately owned land, either along field bunds or in the fields themselves. In addition to these privately owned trees, there were community owned trees on the village commons and along roadsides. Other communal lands, designated as *gomal* lands, were used predominantly for grazing, but also produced communally available tree products.

All of the traditional species played a significant role in maintaining soil fertility, preventing soil erosion and conserving underground and surface water resources. Using its traditional store of knowledge of silviculture, the species chosen by the community and the lands on which they were planted were carefully chosen to maximize their ecological, as well as their economic, value. Thus, trees were planted along the tank bunds, field boundaries, and on common land to hold the soil and conserve moisture. Hence, the distribution of trees, together with the choice of species, lent itself to maximizing material benefits for the community as a whole.

Erik Eckholm has argued that the cooperation required for communal forestry is largely ruled out in settings of significant social inequality such as exist in Kolar.[6] This goes against the evidence of India's historical reality. Relics of village woodlots or roadside plantations can still be easily found. In the traditional village, private and unequal landholdings existed side-by-side with common and equally shared resources.

The Breakdown of Community Norms

While self-interest might guide a landlord's use of his own land, the use of common resources such as village woodlots was guided by shared community norms, even for the private landlord. The efficacy of these norms was sustained until the simultaneous operation of individual and community obligations was made impossible through the opening up of the village economy to large urban and industrial markets. By and large, access to the larger markets was, and still is, possible only for the most privileged members of the community who had easy access to educational, bureaucratic, and financial institutions. That started a process that gradually broke down the traditional social bonds between the rich and the less fortunate members of the village—leading gradually to a breakdown of the community. Furthermore, the introduction of new agricultural techniques that were adopted only by the rich farmers made them less dependent on local resources, as for example, the substitution of chemical fertilizer for green manure. Under such circumstances, the participation of rich villagers in community efforts to maintain local resources was reduced, leading ultimately to the slow decay of those community norms that had previously governed the use of local resources. Where social organization is based on cooperation amongst members and production based on need, the logic of gain is entirely different from that of societies based on competition and profits through exchange.

The survival of such community property as pastures and villge woodlots, or "common goods" like a stable ecosystem, is only possible under a social organization where checks and controls on the use of resources are built into the organizing principles of the community. On the other hand, the breakdown of a community, with the associated collapse in concepts of joint ownership and responsibility, can trigger the degradation of common resources. This is what has happened in forest ownership and land use in India.

Eucalyptus: The Great Encroacher

In the second half of the 1970's, significant changes in land use in Kolar emerged as a result of the Karnataka social forestry program. Through the distribution of free seedlings, farmers have put a large amount of land under farm forests. Although the social forestry scheme was supposed to make a variety of species available for farm forestry, in fact very few species other than *Eucalyptus tereticornis* (also called Mysore hybrid) have been planted. According to our observations in Kolar district, about 55,000 acres had been committed to eucalyptus by 1980-81. The government estimated that 14,000 acres had been planted to eucalyptus in that year alone, and that 93.1 percent of the extension had taken place on agricultural and cultivatable waste lands.[7]

As was noted earlier, the primary objective of the social forestry program is to meet the basic needs of the rural population for forest products, in particular for firewood and fodder. Yet, while for cooking purposes the need is for a slow, controlled heat, eucalyptus—the primary product of the social forestry project—burns too fast to be a preferred cooking fuel among residents of the area. Furthermore, because it is so fast burning, the quantities of eucalyptus wood required to sustain a fire for the length of time required to cook a meal can be prohibitively expensive at its current market price, which is set by the demand for it as a pulp source for the manufacture of paper and rayon. (More than 80 percent of the eucalyptus from Kolar is earmarked for the polyfibre industry in Harihar.) The small number of families using eucalyptus for cooking are usually poor families who collect it from reserved forests in the absence of any other species.

Because of the decline in traditional tree species like honge, tamarind, etc., the supplies of traditional cooking woods that were once available are becoming increasingly restricted. If that trend continues, the firewood crisis will worsen during the years to come, despite the impressive growth of eucalyptus plantations in the villages. Furthermore, eucalyptus tereticornis provides no fodder and in arid regions where it drives out herbaceous annuals, which cannot compete with it for the limited available water, thus allowing no undergrowth which might be used for grazing. Consequently the widespread planting of this species on farmland and communal lands has succeeded in further depleting the already scant fodder resources of the area.

By increasing fodder shortages, the planting of eucalyptus has also indirectly affected the viability of two alternative, renewable energy resources: animal energy and biogas energy. Less fodder reduces the inputs to biogas plants, thus accentuating the already acute problem of firewood shortages.

SIMPLISTIC ASSUMPTIONS

Why has the social forestry program failed so conspicuously to achieve its primary objective of satisfaction of the basic biomass needs of the rural population? The answer, in our view, lies in the simplistic assumptions that have been made about the production and distribution of primary forest products. It has been assumed implicitly that just growing more trees will satisfy basic needs. No distinction has been made between what trees are grown or who grows them, even though the evidence suggests that the tree species that get planted determine to a large extent which groups will benefit. It has also been assumed erroneously that if more of a particular commodity is produced in a particular area, that commodity will automatically become more available to the local people. That assumption takes little account of the nature of the market economy. In a market economy, it is those with the highest purchasing power who have command over resources. And in this case, those with the highest purchasing power are not the local people but distant unban based industries.

Also neglected is the relationship between wood fibre production and food production. There has been a tendency for the government to be concerned with food productivity, food shortages, and food surpluses only in relation to urban consumption needs. Thus, we have instances of importing wheat to check inflation in response to a rising price of wheat, but wheat is not the staple food of most of the rural poor in India. In Karnataka the basic staple is *ragi*, a millet. Price increases of 200 percent in two years have made ragi nearly as expensive as wheat and rice, with little reaction from the government. Among the consequences is a decline in physical health and nutritional status as a result of shifting from the traditional staple diet of millets and pulses to diets (made possible through debt or food for work programs) of wheat or rice.[8]

Significantly the area under ragi has been systematically shrinking in Kolar (from 141,772 acres in 1977 - 78 to 48,406 in 1980-81) as it has throughout Karnataka, primarily through the conversion of these lands to eucalyptus plantations. It may be anticipated that this conversion will continue in response to further expansion of the social forestry program.

A related consequence is a decline in the demand for labor. By growing eucalyptus, a farmer becomes relatively independent of labor for his farm operations while simultaneously retaining the returns from his land. The cost of mixed and rotational cropping of traditional food crops in rainfed areas requires an annual expense of at least Rs. 1,500 per hectare, with a labor requirement on the order of 250 man-days. By contrast, eucalyptus plantations require only an initial expenditure of Rs. 1,500 per hectare plus harvesting costs, with a guaranteed high return. Labor costs during the growth period are negligible. Farmers currently sell eucalyptus at around Rs. 300 per ton to the pulp based industries, easily providing an annual return of Rs. 2,500 per hectare.

Despite its proclaimed objectives, the present social forestry program thus appears to be little more than yet another policy for supplying industrial raw materials. Unlike conventional forestry, which simply supplied industry its raw material from land specially earmarked for reserved forests, social forestry is ultimately performing the same function by putting new demands on lands that have been used for production of the basic food requirements of the rural population. At worst, such calculated displacement of basic food production must lead to slow emaciation and death through starvation of a significant number of the rural poor.

Perversely this in turn may in fact have a detrimental impact on non-eucalyptus forest production, since the survival of the displaced labor is dependent on searching out alternative means of livelihood. One such option is the collection of firewood in the reserve forests, not for their own consumption, but for sale in urban and semi-urban centers. In one of the villages in our survey, fifteen out of sixty households were found to be fully dependent on the firewood trade. Villagers spend nearly eight hours a day walking six to eight kilometers to the local market where a headload of firewood sells for some Rs. 4.00. Further deforestation is one of the consequences of this firewood trade, and the theft of firewood through stripping forest reserves of their remaining trees is the only option left to more and more villagers.

Earlier afforestation programs of the forest department, which raised eucalyptus on forest land, presented the argument that eucalyptus was often the only species that could survive on degraded soils. But now, through social forestry, eucalyptus is being introduced for the first time on fertile land in arid and semi-arid regions where crops could grow. Since eucalyptus leaves do not contribute to the building up of humus, and the tree does not allow undergrowth, the long-term impact of eucalyptus on the fertility of agricultural lands in these regions is quite deleterious.[9]

THE CHALLENGE

Our study has demontrated a substantial gap between the high-sounding objectives of social forestry and the realities of its implementation in the Indian district studied. Unfortunately the evidence suggests that the negative consequences described are not limited to this district. The task of developing social forestry programs that can in fact meet their intended objectives becomes a major challange for those who believe in people's participation in development. The organized will of the people, instead of the availability of foreign funds, should be the starting point for social forestry. In various parts of the country, nongovernmental organizations have done excellent afforestation without foreign aid. Perhaps ultimately the answer can be found in some form of collaboration between the government foresters, nongovernmental organizations, and the village people.[10] Only if the people and the government learn to work together in a new relationship is it likely that the laudable objectives of social forestry will be realized.

NOTES

1. Revised and abstracted version of "The Challenge of Social Forestry" by the same authors published in W. Fernandez and S. Kulkarni, *Towards a New Forest Policy*, Indian Social Institute, New Delhi 110003 (1983). Reprinted by permission.

2. B. B. Vohra, "The Greening of India" in J. Bandyopdahyay, N. D. Jayal, U. Schoettli, and Chhatrapati Singh (eds.), *India's Environment: Crises and Responses*, (Dehradun: Natraj Publishers, 1985), p. 27.

3. C. T. S. Nair, "Crisis in Forest Resource Management" in Bandyopadhyay, *loc. cit.*, pp. 10-3.

4. Government of Karnataka, *Social Forestry Programme with World Bank Aid* (Bangalore), 1980, p. 9.

5. Vandana Shiva and J. Bandyopadhyay, *Ecological Audit of Eucalyptus Cultivation*, (Dhradun: The English Book Depot, 1985), pp[. 31-46.

6. Erik Eckholm, *Planting for the Future: Forestry for Human Needs*, World Watch Paper No. 26, World Watch Institute, Washington, D. C. 1979, p. 36.

7. See Bureau of Economics and Statistics, Government of Karnataka, *Report on the Impact of Social Forestry Programme on Land Use in Kolar and Bangalore Districts*, Bangalore, 1984, p. 6.

8. Vandana Shiva, et al., unpublished, 1979.

9. Shiva and Bandyopadhyay, *Ecological Audit*, op. cit.

10. Vandana Shiva, J. Bandyopadhyay and N. D. Jayal, "Afforestation in India: Problems and Strategy," *AMBIO* (forthcoming).

CHAPTER EIGHTEEN

Government as an Agent of Social Development—Lessons from the Bangladesh Experience

Shaikh Maqsood Ali

> To commemorate tree plantation week a Subdivisional Officer was instructed to plant a tree at the local police station. Arriving there he asked the assembled officials where he should plant the tree. A heated debate followed with many opinions forcefully expressed, until a member of the village police appeared and insisted he knew exactly the proper place. Accepting the guidance, the official asked after the tree was planted what was special about this particular spot. The policeman replied: "Every year at this time an official comes to plant a tree and always it has been planted in this same place."
>
> —Anonymous

Like the planting of the tree we have experimented with many different rural development programs in Bangladesh, planting our seedlings in the same ground time after time, without proper care and time to mature; and without evaluation to determine why previous seedlings have prospered or failed on the same ground.

We set up credit cooperatives in 1905 throughout the rural areas of what is now Bangladesh at the initiative of enlightened British adminstrators who identified the money lenders as the main exploiters of the rural poor. Ultimately these cooperatives failed because the funds available were negligible compared to the growing needs of the poor. They also neglected the need of poor farmers for inputs such as better seed and fertilizer, which were always in short supply. Finally, since the poor were not in a position to organize themselves, their management remained in the hands of the relatively well-to-do who captured a major portion of the benefits.

After the British left India there was a series of new experiments. Efforts were made to expand the existing credit cooperatives and convert them into multi-purpose societies that would provide farmers with a range of inputs. Then in the 1950's we tried the community development approach with the assistance of AID. Later we become captivated by the Comilla approach, which had apparent success in Comilla District, and used it as the basis for a national Integrated Rural Development Program. But by 1974 we found once again that the cooperative societies had become the closed clubs of the local elites. So then we moved to the Reformed Cooperatives.

Many of us in government continue to believe that for rural development to be effective in Bangladesh the poor must be organized so that they can reduce their dependence on an administrative and planning system based to benifit the relatively rich and powerful. But important questions are raised by past experiments.

–Is it inevitable that local organizations only strengthen the power of local elites to further serve their own interests at the expense of the poor?

–Can civil servants play a leadership role in organizing the poor into viable interest and functional groups? Or do the bureaucratic structures within which they work inevitably doom such efforts to failure?

–Are there ways in which governments can stimulate and enable broadly based local initiatives that do not depend on the dierct intervention of civil service personnel?

It is perhaps significant that the failures of many ambitious government initiatives stand in rather pointed contrast to the many spontaneous local development initatives that have emerged throughout Bangladesh over the years and made important differences in the lives of their participants. There are crucial lessons to be learned from these truly spontaneous and voluntary efforts and from subsequent efforts to turn them into national initiatives.

It will be helpful in understanding the cases that follow to know that Bangladesh administration today is divided into four divisions, sixty-four districts, and about 460 *upazilas* (thanas).[1] At the upazila level there are about thirty-five class I officers of various national departments with responsibility for assisting the development of the villages under their jurisdiction. Below the upazila come the Union Councils (*parishads*), each responsible for about fifteen villages. The chairman and members of the Union Council are elected directly by the people, normally with one representative coming from each village. However, experience shows that the elections are effectively controlled by local faction leaders who bring factional politics into local government, often with limited concern for the broader interests of the community. On the other hand, government officials posted at upazila level remain largely unaccountable, irresponsible, and unresponsive to the people. There is, therfore, no real integration of the local government institutions with upazila administration. Consequently anyone exercising leadership at village level in local development activities is largely isolated from these institutions and the resources they control.

VOLUNTARY VILLAGE DEVELOPMENT INITIATIVES

The very poor who inhabit the deltaic region of Bangladesh have long accepted natural disaster as a part of their lives. Because government assistance to meet these crises always has been negligible, they of necessity developed a special self-reliance, resilience, and cooperative spirit as a requirement of survival. These qualities came strongly into play during the liberation war when outside aid to the region that is now Bangladesh dropped to its lowest level.

But the immediate post-liberation period saw a huge influx of relief assistance. This so undermined the traditional spirit of self-reliance that when a devastating flood occurred in 1974, people in the flood-affected areas, particlarily in North Bengal, took little action on their own behalf, waiting instead for the relief agencies to rescue them. But by this time most of the relief agencies were winding down their programs and departing. Many people suffered as a result.

Some people recognized this tragedy and acted. In many places self-help projects intended to rapidly boost food production were undertaken. Sometimes the initiative came from an energetic district officer, a teacher, or a public spirited member of the village elite. In others it might be an educated housewife or one of the better educated but unemployed young villagers. In the earlier days these village "social workers" came from reasonably good family backgrounds and were able to support themselves from their own resources even as they gave significant time to community work. Subsequently they were joined by growing numbers of volunteers from lower socio-economic backgrounds. Some of these initiatives were assisted by private, indigenous development agencies, others emerged wholly spontaneously, but the local initiatives that resulted all had the quality of being the products of individual concern, and their resources were largely limited to the commitment and creativity of those who participated.

Spontaneous village self-help efforts gained particular impetus in late 1974 and early 1975 in response to the flood. By mid-1975 such efforts were springing up all over the country. Their organizers gave them beautiful names: *Shabuj* in Comilla, *Barnali* in Tangail, *Shamali* in Sylhet and so on. Commonly the prospective social worker or village organizer began by identifying those elders in the village respected for their honesty, integrity, sense of judgement and impartiality, and encouraged them to exert their leadership. The more successful social workers attributed their achievements in part to being "invisible like the air" meaning that they worked quietly behind the scenes, giving the credit to the traditional village leaders. This gained acceptance for their activities from the local power holders. Many also spoke of "learning to flow like a river." When a flowing river faces an obstacle it cannot turn back or lodge a complaint with a higher authority. The river must find an alternative course. Similarily the skilled social workers devised alternative strategies suited to the circumstances.

While they made mistakes, the more successful also learned quickly and sometimes evolved quite sophisticated methods, as demonstrated by the story of a social worker from the village of Mokshedpur in Kishorgan District who established a village literacy campaign. Originally he had done what the government literacy programs normally did. He attempted to set up a night school with papers, pencils, blackboard, mats, lanterns, etc., for the illiterate adults. But the students he enrolled quicky lost interest. So he changed his strategy.

He found that illiteracy was highest among the thirty-seven landless farming families in the village. He also found that a road was to be repaired in his village by the Thana administration through contractors at a cost of Tk. 2000. He approached the local adminstrator and requested that he allow the villagers to repair the road at the same cost. When the adminstrator agreed, he organized the landless to repair the road during their off time (from five to nine o'clock in the evening). Expenditures for incidental charges were Tk. 700, leaving Tk. 1300 for distribution among them as wages.

He then convinced the farmers to put the money into a postal savings bank in a joint account in the name of all the members to be used as a revolving fund which members could use to invest in income producing activities. But only those who could sign their names would be able to participate. They were soon chasing after educated people to teach them how to sign their names correctly. By the end of the first week all had learned. Capitalizing on the enthusiasm for learning that this experience generated, the night school was re-established and subsequently well attended.

The sophistication and resourcefulness of the bettter social workers was demonstrated to me in a village to which I had taken thirty-five medical doctors for action training. For those landless farmers who were good cultivators they had obtained a piece of land on lease from a local businessman using a self-reliance fund. They obtained two derelict tanks for a pisciculture project for another group who could maintain themselves from other sources while the fry matured. For the very poorest who were strong but not good farmers, they rented two cycle-rickshaws. For those too weak for physical labor they bought old clothes in Dhaka for them to clean and mend for sale in the market.

Such examples attracted growing attention and provided inspiration for others, leading some concerned individuals to look for the means by which the successes could be replicated on a national scale. The Swanirvar Movement was one such effort.

EMERGENCE OF THE SWANIRVAR MOVEMENT

In September 1975 a national seminar was organized by the Agricultural Research Institute at Joydevpur. Selected village volunteers came from all over the country, along with concerned government officials, including those from disrtict and division commissioner level. The participants endorsed the idea of a national movement and agreed that it should be called *Swanirvar,* meaning self-reliance.

While some of the government officials present were enthusiastic, others raised questions regarding the official status of Swanirvar activities. They noted that if it were a government program, it would be easier for them to assist in their official capacities. The seminar organizers replied that they were strongly opposed to the opening of yet another department of rural development with its inevitable generations of rules and regulations that would mire the movement in red tape. The officials responded that if there were no official status they could not recieve travel and other allowances for their participation.

Eventually a compromise was reached. Swanirvar would be a movement, not a program. And it would be outside of, but indirectly backed by Government. Official recognition would be provided by appointing a special secretary for agriculture (Swanirvar). He would have a small office, with other officers obtained on secundment from cooperating offices when necessary. It was expected that he would spend most of his time in the field away from his Secretariate.

Then, having reached agreement that Swanirvar would be a movement rather than a program, the participants immediately set about to design a program to be implemented through the local units of the national government. Activities would be coordinated by a Central Swanirvar Committee with members carefully selected from among persons who were strong believers as well as action workers in the movement. The committee included some veteran social workers who were experimenting with innovative rural development practices in their own villages. A number of high-level government officials served as ex-officio members.

It was decided that each district administration would select one village from each thana in its jurisdiction for inclusion in the movement the first year. The development of each selected village would be undertaken as a joint venture of the local thana officers and the villagers. A manual would be developed for use by villagers in surveying village resources and organizing village interest groups. Training on the application of the manual would be organized for concerned divisional and district officials by Central Committee. These officials would in turn conduct training for subdivisional officers in district training camps. The subdivisional officers would then train thana officers who would in turn train the Swanirvar villagers.

Developing a Manual

A group of experts from various research and training institutions, universities, and government agencies was assembled to draft a manual. When tested in four villages near one of the participating universities it was found to be too long and difficult for the villagers to understand, let alone apply.

The assignment was then turned over to a group of villagers and social workers who drafted a short simple version. The scheme proposed recognized four main village occupational groups: the rich farmers, the middle farmers, the small farmers, and the landless, each of which had different economic problems. In addition there were to be two social groups, youth and women, also with distinctive needs and interests. The cooperative was taken as the basic instrument of rural organizing in the belief that past failures could be overcome by organizing on the basis of interest groups. Each cooperative would have two representatives on a Central Village Swanirvar Committee, which was intended to integrate the village into an effective development unit. The committee would function through a number of technical subcommittees which would deal with matters such as agriculture and sanitation on a villagewide basis.

The final Swanirvar training manual provided guidance on how to train village workers to mobilize the village people to form the various organizations. It also indicated how village resources could be surveyed and projects prepared and implemented through these organizations with minimum reliance on outside help.

Training of Trainers Program

The district-level training of trainers programs for division and district officers were held between June and September 1976. By this time many of the initial Swanirvar villages had already been selected and development work begun. Consequently many of the officials involved in this were able to share their early implementation experiences.

As head of one of these division training centers I had a very revealing experience with my first group of trainees. The course was scheduled for three days and the training plan called for the trainees to do a village survey following procedures outlined in the manual. The trainees returned from this assignment with their "data" in only a few hours, having obtained it from the files of the school and the union office.

In response to my inquiry about their apparent lack of interest in the assignment they came forward with a number of criticisms of Swanirvar. They had seen government officials arriving at villages in government cars powered by government petrol as if at a picnic outing. The officials were hosted and fed, finally paying Tk. 5 per head to the organizer for food actually costing much more. At the end they had driven back to their offices and not given the village and its needs further thought.

With respect to their own behavior on the survey, they argued that they could not get correct statistics from the villagers because the villagers do not trust government officers. Never in the history of this region had an officer gone to a village to work with the villagers as their partner. They had come either as tax collectors, process servers, or to exploit the villagers in some other way. Having gotten this all out they seemed more relaxed and committed. Finally they agreed to return to the village to do the job for which they had come.

The next day I went to the village. I found the officials inside the houses of the small farmers smoking huccas and talking as intimate friends. Later they commented on how the accuracy of the information improved as trust was developed. For example, a farmer might initially admit to having only one cow. Then as they became more friendly it might increase to two, three, or even more.

The implications were clear. To work together with the villagers as partners, the officers would have to spend a good deal of time in the village and become a part of the rural society.

Expansion

Early in 1977 the progress made by the 354 villages that had undertaken the program in 1976 was evaluated by a group of experts belonging to a number of Bangladesh research and educational organizations. It found that of the 354 villages, thirty-seven had done quite well. Their total income was claimed to have increased on the average by about 37 percent during the year, with particular improvement in the production of food and vegetables, fish raising, poultry production and literacy rates. There were complementary decreases in the rate of population growth and number of crimes.

Cooperation between the thana officers and social workers in these villages had improved and some villages were trying to prepare annual development plans. These thirty-seven villages were rated as category "A". Another ninety-six villages were rated as category "B", which meant that

on the whole they had performed well. A "C" rating for "average" performance was given to 147 villages. The remaining seventy-four villages,
which had not undertaken any development work, were rated as "D".

Though some more cautious members were urging a period of consolidation, the more expansionist members focused on the rather
remarkable success of the thirty-seven category A villages, obtaining agreement from the National Central Committee to expand immediately to one
village in each union, or a total of 4,352 villages. In addition, twenty thanas
of five districts were urged to introduce the movement to all their villages.[2]

Formalizing Linkages to Local Administration

As serious efforts were made to expand the Swanirvar movement, attention was necessarily directed to the question: How should the elected
members of the Union Councils, the thana officers and the Swanirvar
workers cooperate in the preparation and execution of local development
projects? Examination of Swanirvar experience in different districts revealed
two distinctive approaches.

The Kushtia Model initiated by the deputy commissioner of the Kushtia
District added to the basic village structure proposed by the Swanirvar
training manual, a Village Assembly (Shava) comprised of the head of
each family in the village. This assembly assumed collective responsibility for all of the members of the village. In addition two representatives
of each of the five main groups in the village, the landless, the youth,
the women, and people belonging to other professions, formed a Central
Village Committee known as the Village Parishad (Cabinet). The largest
group in the village would send one additional member. Each of the eleven
members of the Village Parishad assumed responsibility for one area of
development such as agriculture, education, health, etc. Each Parishad
member was helped by the relevant technical sub-committees.

The significant feature of this model was that the Union Council was
essentially by-passed, as was the thana level of administration. The village
related directly to government officials at the district level, and village
activities depended heavily on their direct support. Consequently when
the particular deputy commissioner who initiated it was transferred out
of the district, much of the momentum of the movement in Kushtia villages
seemed to have been lost.

The Sadullapur Model was the innovation of the chairman of the
Naldanga Union Parishad in Sadullapur Thana of Rangpur District. Instead of only the heads of families, all the adult members of the village
were members of its Village Assembly. Another difference was that the
local member of the Union Council served as ex-officio chairman of its
Union Council. At union level, each member of the Union Council was

assigned responsibility for the "portfolio" of at least one development sector corresponding to the sector responsibilities of their counterparts on the village council. The members of both the Village and Union Council[3] were referred to as village and union ministers, respectively—to the substantial displeasure of some of their national level counterparts.

This structure achieved much better coordination between the village and the union than did the Kushtia model. At the same time the district level had little involvement. Consequently, as the movement spread to other unions of the Sadullapur Thana, the commitment and support of district-level officials were limited.

Thus, we had one model in which both district and village levels were active, with union and thana levels remaining largely dormant; and another with strong union and village involvement, without effective participation from either thana or district levels. Either seemed adequate to initiate the effort, but it appears that sustaining it required a more effective involvement from all levels.

From Spontaneous to Formalized Self-Reliance

As praiseworthy and well intentioned as these efforts were, they were gradually and subtly shifting the impetus for village self-reliance from the villagers to an external body of adminstrators and intellectuals. This introduced a basic dilemma faced by all efforts to develop self-reliance as a significant national development force. Actions that formalize the organization of such a movement inevitably change its nature.

While it might be argued that for this reason local movements should be left to their own devices, there are serious limits to what a village can accomplish entirely on its own. This is at least in part because it inevitably belongs to a larger local and national system which can, and often does, overwhelm local initiatives based on pure self-reliance. Furthermore, spontaneous initiatives are likely to emerge on only a sporadic basis, particularly within a basically hostile political and administrative setting.

Consequently those who would seek a development path based on the concept of local self-reliance must eventually come to terms with the question of how these local efforts will relate to larger national structures. Dealing with this issue in a way that does not sap the vitality of local self-reliance efforts through their colonization in the service of a central administration poses a delicate challenge.

THE "OWN VILLAGE DEVELOPMENT PROGRAMME"

The "Own Village Development Programme" (OVD) was initiated by the Cabinet Division of the Government of Bangladesh in January 1977. The National Institute of Public Administration of Dhaka University was to provide two days of orientation sessions for the middle level government officers selected for the program. Once oriented, they were to be allowed by government to spend an initial period of one month in their home villages to promote rural development. The program was based on the theory that working in their own villages would enhance both the access and motivation of the officials. Up to two follow-up visits were to be allowed each year.

The program was coordinated by a joint secretary in the Cabinet Division but operated with only the most minimal resources. The Institute of Public Administration provided training and such follow-up support as it could with its own resources. Participating officials received their normal pay and transportation allowances for visits to their villages, but not the extra daily living allowance they normally received when on travel status. Nor were any financial resources provided for use in local development projects.

The first group of OVD officers reported to the National Institute of Public Adminstration (NIPA) in February 1977 for their orientation. Since it was intended to be an unconventional program for the civil servants, the orientations were also organized in an unconventional way. Social workers were brought in from villages that had demonstrated effective performance in self-reliant village development to serve as instructors for the OVD officers. Much to our surprise the officials readily accepted this novel approach. We were further surprised by the generally high level of interest of the participants in both the specific development fields identified for examination and in the organizational mechanism by which villages might achieve integrated self-reliant development. Follow-up workshops were held for each group of trainees upon their return from their initial village visits, again with the participation of successful social workers.

Although relations between the officials and the social workers were cordial and members of each group often made similar observations and recommendations, marked differences were observed in their attitudes and problem-solving approaches. By and large, the OVD officers were inclined to solve problems through bureaucratic means by obtaining commitment of government resources, and they felt that to get necessary action from local officials they needed some formal authority over them. By contrast, the social workers recognized they had no possibilities of getting any such "authority" or "power" so they were more inclined to give credit to the village elites and to be more creative in finding ways around obstacles.

The president of Bangladesh, who had a significant interest in rural development, met wiht the OVD officers at his own initiative. A report prepared by the officers for the president in preparation for this visit further revealed their predisposition to rely on authority and central resources in dealing with local development problems. Among their recommendations they asked that: A reporting cell be established in the Cabinet Division to act on cases of irregularities and corruption reported to it by the OVD officers; clear instructions be issued to both district and central ministry authorities to support the OVD officers in their rural development activities; their vilalges be given priority in receiving government-provided services and inputs; and a development fund be established to provide them with matching grants for local development activities.

Eventually the OVD experiment fell from grace. One important reason was that the OVD officers, by and large, remained bureaucratic in their approach to development, continuing to seek increased funding from government for their work. It proved impossible for most of them to "float like a river" as was the case with the Swanirvar workers.

It was determined that by March 1981, 1,574 officers had participated in the program. While all had visited their villages at least once, only 300 had visited more that once. Some officials participated only because the government wanted them to do so, or had lands in their village which they welcomed an opportunity to supervise at government expense. Others simply went to their villages for a paid holiday. Many of their reports reflected only a superficial understanding of rural development problems.

REFLECTIONS ON LESSONS LEARNED

Moving from a centralized, rule-bound bureaucratic system known for its unresponsiveness to, and exploitation of, villagers to a decentraliz-ed system of locally accountable adminstration that stimulates local self-reliant development action takes a combination of patience and sustain-ed commitment. It also requires difficult-to-achieve changes in value and skills backed by changes in formal authorities and structures and an in-vestment in building the trust of village partners.

The cases examined here were premised on the initiative of govern-ment officials more than that of the villagers, and the actions directed to achieving the changes in roles and attitudes supportive of this initiative were limited largely to training interventions. Ultimately change depend-ed on the motivation of the officials so trained being sufficiently strong to withstand the contrary pressures exerted on them by the bureaucracies in which they worked. Neither case involved any effort to change selec-tion or assignment criteria, job rotation patterns, promotion procedures and criteria, compensation, lines of authority, formal job descriptions, supervision styles, budgeting procedures, funding allocations, other train-ing programs, or any of the other incentive systems of the bureaucracy that shape the behavior of its members. given the deeply entrenched nature of existing bureaucratic structures, achieving supportive structural changes probably would not have been feasible.

The two national experiments outlined above demonstrate the difficulty, within the Bangladesh setting, of seeking to build local self reliance by calling on government officials to take the lead in increasing the people's capacity for participation. While such experimentation must surely continue, it seems prudent at the same time to look for alternative approaches to meeting this need.

Concurrent with the numerous experiments outlined above, a number of private voluntary groups indigenous to Bangladesh have acquired strong national and international reputations for the success and scope of their efforts in support of self-reliant local development. Working with relative independence of existing political systems, they have been able to work directly with the rural poor, organizing them to improve their livelihood activities, to obtain credit, to gain access to public and idle lands, to organize their own public services, and to demand the services due them from government. These efforts are an important force in Bangladesh toward creating a basis for effective local democracy.

Perhaps, rather than looking to government officials to themselves accomplish the organization and mobilization of the rural poor, the government should encourage the private voluntary sector in its already substantial efforts. The governmental role in such a partnership would be to create a favorable policy setting and respond in supportive ways to the local initiatives so generated.

This would define the role of government training institutions in the larger rural development effort in terms of sensitizing members of the career civil service to the essential and constructive role of these private development organizations, while training them in how to create a positive policy setting and to make their programs more responsive to locally generated initiatives. At the same time we must surely give attention to helping them see the possibility of nonbureaucratic approaches to basic problem solving essential to their effectiveness in an enabling role.

However, not all private voluntary organizations may play the constructive role we envisage for them in the field of rural development. They can acquire their dynamism only through a painful process of trial and error over a prolonged period of time. They will survive only if they are guided by dedicated leaders who derive their power from an inner conviction that the purpose of their lives is to serve the poor and the disadvantaged. Since such people are quite few in number in any country, the government has to be selective in coordinating its development activities with these private voluntary organizations.

On the other hand, we also face the danger that, in embracing such private voluntary effort, government may have a tendency to seek to control and direct it in the name of coordination. In so doing it would almost surely render it an ineffective extension of central control. Avoiding such tendencies would be crucial to the success of such a partnership between the public and the private voluntary sectors.

Bangladesh has reached a threshold in the development of its political and administrative process toward achieving local self-reliant development. It reflects a combination of a maturation in its public policies, the growing capacities of its private voluntary development sector, and the experience of its many public and private experiments with self-reliant local development. The opportunity is at hand, but realizing it will require a vision that recognizes the creative potentials of all the peoples and sectors of Bangladesh society and helps them to find their legitimate place within the national development effort.

NOTES

1. In 1984 a decision was taken to upgrade the function of the thana and its name was changed to Upazila. When referring to events which occurred before the change the term thana will normally be used.

2. The expansionists gained further strength for their argument from a 1976 Presidential announcement that in the future the development of Bangladesh would be village and people based; and a government announcement that during 1977-78 the Union Councils would be given increased authority to carry out local development projects.

3. The actual term is "parishad" which may also be translated "cabinet."

4. Another reason was that many of the OVD officers chose to emphasize water control projects because they felt agricultural development was the most important aspect of rural development. Often this invloved fairly large projects which, due to considerations of topography and hydrology, involved two or more thanas. Thus, they were difficult to accommodate within the existing planning framework base on administrative units like the thana and the union. They also were clearly beyond the capacity of the village to implement and gave little impetus to development of village self-reliance.

CHAPTER NINETEEN

Averting the Bureaucratization of a Community-Managed Resource— The Case of the Zanjeras

Robert Y. Siy, Jr.[1]

Many large-scale technically sophisticated government-managed irrigation systems throughout the world irrigate much less area than they
were designed to serve, experience rapid rates of deterioration, and leave
water users frustrated and dissatisfied with unreliable, unpredictable
deliveries of water.[2] Yet there are also many reports of relatively high performing irrigation systems constructed, operated, and maintained by long
established indigenous water users organizations.[3]

It is unfortunate that irrigation engineers have for many years
dismissed such indigenous systems as primitive and inefficient and have
seldom sought to learn the lessons of their experience.[4] Few irrigation
bureaucracies even include the areas served by such systems in their
reports of area under irrigation. The tendency to ignore these systems
becomes particularily disturbing when, as is common throughout the
humid tropics, so called modern systems are built in areas where
community-operated irrigation systems already exist.[5] The problem is illustrated by the following case.

The province of Ilocos Norte in the northern Philippines is well known
internationally as the domain of the zanjeras, farmer irrigator organizations that have been unusually effective at managing water resources.[6]
Some are as large as 1,000 hectares, many are centuries old and all are
recognized for their highly appropriate and systematic rules and procedures for water allocation and system maintenance.

These zanjeras managed their irrigation systems through heavy monsoons and scorching summers with only minimal external assistance or
intervention—until 1978. In that year, a 22,600 hectare irrigation project

was proposed for funding by the Japanese overseas development assistance program. A "modern" irrigation system, designed by a joint Japanese-Filipino consulting team, was to cover the entire project area, an area already served by over two hundred zanjeras, each with its own social organization and canal facilities. The proposed design would have almost completely obliterated the existing indigenous irrigation systems. This article tells of how a potential tragedy was averted by a combination of active, persuasive farmer resistance and the wisdom of an enlightened, sympathetic agency administrator. What followed in the wake of the near tragedy was the establishment of a precedent-setting experiment of farmer-agency collaboration in the design and implementation of a large-scale irrigation project.

THE ZANJERA IRRIGATION SYSTEMS

As of 1978 the landscape of the province of Ilocos Norte was dotted with hundreds of community-built and managed irrigation systems, many of which were constructed over two hundred years ago. The groups that operated and maintained these systems were known to the local people as *zanjeras*, a term taken from the Spanish word *zanja*, meaning canal. In recent years, documents have been found in the possession of a few zanjeras that prove their existence as far back as the eighteenth century.

A number of these documents also describe how some of these irrigation societies were formed. In areas where unirrigated arable land was held as private property, groups of skilled and resourceful individuals seeking land for cultivation offered to construct irrigation systems in exchange for the right to farm portions of the newly irrigated area. This novel arrangement permitted landowners to increase the productivity of their farms while permitting even landless individuals to gain access to land. Other farmers in the province, encouraged by the experiences of these enerprising individuals, formed zanjeras to irrigate the lands they were already cultivating. By the end of the nineteenth century, hundreds of zanjeras were already in operation in the province and their brush dams and earthen canals were a common sight along the waterways of Ilocos Norte.[7]

Operated without government assistance, they relied on the mobilization of local labor for operation and maintenance. It was common for individual members to contribute an average of twenty to thirty days of labor in a year. In a number of zanjeras, members each contributed as many as eighty days of labor annually.

The activities involved in the upkeep of the facilities included construction and repair of temporary diversion dams destroyed by the annual typhoons, reinforcing canals, and cleaning out vegetation and silt accumulation. Communal labor was also required for activities such as water distribution. Over the years, systems were expanded and technical improvements were gradually introduced. Members' contributions of labor and materials were called for according to need and thus varied from year to year. For example, a particularily bad typhoon might create the need for extensive repairs.

The sucess of the zanjeras in mobilizing local labor for irrigation system management was greatly facilitated by: (1) a pattern of land distribution that helped to mitigate conflicts; and (2) assessment of labor contributions in proportion to the area of land a member cultivated.

Within each zanjera, individual landholdings usually consisted of several parcels of nearly equal size, one parcel in each of the sections of the service area, i.e., at the head, middle, and tail of the canal system. This situation helped to avoid the usual "upstream-downstream" or "head-tail" distinctions among farmers and eliminated one of the most common sources of conflict among irrigation users. It served as a strong incentive for cooperating to maintain the system at maximal efficiency in order to adequately irrigate the entire area, greatly facilitating the tasks of water allocation and system maintenance.

The other factor that seemed to explain the longevity and cohesiveness of the zanjeras was their method of regulating members' contributions. In each zanjera, members were assigned "shares," called *atar,* in the organization. These represented the member's share in the water produced and delivered by the irrigation system, and were directly proportional to the area of land that he cultivated within the area irrigated. The ratio of an atar to land area was constant over time and unique to each zanjera. For instance, in one zanjera a member was assigned one atar for every one-fourth of a hectare he farmed, in another organization, members were assigned one atar for every three-fifths of a hectare.

The atar also defined each member's obligation to contribute labor and materials to operate and maintain the irrigation system. The basic rule was that each member was obligated to provide one man-day of labor during each work session for every atar assigned to him.

Over the years these shares were passed on to the heirs of founding members; they were also transferred whenever zanjera land was sold, leased, or tenanted. Through this process, the landholdings of founding members were subdivided. Atars were fractionalized accordingly whenever the lands of founding members were transferred to new members. Thus, if a person now farmed half of the lands of the founding member, he would be assigned one-half atar and would have to fulfill half of the labor obligations of that atar.

Since work obligations continued to be assigned in proportion to the area farmed by each member, the ratio of individual benefits to labor contributions remained roughly equal for all members of a given organization despite changes in the distribution of landholdings. This equitable sharing of benefits and costs, deeply embedded in the norms of the local culture, contributed to a more open and unconstrained atmosphere for cooperation.

These features of the zanjera help to explain why they were able to survive for generations, successfully resolving conflicts and mobilizing local labor and materials as required.

THE PROPOSED IRRIGATION DEVELOPMENT PROJECT

In 1978 a Japanese engineering survey team contracted by the Overseas Economic Cooperation Fund (OECF) and the Japanese International Cooperation Agency (JICA), Japan's two institutions responsible for overseas aid, submitted a report to the Government of the Philippines recommending for the province of Ilocos Norte a two-phase integrated agricultural development project that would include the construction of irrigation facilities, a dam, and two hydroelectric power plants.

The Plan

The report presented a convincing case for the project. First, the province was the birthplace and political base of the Philippine president and there was yet to be a major foreign-funded development project in the area. Second, the proposed power generating facilities would permit the province to become self-sufficient in electrical energy. Third, the project was estimated to benefit roughly 17,500 farm families in the 22,600 hectare project area through improved irrigation.

Although the survey team recognized the existence of many community managed irrigation systems within the project area, their report noted a lack of modern facilities for water regulations, water losses resulting from seepage through the earthen canals, and the use of temporary dams made of wood, stone, and sand, which had to be rebuilt after the yearly storms and floods. According to the survey team,

> no systematic water distribution facilities are provided to convey water to the terminal areas, and the so-called continuous flowing irrigation has been practiced for both the wet and dry season cultivations... Under the circumstances, water resources development as well as the provision of systematized irrigation facilites inclusive of the on-farm facilities are the prerequisites to achieving double cropping of high yielding rice and upland crops.

The economic potential of the area, it was argued, could only be realized through the moderniztion of the area's agriculture. This, in turn, would mean introducing an irrigation system that would permit a more efficient and equitable distribution of water, dams that could withstand the regular typhoons and monsoon rains, and an organizational structure that would ensure coordination and cooperation among water users.

The first phase of the project was to involve an area covering 10,200 hectares, and was expected to cost U.S.$65.5 million. The engineering studies reported that this initial development site contained 136 indigenous water users' organizations (the actual number was later determined to be 186) ranging in size from two hectares to one thousand hactares in service area, and irrigating a total of 8,041 hectares. Although the consultants' report acknowledged that a large part of the project area was already under irrigation by local water users' groups, it contained minimal description of these organizations. There was no mention of the skills, organizational resources or management practices of the groups which were already bringing irrigation to roughly 80 percent of the the Phase I project area. Their irrigation systems were merely regarded as being below acceptable engineering standards. This conclusion, however, was reached without conducting formal hydrological and engineering studies to determine the actual water use efficiencies of the zanjera systems.

Although the survey team had made several visits to the project site and had spent a total of 31.3 man-months of time in the area, most of their work had centered on technical aspects of the project design. Among the members of the survey team, there was only one social scientist, an agricultural economist, who spent two months at the project site collecting statistics on land use and crop yields in order to generate the project cost-benefit calculations.

The plan called for the construction of five dams, 159 kilometers of irrigation canals, 200 kilometers of drainage canals, and nearly a thousand kilometers of main and supplementary farm ditches. The five concrete dams would be built on the upstream sections of each of the five major rivers serving the area. From the dams, the water in each river would be diverted into the new canal system. Water would flow from each dam into a main canal from which it would be conveyed to secondary canals, flowing from these into main farm ditches each serving a thirty-hectare area called a Compact Farm.

The project planners envisioned that the farmers in each Compact Farm would be organized into a Farmer Irrigator's Group (FIG). The FIG's in each 500-hectare area would then compose a Farmer Irrigators Association (FIA). A water management technologist, provided by the irrigation authority, would be assigned to each FIA to assist them in system operation and maintenance activities. The FIA's in each 2,500-hectare area would be formed into a Farmer Irrigators Federation. The federations in the 10,200 hectare (Phase I) area would then form the Farmer Irrigators Union.

The project plan entrusted the NIA with the responsibility for controling and allocating water within the new system. Farmers were to pay for the services of the irrigation authority with a standard irrigation fee equivalent to 250 kilograms of paddy rice per hectare per year.

During construction, a total of 675 hectares of farmland in the Phase I area would need to be expropriated by the government for the construction of new canals and access roads.

Project Implementation

By November 1980, Phase I of the project had been approved for funding by the OECF and the JICA. Detailed plans and engineering designs had been completed by a team of Japanese and Filipino consultants at a cost of approximately U.S. $1 million. A large contracting firm, a Filipino-Japanese joint venture, had already mobilized to begin construction on the first 1,000 hectares of Phase I, which was called the "Pilot Area."

This area was intended to serve as a demonstration site—to prove to farmers in the rest of the project area the benefits of a systematically designed irrigation system and to convince them to cooperate with NIA. Unlike the rest of the project, which was to be financed by a low interest loan from the Japanese government, the Pilot Area construction was consider to be a "gift" from the Japanese government. The provision of a direct grant of U.S.$4.3 million permitted the NIA to initiate Pilot Area construction activities ahead of the implementation schedule for the rest of Phase I.

The construction of facilities for the Pilot Area was to be completed by March 1982, including:

a) a temporary diversion dam forty-eight meters long and .8 meters wide;

b) a main canal of 9,170 meters with related structures;

c) 4,885 meters of lateral canals and structures;

d) 13,762 meters of drainage canals; and

e) 46,000 meters of farm ditches, farm roads, and drains.

Construction on the remaining Phase I area, which covered 9,200 hectares, was to begin in the third quarter of 1981. The completion of Phase I construction was programmed for the year end of 1984.

By December 1980 an agency project management team had assembled at the site—a total of 276 persons, all eager to get the project off to a good start. Nearly all senior management positions were staffed by civil and agricultural engineers.

It did not take the team long to realize that serious difficulties were in store. The first indication of trouble came when farmers refused permission to project staff and engineers to conduct surveys on their lands. In a few districts, trees were felled by farmers to block the vehicle of project staff. Project employees were viewed with suspicion and treated with hostility.

The strongest reactions came from the members of zanjeras located along the upstream sections of the rivers. One of the largest federations, composed of over a dozen upstream zanjeras, not only barred the project staff from entering their irrigation service areas but also sent a delegation of their representatives to Manila to meet with the agency administrator, Dr. Fiorello Estuar, to demand they be excluded from the project. Various explanations were offered for their resistance. Members of zanjeras with good access to water contended that the project would not provide them with additional benefits, yet it would give the NIA authority to collect irrigation fees, thus reducing their incomes.

More surprising to the engineers was opposition from members of zanjeras that would gain by improved access to irrigation. They feared the project, with its wide canals and access roads, would reduce their already small landholdings. In certain areas, the paths of the main canals would completely consume the farmlands of a number of farmers. Many of these farmers were sharetenants and therefore the compensation for expropriated land would be given to their landlords, leaving them without any means of subsistence. In many other cases, parcels would be cut in two by the lines of the new canals making these farms more difficult to operate.

Perhaps the most compelling reason for the resistance of the local community was that the project would install a completely new and different irrigation system. It would level and erase the community-built systems and destroy along with them the local institutions and organizational structures that had been in existence for generations and that would be essential to the effective management of the proposed irrigation system.

Alarmed by the local dissent among the farmers and by the message delivered by the zanjera leaders to his own doorstep, NIA's Administrator made a series of visits to the project site. In addition he endorsed visits by a number of concerned social scientists to the area. His own observations confirmed those of the social scientists that implementing the project as designed would result in the eradication of the indigenous water users' organizations, would create much dissatisfaction and resentment among farmers, and would seriously jeopardize prospects for successful operation of the new system.

In August 1981 the Japanese design consultants submitted to the administrator several bound volumes of their final detailed design for the entire Phase I area. These three volumes provided detailed engineering drawings, construction time-tables, descriptions of specific activities and tasks, financial data, and other specifications to guide project implementation over the next seven years. The government of both Japan and the Philippines were waiting anxiously for the approval of the plan. Approval would initiate the influx of needed foreign exchange to the Philippine government, and delay in the project implementation would mean cost increases.

A NEW PLAN

In October 1981, after consultation with key NIA staff, Dr. Estuar took the difficult decision of setting aside the project design. When asked to explain his decision, he remarked that he "refused to go down in history as the NIA administrator during whose term the zanjeras were eradicated." Along with this bold step, Dr. Estuar laid down guidelines for the preparation of the new design.

a) The integrity and identity of each zanjera in the project area should be preserved.

b) The existing canal lines should be utilized to the extent possible and farmers should be consulted regarding additional canal lines.

c) The farmers should be fully and actively involved in planning and implementing the project.

d) The likely operation and maintenance schemes should be disseminated to the farmers as early as possible to insure that they fully understand their roles and responsibilities in managing the system.

e) The project should be conceived as one involving the rehabilitation of many small community-managed irrigation systems rather than as the construction of a new, large-scale irrigation project.

Many of the engineers and designers at the project site had had extensive experience in building large-scale irrigation systems, but never had they been required to follow such guidelines. In other large projects, farmer participation had been limited to the hiring of a few skilled laborers from the community and to meetings where the agency personnel informed the farmers about the project. The reason for limiting farmer involvement in decision making were well understood; design and construction work had to be accomplished according to a tight schedule and there was not enough time to discuss issues with the farmers. Besides, what did farmers really know about the design and construction of large irrigation systems?

But it was also understood that a project of this magnitude would be seriously impeded by open and hostile farmer opposition. The farmers could easily make work difficult for the project staff, even destroying structures that would not serve their interests. Moreover, the operation of the proposed system would need to be financially sustained by collection of irrigation fees. Dissatisfied water users were not likely to pay those fees.

The rationale for a new approach and a new design was evident, but

8

how it would be accomplished was not apparent to the project implemen-
tors. Particlarly difficult to concieve was how participation in the project
design could be realistically obtained from over 115,000 farmers belonging to nearly two hundred indigenous water users organizations of diverse
sizes, circumstances and characteristics.

The NIA, by this time, had some experience in implementing small-
scale community-managed irrigation projects with an approach that directly involved farmers in planning and construction activities. However, the
application of similar approaches in larger, agency-managed irrigation
system projects was something very new to the irrigation authority. Clearly,
an approach specific to this project would need to be developed and the
design itself would have to evolve over time.

The Pilot Area

By the time the decision had been made to reject the original project
design, construction work was already well underway in the 1,000 hectare Pilot Area of Phase I, as originally planned—with new canals, standardized rotation areas, and completely different organizational requirements. New farmer organizations with newly elected leaders were
formed by NIA institutional personnel to correspond to the new canal
network, with the new groups commonly consisting of farmers from
several former zanjera organiztions. Although by October 1981 the implications of these changes had to become clear to the NIA management
and staff, the Pilot Area implementation was already too far along to allow
for any changes.

The results were tragic. Although Pilot Area construction was scheduled for completion by March 1982, as late as June 1982, when the main
season cultivation activities should have been started, major irrigation
structures were still inoperative. Over a dozen turnout facilities were defec-
tive and the main canal suffered leaks in several places. Furthermore, the
construction activities in the pilot area had disrupted planting schedules,
and the right-of-way requirements of the design had forced many farmers
to give up parts of their farms in order to accommodate the new canals,
laterals and access roads. Most of the new canals actually crossed over
the existing zanjera canals and prevented the farmers from operating their
system during the construction period.

Facing the start of the main 1982 cropping season with inoperable irrigation facilities, the farmers took it upon themselves to bring irrigation
water to their fields by reviving their original zanjera systems. They rebuilt
their brush dams and restored their old canals. In several sectors of the
Pilot Area, farmers resorted to destroying the new farm ditches in order
to permit their old canals to bring the water to their fields. They also found

ways of rerouting their canals to bypass the newly built structures. Irrigation water was soon flowing again through the "traditional" zanjera systems, while the main canal of the new system was almost totally dry.

The institutional situation was also problematic. The radical change in organizational affiliation and leadership structures generated much confusion and conflict within the community. Friction erupted between traditional zanjera leaders and the new officers of the rotational units. The situation became even more strained when the engineering defects in the new structures forced the farmers to reactivate their zanjera systems. For a time two different systems for delivering water co-existed within the same area, each with its own organization and leaders.

This experience was clearly a frustrating and demoralizing one for the project staff. However, the Pilot Area experience permitted the NIA managers to view first hand the serious weakness of the original design and its damaging consequence for the affected farmers. It also provided a constant reminder of what should not be permitted to happen in the implementation of the rest of the project, serving to convince many of the cynics at NIA of the importance of farmer participation in each of the stages of project planning and implementation. For these reasons, the Pilot Area was a valuable component of the project though the purpose served was quite different from that which had been intended.

A Participatory Planning Process

The new participatory planning approach introduced outside the Pilot Area was intended to avoid just these problems. Here the project staff began by holding meetings with each of the water user organizations. These were meetings where, first, they assured the zanjera members that the identity of each zanjera would be respected and that the new design would, to the extent possible, make use of existing canals. Second, they used the meetings as opportunities for dialogue where the engineers tried to win trust and support rather than convey information. Following these zanjera-level meetings, the project staff organized conferences among the leaders of all the zanjeras in the area. These conferences permitted the exchange of views between different local leaders and the sharing of experiences in managing local organizations. One of the most ambitious events was a field trip hosted by the project managers for fifty zanjera leaders to another large-scale irrigation project in the neighboring province. There, the zanjera leaders interacted as equals with the agency staff, and closer personal relationships were established between farmers and engineers. Never before in a project of this scale had NIA officials gone to such lengths to develop rapport with farmers.

As the two sides grew more familiar with each other, the farmers became aware of the benefits that the external assistance could bring. They came to respect the advice of the engineers and recognized their sincerity. The engineers, likewise, came to appreciate the traditions and values of the farmers and the leadership and organizational resources that the farmers had sustained over many years. They then realized and understood the serious threat that the original project design had posed for the farmers.

In the months that followed, new plans and designs were formulated, this time in close consultation with the farmers. Canal lines were laid out, revised and finally approved by the zanjera members. In most cases, the canal lines followed the existing zanjera canals; in others the farmers opted for alterations in the old zanjera lay-out, approving designs that would be more efficient or durable than what was currently in place. The granting of rights-of-way was greatly facilitated by the consultations on canal locations, and since most of the project canals would follow existing zanjera canals, the need to negotiate for additional land was minimized. In the new design as finally approved over 80 percent of the canal lay-out followed existing zanjera canals, in contrast to 20 percent in the original plan, and would permit each zanjera to retain its identity. The new design, using the participatory approach, generated savings estimated at over US$1 million in two cost items: a) expenses for land acquisition; and b) construction costs for the on-farm canal system.

Under the new design upstream dams would divert water from a river and channel it to specific zanjeras. Beyond the point of delivery the zanjera would have full control of the operation of its own distribution system, being free to adopt its own procedures for water allocation and system manintenance in accord with its time-tested rules and policies.

While the concept was acceptable to the zanjeras and was consistent with existing practices, there remained other critical issues to be resolved. For example, How would water be allocated to different zanjeras? Who or what body would make the water distribution decisions or policies at the main system level? Should the irrigation agency step in or would it be left to the zanjeras to come to an acceptable agreement?

In the past, the zanjeras operated almost independently of one another, with each zanjera simply maintaining its own temporary dam along the river. Commonly, the upstream zanjeras enjoyed more plentiful supplies while downstream zanjeras often suffered water shortages in the dry season—except in selected cases where water sharing—agreements existed between neighboring zanjeras specifying how available water supplies would be allocated among them.

Management of the Main System

By establishing physical "links" between different zanjeras, the new

system created the need for closer coordination on matters of water allocation among zanjeras and the distribution of responsibilities for the
maintenance of common facilities. Even with the construction of the new
dams and canals, the engineers estimated that available dry-season water
supplies would be inadequate to irrigate the entire project area. Within
each zanjera, there were strong organizational capacities and skills. The
question was how to build on those in order to develop cohesion and
cooperation at the next level above the individual association.

One option would have been for the NIA to assume the responsibility for main system operation and for making the critical water allocation
decisions. But this involved hidden costs. An external institution responsible for regulating and allocating water would naturally come under at-
tack or criticism during periods of scarcity, and it is difficult for the agency to keep people on the spot twenty-four hours a day to enforce the allocations. There were also expenses involved in deploying system management staff at the project site after project completion. The agency therefore
has opted to examine alternatives that would encourage the farmers to
assume a larger responsibility.

IMPLICATIONS

The case points to several features of conventional irrigation project
planning and implementation that can be very costly. The first is the
assumption that the design of the physical structures is the most important determinant of an irrigation system's effectiveness and performance,
and that the choice of structures and their location should be based
primarily on the analysis of hydrology, topography, and crop requirements.
A corollary assumption is that the required management and organizational capacities can be developed at later stages of project implementation, and that these can be shaped to suit the demands of the optimal
engineering design.

These features of conventional irrigation project planning lead naturally to: 1) a failure to adequately understand prevailing social and institutional conditions in the project area; and 2) poor flow of communication
between the government agency and the local community, especially during the stages where the most crucial decisions are being made. Consequently opportunities are lost for securing farmer assistance in generating
both social and technical information on the project area, and for
strengthening local organizational capacities by involving the farmers in
the decision-making process. The poor flow of communication likewise
invites the risk of future resistance and opposition from the local community. More important, there is the danger that alternations or so-called
improvements in existing physical facilities may undermine sometimes

quite effective local organizational arrangements while imposing demands for new arrangements alien to the experience of the local people.

The case presented here is not intended to focus criticism or blame on one country, agency, or set of advisors. Rather, its purpose is to reveal serious inadequacies in conventional approaches to planning and implementing rural development programs. At the same time the case directs attention to alternative planning approaches which appear to hold promise of more positive results. These alternatives are founded on the premise that existing community organizations, as exemplified by the zanjeras, are a strategic resource in rural development and have much to contribute to the extent that their identity and essential autonomy is maintained.

A tragedy was averted in this case as a result of the willingness of the key actors—the agency officials, the team of consultants, and the donor agency—to abandon an unrealistic and undesirable plan in favor of a fresh start based on a more appropriate approach. Even with the changes made it remains to be seen whether the expensive project assistance will result in more than marginal imrovements in water distribution. Considerable personal courage and conviction were necessary in order to redirect efforts and to reorient established agency procedures and policies. There are many other situations in the developing world similar to the one described in the case. The opportunities for corrective action and change in those situations are likewise present. The relevant question is not whether existing procedures and project covenants in other projects are more rigid or more flexible, but whether the key actors in those situations possess sufficient courage and conviction to take the less expedient but more productive path.

Yet even with decisive action by NIA management in redesigning the project, as of March 1986, with Phase I construction as yet incompleted, the project engineers were concerned that the project might not produce sufficient improvements in area irrigated to show an economic return on investment. At that point they expected some expansion in the area irrigated during the primary cropping season, but an expansion of the area able to support second cropping was not anticipated. Hope was expressed that improvements in agricultural technology planned for introduction following the construction phase, though unrelated to water management, might increase production sufficiently to allow the project to show some improvements in economic performance. Thus, in the final analysis a less ambitious project tailored from the beginning to actual needs and existing capacities likely would have been considerably more cost effective.

NOTES

1. The author would like to acknowledge the valuable assistance of Ms. Ruth Yabes in reviewing various drafts of this paper.

2. See *Report of a Planning Workshop on Irrigation Water Management* (Los Banos, Laguna: The International Rice Research Institute, 1980), and Kunio Takase and Thomas Wickham, "Irrigation Management as a Pivot of Agricultural Development in Asia," a Report by the Associate Experts in Irrigation for *Asian Agricultural Survey II* (Manila: Asian Development Bank, November 1976).

3. See E. Walter Coward, Jr. (ed.), *Irrigation and Agricultural Development in Asia: Perspectives from the Social Sciences* (Ithaca: Cornell University Press, 1980).

4. This situation was one of the major concerns discussed in "Organization as a Strategic Resource in Irrigation Development: A Conference Report," prepared by E. Walter Coward, Jr., Bruce Koppel, and Robert Y. Siy Jr., published under the auspices of the Asian Development Bank and the East-West Center Resource System Institute, 1983.

5. *Ibid.*

6. Studies of the culture, organization, and practices of the zanjeras include: E. Walter Coward, Jr., "Principles of Social Organization in an Indigenous Irrigation System," *Human Organization*, Vol. 38, No. 1 (Spring, 1979), pp. 28-36; Henry T. Lewis, *Ilocano Rice Farmers: A Comparative Study of Two Philippine Barrios* (Honolulu: University of Hawaii Press, 1971); and Robert Y. Siy, Jr., *Community Resource Management: Lessons from the Zanjera* (Manila: University of the Philippines Press, 1982).

7. Emerson B. Christie, "Notes on Irrigation and Cooperative Irrigation Societies in Ilocos Norte," *The Philippine Journal of Science*, Vol. IX, No. 2 (April 1914), pp. 99-113.

8. See Felipe B. Alfonso, "Assisting Farmer Controlled Development of Communal Irrigation Systems," In David C. Korten and Felipe B. Alfonso (eds.), *Bureaucracy and the Poor: Closing the Gap* (West Hartford: Kumarian Press, 1983); and Frances F. Korten, "Building National Capacity to Develop Water Users' Associations: Experience from the Philippines," *World Bank Staff Working Paper No. 528* (July 1982).

PART VI

CREATING AN ENABLING SETTING

CHAPTER TWENTY

The Policy Framework for Community Management[1]

Frances F. Korten
The Ford Foundation

A striking feature of the last two decades of development in Asia has been the rise of central government influence on the management of local resources. Where once the management of small irrigation systems, forest areas, grazing lands, or coastal fisheries was primarily determined by the people using those resources, today we see a variety of national laws, policies, and programs directly affecting them.

Several key factors interact to create this trend. Population growth has increased the pressure on all of these natural resources, creating national-level concerns about their effective and sustainable use. Funding for central government projects has risen dramatically generating a plethora of programs directed at improving the management of these natural resources. Bureaucratic infrastructure and personnel has grown, resulting in capacity to reach into much more remote areas.

Do these modernizing influences strengthen or weaken local capability for resource management? The rhetoric of project documents increasingly stresses the objective of strengthening it. Projects now often include a component for developing local organizations to handle some aspect of local resource management. But seldom is attention to questions regarding the institutional framework that defines the legal status, rights, and authorities essential to the organization's effective performance. While once

275

it was primarily local customs and authorities that determined the framework within which such organizations operated, currently that framework is increasingly determined by national law, agency policies, and bureaucratic procedures.

One important type of organization designed to manage a local resource is a water-user organization, a group of farmers who manage some aspect of an irrigation system. Experience in Southeast Asia illustrates the types of laws, policies, and procedures that influence the significance of a water user organization in the eyes of its members, the community, and the nation.

WATER USER ORGANIZATIONS IN SOUTHEAST ASIA

There is growing worldwide interest in the role of farmers in operating and maintaining irrigation systems.[2] As government-built irrigation systems expand, it is increasingly recognized that irrigation is not a task that governments can do alone. They simply cannot field enough personnel to guard every gate, clean every canal, settle every conflict that arises throughout an irrigation system. The farmers themselves need to share an important part of this task.

But for farmers to play an effective role in irrigation management they must be organized so that their mutual and conflicting interests can be addressed. The need for organization is fundamental in irrigation because of the high level of interdependency of users who share the same irrigation system. If a farmer upstream fails to clean a canal, water may not reach a downstream farmer. Or if one farmer uses too much water, it may cause flooding for a nearby neighbor and drought for one farther away. A major washout of a canal may require the mobilization of labor far greater than could be handled by any single individual. These interdependencies call for organizational arrangements through which farmers can voice their needs and enforce their agreements.

This paper examines key aspects of national law, agency policy, and bureaucratic procedure relevant to water-user organizations in four Southeast Asian countries: the Philippines, Indonesia, Thailand, and Malaysia. The comparison illustrates how the institutional framework created by government affects the extent to which the water-user organization is meaningful to its members and hence effective in attracting their support.

While the climate, topography, and cultures of these four countries bear strong resemblances, the institutional frameworks for water-user organizations are strikingly different. Each has strong traditions of community management of small-scale irrigation systems. Particularly well known are the People's Irrigation Systems in northern Thailand,[3] the *zanjeras* of Ilocos Norte in the Philippines,[4] and the *subaks* of Bali, Indonesia.[5]

But these represent only the most famous among thousands of somewhat similar, farmer-developed and managed irrigation systems throughout the region.

Examination of the histories of farmer-built irrigation systems reveals a common pattern in which farmers develop understandings of the obligations and authority of the members and their leaders.[6] The water-user groups often received clear recognition by other bodies within the local area, but this institutional framework was based on community understandings, customary law, or local jurisdiction that generally had little relationship to national law, policy, and bureaucratic procedure.

In the last two decades, these local understandings have often been overshadowed as national influences permeate local environments. This is to be expected as a process of modernization and nation building occurs. But what is it that is replacing those local understandings? What does the national institutional framework offer to make these organizations meaningful?

Government officials in all four countries have indicated a desire to develop stronger water-user organization. All share the basic concept of a water-user organization as a mechanism through which farmers can actively participate in irrigation management. But behind this similarity lies a diversity of conception regarding the powers, authority, rights, and obligations of these organizations. Of particular significance are issues of the organization's legal status; its ownership of the physical system; its right to use water; its hydrological area of authority; its financial obligations and authority; and its involvement in the design and construction of its physical facilities.

Legal Status

Businesses, government bodies, educational institutions, foundations, research institutes—the organizations of modern society have their status defined in law through the registration of their charters. Thus, they achieve legal recognition and are formally placed within a framework of laws that determine what the organization can and cannot do, how it relates to other organizations and individuals and how it can protect its rights and enforce its authorities. Such status, for example, determines whether an organization can legally own property, sue and be sued, enter into contracts, be granted legal rights and authorities and in general function as a recognized legal body within the context of the broader national society. In the nations of Southeast Asia, considerable attention is given to defining the legal status of modern, urban organizations. Yet it is common that, in regard to rural organizations, such considerations are neglected or not raised at all.

For example, in Malaysia the Drainage and Irrigation Department has been developing irrigators' organizations in its large Muda Irrigation Scheme for some years, but these are viewed strictly as "informal groups" with no provision for registration or legal recognition.[7] In Indonesia water-user organizations are recognized in law,[8] but there is no registration process by which such organizations can obtain legally enforceable recognition of their identity and rights within the society.

In Thailand, for small systems, the law recognizes the existence of "People's Irrigation Systems" and specifies decisions that must be based on the agreement of the "majority of the people who gain benefit from the irrigation," including the approval of appointments of local irrigation officials.[9] Thus, the authority of the water users is recognized in law. However, the law does not make explicit mention of a water-user organization but rather focuses on the role of local government officials in regulating the activities of users of the irrigation systems. On larger systems the Royal Irrigation Department (RID) creates water user organizations of which it maintains a list, but these organizations seldom achieve status as legal bodies through formal registration.

The Philippines presents a distinctive contrast, providing water-user organizations with full and independent legal status. A formal procedure for registering with the national Securities and Exchange Commission confers upon the organization a legal personality and embeds it in the set of national laws governing other corporate organizations. Any irrigation system receiving government assistance is required to become legally registered.

System Ownership

The legal status of a water-user organization often has a direct effect on whether it can be viewed as the owner of the irrigation facilities it uses. Traditionally when farmers, through their formal or informal organization, built an irrigation system primarily through their own initiative and funding, their ownership of the systems, as well as the rights and obligations of members, was generally recognized in local customary law.[10] But when governments undertake construction or rehabilitation of structures to be used by farmers, the question arises as to who owns the new or improved structures. This has implications for who views themselves as responsible for the system's operation, maintenance, and subsequent improvement.

For large systems in the Philippines, Malaysia, Thailand, and Indonesia, the ownership of the main canals and structures is both clear and uniform. The government owns them and water-user organizations simply represent users. But for small-scale systems, the four countries treat the issue of system ownership quite differently.

The two clearest, though contrasting, cases are Malaysia and the

Philippines. In Malaysia, if the government has built the system, no matter what its size, then the government owns it—even a system as small as eleven hectares.[11] In contrast, in the Philippines when the government builds small systems called communals (generally under 1,000 hectares) the irrigation facilities are turned over to the water user organization in a formal ceremony. Signed documents clearly establish the organization's legal ownership of the facilities and leave no question regarding its full responsibility and authority for operation and maintenance.

In Thailand the People's Irrigation Law does not explicity discuss the issue of system ownership. However, it does establish the right of the people using an irrigation system within a district to determine, together with district government officials, any physical changes in their irrigation systems, thus implying the rights associated with ownership.[12] In the case where an irrigation system covers more than one district or province, the law provides that a government official can appoint a committee to make decisions about physical changes, thus potentially removing from the users a role in the decision making. In recent times many of the small systems have been consolidated into larger, government-owned and managed systems, leaving system ownership clearly in the hands of the government.[13]

A similar ambiguity exits in Indonesia where system ownership is not treated explicitly either in national law or government agency policy. Generally it is assumed that farmers who built an irrigation system themselves are the owners of that system. But if it receives assistance from the public works agency, the system becomes classified as a "public works" system, implying that ownership has been transferred to the government. The lack of a clear, legal status for the water-user organization contributes to the ambiguity, since it is not clear whether facilities built by government can legally be turned over to a group that does not have the status of a legal body. While the Ministry of Public Works does turn systems over to local governments, they are not generally further transferred to the water-user organization.

The Right to Use Water from a Public Source

Water is the raison d'etre of a water-user organization. An important part of its legitimacy rests upon its possessing an enforceable right of access to water from the irrigation system's source—a river, lake, spring, or underground reservoir.

The Philippines is the only country in the region with an operational program for allocating water rights, and it is in the Philippines that the clearest connection exists between the water-user organization and the right to use water. Any individual or group that wants to use water from a public source must apply for a water permit from the National Water

Resources Council.[14] Water-user organizations that have attained legal status by registering with the Securities and Exchange Commission can legally hold the water permit. When the government assists a small-scale irrigation system, part of that process entails registering the water-user organization and obtaining a water rights permit. The importance of holding that permit has become increasingly apparent as the competition for water has increased, and obtaining the water permit has become a motivation for farmers to spontaneously form themselves into organizations as a means of protecting their access to water.[15] The law, in fact, favors organizations over individuals, stating that any individual who can be served by a communal irrigation system should not be granted an individual water right.[16]

In the other three countries there are no comprehensive systems for allocating water. Competition for water in this humid region has generally not been sufficiently severe to encourage the development of clear national laws. But population pressure is rapidly changing this and governments are searching for ways to systematize water allocation.

In the absence of procedures to allocate rights to some specified flow of water, most governments implicitly allocate water rights by requiring approval to build structures taking water from a public source. When that approval is given to a water-user organization, it implies that the organization has a legitimate claim on water. However, if there is no such permission, or if the permission is given to some body other than the water-user organization, this weakens the organization's status since it does not have any clear claim on water. While the organization can manage water once the water enters its appointed area, it has no legal role in determining how much water it can access. Yet as Wickham has noted, farmers care intensely about protecting their access to water since their very livelihood depends on it.[17]

In Indonesia for example, a water law exists which specifies the priorities of water use and states that users must get a license in order to use water, with the licensing to be done by the Ministry of Public Works and the provincial government.[18] Nevertheless, while the law has existed since 1974, a procedure for licensing has not actually been developed. Rather, the allocation of water has been linked to the management of the structure that takes water from a river. The public works agency manages the structures it has built while villages manage structures they have built. Thus, there is no unified system for allocation of water along a river course. This has resulted in a certain amount of conflict and confusion, and has developed within the public works' agency an interest in managing the intakes of any system using sufficient water to affect water availability of other systems.

In Malaysia a system exists for allocating water permits, but the of government do not need to apply. It is assumed that the government body building the structure has a recognized right to do so. Consequently all of the dams built by the Department of Drainage and Irrigation are automatically assumed to have permission to use water in accordance with the characteristics of the structure built. In cases where farmers have built dams on their own—often of a temporary nature—they have no state-recognized right to use that water. Since there is no such thing as a legally recognized water-user organization, it is not possible to confer on the group of water users the legal right to use water.

In Thailand there is no comprehensive legal system for allocating specified water flows from a public source. To some degree, control over water allocation is exercised through the granting of permission to build a structure on a river. In northern Thailand where there are many people's irrigation systems, a group wishing to build a dam on the river must apply to the district chief, who in turn must obtain approval from the provincial governor. Once this is granted, the people's irrigation system has a recognized right to use the water from that river. Under conditions of water shortage, the people's irrigation law further provides that, for rivers serving areas in more than one province, water allocation decisions are to be carried out by committees comprised of representatives of the provinces as well as the RID but does not specify how a given group of water users could protect their claim on water.[19]

Hydrological Area of Authority

The definition of the hydrological unit under the authority of the water user organization varies significantly among the nations of Southeast Asia. These area defenitions have important implications for the ability of the organizations to address one of the most basic issues of irrigation, namely conflicts between "upstream" and "downstream" users within the system. Since water flows downhill from a source through canals and sub-canals to the far reaches of the system, farmers whose lands lie closer to the source have first access. In most irrigation systems, both large and small, farmer managed or government managed, the upstream farmers use larger quantities of water per hectare than their downstream neighbors. Restraining upstreamers' use of water and sustaining irrigation facilities so they serve the entire system are the most essential yet difficult tasks of the water user organization.

The most meaningful management unit in irrigation is the total hydraulic command—that is all of the irrigation facilities from the main water source (such as the dam on a river) on down to the last fields watered by those facilities. If a water-user organization has as its management unit the entire hydraulic command, then it can serve as the forum for the interplay of all upstream-downstream interests.

In Southeast Asia water-user groups have such unified hydrological authority on a number of types of the smaller irrigation systems. In Indonesia subaks, traditional water user organizations found on Bali and nearby islands, generally have authority over their entire system. So do the users on people's irrigation systems in northern Thailand and on communal irrigation systems in the Philippines, even when the command of the systems includes the territory of, and water users from, more than one village.

But in other instances this is not the case. In many places in Indonesia water-user organizations are based on villages. Since even small systems often cut across villages, this leaves the organization without a clear mechanism for handling the basic upstream-downstream issues. Often the organizations reach informal agreements among themselves,[21] but these arrangements, being informal are easily ignored by the government and other outside forces and hence remain fragile. Under these conditions farmers often depend on some outside agent, such as the irrigation agency or a higher level of local government. Since these outside agents do not have sufficient time to handle all the issues that arise, there is a vacuum of authority which leads to poor water management.[22]

On larger systems the question of the hydrologic area of authority for the water-user organization becomes even more complicated. In all four countries government is responsible for "main system management" and farmers are responsible for sub-units of that system. But the definition of the sub-units vary substantially between the four countries.

In Indonesia national law provides that farmers are responsible for management of the sub-unit called "the tertiary," meaning the third level canals, while the government is responsible for main systems (primary and secondary canals).[23] However, two problems are observed in implementation.

The first is the fact that the water-user organization is often village based, so while "farmers" are responsible for tertiaries, their organizations are not! Their organizations are responsible only for the section of the tertiary that falls within their village. For example, a study of two 800-hectare systems in East Java reveals that only two of the fourteen tertiaries on these two systems fell entirely within one village. On the average each of these fourteen tertiaries crossed three different villages. Conflict frequently arose between the villages sharing a single tertiary canal without adequate mechanisms for resolving it.[24]

The second problem is that this definition has extended government responsibility down to very small areas for some irrigaion systems. When a canal takes water directly from a river, it is generally considered to be a main canal. If it has been built or repaired by the public works agency, this implies government management responsibility. The law assigning farmers responsibilities for tertiaries makes no distinction between large- and small-scale irrigation systems. The result is that government has become responsible for main system management on irrigation systems as small as twenty hectares, even though this is an area one-tenth the size of most tertiaries on larger systems.[25]

The Royal Irrigation Department in Thailand has experimented with two different groupings of water users. Water-user associations are based on areas covering an average of approximately 3,000 hectares.[26] While these are likely to represent a highly significant hydrological area, the associations have little authority within these areas. Water allocation and maintenance is carried out by paid employees of the RID. A problem has been that these groups were basically created "on paper" without the gradual build up of organizational capacity and authority at lower levels. In response to this problem the RID more recently has focused on creating *chaek* groups, which are groups of farmers receiving water from the same outlet, serving between twenty-five and fifty hectares. These groups are intended as sub-units of larger water-user organization. However, studies of these smaller groups indicate their actual authority remains weak, with government irrigation agents playing the primary role in operation and maintenance even within these smaller areas.[27]

On large systems in the Philippines, water-user organizations in the past have been formed at the turnout level, which generally covers about fifty hectares. While having full authority over water management within their areas, studies indicated that farmers viewed the more important water management issues as being those between, rather than within the turn-outs. Although the turnout groups have no formal responsibility for these between-unit problems, farmers often work out their own organizational arrangements for resolving problems at this higher system level.[28]

Recognizing that the higher levels of system operation appear to be more meaningful to water users, the National Irrigation Administration is now taking steps to form the organizations at higher hydrological levels while still maintaining the lower level units as sub-units of the larger water-user organizations.[29] Where previously perhaps five different water-user organizations would have been formed for five different turnouts all taking water from the same canal, under the new approach there is only one legally recognized organization managing the entire canal and having the turnout-level organizations as sub-units within its structure. Heightened farmer interest in the organizations having such responsibility has validated the concept that such higher level authority is meaningful to them.[30]

Financial Authority and Obligations

Financing irrigation system development and management can take several forms including land taxes, irrigation fees paid to the government, and fees paid to the water-user organization. These different forms have very different implications for the strength of water-user organizations. While fee collection represents a burden for an organization, if the resulting funds are clearly under its control accompanied by authority for system operations, such funds strengthen the organization's role and power. Funds give the organization the ability to hire personnel to manage the system, purchase materials needed for repairs, and contract with outside agents for services. Since farmers will only pay fees if they have received irrigation service, this helps keep the organization accountable to its members.

In all four countries land owners pay a land tax based on the value of the land, and irrigated land is more highly valued than nonirrigated land. Thus, in the sense of a general contribution to government revenues, farmers in all countries make a contribution, but water-user organizations generally have no role in this. They neither collect the money nor control its use. In fact, as Bottrall points out, because land taxes are collected through the general revenue system and go directly to the central treasury, there is no direct connection between the collection of these taxes and any aspect of irrigation management.[31]

In Malaysia these taxes represent the only costs of irrigation to the farmers and cover approximatly 30 percent of the government's costs for irrigation system operation and maintenance.[32] Thus, water-user groups have no officially sanctioned financial authority or responsibility. In Indonesia farmers often pay fees to their water-user organization, if one exists, or to an individual designated as the water master for the area under farmer jurisdiciton,[33] but they are not asked to pay for government costs of irrigation development or management.

In Thailand farmers on people's irrigation systems have elaborate rules at the local level for eliciting contributions from farmers in labor, materials and rice; rules that are legally sanctioned by the People's Irrigation Law. Studies show that these arrangements have been highly successful in eliciting substantial contributions from farmers.[34] The water-user organizations on the government-run systems, however, have generally not collected fees. While in selected systems there have been some efforts to require farmers to pay irrigation fees to their water user organizations, reports have indicated poor results. Researchers have attributed the poor results to the fact that membership in such organizations is voluntary, they have little authority for system management, mechanisms for assessing and collecting water charges have not developed, the farmers feel the government owns the system and should be responsible for it.[35]

The clearest and most extensive responsibility for irrigation financing is found in the Philippines on the communal irrigation systems. Here, since the system is entirely under farmer jurisdiction, the farmers are completely responsible for operation and maintenance costs from the entire system as well as for any construction they undertake on their own. Even when government provides construction assistance, it does so on the basis of a subsidized loan. The water-user organization is expected to pay 10 percent of the cost of the assistance at the time it is provided, and pay back the remainder annually, based on a minimum payment of 150 kilos of unhusked rice per hectare. The loan is subsidized because there are no interest charges on the unpaid amount.

This presents a substantial burden to the water-user organization. Not only must it collect fees for its own operations but it must also collect funds to repay the government. However, the financial responsibility also helps strengthen the concept of the organization's authority, both in relation to its own members and in relationship to the broader society. It adds to the clear sense of ownership of the system, of the authority to manage water in the system, and of its client relationship to the government, with the power to reject or modify as well as accept assistance offered. Also, because collections go directly to the agency that provides the assistance, this gives the agency powerful incentive to support strong water-user organizations.[36]

Role in System Design and Construction

When a group of farmers develops an irrigation system entirely or largely on its own, as has been a common tradition throughout much of Southeast Asia, the farmers are forced to develop an effective social organization to achieve planning, design, and construction of the system. This then provides the organizational fundation, including leadership structure and shared commitment, required for subsequent system operation. The significance of the link between construction and operations can be particularily striking where the construction task is unusually difficult.

For example, in Bali a study has been conducted of a group of farmers who built a two-kilometer tunnel through a mountain to bring water to their fields.[37] The farmers carefully calibrated their contributions to construction, which later provided the basis for determining the share of water they would receive from the system. The organization and leadership developed to mobilize the labor for construction was then used to mobilize and direct labor for maintenance and to adjudicate disputes relating to water distribution. Similar processes linking construction contributions to subsequent water rights have also been documented elsewhere in Indonesia as well as in the Philippines and Thailand.[38]

When irrigation systems are constructed or rehabilitated by the government, a role for the farmers is seldom envisioned prior to the system's completion. Government itself provides the social organization for the planning, design, and construction process. Generally the water-users are ignored until after the construction is finished, even in situations where farmers have been irrigating for many years prior to the construction intervention. Once construction is completed, farmers are suddenly expected to clean canals, develop and obey water allocation systems and cropping calendars appropriate for their new or improved system. At this point the lack of prior attention to organizational issues becomes painfully apparent.[39]

Experience in the Philippines points to the advantages of giving farmers a significant role from the very earliest design stages. Not only does this result in technical improvements in the system, which make it more responsive to farmer needs, but it also provides the farmers an opportunity to develop their organizational capacities at a time when their interest is likely to be at a peak. Results indicate that an approach involving farmers from the earliest stage creates organizations more representative of their users, that contribute more to system development, are better able to pay the government for the construction cost, and have more sophisticated approaches to water management.[40]

Drawing in part on the Philippine experience, Indonesia since 1982 has begun involving farmers more fully in system design and construction in experimental projects in a total of nine provinces. Results in these pilot projects indicate a positive impact.[41] In 1985 the Royal Irrigation Department in Thailand initiated projects explicitly calling for farmer participation in system design and construction.[42] In Malaysia the Drainage and Irrigation Department has developed approaches to involving farmers in the design of tertiary facilities in their large Muda Irrigation Scheme.[43]

CONCLUSIONS

Effective community-level management of resources commonly depends on the strength of local organizations, including their ability to command the loyalties of their members and to enforce their decisions. Governments are often quite willing to call for greater local involvement in the mobilization and management of development resources. But the government focus is often exclusively on the tasks the local groups must perform, with the local group viewed primarily as a village-level extension of the government agency in charge. Such a conception fails to acknowledge the extent to which the development of local capacities depends on establishing commensurate rights and authorities. Local organizations can seldom command the respect of their own members if they cannot also command the respect of the agencies of state, and the latter commonly depends on their having a clear and independent mandate.

There is a natural dilemma involved. It is unlikely that strong local organizations will flourish in the absence of a supportive policy framework that gives them requisite recognition. Yet governments are reluctant to give significant authority to local organizations that have not demonstrated the capacity to use it effectively. Too often, however, those in a position to make such choices have a vested interest in understating capacities, existing and potential, of local organizations as a means of protecting the authority of their own agencies.

The issues are not easily resolved. Each policy bearing on a community management organization is embedded in a broader network of laws, policies, and procedures and consequently may be extremely difficult to change. However, if the need is recognized, and strong community management organizations are genuinely desired, a gradual process of change can be instituted.

Sometimes leaps of faith may be needed, where organizations are given authority, even though all are not ready for it, as a stimulus to build organizations actually able to exercise authority. But in addition to the leap of faith, concerted attention and resources are needed for building the organizations that can exercise that authority responsibly. It is this combination of attention to institutional context and the process of community-level change that is needed if effective community management strategies are to be pursued.

NOTES

1. Based on presentation at Irrigation Seminar, LP3ES, Jakarta, October 8, 1985.

2. Food and Agriculture Organization, *Participatory Experiences in Irrigation Water Management* (Rome: FAO, 1985); E. Walter Coward, Bruce Koppel, and Robert Siy, "Organization as a Strategic Resource in Irrigation Development" (Conference report, Honolulu: East-West Center, 1983); Michael Cernea ed., *Putting People First: Sociological Variables in Rural Development* (Oxford University Press for the World Bank, 1985).

3. Abha Sirivongs na Ayutthaya, "A Comparative Study of Traditional Irrigation Systems in Two Communities of Northern Thailand" (Bangkok: Chulalongkorn University Social Research Institute, 1979); Jack M. Potter, *Thai Peasant Social Structure* (Chicago: University of Chicago Press, 1976); Uraivan Tan-kim-yong, "Resource Mobilization in Traditional Systems of Northern Thailand: A Comparison between the Lowland and the Upland Irrigation Communities," unpublished PhD. dissertation, Cornell University, 1983.

4. H. T. Lewis, *Ilocano Rice Farmers: A Comparative Study of Two Philippine Barrios* (Honolulu: University of Hawaii Press), 1971; E. Walter Coward, "Principles of Social Organization in an Indigenous Irrigation System," *Human Organization* Vol. 38 (1979), No. 1:28-36; Robert Y. Siy, *Community Resource Management: Lessons from the Zanjera* (Quezon City: University of the Philippines Press, 1982).

5. Clifford Geertz, "Organization of the Balinese Subak," in E. Walter Coward, ed. *Irrigation and Agricultural Development in Asia* (Ithaca: Cornell University Press, 1980) pp. 70-90; N. Sutawan, M. Swara, N. Sutjipta, W. Suteja, and W. Windia, "Studi Perbandingan Subak

Dalam Sistem Irigasi Non-PU dan Subak Dalam Sistem Irigasi PU," (Denpasar: University Udayana, September 1984).

6. Numerous studies have revealed the detailed attention that indigenous water user organizations pay to the issues of the rights and authorities of leaders and members and how these are continually refined over time. Examples of such studies from Southeast Asia include: Douglas Lynn Vermillion "Rules and Processes: Dividing Water and Negotiating Order in Two New Irrigation Systems in North Sulawesi, Indonesia," (unpublished PhD. dissertation, Cornell Unniversity, Ithaca, N.Y., 1986); Abha, "A Comparative Study of Traditional Irrigation Systems in Two Communities of Northern Thailand"; Siy, *Community Resource Management: Lessons from the Zanjera*; Potter, *Thai Peasant Social Structure*; Sutawan et al., "Studi Perbandingan Suba Dalam Sistem Irigasi Non-PU dan Subak Dalam Sistem Irigasi PU"; Romana de los Reyes *Managing Communal Gravity Systems* (Quezon City: Institute of Philippine Culture, 1980); Sarnubi Abuasir "Perkembangan Organisasi Pengairan Pedasaan de Sumatera Selatan" (Jakarta: University of Indonesia, Fakultas Pascasarjana, 1985); Tan-kim-yong, "Resource Mobilization in Traditional Systems of Northern Thailand."

7. Cheong Chup Lim, "Irrigation Development and Farmers' Participation in Malaysia," in *Participatory Experiences in Irrigation Water Management* (Rome: Food and Agriculture Organization, 1985), pp. 159-162.

8. The Law of Republic of Indonesia Number 11, 1974 on Water Resource Development; Government Regulation of the Republic of Indonesia, Number 22 and 23 on Irrigation, 1982.

9. People's Irrigation Law of 1939, section 12 as reported in Abha, "A Comparative Study of Traditional Irrigation Systems in Two Communities of Northern Thailand"

10. Coward stresses system ownership as being a key factor accounting for much of farmers' behavior in traditional irrigation systems. He comments "the remarkable ability of many of these groups to mobilize extraordinary amounts of labor for repairing and maintaining the [irrigation] works can be viewed as collective activity to protect and sustain the common property which they own and control." E. Walter Coward, "Traditional Irrigation Systems and Government Assistance: Current Research Findings from Southeast Asia," (Paper presented at the Symposium on Traditional Irrigation Schemes and Potential for their Improvement, German Association for Water Resources and Land Development, Darmstadt, Germany April, 1985), p. 2.

11. Donald C. Taylor with Kanaengnid Tantigate "The Nature and Performance of Malaysia's Irrigation Schemes: A National Analysis," in Donald C. Taylor, ed., *The Economics of Malaysian Paddy Production and Irrigation* (Bangkok: Agricultural Development Council, 1981).

12. The People's Irrigation Law of 1939, Section 22 as reported in Abha, "A Comparative Study of Traditional Irrigation Systems in Two Communities of Northern Thailand."

13. Tan-kim-yong, "Resource Mobilization in Traditional Systems of Northern Thailand."

14. National Water Resources Council, *Philippines Water Code* (Quezon City: National Water Resources Council, 1976). For a discussion of the evolution of water law in the Philippines and implementation of the Water Code, see Concepcion Cruz, Luzviminda Cornista, and Diogenes C. Dayan, "Water Rights in the Philippines" (Los Banos: Agrarian Reform Institute, 1986).

15. Honorato Angeles, Romeo B. Gavino and Arturo Cubos, *Community Managed Irrigation System* (Munoz: Central Luzon State University, 1983): Siy, *Community Resource Management: Lessons from the Zanjera*.

16. Benjamin Bagadion "Water User Organizational Needs and Alternatives" (Paper presented

at the Regional Symposium on Water Resources Policy in Agro-Socio-Economic Development, Dacca, Bangledesh, August 4-8 1985).

17. Thomas Wickham, "Scale and Type of Irrigation" (Paper presented to the workshop on Investment Decisions to Further Develop and Make Use of Southeast Asia's Irrigation Resources", Bangkok, Thailand, August 17-21, 1981) p. 6.

18. The Law of the Republic of Indonesia #11, 1974.

19. People's Irrigation Law of 1939, as reported in Abha, "A Comparative Study of Traditional Irrigation Systems in Two Communities of Northern Thailand."

20. Daniel W. Bromley, Donald C. Taylor, Donald E. Parker, "Water Reform and Economic Development: Institutional Aspects of Water Management in the Developing Countries," *Economic Development and Cultural Change*, Vol. 28, pp. 265-387.

21. An example of such an arrangement has been documented in East Java where several separate water-user groups all taking water from the same canal meet regularly to determine their water use schedule. See Lembaga Penelitian, Universitas Kristen Satya Wacana, "Proses Dokumentasi Dalam Rangka Pilot Proyek Pengembangan Tersier Dengan Tenaga Penuntun Petani Pemakai Air," Salatiga, Indonesia, Satya Wacana, 1983.

22. Richard Hutapea, *Peranserta Petani Dalam Pembangunan Jaringan Irigasi Tersier* (draft PhD thesis, Institut Pertanian Bogor, Bogor, Indonesia 1986).

23. Government Regulation of the Republic of Indonesia, Number 22 and 23 on Irrigation, 1982.

24. Kutut Suwondo, *Pola Pengelolaan Pengairan* (Bogor: Institut Pertanian Bogor, 1985).

25. Kelompok Kerja Irigasi, Universitas Andalas, "Pengelolaan Irigasi Berskala Kecil di Sumatera Barat." (Paper presented at the workshop on Research on Traditional Irrigation, Palembang, Indonesia, December 11-14, 1985).

26. Kanda Paranakian, "Summary Report on Terminal-Level Irrigation Organizations in the Nong Wai Pioneer Irrigated Agriculture Projects Areas, Khon Kaen, Thailand" (Bangkok: Kasetsart University, 1978).

27. *Ibid.* ; Scott Duncan, "Local Irrigators' Groups: Assessment of their Operation and Maintenance Functions," in Donald C. Taylor and Thomas H. Wickham, eds., *Irrigation Policy and the Management of Irrigation Systems in Southeast Asia* (Bangkok: The Agricultural Development Council, 1979), pp. 185-192.

28. Mark Svendsen, "Group Behavior of Farmers in Three Types of Philipppine Irrigation Systems," in T. Wickham ed., *Irrigation Management: Research from Southeast Asia* (New York: The Agricultural Development Council, 1985).

29. Chambers has also noted that farmers often organize extensive activities above the outlet, even though these are not officially sanctioned or encouraged. See Robert Chambers, "Farmers above the Outlet: Irrigators and Canal Management in South Asia" (Institute of Development Studies, University of Sussex, 1984).

30. Bagadion, "Water User Organizational Needs and Alternatives"; Jeanne Frances I.Illo and Ma. Elena Chiong-Javier, *Organizing Farmers for Irrigation Management: The Buhi Lalo Experience* (Naga City, Philippines: Ateneo de Naga, 1983); Ted Ehera, "Irrigators' Organization of the Rinconanda/Buhi-Lalo (BIAD III) Project: The Experiment on NIA's New Orientation for National Irrigation Systems" (Paper presented to the BRBDP, Iriga City, July 16, 1981).

31. Bottrall points out the unfortunate consequences for irrigation management when income, services, and expenses bear no relationship to each other. See Anthony Bottrall, "Issues in Main System Management," in T. Wickham, ed., *Irrigation Management: Research from Southeast Asia* (New York: The Agricultural Development Council, 1985), pp. 230-248.

32. Personal communication, Eng. Cheong Chup Lim, Deputy Director General, Drainage and Irrigation Department, Malaysia.

33. Pasandaran notes that farmers using irrigation systems they consider their own pay higher water-user fees than do those on systems under the jurisdiction of the government. Effendi Pasandaran, "Exploitasi dan Pemeliharran Sistem Irigasi: Masalah dan Alternatip Pendekatan." (Paper presented at LP3ES Irrigation Seminar, Jakarta, Indonesia, February, 1986.)

34. Abha, "A Comparative Study of Traditional Irrigation Systems in Two Communities of Northern Thailand".

35. Duncan, "Local Irrigator's Groups: Assessment of their Operation and Maintenance Functions"; and Kanda, "Summary Report on Terminal-Level Irrigation Organizations in the Nong Wai Pioneer Irrigated Agriculture Project Areas, Khon Kaen, Thailand."

36. In the Philippines even with a strong policy framework creating incentives for attention to water-user organizations, it was still a major task to reorient the National Irrigation Adminstration, a primarily engineering organization, to incorporate issues of social capacity building into their work. For details on how this was done see Benjamin U. Bagadion and Frances F. Korten, "Developing Irrigator's Organizations: A Learning Process Approach," in Michael Cernea, ed., *Putting People First: Sociological Variables in Rural Development* (Oxford University Press for the World Bank, 1985).

37. Sutawan et al., "Studi Perbandingan Subak Dalam Sistem Irigasi Non-PU dan Subak Dalam Sistem Irigasi PU."

38. Siy, *Community Resource Management: Lessons from the Zanjera.*

39. The lack of attention to organizational issues prior to construction is equally a problem in areas where there was previously no irrigation and in areas where there has been irrigation. An example of the latter is provided in Siy's chapter in this volume, which discusses the problems resulting from a project where existing irrigation groups were not involved in the design of the rehabilitated structures. Once the rehabilitation was completed, old and new structures, procedures and social groupings existed side-by-side, creating considerable confusion. Robert Siy, "Averting the Bureaucratization of a Community Managed Resource: The Case of the Zanjeras" (Chapter Nineteen of this volume).

40. Romana de los Reyes and Sylvia Jopillo, "An Evaluation of the National Irrigation Administration's Participatory Irrigation Program" (Draft report, Quezon City: Ateneo de Manila, 1986).

41. David Robinson, "Farmer Participation in Design and Construction of HPSIS Irrigation Systems in Indonesia" (Jakarta: U.S. Agency for International Development, 1985); Rene Masa, "Farmers' Participation in Irrigation Development and Management in Indonesia" (Final consultancy report to the U.S. Agency for International Development, Jakarta, 1985); Michael Morfit and Mark Poffenberger, *Community Participation and Irrigation Development.* A case study of the Asia Regional Committee on Comunity Management, (Washington, D.C.: NASPAA, 1985); Institute for Socio-Economic Research, Training and Information, "Studi Monitoring: Lima Kasus Lokasi" (Jakarta: LP3ES, 1985).

42. Water Resources and Environment Institute and Faculty of Engineering, "Small Scale Irrigation System Project," (Proposal presented to the Ford Foundation, Khon Kaen: Khon

Kaen University, 1985); Alan C. Early, David M. Freeman, Kanda Paranakian, Nukool Thongtawee, Prasert Kanoksing, "Thailand Irrigation Organization Project" (Proposal presented to the U.S. Agency for International Development under the Water Management Synthesis Project, October, 1985).

43. Yem Othman, "Farmer Participation in Tertiary Irrigation Development: The Muda II Project in West Malaysia," in T. Wickham, ed., *Irrigation Management: Research from Southeast Asia* (New York: The Agricultural Development Council, 1985), pp.217-229.

CHAPTER TWENTY-ONE

Government Protection of Traditional Resource Use Rights—The Case of Indonesian Fisheries[1]

Conner Bailey

Competition and conflict between small-scale and commercial fishermen is a persistent problem facing policy makers responsible for fisheries development and management in the Third World. The rapid growth of commercial fisheries, especially trawl fisheries aimed at export-quality penaeid shrimp species has contributed valuable foreign exchange earnings and has introduced new technologies into the fisheries sector. In many cases, however, these gains have been won at the expense of small-scale fishermen who over many generations have established traditional resource use rights over coastal fishing grounds where shrimp are most abundant and where, as a consequence, trawlers are most active. Most Third World countries have attempted, but with little success, to restrict trawlers from operating in these coastal waters. A notable exception to this experience is Indonesia, which imposed and effectively enforced a nearly complete ban on all trawling beginning during the period 1981-83.

This chapter traces the development of commercial trawling in Indonesia and the impact this had on resource allocation and distributive equity within the fisheries sector. The Indonesian government's decision to ban all trawling represents a significant reorientation of development priorities in favor of small-scale fisheries and a reaffirmation of government support for traditional resource use rights. The chapter concludes by assessing the largely favorable impact of the trawler ban on employment, incomes, and landings within the sector.

COMMERCIAL FISHERIES DEVELOPMENT

Over the past two decades, marine fisheries in many tropical developing countries have experienced a technological transformation of major proportions. This "blue revolution" has been especially significant in Southeast Asia, a region with a long maritime tradition, a large number of fishermen, and a high degree of dependence on fish for dietary protein.[2] More recently fisheries products have gained increased importance as a source of foreign exchange.[3] Indeed, it is this shift in emphasis toward integration into world commodity markets that is the driving force behind the "blue revolution."[4]

Prior to the 1960s the fisheries of Southeast Asia were almost exclusively small-scale in nature and were oriented to supplying local domestic markets. The opening of international markets for shrimp, and to a lesser extent tuna and other highly valued species, has made adoption of capital-intensive fishing technologies commercially attractive. Governments throughout Southeast Asia actively supported development of commercial fisheries through gear trials, exploratory fishing surveys, extension of technical advice and training, construction of ports and related infrastructure, and provision of subsidized loans.[5] Multilateral development assistance agencies, including the World Bank, the Asian Development Bank, and the Food and Agriculture Organization, encouraged development of export-oriented commercial fisheries by providing technical and financial support for these government programs.[6] Various bilateral donors, notably the German Agency for Technical Cooperation, also supported development in this direction. Commercial fisheries development promised to transform marine fisheries into a technically modern and highly productive sector which, in the view of national policy makers and foreign experts alike, would generate profits and foreign exchange through the efficient exploitation of what were perceived to be abundant untapped marine resources.[7]

The rosy glow of this optimistic forecast gradually has become more subdued. Policy makers have been forced to recognize the inherent vulnerability of biologically renewable resources to over-exploitation and depletion. Evidence that the rapidly expanding use of powerful commercial fishing technologies posed a significant threat to sustainability of fisheries landings gradually forced Southeast Asian governments to recognize the need to balance development programs with effective resource management policies.[8]

In Southeast Asia, commercial fisheries first were established with the introduction of trawlers, and these continue to be the most common type of commercial fishing unit throughout the region. Trawling is a particularly effective means of capturing large penaeid shrimp species, which are highly valued by consumers in Japan, the U.S., and Western Europe.[9] During the period 1978-1981, the total combined value of shrimp exports from Indonesia, Thailand, Malaysia, and the Philippines was more than US $1.3 billion.[10] Indonesia accounted for more than half of this total, most of which came from the operations of commercial trawlers.

TRADITIONAL RESOURCE USE RIGHTS

It was not, however, concern regarding the resource itself which forced the governments of Southeast Asia to recognize the need to regulate commercial fisheries development. Far more effective in attracting governmental attention was a rising chorus of protest by small-scale fishermen, who claimed that commercial fishermen were encroaching on fishing grounds over which they had long-standing traditional use rights.

These claims were supported by individual politicians and academicians, and by a variety of nongovernmental organizations involved in social and environmental issues. Small-scale fisherman and their allies throughout the region argued that government support of commercial fisheries skewed the benefits of development in favor of a small economic elite and had a direct negative impact on incomes and standards of living among hundreds of thousands of small-scale fishing households. Thus, issues of distributive justice and resource allocation were added to the policy agenda. Resolution of these issues became a major concern of Southeast Asian governments, particularly as small-scale fishermen increasingly resorted to violence as a means of defending their rights over traditional fishing grounds.[11]

Nowhere in Southeast Asia was a conflict between commercial and small-scale fishermen more intense than in Indonesia. Unlike other nations in the region, Indonesia has taken effective steps to resolve this conflict through a dramatic reorientation in national priorities in favor of small-scale fisheries development. The full force of the government has been put behind protection of traditional resource use rights of small-scale fishermen. Initial governmental support for commercial trawling in the 1960s gave way in the 1970s to policies that sought to restrict trawler operations from coastal fishing grounds, where conflict with small-scale fishermen was most intense. These regulations proved difficult if not impossible to enforce and were largely ignored by trawler operators in Indonesia.[12]

Frustrated by these regulatory failures, concerned about mounting violence, and aware that some form of management action needed to be taken to guard against resource depletion, between 1981 and 1983 the Indonesian government imposed a total ban on virtually all commercial trawling. Unlike previous regulatory efforts, this total ban on trawling has been effectively enforced. Two factors account for this. It was physically easier to enforce a total ban compared with other, more limited restrictions. Equally important, the ban on trawling reflected the mobilization of significant political will by the highest authorities in the land. The trawler ban was promulgated by means of Presidential Decree No. 39 in 1980. Although considerable local autonomy exists in the governance of this far-flung archipelagic nation, at all levels the government is dominated by the military. President Suharto, a retired general in the Indonesian Army, enjoys the unquestioned support of civil and military authorities.

National governments do not frequently adopt forceful policies contrary to the interests of powerful groups. The case of the Indonesian trawler ban appears to be an exception. A central purpose of this chapter is to understand why the Indonesian government took this action. To accomplish this, the chapter describes Indonesia's marine fisheries sector, examines the development of commercial trawl fisheries in Indonesia, the impact of this development on marine resources and small-scale fisheries, and the evolution of government policy. The paper will conclude by assessing the generally favorable consequences of the trawler ban on development within Indonesia's fisheries sector.

INDONESIA'S MARINE FISHERIES SECTOR

Indonesia is a vast archipelgic nation of over 13,000 islands straddling the equator. The national Central Bureau of Statistics reported 1980 population of 146.5 million,[13] making Indonesia the fifth largest nation on earth. Data published by the Directorate General of Fisheries indicate that in 1982 nearly 1.2 million people were directly employed as marine fishermen in Indonesia;[14] a comparable number probably were employed in supply, processing, distributing, marketing, and other activities supporting this sector. Fish provides approximately 60 percent of all high quality protein in the national diet, 75 percent of which comes from marine capture fisheries.[15]

Indonesia's marine fisheries sector is overwhelmingly small scale in nature. More than 215,000 boats, over 70 percent of the nation's fishing fleet, are powered only by sail or paddle.[16] An additional 55,000 small-scale fishing boats are powered by small outboard engines, an increasingly popular innovation. Dependence on wind or paddle power served to limit the operational range of most fishermen to coastal waters adjacent to their home community. Even the adoption of outboard engines by small-scale fishermen has not appreciably changed this pattern of exploitation. This is so primarily because tropical fisheries resources are most abundant in shallow and typically nutrient rich waters near to shore.

Coastal fishing grounds surrounding the archipelago's most populous islands offer limited scope for expanded production and in a number of important cases are either fully exploited or depleted due to heavy fishing pressure by both small-scale and commercial fishermen. Of most pressing concern to Indonesia's fisheries policy makers are the Malacca Straits and the north coast of Java where in 1980 over 379,000 fishermen (39 percent of Indonesia's total) accounted for 44 percent of total marine fisheries landings.[17] Prior to the trawler ban, these two areas experienced the greatest concentration of fishing efforts by commercial trawlers within Indonesia.

DEVELOPMENT OF INDONESIA'S COMMERCIAL TRAWL FISHERIES

The trawlers of Southeat Asia were relatively small and unsophisticated compared with those of Europe or North America, but by local standards they represented a quantum leap in fishing power compared to that available to small-scale fishermen. The typical Indonesian trawler, for example, was a wooden hulled vessel displacing 20-30 gross tonnes (GT) and was powered by a diesel engine generating 100-200 h.p. Total investment cost for a trawler of this class was approximately US $20,000.[18] In contrast, investment levels of typical small-scale fishing units in Indonesia varied from 1 percent to 10 percent of this figure, though most were at the lower end of this range.[19]

Small numbers of trawlers are known to have operated in Southeast Asia prior to 1940, but first became prominent in Thailand during the late 1950s. By the mid-1960s trawlers had been adopted by Malaysian fishermen along the Malacca Straits. From there the new technology diffused across this narrow body of water to Indonesian fishermen on Sumatra. This diffusion-adoption process was facilitated by geographic proximity and the ability of Indonesian fishermen to observe the effectiveness of Malaysian trawlers on a first hand basis.

In both Malaysia and Indonesia, enterpreneurs who first invested in trawlers had established interests in the fisheries sectors. In some cases early adopters were able to recoup capital investment costs in as little as six months.[20] This high level of profitability served as a powerful stimulus for entrepreneurs from other sectors of the economy to invest in construction of new trawlers. It also is relevant to note that on both sides of the Malacca Straits the initial investors were of Chinese descent. The presence of social and economic ties between communities of this economically powerful ethnic group probably was a factor contributing to the rapid adoption and diffusion of trawlers in Indonesia.

By 1971, five years after their introduction, approximately 800 trawlers were operating in the Malacca Straits.[21] The trawler fleet was reported to total 935 in 1974.[22] This rapid growth in numbers of trawlers led to significant increase in pressure on demersal resources (i.e., stocks of species that live at or near the bottom, including finfish and shrimp) and by the early 1970s per unit productivity of trawlers in the Malacca Straits was declining.[23] Even with declining catch rates, however, the numbers of trawlers in this area increased to a peak of 1,300 in 1977 before declining during the two subsequent years (Figure 21-1).

Also by 1971 at least fifty trawlers from Sumatra had shifted their base of operations to the north coast of Java.[24] Also in that year trawleres were established at Cilacap, a port on Java's south coast. By 1977 nearly 800 trawlers were operating in waters off Java's north coast and a further 234 units were based in Cilacap.

Data on Indonesia's demersal fisheries resources have been reviewed by Dwiponggo.[25] His analysis clearly indicates that during the period 1975-1979, each of the three main centers of trawler activity (the Malacca Straits and north and south coasts of Java) experienced levels of demersal fishing effort beyond that necessary to achieve maximum sustainable yields (MSY). In economic terms this means that the demersal fisheries of these areas were over capitalized, with too many fishing units in competition for a finite resource. In biological terms, surplus fishing effort during this period resulted in resource depletion. In sum, surplus fishing effort led to lower total harvests being shared between too many fishing units.

IMPACT OF COMMERCIAL TRAWLING ON DEMERSAL RESOURCES

In Southeast Asia and many other parts of the developing world, the single most important type of commercial fishing gear employed is the trawl, a funnel-shaped net typically towed along near or at the bottom to capture demersal finfish and shrimp. Compared to most types of small-scale fishing gear, trawlers may be characterized as active (rather than passive) and nonselective (rather than selective). Gill nets, simple hand lines, and most other common types of small-scale gear, once deployed, are passive in that they depend on the fish to come to them, as distinct from the more active nature of a trawl net which moves in active pursuit through the water. Small-scale gear also tends to be more selective of larger individuals of commercially valuable species. As used in Southeast Asia, trawl nets typically capture a high proportion of immature fish and shrimp before they have been able to reproduce.[26] Thus, compared to small-scale gear, fishing mortality caused by trawlers is more likely to have a serious impact on the resources's biological renewability by reducing recruitment of succeeding generations.[27]

The potential threat posed by trawlers to the fisheries resources is exacerbated by the common practice of trawling in shallow inshore waters, which serve as breeding and nursery ground for many commercially valuable species.[28] Trawler fishermen prefer operating in coastal waters primarily because penaeid shrimp are concentrated near shore.[29]

No data exists on the composition of trawler catches in Indonesia. However, data from the Malaysian side of the Malacca Straits for trawlers of comparable size and using trawl nets with similar design and mesh size are available and provide some basis for estimating catch composition of Indonesian trawlers: penaeid shrimp (17 percent); finfish for human consumption (17 percent); and "trash fish" for reduction into fish meal (66 percent).[30] One-quarter of this "trash fish" (and 16 percent of total landings) was comprised of juveniles of commercially valuable finfish or shrimp species. Removal of undersized demersal finfish and shrimp threatens the biological renewability of these resources and directly affects the ability of small-scale fishermen who operate bottom set gill nets, trammel nets, fish traps, other demersal gear.

IMPACT OF COMMERCIAL TRAWLING ON SMALL-SCALE FISHERMEN

Direct competition between commercial trawlers and small-scale fishermen is widespread in Southeast Asia. The greater fishing power of trawlers, with their powerful engines and highly effective nets, has placed small-scale fishermen at a disadvantage in competing for a dwindling resource. In the absence of data comparing the catch composition of commercial trawlers and small-scale fishermen, it is difficult to state precisely the extent to which these two groups compete for specific resources. This has, however, been studied in the case of San Miguel Bay (Philippines) where results of a throughly documented two-year study show substantial overlap (and hence direct competition) in the species being landed by trawlers and those being caught using the most important types of small-scale fishing gear.[31]

Based on personal involvement in the San Miguel Bay study and my familiarity with the coastal fisheries by Indonesia, I have no doubt that direct competition existed between trawlers and small-scale fisheries prior to 1980. Several studies conducted along the north coast of Java indicate that this competition between trawlers and small-scale fishermen led to declining incomes among the latter and a consequent withdrawal from fishing among those no longer able to earn an adequate livelihood.[32] The same problems were reported in the area of Cilacap[33] and along the Malacca Straits.[34]

In some cases small-scale fishermen found employment on trawlers or other types of commercial fishing units.[35] More often, however, those small-scale fishermen no longer able to compete at sea sought employment as agricultural laborers or engaged in petty trade.[36] Particularly on

Java, these displaced fishermen added to the already swollen ranks of the underemployed.[37]

Trawlers not only competed effectively against small-scale fishermen for a dwindling resource but, because of their "active" mode of operation, frequently damaged or destroyed more "passive" small-scale gear. This problem was most severe at night, a time preferred by trawler operators because shrimp are more active (and hence most easily caught) then. As an added incentive, trawlers operating illegally in coastal waters were far less likely to be apprehended at night. One observer notes that in the case of Thailand:

> Small-scale fishermen using traditional fishing methods must either abandon those types of gear that are susceptible to destruction by trawlers or change fishing grounds, a choice that can be ill afforded by fishermen with limited fishing range and meagre funds.[38]

Destruction of small-scale gear by commercial trawlers also has been reported in the Philippines,[39] Malaysia,[40] and Indonesia.[41] Damage or destruction of small-scale fishing gear caused by the incursion of trawlers into shallow coastal waters has resulted in serious economic losses to the fishermen involved and a continuous threat to the life and livelihood of others.

Increasingly, small-scale fishermen have responded to these threats by attacking trawlers with (among other things) molotov cocktails, a particularly effective weapon when used at night against wooden boats at sea. In Malaysia between 1970 and 1973, over sixty boats were sunk and twenty-three fishermen killed.[42] Similar vilence occurred during the 1970s in the Indonesian portion of the Malacca Straits and in waters off both coasts of Java.[43]

EVOLUTION OF GOVERNMENT POLICY

Increasingly violent conflict between small-scale and trawler fishermen, combined with mounting evidence that demersal fisheries resources were being over exploited in areas where trawlers were most active, led during the 1970s to a series of regulatory measures designed to restrict trawler operations. There is in Indonesia a long tradition of regulatory measures designed to protect customary rights of small-scale fishermen to exploit their traditional fishing grounds and to preserve marine resources from destructive means of exploitation.[44] Laws to this effect were established by the Dutch colonial authorities in 1916 and 1927 and continued to serve the needs of fisheries management two decades after independence was declared in 1945. By the late 1960s, however, the growth of commercial fishing, and particularily the rapid increase in numbers of trawlers, drastically changed the nature of fisheries management needs.

The first evidence of official concern came in 1973 when the minister of agriculture (whose responsibilities include fisheries) issued Decree 561 calling for the "rational" exploitation of fisheries resources. This Decree specifically noted the destructive impact of trawlers on demersal resources caused by the capture of juveniles of commercially valuable species.

As a statement of concern, this decree is significant, but it provided no operational guidelines or specific regulatory powers. However, through Decree Number 1 of 1975, the minister of agriculture established that ministry's authority to limit access to marine fisheries with respect to (1) seasons of operation; (2) type, size, and number of boats in a particular area; and (3) size of mesh that could be used. The decree also provided the authority to establish quotas for allowable catch on an area-by-area basis. On the basis of this expanded regulatory authority, the minister of agriculture issued two further decrees during 1975 that limited trawler operations to more than 7 km from the shore and restricted them to operations within areas for which they were specifically licensed.

Based on this authority, an attempt was made to restrict numbers of trawlers operating in the Malacca Straits[45] and in waters off Cilacap.[46] However, effective enforcement proved illusive. The physical difficulties of enforcing zones of operation along the thousands of kilometers of coastline, particularily at night, limited the effectiveness of fisheries management efforts. Along the Malacca Straits, restrictions placed on number of licenses resulted in thousands of trawlers operating without licenses. In the Cilacap area, most trawlers simply shifted from one port to another and continued fishing in the same area.[48]

Institutional difficulties also hampered effective implementation. The Directorate General of Fisheries was primarily responsible for establishing specific fisheries management plans but lacked a clear role in actual enforcement, which was the responsibility of local police and Navy units. The number of personnel and patrol vessels made available was insufficient to assure compliance.[49] These problems reflected lack of clear purpose and political will on the part of Indonesia's leaders. In 1980, however, the government acted decisively to resolve conflict in the fisheries sector.

PRESIDENTIAL DECREE NO. 39

Evidence of continued illegal operations by trawlers and the increasingly violent conflict between trawler and small-scale fishermen finally led to the proclamation in 1980 of Presidential Decree 39 banning all trawlers from waters off Java and Sumatra. In 1983, Presidential Letter of Instruction No. 11 extended this ban on trawlers nationwide, with the exception of the Arafura Sea. Personal observations in the affected areas during 1981, 1982, and 1984 indicate that, unlike previous efforts to control trawler operations through ministerial decrees and regulations issued by the Directorate General of Fisheries, Presidential Decree 39 appears to have been effectively enforced.

The imposition of the trawl ban in waters off Java and Sumatra was far more significant than the subsequent extension of this ban because, with the exception of the Arafura Sea, trawling elsewhere in the archipelago was of limited importance. In the Arafura Sea, joint-venture shrimp trawling enterprises formed between Indonesian and Japanese interests were permitted to continue because they did not compete with small-scale fisheries. Moreover, in 1980 the large modern trawlers operated by these enterprises contributed over half of all shrimp exports from Indonesia.[50]

The ban on trawlers led initially to declining harvests and adversely affected both domestic fish supplies and quantities of shrimp available for export. To overcome these expected problems, the Indonesian government initiated three special development programs: (1) a loan program to encourage conversion of trawlers for operations with other types of fishing gear, especially purse seines to harvest highly exploited pelagic species;[51] (2) a program to promote brackish water pond production of shrimp; and (3) expanded loan and technical assistance programs for small-scale fishermen in areas where previously trawlers had dominated the fisheries.

To a large extent, these programs have achieved their goals. By 1982, landings of demersal species along the north coat of Java had surpassed those preceding the trawler ban.[52] Between 1980 and 1982 the number of fishermen operating along this coast increased by nearly 10 percent to over 290,000.[53] The size of the fishing fleet remained relatively constant, but the use of engines increased, as did the per unit productivity of demersal fishing gear, which nearly doubled during this period.[54] Average household incomes increased by 30 percent among small-scale fishermen on the north coast of Java and in the area of Cilacap on the south coast.[55] These figures go a long way to explain the significant increase in numbers of fishermen operating in waters of Java subsequent to the trawler ban.

Unlike the north coast of Java, along the Malacca Straits demersal landings and per unit productivity of demersal fishing gear continued to decline. In this area it appears that the removal of trawlers did not result in a significant reduction in fishing effort. There was, instead, a major increase between 1980 and 1982 in the numbers of small-scale boats (21 percent), demersal fishing gear (40 percent), and fishermen (21 percent).[56] No data are available on changes in household income. The apparent creation of additional employment opportunities in this area is a positive feature, but this also has contributed to continued resource depletion.

The trawler ban's impact on shrimp exports was less serious than initially was expected. Prior to the issuance of Presidential Decree No. 39, trawlers had accounted for the bulk of all shrimp exports.[57] The quantity of shrimp exports did decline (13 percent) between 1980 and 1983, but foreign exchange earning increased by 15 percent,[58] in part due to improved product quality. Unlike the shrimp landed by trawlers, most of which had been on ice for several days, small-scale fisherman land their catch every day. Once logistical problems were overcome, shrimp processors generally seem to have successfully adapted to obtaining supplies from small-scale fishermen and brackish water pond operators.

WHY PRESIDENTIAL DECREE NO. 39?

By issuing Presidential Decree No. 39, Indonesia's President Suharto put the considerable weight of both government and military behind enforcement. The combination of clear political will from the highest authority in the land, and the relative ease in enforcing a total ban rather than previous restrictions, are the primary factors contributing to this improved enforcement performance.

It is clear that the main impetus behind Presidential Decree No. 39 was the widespread and increasingly violent conflict between small-scale and trawler fisherman. The resulting death and destruction dramatized, and made impossible to ignore, the threat that commercial trawling posed to inshore fisheries resources and the livelihoods of large numbers of small-scale fishermen who for generations have fished in these waters.

According to Admiral Sardjono, then Director-General of Fisheries, Presidential Decree No. 39 was clearly, a "political decision" justified primarily in terms of protecting the interests of small-scale fishermen:

> Every sudden change in policies or regulations by a Government might indeed upset certain established systems or investment, but compared with the aim of reaching social peace and stability, by way of providing better protection to the poor traditional fishermen masses, the disadvantages become very minor.[59]

To understand the logic behind Presidential Decree No. 39, it is necessary to recall that, beginning with the colonial era, governmental policy consistently has supported traditional resource use rights of small-scale fishermen. Moreover, recent national Five Year Development Plans have emphasized distributive equity as a primary development goal for all sectors of the national economy. Presidential Decree No. 39, then, is consistent with long established fisheries policies and with current and important national development priorities.

Support for Presidential Decree No. 39 also came from other, more clearly identifiable directions. Government marine biologists had become increasingly concerned about the detrimental impact of trawling on important fisheries resources, and within the DGF and other government agencies, strongly supported the ban on trawling in waters of Java and Sumatra. Researchers from several Indonesian universities began to examine the impact of trawling on small-scale fishing communities and in the process documented serious declines in income, the reduction of employment opportunities within the fisheries sector, and the general marginalization of small-scale fisheries within that sector. Popular awareness of widespread unrest among fishermen was established through the print media. Reporters actively publicized the plight of the small-scale fishermen, characterizing trawler operators as rapacious, an image fostered by the popular Indonesian term for the trawl net: "tiger net" (*pukat harimau*).

Several influential politicians working through the "All-Indonesia Fishermens' Association" (*Himpunan Nelayan Sa-Indonesia*, or HNSI also became effective lobbyists in support of small-scale fishermens' traditional resource use rights arguing that trawler operations should be curtailed or eliminated.

The HNSI is a nominally nongovernmental organization representing the interests of small-scale fishermen. In practice, the HNSI serves as a forum through which small-scale fishermen can communicate their concerns to the government. As such, it fits a general pattern of socio-political organization under the Suharto administration whereby various interests are aggregated into identifiable "functional groups." These groups serve to articulate interests to the government and provide group leaders (i.e., politicians) a political power base. In turn, governmental responsiveness to the needs of these groups and their leaders serves to build and maintain political support. Thus, groups such as the HNSI have influence in government councils because they generally support the government. Politicians closely associated with the government tend to be selected as leaders of such groups, as is the case with the HNSI, to provide assured access to the corridors of power. In return, these politicians are assured of an organized constituency in a political system without direct national elections.

One further factor, the issue of ethnicity, must be mentioned if we are to explain the government's decisions to ban trawlers. Most trawler owners were of Chinese descent. Ethnic Chinese comprise roughly 3 percent of the national population but dominate key sectors of Indonesia's economy, just as they do throughout Southeast Asia. Among all citizens, they are the ones most likely to have acess to the capital resources necessary to invest in shrimp trawling or any other profitable enterprise.

Most small-scale fishermen, however, are not ethnic Chinese but rather Javanese, Sundanese, Malay, or other indigenous ethnic groups known as "princes of the soil" (*pribumi*). There is a long history of ethnic antagonism between the econmically aggressive Chinese and the indigenous population of Indonesia. These facts may have exacerbated tensions and led to the high level of violence between trawler and small-scale fishermen.

There is no evidence that the trawler ban was imposed because trawler owners and many of their crewmen were ethnic Chinese. However, the nature of ethnic tensions may have been a contributing factor to the effectiveness of enforcement. The fact the trawler ban negatively affected relatively wealthy Chinese may have reduced the political costs of this action.

CONCLUSION

Indonesia is not the only country in Southeast Asia where endemic conflict in the fisheries sector is a problem. The banning of trawlers in Indonesia represents an important turning point in that country's fisheries development strategy. Traditional resource use rights of small-scale fishermen have been confirmed in a manner consistent with sound resource management and larger social goals of improving incomes and employment opportunities for the majority of those employed in the fisheries sector. Elsewhere in Southeast Asia, competition and conflict between trawler and those responsible for establishing fisheries management and development policies. The experience of Indonesia in resolving this issue has important implications not only for the pace and direction of fisheries development in that country but elsewhere in Southeast Asia and the developing world.

NOTES

1. Preparation of this chapter was carried out under Auburn University's program in Third World fisheries development, which is supported in part by a strengthening grant from the U.S. Agency for International Development.

2. D. K. Emmerson, *Rethinking Artisanal Fisheries Development: Western Concepts, Asian Experiences.* World Bank Staff Working Paper No. 423, (Washington, D.C.: The World Bank, 1980); I.R. Smith, *A Research Framework for Traditional Fisheries,* ICLARM Studies and Reviews No. 2 (Manila: International Center for Living Aquatic Resources Management, 1979).

3. J. M. Floyd, *International Fishery Trade of Southeast Asian Nations,* Environment and Policy Institute Research Report No. 16 (Honolulu: East-West Center).

4. C . Bailey, "The Blue Revolution: the Impact of Technological Innovation on Third World Fisheries," *The Rural Sociologist* Vol. 5, No. 4 (1985), pp. 259-66.

5. T. Panayotou, *Management Concepts for Small-Scale Fisheries: Economic and Social Aspects,* FAO Fisheries Technical Paper No. 228 (Rome: Food and Agriculture Organization).

6. Asian Development Bank, *Bank Operations in the Fisheries Sector,* Bank Staff Working Paper (Manila: Asian Development Bank, 1980).

7. Smith, *op. cit.*

8. J.C. Marr, *Fishery and Resource Management in Southeast Asia* (Washington, D.C.: Resources for the Future, 1976); D. Pauly, *Theory and Management of Tropical Multispecies Stocks: a Review with Emphasis on the Southeast Asian Demersal Fisheries*, ICLARM Studies and Reviews No. 1 (Manila: International Center for Living Aquatic Resources Management, 1979); Smith, *op. cit.*

9. R. Rackowe, *The International Market for Shrimp*, INFOFISH Market Studies No. 3 (Kuala Lumpur: INFOFISH, 1983).

10. Floyd, *op. cit.*

11. W.L. Collier, H. Hadikoesworo, and M. Malingreau, "Economic Development and Shared Poverty Among Javanese Sea Fishermen," in A. Liberero and W.L. Collier (eds.), *Economics of Aquaculture, Sea-Fishing and Coastal Resource Use in Asia* (Los Banos: Agricultural Development Council and the Philippine Council for Agriculture and Resources Research); A. F. LaPorta, "Pribumi fishermen and the trawlers' (unclassified letter to U.S. Embassies in Jakarta and Kuala Lumpur from U.S. Consulate in Medan, dated December 5, 1978); D.S. Gibbons, "Public Policy Towards Fisheries Development in Peninsular Malaysia: a Critical Review Emphasizing Penang and Kedah," *Kajian Ekonomi Malaysia* Vol XIII, Nos. 1&2 (1976), pp. 89-121; N. Naamin, "Problems Faced in implementation of Presidential Decree No. 39 of 1980 Prohibiting the Use of Trawlers" in Indonesian), *Proceedings of the Workshop on the Socio-Economics of Fisheries*, CRIFT/SOSEK/82/VI-1 (Jakarta, Center for Fisheries Research and Development, Ministry of Agriculture, 1983); I. Sardjono, "Trawlers Banned in Indonesia," *ICLARM Newsletter* Vol. 4, No. 1 (1980), p. 3; Smith, *op. cit.*

12. Sardjono, *op. cit.*

13. Central Bureau of Statistics, *Population of Indonesia by Province; Results of the Complete Population Census of 1980* (in Indonesian) (Jakarta: Central Bureau of Statistics, 1981).

14. Directorate-General of Fisheries, *Annual Fisheries Statistics, 1982* (Jakarta: Directorate-General of Fisheries, Ministry of Agriculture, 1984).

15. Central Bureau of Statistics, *Food Supply in Indonesia* (in Indonesian) (Jakarta: Central Bureau of Statistics); Directorate-General of Fisheries, *Annual Fisheries Statistics, 1982.*

16. Central Bureau of Statistics, *Food Supply in Indonesia*; Directorate-General of Fisheries, *Annual Fisheries Statistics, 1982.*

17. Directorate-General of Fisheries, *Annual Fisheries Statistics, 1980* (Jakarta: Directorate-General of Fisheries, Ministry of Agriculture, 1982).

18. G. A. Baum, "A Cost-Benefit Calculation for 'Bagan Siapi-Api' Trawlers Operating from Semarang/Central Java," *Proceedings of the Symposium on Modernization of Small-Scale Fisheries*, SMPR/78/S21 (Jakarta: Marine Fisheries Research Institute, Ministry of Agriculture, 1978); A. A. A. S. Dominggo, "Comparative Analysis of Costs and Returns of Purse Seiners and Trawlers in the District of Pekalongan" (Unpublished thesis in Indonesian, Faculty of Animal Husbandry and Fisheries, Diponegoro University, Semarang, Central Java, 1978).

19. C. Bailey and F. Marahudin, "The Economics of Marine Fisheries Production: Costs, Earnings, and Incomes," in C. Bailey, A. Dwiponggo, and F. Marahudin, *Review of Indonesian Marine Fisheries*, ICLARM Studies and Reviews (Manila and Jakarta: Directorate General of Fisheries and the International Center for Living Aquatic Resources Management, *in press*).

20. R. G. Boudon *et al.*, *Report on Costs and Earnings Survey of Malaysian Trawl Fisheries*,

1969-70. (Kuala Lumpur: Ministry of Agriculture and Lands, 1970).

21. M. Unar, "Review of the Indonesian Shrimp Fishery and its Present Development," Research Reports on Marine Fisheries No. 1 (Jakarta: Marine Fisheries Research Institute, Ministry of Agriculture, 1972).

22. N. Naamin and A. Farid, "A Review of the Shrimp Fisheries in Indonesia," in *Report of the Workshop on the Biology and Resources of Penaeid Shrimps in the South China Sea Area—Part I*, SCS/GEN/80/26 (Manila: South China Sea Fisheries Development and Coordinating Programme, 1980).

23. Unar, op. cit.; Naamin and Farid, *op. cit.*

24. Unar, *op. cit.*

25. A. Dwiponggo, "Indonesia's Marine Fisheries Resources," in C. Bailey, A. Dwiponggo, and F. Marahudin (eds.) *op. cit.*

26. T. Azhar, "Some Preliminary Notes on the By-Catch of Prawn Trawlers Off the West Coast of Peninsular Malaysia," in *Report of the Workshop on the Biology and Resources of Penaeid Shrimps in the South China Sea Area—Part I*, SCS/GEN/80/26 (Manila: South China Sea Fisheries Development and Coordinating Programme, 1980); D. Pauly, "The Fisheries and Their Ecology," in D. Pauly and A.N. Mines (eds.), *Small-Scale Fisheries of San Miguel Bay, Philippines: Biology and Stock Assessment*, ICLARM Technical Reports No. 7 (Manila: International Center for Living Aquatic Resources Management; Institute for Fisheries Development and Research, College of Fisheries, University of the Philippines in the Visayas; and the United Nations University, 1982).

27. D. Pauly, *Theory and Management of Tropical Multispecies Stocks.*

28. D. Pauly, "The Fishes and Their Ecology."

29. A. Dwiponggo, *op. cit.*; P. Martosubroto and N. Nammin, "Relationship Between Tidal Forests (Mangroves) and Commercial Shrimp Production in Indonesia," *Marine Research in Indonesia* No. 18 (1977), pp. 81-86; R.E. Turner, "Intertidal Vegetation and Commercial Yields of Penaeid Shrimp," *Transactions of the American Fisheries Society* Vol. 106, No. 5 (1977), pp. 411-16.

30. Azhar, *op. cit.*

31. D. Pauly, "History and Status of the San Miguel Bay Fisheries," in D. Pauly and A. N. Mines (eds.), *Small-Scale Fisheries of San Miguel Bay, Philippines: Biology and Stock Assessment*, ICLARM Technical Reports No. 7 (Manila: International Center for Living Aquatic Resources Management; Institute for Fisheries Development and Research, College of Fisheries, University of the Philippines in the Visayas; and the United Nations University, 1982).

32. W. L. Collier, H. Hadikoesworo, and S. Saropie, *Income, Employment, and Food Systems in Javanese Coastal Villages* (Athens: Ohio University Center for International Studies, Southeast Asia Series No. 44, 1977; Mubyarto, L. Soetrisno, and M. Dove, *Fishermen and Poverty; an Economic Anthropology Study of Two Coastal Fishing Communities* (in Indonesian) (Jakarta: CV Rajawali, 1984).

33. G. R. Joenoes et al., *The Effect of Reducing Numbers of Trawlers (Tiger Nets) on the Livelihood of Fishermen and Fish Production in the Area of Cilacap Regency* (in Indonesian) (Semarang, Central Java: Marine Fisheries Research Institute and Diponegoro University); Naamin, *op. cit.*

34. B. Darus, "The Effect of the Trawl Ban in Northern Sumatra," in Indonesian, *Proceedings of the Workshop on the Socio-Economics of Indonesian Fisheries*, CRIF/SOSEK/82/VI-2(Jakarta:

Central Institute for Fisheries Research and Development, Ministry of Agriculture, 1983); M. Unar, "A Note on Marine Fisheries Management in Indonesia," *Proceedsings of the Indo-Pacific Fisheries Council*, IPFC/74/SYM/17 (Jakarta: Indo-Pacific Fisheries Council, 1974).

35. Darus, *op. cit.*; Mubyarto, Soetrisno, and Dove, *op. cit.*

36. Mabyarto, Soetrisno, and Dove, *op. cit.*

37. G. J. Hugo, *Population Mobility in West Java* (Yogyakarta, Indonesia: Gadjah Mada University Press, 1981); B. L. M. Schiller, "The 'Green Revolution' in Java: Ecological, Socio-Economic and Historical Perspectives," *Prisma* Vol. 18 (1980), pp. 71-93.

38. T. Panayotou, "Economic Conditions and Prospects of Small-Scale Fishermen in Thailand," *Marine Policy* Vol. 4, No. 2 (1980), pp. 142-46.

39. C. Bailey, *Small-Scale Fisheries of San Miguel Bay, Philippines: Occupational and Geographic Mobility*, ICLARM Technical Reports No. 10 (Manila: International Center for Living Aquatic Resources Management; Institute for Fisheries Development and Research, College of Fisheries, University of the Philippines in the Visayas; and the United Nations University, 1982); Smith, *op. cit.*

40. C. Bailey, *The Sociology of Production in Rural Malay Society* (Kuala Lumpur: Oxford University Press, 1983); Gibbons, *op. cit.*; Smith, *op. cit.*

41. La Porta, *op. cit.*; Sardjono, *op. cit.*

42. Smith, *op. cit.*; Gibbons, *op. cit.* See also the undated (1978?) pamphlet "Small-Scale Fishermen in Asia Speak Out" (Bangkok: Asian Cultural Forum on Development, n.d.); see also "Trawler Invasion Persists," *Asian Action* Vol. 26 (Newsletter of the Asian Cultural Forum on Development), p. 4.

43. Collier, Hadikoesworo, and Malingreau, *op. cit.*; LaPorta, *op. cit.*; Naamin, *op. cit.*; Sardjono; *op. cit.*

44. C. Bailey, "Marine Fisheries Mangement and Development: Policies and Programs," in C. Bailey, A. Dwiponggo, and F. Marahudin, *Review of Indonesian Marine Fisheries.*

45. LaPorta, *op. cit.*; "Small Fishermen in Asia Speak Out," *op. cit.*

46. Joenoes *et al.*, *op. cit.*; N. Naamin, "The Present State of the Shrimp Fishery in the Cilacap Area and Some Problems of its Mangement," *Report of the Workshop on the Biolopgy and Resources of Penaeid Shrimps in the South China Sea Area—Part 1*, SCS/GEN/80/26 (Manila: South China Sea Fisheries Development and Coordinating Programme, 1980).

47. Central Bureau of Statistics and Directorate General of Fisheries, 1979.

48. Naamin, "The Present State of the Shrimp Fishery in the Cilacap Area and Some Problems of its Management."

49. Sardjono, *op. cit.*

50. A. Rachman, "The Development of Industrial Fisheries in Indonesia" (mimeo, report prepared by the Director-General of Fisheries, Ministry of Agriculture, Jakarta, 1982).

51. Pelagic species are those which customarily live at or near the surface or at varying points in the water column, and are distinguished from demersal (bottom dwelling) species. A purse seine is a net used to encircle a school of fish. The net is suspended at the surface with

floats. Along the bottom edge are a series of rings through which a rope or cable is run. When this is pulled in, the bottom of the net is "pursed" or closed, preventing escape as the net is hauled aboard.

52. Directorate-General of Fisheries, *Annual Fisheries Statistics, 1980* and *Annual Fisheries Statistics, 1982* (Jakarta: Directorate General of Fisheries, Ministry of Agriculture, 1982 and 1984).

53. *Ibid.*

54. *Ibid.*

55. Naamin, "Problems Faced in Implementation of Presidential Decree No. 39 of 1980 Prohibiting the Use of Trawlers."

56. Directorate-General of Fisheries, *Annual Fisheries Statistics, 1980* and *Annual Fisheries Statistics, 1982* (Jakarta: Directorate General of Fisheries, Ministry of Agriculture, 1982 and 1984).

57. B. Gafa and R. Rustam, "Condition of the Fisheries Resources in West Java Province after Issuance of Presidential Decree No. 39 in 1980," mimeo report in Indonesian from the Semarang (Central Java) office of the Marine Fisheries Research Institute, Ministry of Agriculture, 1981; D. Nugroho and I. Murtoyo, "Monitoring the Cold-Storage Industry in the Areas of Cirebon and Cilacap," mimeo report in Indonesian from the Semarang (Central Java) office of the Marine Fisheries Research Institute, Ministry of Agriculture, 1981; N. Naamin (1982), *op. cit.*

58. Food and Agriculture Organization, *Yearbook of Fisheries Statistics, 1983,* Vol. 57 (Rome: FAO, 1983).

59. Sardjono, *op. cit.*

CHAPTER TWENTY-TWO

Micro-Policy Reform—The Role of Private Voluntary Development Agencies

David C. Korten

Current development thinking stresses the need for policy reforms supportive of more effective and sustainable outcomes from both centrally and locally initiated development actions. In addressing the needs for policy reform, it is useful to make a distinction between two quite different classes of policy reform: macro-reforms and micro-reforms.

MACRO- VERSUS MICRO-POLICY REFORM

Macro-policy reforms are those which can be accomplished through preemptive central actions—the stroke of an authoritative pen. Usually they involve a fairly clearly defined and specific decision. Strong political interests opposing the reform may make it extraordinarily difficult to reach that decision. But once the decision is clearly made and formalized by the signature of the component political authority, the implementation is a comparatively straightforward process involving minimal requirements for the development of new institutional capacities as a precondition to effective action. The decision to remove a subsidy from fertilizer imports tends to be of this nature, or a decision to move from subsidized to market-level interest rates for agricultural credit. In the latter case the administrative mechanisms presumably are in place to administer agricultural loans. The primary change will be in in the regulation specifying the interest rate to be charged. Many policies relating to pricing decisions, subsidies, and trade policies are of this nature. Macro-policy is the natural and appropriate realm of the policy analysis studies, which are focused on projecting the consequences of alternative policy choices so that the "correct" answer can be chosen.[1]

Micro-policy reforms are those which depend for their implementation on the accomplishment of sometimes highly complex and difficult institutional changes commonly involving the development of significant new institutional capacities and norms and a redefinition of institutional roles. The introduction of a credit program for small farmers where none has existed before would be of this nature. In this case, credit institutions may already be in place, but making their services accessible to small and often remote client populations will require capacities quite different from those involved in reaching larger, often more urban, clients. Most complex of all are likely to be those micro-policy reforms calling for a sharing of power between national and local levels and the development of self-reliant beneficiary organizations. Micro-policy reform is the natural realm of social learning, where the most difficult questions relate to how to make a given reform effective.

The differing nature of macro- and micro-policy reforms has important implications. In dealing with macro-policy, the presence of a strong authoritarian leader can offer significant advantage. The problem then becomes primarily one of making it worth his or her while to accept the political costs of the decision. Commonly this can be accomplished through offering financial resources as an "incentive." These resources may be used either to make it worth the while of the opposition to give up its benefits under the old policy, or to buy countervailing political support from influential interests. These are the types of policy reform that lend themselves to application of the substantial financial leverage of large donor organizations.

Micro-policy reform is quite a different matter. In the micro-policy arena both political leaders and the large donors commonly find their leverage to be very limited. While they can demand formal compliance, pre-emptive action carries little or no real force unless backed by persistent action to achieve what must be essentially bottom-up processes of rebuilding institutional structures and supporting norms. Here the large donors may even be at a disadvantage. Demands to keep the money moving divert their attention from the careful coalition building and learning process facilitation through which micro-policy reforms are worked through and institutionalized. They may also tend to confuse formal acceptance of project conditions with actual compliance, failing to recognize that there may in fact be no institutional capacity to act on these conditions irrespective of intent.

For example, the conditions of a major irrigation loan can demand a role for water user associations, but unless the capacity to develop and support such associations already exists there is seldom any action. Faced with competing political interests within their own organizations and having little time for the details of internal management, even the top administrators of the irrigation agency may face similar limitations in their ability to achieve such changes irrespective of the strength of their personal commitments. Agricultural extension projects can demand that the research extension system be responsive to farmer realities and inputs, but if existing structures are geared to enforcing farmer compliance with centrally mandated recommendations, and there is no tradition of researchers seeking feedback from extension agents, such response is unlikely. Community health projects can call for the development of self-sustaining, self-financing village health committees to assume the leadership in local health matters, but if the health system is geared to centrally funded physician care, formally established local committees will be sustained only so long as central project funds are available.

The list could be extended to include most all people-centered development activities. Commonly, basic changes are required in deeply held personal and professional values as well as a reversal of existing professional and managerial practice. These are not easily achieved.

THE CATALYST ROLE IN MICRO-POLICY REFORM

Though authoritative support is commonly needed, the reform of micro-policy is more an outcome of social process than of legal proclamation. Prospects for successful outcome can be considerably enhanced by the involvement of one or more catalyst organizations with a sustained commitment to facilitating coalition building and institutional learning basic to the types of social process involved.

The methods and potentials of such a catalyst role have been demonstrated with particular effect by the Southeast Asia Office of the Ford Foundation through its support for community management approaches in irrigation and forestry in Indonesia, the Philippines, and Thailand. While each country and sector effort has its own distinctive features, the common pattern is one in which Ford staff start by identifying those agencies that dominate the policy and program environment with regard to the management of a particular resource such as irrigation water or forest lands. Then they identify key individuals within these agencies with an interest in community-based approaches to the management of that resource. Funds are provided to the focal agency through these concerned individuals to support studies, often carried out by local universities, focusing on existing community management practices and the impact of existing agency programs on those practices. The results of these studies are examined on an iterative basis by the researchers and agency officials in local and/or national forums. Representatives from one or more private voluntary agencies with interest and expertise in the topic may also be invited to participate.

Gradually those individuals who demonstrate a serious interest in the problem are formed into a working group which assumes a growing leadership role in the analysis of the experience.[2] In addition to agency staff and the responsible Ford Foundation program officer, a mature working group may include participants from four or five research and training institutions plus one or more PVOs. The working group is invariably chaired by a senior official of the responsible agency.

As understanding of the resource management problem increases, and possible ways of dealing with it using community management approaches are identified, one or more pilot projects are established under agency auspices to serve as learning laboratories in the development of new approaches. These pilot efforts may involve one or more private voluntary development agencies assisting in the training and supervision of field staff—plus social scientists from one or more in-country institutions who develop site assessment methods and document implementation processes. The experimental field activities are intensively monitored by the working group so that approaches may be modified and implications for the larger organization can be assessed. Through workshops, conferences, and training programs, the experience base and the number of persons engaged in the review of these experiences is expanded. Gradually additional learning laboratories that build from the experience of the earlier efforts are established.

Ford staff working in facilitator roles identify prospective working group members, engage them in relevant activities, and gradually help them establish roles within the working group. At the same time they play a key role in agenda setting, in facilitating relations among participants, and in providing flexible funding to the sponsoring agency to support activities of the working group while also making small grants to participating institutions to pursue related initiatives designed to strengthen their own programs. Occasionally Ford staff develop their own studies illuminating key program and policy issues for exposure in workshops with agency personnel.[3]

Organizations that assume such catalyst roles must have experienced staff combining in-depth country knowledge, professional credibility, and well-developed facilitation skills. Expatriate organizations may at times perform this catalyst role, as the Ford Foundation has demonstrated in Southeast Asia, but where expatriate staff are involved, their effectiveness is likely to depend on stable country assignments and established professional credibility. Their jobs must be structured to leave them relatively free of routine administrative duties so that they may concentrate their energies on problem-centered collegial interactions with counterparts. There must also be a capacity to quickly and flexibly fund a range of activities through small grants and contracts as needs and opportunities arise.

Unfortunately, relative to the need, there are at present all too few organizations with the commitment and capacity to perform catalyst roles in support of needed micro-policy reforms. However, there are within the development community a number of private voluntary development agencies (PVOs) with a natural interest in micro-policy reform, that view development as primarily a people-to-people process, and that lack the inherent structural constraints faced by the large donors.

THREE GENERATIONS OF PRIVATE VOLUNTARY DEVELOPMENT ACTION

Private voluntary and humanitarian development assistance efforts directed to the relief of Third World poverty have undergone important changes over the years as their practitioners have grown in sophistication and professionalism. Yet the full potentials of the private voluntary development community to be a major force for self-sustaining, broadly based development have yet to be realized.

In formulating actions directed to actualizing this potential, it is useful to differentiate between three generations of private voluntary development strategies, each subsequent generation of thought and action bringing to bear a longer time perspective and a broadened definitition of the development problem. The programs and capacities created by each of the three generations have a continuing place within the overall scheme of development action. Yet, just as within the human family it is important at times to give special recognition to the distinctive needs and potentials of the most recent generation.

Generation 1: Relief and Welfare. Many of the larger international PVOs such as Catholic Relief Services, CARE, Save the Children, and World Vision began as charitable relief organizations, relying on private contributions to deliver welfare services to the poor and unfortunate throughout the world. Such efforts represented a first generation of private voluntary development assistance. Relief efforts are an essential and appropriate response to emergency situations, which demand immediate and effective humanitarian response. Such situations may forever be a part of the human experience, and there will always be those within any community whose circumstances are such that they necessarily depend on some form of welfare assistance. But as a development strategy, relief and welfare approaches currently have few serious proponents.

Generation 2: Small-Scale Local Development. In the early and mid-70's, individuals and organizations throughout the development community came to recognize that sustainable improvements in the lives of the poor depend on increasing their capacity to meet their own needs with their own resources. The issues were ably articulated in a study by the Overseas

Development Council.[4] Within the PVO community, as elsewhere, recognition grew that attempting to relieve poverty through the direct delivery food, health care, and shelter attacked only its symptoms without addressing its causes. Thus, many PVOs undertook development of program capabilities to promote and fund local development activities in areas such as preventive health care, improved farming practices, local infrastructure, and other community development activities intended to promote local self-reliance. Thus emerged a second generation of private development effort. AID Development Program Grants made available during the period of 1975-79 encouraged and assisted interested PVOs in developing the necessary capacity to implement these second generation strategies, contributing to their substantial increase over the past ten years.

Some governments have attempted to discourage and/or control PVO efforts, seeing them as competitive with their own public development programs and fearing that independently created local organizations might represent competing political interests. Some PVOs, perceiving government as incompetent and hostile to their efforts, have sought to avoid or bypass it, even when claiming that their own activities are intended as models for emulation by public programs. Examples of effective cooperation to realize the comparative strengths of each, while they exist, are all too rare.

Generation 3: Sustainable Systems Development. Currently segments of the PVO community are again engaged in a re-examination of basic strategic issues relating to sustainability, breadth of impact, and recurrent cost recovery. At the heart of this re-examination is the realization that sustaining the outcomes of self-reliant village development initiatives depends on systems of effectively linked local public and private organizations which integrate local initiatives into a supportive national development system.[5] Unfortunately in many instances the necessary institutional linkages and policies either do not exist or, if they do, work to the detriment of local control and initiative. There may be no provision for independent local groups to obtain legal recognition or enforceable rights over productive resources, or local income generating activities may be undermined by publicly subsidized corporations competing for control over productive resources and markets. In many instances local initiative is substantially discouraged and/or overshadowed by bureaucratically sponsored and administered service delivery programs, which create local dependence on central subsidies and extend central bureaucratic control to the lowest societal levels.

In such instances the successful outcomes of a rural development initiative may depend on the PVO assuming a catalytic role involving collaboration with government, and a wide range of other institutions, both public and private, to put into place new policies and institutional linkages that enable self-sustaining local private initiative. Acceptance of this role leads the PVOs to a third generation strategy, which brings with it substantial new demands.

Third generation strategies, which cast the PVO into the role of catalyst of broader policy and structural change, are by no means new to the PVO community. For example, in the field of population, private organizations such as Pathfinder Fund pioneered public education and service delivery programs several decades before governments began to take population growth seriously, preparing the way for a major shift in public attitudes and policies. In the late 1960's and early 70's, national affiliates of the International Planned Parenthood Federation throughout the world committed themselves to sophisticated strategies, which in country after country resulted in important changes in public policy and achieved government commitment to the provision of family planning services. These efforts combined direct lobbying at policy levels by influential boardmembers, sponsorship of policy research, public education campaigns, and services delivery programs that proved the extent of demand and served as models for government programs.

The 1980's have seen a growing number of PVOs, both large and small, in areas such as local development, health, and small enterprise, become increasingly conscious of their potential for contributing to improved human well-being by serving as catalysts in support of needed reforms in public policies and programs. As of 1986 Technoserve, Partnership for Productivity, CARE, Philippine Business for Social Progress, the Bangladesh Rural Advancement Committee, and Helen Keller International were among the PVOs at the forefront of thought and action in this regard. Yet most of these efforts are still in their infancy, presenting demands on the PVOs that undertake them to achieve a clearer definition of their own purposes and distinctive competence, while simultaneously developing a range of new capacities, for example, in stategic management, policy and institutional analysis, networking, and coalition building.

BUILDING THIRD GENERATIONAL STRATEGIC CAPACITY

The PVO choosing to undertake a third generation strategy works in part in the mode of a foundation, directing its attention to facilitating development by other organizations, both public and private, of the capacities, linkages, and commitments required to address the designated need on a sustained basis. The organizations involved may include local PVOs, cooperatives, private firms, line agencies of central government, local governments, universities, research institutes, etc.

PVOs committed to third generation strategies cannot be guided by good intentions alone, they must develop disciplined organizations led by well trained and motivated professional managers.[6] Development of such capacities requires a major committment involving actions such as: 1) sending key senior staff for advanced management training at top ranked management schools; 2) developing collaborative relationships with groups that have advanced capabilities in relevant social and policy analysis; 3) carefully documenting and critically assessing their early third generation efforts to strengthen learning from their own experience; 4) conducting strategic assessment workshops with their staff; and 5) participating in experience exchange with other similarly committed PVOs.[7]

The need for innovative thinking leading to expanded roles for private development agencies is becoming particularly evident in Asian countries. Throughout the region it is becoming clear that financial realities preclude continued reliance on expensive and wasteful public projects and programs as the basis for continued development progress. For many Asian nations, a greater reliance on broadly based, local private initiative may be essential. Further, while it is important that governments recognize and give effective support to such initiative, much of the leadership must ultimately come from the private sector itself.

NOTES

1. This fit between macro-policy and the concerns and methods of policy analysis, and the corresponding fit (as noted below) between micro-policy and the concerns and methods of social learning have been identified and elaborated by Frances F. Korten, "Making Research Relevant to Action: A Social Learning Perspective," Paper presented at the Workshop on Public Intervention in Farmer Managed Irrigation, International Institute for Irrigation Management (Sri Lanka), held in Kathmandu, Nepal, August 4-6, 1986.

2. For an examination of the working group concept and its application in one change effort, see David C. Korten, "The Working Group as a Mechanism for Managing Bureaucratic Reorientation," NASPAA Working Paper No. 4 (Washington, D. C.: National Association of Schools of Public Affairs and Administration, May 1982).

3. Chapter Twenty by Frances Korten is is an example of one such contribution. The original analysis was presented at a seminar in which the issues were jointly examined by a number of Indonesian government officials, as well as representatives of private voluntary organizations. This led to a more intensive study of the issues in specific relation to Indonesia by a major Indonesian PVO with extensive experience in irrigation development.

4. John G. Sommer, Beyond Charity: U.S. Voluntary Aid for a Changing World (Washington, D. C.: Overseas Development Council, 1977).

5. Milton J. Esman and Norman Uphoff, Local Organizations: Intermediaries in Rural Development, (Ithaca: Cornell University Press, 1984). See also Norman, Uphoff Analyzing Options for Local Institutional Development, Special Series on Local Institutional Development No. 1, (Ithaca: Rural Development Committee, Cornell University, 1984).

6. This by no means implies an authoritarian style of management, but it does imply well-developed management systems, a strong commitment to performance, and an ability to set and sustain directions of effort, while still being able to make adaptive decisions quickly in response to changing circumstances. The model is that of the strategic organization described in David C. Korten, "Strategic Organization for People-Centered Development," *Public Adminstration Review*, Vol. 44, No. 4, July/August 1984, pp. 341-352.

7. For many of the PVOs that attempt it, the transition from second to third generation strategies is likely to be as wrenching as was the former transition from first to second generation strategies. Indeed, questions have been raised as to how complete this first transition has been in many instances. See Brian H. Smith, "U.S. and Canadian PVOs as Transactional Development Institutions," in Robert F. Gorman (ed.), *Private Voluntary Organizations as Agents of Development* (Boulder: Westview Press, 1984), pp. 115-64. For case studies of aspects of internal organizational culture that inhibit development of strategic competence in some PVOs see L. David Brown and Jane Covey Brown, "Organizational Microcosms and Ideological Negotiation," in M. H. Bazerman and R. J. Lewicki, *Negotiating in Organizations*, (Beverly Hills: Sage, 1983).

CONCLUSION

COMMUNITY MANAGEMENT AND SOCIAL TRANSFORMATION

David C. Korten

For several decades development has been viewed as largely synonymous with the industrialization of formerly agrarian societies. Development transformation so conceived is commonly characterized by urbanization, centralization, bureaucratization, concentration, and mechanization. In many respects community-based resource management, with its emphasis on rural development, decentralization, development of nonbureaucratic organizational forms, and the broadly based control of productive resources and technologies, might well be viewed as antithetical to such a transformation. In many respects it represents an inversion of the resource management system widely considered necessary to achieve rapid industrialization. Indeed, so it has been viewed within many of the leading schools of development thought.[1]

The conventional image of development as industrialization was defined largely by the features that characterized a number of Western countries in the 1950's. But development is not an end state, it is a process, and those countries that gave a particular meaning to the term "developed" in the 1950's have been undergoing continuing changes in response to the opportunities created by new technologies, changes in social values, and the confrontation of ecological realities. These changes create both a demand for and the possibility of a truly modern society based on diversity, decentralization, and distributed control—representing essentially an inversion of the resource management system of the modern industrial state. Here the development of community-based resource management systems emerges as a central, even essential, element of the development strategy.

INDUSTRIALISM: DEVELOPMENT PROTOTYPE
OR A FORM OF UNDERDEVELOPMENT?

The features of the prototype industrial society are well known. Its population tends to be highly concentrated in a few dominant urban areas. Large corporate production units with broadly diffused ownership and little attachment to place command massive financial resources and serve national and even global markets with standardized products. Specialized by function, each individual, organization, and geographic area is highly dependent on exchange relationships with others. The mechanical, materials-intensive technologies of such a society are dependent on the abundant availability of nonrenewable resources, including cheap, highly concentrated energy sources.

The dominant relationships are those defined by markets and the hierarchical structures of large bureaucratized corporate bodies, which emerged as a hallmark of industrial society. These relationships, at least in the forms most idealized in industrial culture, tend to be formalized, impersonal, and temporary, breaking down the constraints of tradition and personalism. By comparison with traditional society, associations based on family and neighborhood are considerably weakened by these macro-structures. Organizational boundaries tend to be clearly defined and information flows are predominantly vertical. A massified culture, highly responsive to the dominant values and products of the moment, tends to overshadow local cultural variety.

Productivity born of standardization, specialization, and extensive exploitation of stored surpluses of nature made possible unprecedented standards of living for that portion of the world's population in a position to benefit from it. The institutional and technical forms that made this possible understandably captured the imagination of the world.

Yet there is serious question as to whether, due to resource and environmental limits, these forms are replicable on the scale required to be inclusive of all the world's people. There are challenges to the premise that purely materialistic values are a valid basis for assessing human progress. There is concern that ever increasing specialization has resulted in global structures so interdependent that a perturbance in one part of the system can have disastrous and often far reaching consequences throughout the system.[2] On a more personal level, there is the alienation born of impersonalized bureaucratic structures. There is evidence that these and other environmental, technical, and social forces are converging to fundamentally reshape the basic nature of industrial societies, resulting in shifts in dominant technologies, organizational forms, and values.

It is ironic that, having once defined the very meaning of modernity and development, the industrial nations of the 1950s and 60s are rapidly becoming something rather different. Some futurists see the emergence of a new "information" society in which information constitutes the basic resource, and information-based technologies significantly reduce the constraint to broadly shared improvements in human well-being posed by physical resoure limits.[3] Information-based technologies are also rapidly reshaping the structure of employment, away from jobs involving the direct manipulation of things, the hallmark of industrial society, to jobs involving the manipulation of information.[4]

While advances in technology may seem more dramatic and certainly are more visible, there is evidence that changes in dominant organizational forms are also occurring in the former industrial nations. The direction seems to be away from control-oriented hierarchical organizational forms to more distributed self-regulating organizations featuring self-managing local units—work groups, small business units, and geographically defined communities. Such trends are widely documented in the corporate sector where studies of the most progressive and successful organizations suggest that management information systems are used increasingly not as weapons to force compliance but as tools to guide action, providing rich and rapid performance feedback to all organizational levels in support of self-corrective action. Rather than fromal management control systems, it is the institutional culture that provides the dominant force sustaining the direction of such organizations while nurturing individual initiative in the pursuit of ideas and responses appropriate to new circumstances.[5] While these developments do not imply the elimination of hierarchy, they do suggest that a better balance may be emerging between vertical structures and communication flows and horizontal structures and communication flows within organizations than has previously been the case.

Parallel trends are being observed in the re-emerging importance of local government, with more needs met and critical decisions made at the local level. Some observers believe that more generally, face-to-face groups in which the individual has an identity and a role as a valued participant may be regaining some of their former importance.

The combination of advanced information communication and processing technologies and new organizational forms results, overall, in a greatly enhanced capacity to manage variety, consequently reducing the advantages of scale, standardization, and specialization, while allowing greater flexibility in choosing socially, as well as economically appropriate, technologies. Even within larger corporations, there are reports of a growing recognition of the economic advantages of small production units.[6] Equally significant are findings regarding the substantial role of the small entrepreneurial firm in innovation and employment generation.[7]

It appears that an increasingly common model is that of smaller, self-managing units able to produce a complete product or service, but which work within a larger system of technical and marketing support. This is rapidly becoming a dominant model for retailing in the United States.[8] Each store unit may be individually owned and operated, providing both the incentive and the scope for local problem solving. At the same time the unit is able to gain the advantage of highly specialized technical support and mass advertising normally available only to a larger firm. A parallel phenomenon in the Third World is the growing popularity of the nuclear estate model of agricultural development, in which numerous independent farms are serviced by a central technical, processing, and marketing facility.[9]

There is also within the United States a recent growth of interest in local economic self-reliance, calling on communities to produce more of their own basic food and energy needs, to recycle wastes as a valuable local resource, and to retain control of locally generated financial resources.[10] Here we see the explicit emergence of the theme of community management of resources, which seemed to have little relevance for countries such as the United States at the height of the industrial era.

While predicting specific characteristics of information-era societies remains a highly speculative undertaking, it seems evident that whatever the specifics, the emergent information societies will differ substantially from the industrial societies they transcend. There seems to be a realistic prospect that the resulting societal forms will be better able to meet the needs for physical, intellectual, and spiritual growth of all their members. To the extent that these potentials are realized, we shall likely, one day in the very near future, look back on economically, environmentally, and socially convetional industrialism as the mark of a relatively backward and underdeveloped society.

Given this possibility, it seems prudent for the intellectual leaders of Third World societies to question seriously whether the development prototypes that continue to dominate development thought and action actually provide valid guides to their own futures. If not, it may be necessary to approach development not as an act of replication but as an act of creation, seeking to actualize potentials not previously realized by any human society. Releasing the creative energy necessary to accomplish this is likely to depend on development of new institutional forms that will enable local control and initiative. As noted in the introduction to this chapter, a serious commitment to the development of such institutional forms may easily be perceived as a strategic anomaly by those who continue to define their futures in terms of 1950s industrialism. They will naturally fear that local control over crucial development resources will inhibit the development of system specialization under central bureaucratic control and the concentration of capital, both of which have been widely viewed as basic to achieving a modern industrial state. But if the industrial state no longer defines modernity, the picture changes dramatically.

With the data now available, there is reason to believe that, beyond a point, specialization, bureaucratic control, and concentration of capital all become barriers to, rather than facilitators of, true modernization. The most advanced societies are more likely to feature distributed self-managing local units which, in turn, serve as the building blocks of larger self-organizing systems; and more broadly distributed control over productive assets. If this becomes an element of one's definition of modernity, the development of community-based resource management systems naturally becomes a central element of the preferred modernization strategy.

QUESTIONING CORE VALUES: FROM SOCIAL ENGINEERING TO SOCIAL LEARNING

> ...if there existed a universal mind that projected itself into the scientific fancy of Laplace; a mind that could register simultaneously all the processes of nature and society, that could measure the dynamic of their motion, that could forecast the results of their interaction, such a mind, of course could *a priori* draw up a faultless and an exhaustive economic plan, beginning with the number of hectares of wheat and down to the last button for a vest. In truth, the bureaucracy often conceives that just such a mind is at its disposal.
> —Leon Trotsky[11]

The appeal of comprehensive central plans implemented through authoritarian structures as the guiding force in modern development can be traced back to the early decades of the 19th century in the writing of Saint Simon and Auguste Comte. Deeply influenced by the Newtonian model of a predictable, machine-like universe, they concluded that, by applying the methods of positivistic science to the study of human affairs, it would be possible to predict, and ultimately to control human social behavior. With this knowledge a more perfect human society could be created, governed by the objective application of scientific principles rather than by the vagaries of political process. It followed naturally that the good society must be led by a strong central authority figure who would make judgements for society based on the objective application of scientific knowledge.[12]

Such a model for societal decision-making structures and processes is implicitly accepted as the ideal to this day by many intellectuals and technocrats. The model finds its fullest application in totalitarian socialist countries. It has had a powerful influence on the models of development planning and administration that have dominated development thought and practice in countries throughout the Third World irrespective of political persuasion.[13] Providing legitimation for the centralization of power and the emasculation of political process, these models call for the creation of strong central planning units to allocate public development resources on the basis of returns to available capital. Implementation is to be carried out through strong central bureaucracies able to ensure adherence to plan.

Though attainment of the ideal in actual practice has proven illusive, its pursuit is reflected in institutional structures throughout the Third World.[14] In many cases, the resulting concentration of control over political and economic resources has worked more to the advantage of political elites than to the advantage of the people. The former have all too easily seized these instruments of control to sustain their personal power and enrich themselves and their supporters. It is sad and ironic that idealistic technocrats, who believe deeply in the ability of their knowledge and tools to benefit human society, by their very denial of political process and the legitimacy of exercising individual value choices, seem defenseless against co-optation by those who are masters at the manipulation of both.

The predispostion for analysis over political process, and for central control over local choice, are only two elements of a much broader set of preferences which Robert Chambers suggest define the core, or "first," values of what he calls *normal* development professionalism.[15] According to Chambers, normal development professionalism gravitates toward power, wealth, core locations, uniformity, and certainity. It gives preference to industry over agriculture, things over people, modern over traditional technology, market oriented over subsistence oriented production, objective quantification over subjective experience, and peer evaluation over user-client assessment.[16] These perspectives have generally dominated thought and action in Post-World War II development and account in part for its dismal record in dealing with problems of poverty.

Chambers finds cause for hope in an emerging counterforce that inverts the perspectives and value preferences of normal professionalism. He labels this counterforce a *new* development professionalism. Where normal professionalism asks what must be done to increase returns to capital, new professionalism asks who are the poor and how might available resources better be allocated to allow them to improve their lives through improving the returns to their labor. Where normal professionalism asks how can the state and its instruments of bureaucratic control be strengthend to ensure the proper implementation of centrally determined investment plans, the new professionalism asks how can the people be strengthened, particularly the poor, to control and mobilize assets in the service of their own locally defined needs. Where normal professionalism seeks prescriptive, centrally imposed blueprints, new professionalism seeks the enhancement of social learning processes.

The perspectives of the new professionalism may provide a key to unlocking the grip that poverty maintains on the majority of the world's population. Its tolerance for diversity and distributed decision making leads to a preference for institutional structures and processes consistent with the requirements of community management, and not incidentally, those associated with the emerging information age as well. Its recognition of the importance of individual value choice, its acceptance of political process, and its preference for local control insulate it from easy co-optation by self-serving political elites. These are important matters for individual and collectve assessment by members of the development professions. The growing interest in community management in Asia appears to parallel, indeed is in part a product of, the emergence of a new development professionalism.

MEANS AND ENDS: LEADERSHIP BEYOND GOVERNMENT

One of the many important lessons taught by Mohandas K. Gandhi is that in achieving social change the means must be consistent with the ends being sought. A community-management approach to resource management seeks an increase in local control and initiative within larger national and international systems. To look to government to assume the sole responsibility for achieving this outcome would be inconsistent with the outcome itself.

Furthermore, the changes in perception, commitment, and individual action involved in developing a national resource management system based on local control are likely to emerge only as products of a social learning process.[17] Social learning cannot be mandated by the pre-emptive action of central political authority. Nor can it be programmed by bureaucratic procedures. It is a product of people, acting individually and in voluntary association with others, guided by their individual critical consciousness and recognizing no organizational boundaries.[18] Its organizational forms are found in coalitions and networks, which become aggregated in larger social movements, driven by ideas and shared values more than by formal structures.

In the present instance, such coalitions, networks, and movements appropriately find their basis in action directed to strengthening broadly based local control over resources, and local capacities to manage those resources. Generally such local action will itself involve broadly based coalitions of local actors and organizations, including local beneficiary groups, local service organizations, local governments, rural banks, and others. Such local action has a two-fold purpose. The first is the creation of a new social reality. The second is the generation of experience supportive of social learning at higher institutional and policy levels. Achieving this learning depends on the use of multiple channels and forums to disseminate the experience and encourage critical dialogue on its larger implications.

The actors in this process appropriately come from all walks of life ranging from senior public officials and private business leaders, to the poor landless worker who joins with his landless neighbors to obtain the rights to cultivate a piece of public forest land. Often the organizational leadership will come from private voluntary development groups which combine the commitment and the freedom of action required to serve as catalysts in forming the sustaining the coalitions, networks, and movements that serve as the driving force in social transformation processes. [See Chapter twenty-two]

Those participants with access to the instruments of state power are properly advised to use those instruments with care. There is need for considerble self-awareness to avoid the instinctual reactions to which most of us have been conditioned by normal professionalism and by the social engineering models of societal governance. The instruments of the state must be used to enable, allowing the initiative and direction to come from the people. To impose a community-based resource management system by central fiat or to attempt its central control would be to preclude the very outcomes sought.

NOTES

1. Milton J. Esman and Norman T. Uphoff, *Local Organizations: Intermediaries in Rural Development* (Ithaca: Cornell University Press, 1984), pp. 47-52 review the dominant development theories of the 1950's and 60's. They observe that the technology transfer school saw little role for local organizations except as conduits for receiving new technologies from outside. Sociological theories saw indigenous local orgainzations as hopelessly tradition-bound and obstructive to modernization. Marxist theorists saw peasants as an inert class and basically irrelevant. Neoclassical economists, who considered the reduction of consumption essential to capital formation, feared that local organizations might make claims through the political process and thus limit the extraction of resources from agriculture for state directed investment. Political theorists, such as Huntington, Mydral, and Binder called for state imposition of discipline on the masses and warned against self-directed popular mobilization.

2. Examples have become commonplace. A breakdown in one point of a power grid brought the entire northeast U.S. to a standstill. The economy of a major portion of the Philippines was devestated by a fall in the price of a single commodity—coconut oil. An increase in oil prices sent world economy into a recession. And there are realistic fears that a default by two or three countries on their outstanding loans could result in the collapse of the international banking system.

3. The information-based technologies of fields such as bio-engineering and materials science advance our ability to manipulate basic biological and molecular structures in ways that reduce the physical mass of resources required to meet a given human need. Thus, the manipulation of genetic structures makes possible reductions in requirements for chemical pesticides and fertilizers. The creation of stronger and more durable materials allows for a reduction in the weight and energy consumption of cars, airplanes, and innumerable other products. Particularly visible have been the advances that make possible the processing and transmis-

sion of every growing quantitites of data with equipment produced with increasingly negligible investements of physical materials and energy. Among the various development resources, information has the distinctive quaility that its use by one person does not diminish the possibility of its use by another. To the contrary, the more information is used and shared the more its stock and utility increases.

4. These include programmers, teachers, clerks, secretaries, accountants, stock brokers, managers, insurance people, public officials, lawyers, bankers and technicians. According to John Naisbitt, *Megatrends* (New York: Warner Books, 1982), p. 14, only 17 percent of Americans worked in jobs that primarily involved the manipulation of information in 1950, compared to 60 percent in 1980.

5. Such studies include Thomas J. Peters and Robert H. Waterman, Jr., *In Search of Excellence: Lessons from America's Best-Run Companies* (New York: Harper and Row, 1982); William G. Ouchi, *Theory Z: How American Business Can Meet the Japanese Challenge* (Reading: Addison-Wesley Publishing Co., 1981); James Brian Quinn, *Strategies for Change: Logical Incrementalism* (Homewood: Irwin, 1980); and Rosabeth Moss Kanter, *The Change Masters: Corporate Entrepreneurs at Work* (London: George Allen & Unwin, 1983).

6. "Small is Beautiful Now in Manufacturing," *Business Week*, October 22, 1984, pp. 152-6.

7. Naisbitt, *op. cit.*, pp. 145-9.

8. Growing at a current rate of 9.4 percent in the U.S., franchised businesses were expected to account for 33 percent of all sales and 5.6 million jobs in the U.S. by the end of 1985. *John Naisbitt's Trend Letter*, Vol 4, August 8, 1985.

9. *Agribusiness and the Small-Scale Farmer*, A Study by Business International Corporation for the Bureau for Private Enterprise, Agency for International Development (Undated).

10. David Morris, "The Self-Reliant City" in David C. Korten and Rudi Klauss (eds.) *People-Centered Development: Contributions toward Theory and Planning Frameworks* (West Hartford: Kumarian Press, 1984), pp. 223-39; and Medard Gable, Ellen Pahl, Ron Shegda, and Robert Rodale, *Regenerating America: Meeting the Challenge of Building Local Economies* (Emmaus: Rodale Press).

11. As quoted by Albert Waterston, *Development Planning: Lessons of Experience* (Baltimore: Johns Hopkins University Press, 1969), p. 45.

12. See John Friedmann, Chapter on "Four Traditions in Planning Theory" in *Planning in the Public Domain*, forthcoming. Henry Jacoby, *The Bureaucratization of the World* translated from the German by Eveline L. Kanes (Berkeley: University of California Press, 1973), pp. 37-9 also notes Thomas Hobbes as a foremost advocate of the absolute state managed according to rational principles transcending the errors of individual conscience and judgement and the vagaries of political action. Max Weber identified the central role of bureaucratic administration in this process.

13. Ironically the dominant influence has probably come from Western economists and in particular from the World Bank.

14. The experience is reviewed in authoritative detail by Waterston, *op. cit.*

15. Robert Chambers, "Normal Professionalism, New Paradigms and Development," paper for the seminar on Poverty, Development and Food: Towards the 21st Century, Institute of Development Studies, December 13-14, 1985, University of Sussex, Brighton; and Robert Chambers, *Rural Development: Putting the Last First* (London: Longman, 1983).

16. *Ibid.*

17. For further discussion of the concepts and methods of social learning, see contributions by Dunn, Korten, Friedmann, and Ackoff to "Part 5: Social Learning and the Nature of Planning" in Korten and Klauss, *loc. cit.*, pp. 169-198.

18. The importance and legitimacy of exercising individual critical consciousness in performing managerial roles in public organizations is articulated by Louis C. Gawthrop, *Public Sector Management, Systems, and Ethics* (Bloomington: Indiana University Press, 1984).